THE NEW NATURALIST

A SURVEY OF BRITISH NATURAL HISTORY

SCOTLAND

EDITORS
SARAH A. CORBET, ScD
Prof. RICHARD WEST, ScD, FRS, FGS
DAVID STREETER, MBE, FIBiol
JIM FLEGG, OBE, FIHort
Prof. JONATHAN SILVERTOWN

*

The aim of this series is to interest the general reader in the wildlife of Britain by recapturing the enquiring spirit of the old naturalists. The editors believe that the natural pride of the British public in the native flora and fauna, to which must be added concern for their conservation, is best fostered by maintaining a high standard of accuracy combined with clarity of exposition in presenting the results of modern scientific research.

Contents

Editors' Preface vii
Authors' Foreword and Acknowledgements ix

1. Looking at Scotland's Landscapes 1
2. Surface Modifications 6
3. Movements of the Earth from Within 16
4. Episodes in the Bedrock History of Scotland 29
5. Later Surface Modifications 51
6. Area 1: Galloway 63
7. Area 2: Southern Borders 92
8. Area 3: Jura to Arran 111
9. Area 4: Glasgow 138
10. Area 5: Edinburgh 161
11. Area 6: Mull 180
12. Area 7: Rannoch 204
13. Area 8: Dundee 227
14. Area 9: Uists and Barra 241
15. Area 10: Skye 264
16. Area 11: Affric 289
17. Area 12: Cairngorm 305
18. Area 13: Aberdeen 322
19. Area 14: Lewis and Harris 342
20. Area 15: Cape Wrath 370
21. Area 16: Inverness 383
22. Area 17: Caithness 398
23. Area 18: Orkney 413
24. Area 19: Shetland 427
25. Overview 444

Further Reading 452
Index 458

Editors' Preface

IN HIS EARLIER NEW NATURALIST VOLUME on the natural landscapes of Southern England, the author, Peter Friend, presented a new vision of landscape, providing a geological background for our understanding of the distribution and variation of flora and fauna in the lowland parts of Britain.

A division of Britain into lowland and highland regions has often been made in descriptions of our flora and fauna, for example by Arthur Tansley in his classic book on *Types of British Vegetation* (1911). Now Peter Friend has turned his attention to Scotland, the major highland part of Britain. In contrast to the sedimentary origin of the 'soft' rocks of the lowlands, the 'hard' rocks of Scotland arise from a series of events in the Earth's crust dating back to the earliest years of the planet, which were far less understood in the days when Dudley Stamp's New Naturalist volume on *Britain's Structure and Scenery* was published in 1946. The resulting structures, now much better understood, underlie Scotland's great variations in rock type and altitudes. Allied to this is the effect of the northern climate on the distribution of plants and animals, making the Highlands an area of particular interest from the biogeographical point of view, a mountainous region in the far west of Europe, adjacent to the Atlantic.

The illustrations featured in this book take full account of the possibilities of aerial and satellite photography in analysing topography, showing the relation between the geology, the soils, and the directions and angles of sloping features – all factors which must affect flora and fauna. The arrangement into areas, each with a similar treatment and analysis of the landscape, makes the subject very accessible to those interested in the geology or visiting the areas, and to those studying the fauna and flora and wishing to understand the physical background of the natural history. This book is a welcome addition to the New Naturalist Library, and will strengthen our understanding of the important and basic relationships between geology and natural history.

Authors' Foreword and Acknowledgements

THE PLEASURE OF ENJOYING A LANDSCAPE is greatly increased and deepened by developing some feeling for the events in the history of the Earth that may have caused it. This approach was followed in 2008, when *Southern England*, by Peter Friend, appeared as New Naturalist 108. The object was to provide a systematic general review of the landscapes visible in the countryside extending from Land's End in the southwest to East Anglia in the east. Peter has now been joined by two others, Leah Jackson-Blake and James Sample, to apply a similar approach to Scotland.

Peter and his two brothers were brought up in Edinburgh, in the Midland Valley of Scotland, moving with the family for a few years to Peebles in the Southern Uplands, during part of the Second World War. Many of the family activities involved visits to the countryside, and the pleasures and interests of these visits have continued into new generations of the family. The other two authors of this book have recently moved from southern England, where the book has been written, and now enjoy the landscapes of northern Scotland where they live and work.

Landscapes are easy to look at, given reasonable weather conditions, but difficult to describe in words. But developments in computer technology now offer many ways of analysing landscapes using different mapping methods, and these, along with diagrams and photos, form the framework of this book. Working on this imagery has been the main contribution of a succession of enthusiastic helpers. Lucinda Edes, Emilie Galley and Liesbeth Renders, and the second and third authors of this book, have all contributed great skill and enthusiastic innovation to this work, and made the project enjoyable as well as successful.

The home of this project has been the Department of Earth Sciences in the University of Cambridge. Peter Friend walked into the department as a first-year student some 57 years ago, to meet his supervisor, W. Brian Harland, for the first time. Apart from a period in the Scott Polar Research Institute, he has been based in Cambridge Department of Earth Sciences ever since, teaching and exploring the scenery and geology of many parts of the world. This work has included many visits to Spitsbergen (under the guidance of W. Brian Harland), Greenland, Spain, the Arabian Gulf, India and Pakistan. This has been an exciting period to be working in geology in Cambridge, because many key advances in the subject have been made by people working in Cambridge. CASP, originally the Cambridge Arctic Shelf Programme, made a valuable donation in support of the aerial photography used in this book.

All three authors would like to acknowledge their debts to the Cambridge college system. In the case of Peter Friend, his college, Darwin, has provided him with the congenial friendship of many people from diverse backgrounds, and their skills have helped him to remain a generalist in his interests.

Any work of this sort on the British Isles owes a fundamental debt to the British Geological Survey (BGS), now based at Keyworth near Nottingham. The numerous Survey maps and reports provide a remarkable source of carefully observed and objective information. The BGS has readily provided advice and help for this project, and helped to determine the sort of coverage and level that would be best.

The photographs that form such an important part of this book have come from many sources, and we are grateful to the following organisations and individuals for allowing us to use the results of their work (individually credited in the figure captions): Aerographica (Patricia and Angus Macdonald), Nicholas Branson, British Geological Survey, Lorne Gill, Last Refuge Limited (the late Adrian Warren, and Dae Sasitorn), David Law, Planetary Visions/Science Photo Library, Scottish Natural Heritage, Nigel Trewin.

Many other people have made important contributions by providing ideas and materials. These include John R. L. Allen, Wendy Annan, Phillip Gibbard, Alan Smith, Nigel Trewin, Nigel Woodcock and Richard West.

As with the New Naturalist volume on Southern England, this volume is dedicated to the **Dr John C. Taylor Foundation**, which has provided the financial support essential for the production of the imagery that is such a key part of the book's presentation. Some 50 years ago, John spent two summers exploring the geology of Spitsbergen with Peter Friend, and the support of his foundation has made both books possible.

We wish to thank HarperCollins Publishers for their support of the New Naturalist series, and particularly Myles Archibald, and then Julia Koppitz, for enthusiasm and help throughout. Hugh Brazier, Martin Brown and Robert Gillmor have brought great talents to different aspects of preparing this book.

The cover shows a view at Siccar Point, Berwickshire (Area 5). When James Hutton and some friends visited in 1788, they recognised what is now known to be an unusally good example of an unconformity. They made geological history by seeing it as evidence of the folding, erosion and deposition of strata over an incredibly long series of episodes in the Earth's past history (see also picture on page 163).

CHAPTER 1

Looking at Scotland's Landscapes

LANDSCAPES AND LANDFORMS

FIGURE 1 IS A SCOTTISH VIEW, showing landscapes that are typical of the confections of topographic shapes, sea, light, colour and atmosphere that are enjoyed by all. The object of this book is to contribute further to that enjoyment by surveying the varied landscapes of Scotland, and to help the reader to discover the stories that lie behind the rich variety.

At least two landscapes are present in this photograph: (1) in the middle distance, terraced hills in autumn gold vegetation extend down to the shores of Loch Slapin in the foreground, about 2 km in coastal length, and (2) behind this landscape rises the dark mass of the Cuillin mountains, providing one of the most famous and distinctive of Scottish landscapes, covering an area some 10 km across and giving a skyline to this photograph that is about 15 km from the photographer.

Many enthusiasts have written about the scenery of specific parts of Scotland. In this book the aim has been to cover the whole country relatively uniformly, because the variations from place to place are interesting in themselves. But this uniformity of approach has made it necessary to adopt a rather broad-brush treatment, whilst establishing the linear scale of features by the use of maps and aerial photographs in which the scale is clear in general terms. It is useful to follow earlier authors who regarded a landscape as an area of land that can be seen from one vantage point. In the case of Figure 1, the oblique aerial view covers two landscapes that are kilometres to tens of kilometres across.

Figure 1 provides a fine example of Scottish scenery that not only allows some questions of scale to be considered, but also illustrates the sorts of features that can be used to investigate the stories behind landscapes. Numerous small cliffs and bays of the coastal cliffs are visible in the foreground, where resistant *bedrock*

FIG 1. Aerial oblique photograph looking northwestwards towards the Cuillin mountains, Skye. (© Patricia & Angus Macdonald/Aerographica)

provides information about the early history of events in this landscape area. The Cuillin mountains themselves are very special in the amount of bedrock that is visible in their slopes, and in the roughness that this bedrock has given to the peaks and ridges. As we shall see, the bedrock history of the Cuillin provides an explanation of the size and surface style of these remarkable hills. In the middle distance, various smaller landscape features, *landforms*, are visible, particularly some clearly developed terraces and cliffs. There are also smaller ridges, crosscutting the terraces and cliffs, and often occupied by small stream valleys. These landforms directly reflect erosion of different features of the bedrock. The middle distance also illustrates the way that the gentler slopes tend to have a covering of *surface blanket*, often made of peat, soil or relatively weak and young sediment.

PEOPLE

Much has been written about *landscape history*, and by many people the phrase tends to have been used for the way that mankind has modified landscapes. This approach is not the main focus of this book, which deliberately concentrates on natural landscape features. However, all the landscapes described contain roads and settlements. In some cases, such as in Figure 1, these are visible but have had little impact on the landscape as a whole. In other Scottish cases, landscapes have

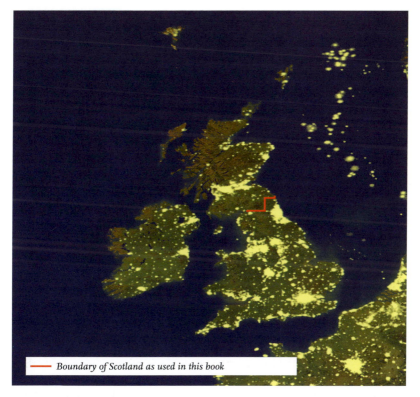

FIG 2. Satellite image covering the British Isles, showing population centres (including the Midland Valley of Scotland) picked out by man-made lighting at night. Note also the lighting on oil and gas platforms in the North Sea. (© Planetary Visions Ltd/Science Photo Library)

been changed profoundly by the building works of man, and the city and town landscapes of the Midland Valley are obvious examples (Fig. 2). In other cases, subtle changes of landscape vegetation across Scotland may well be the result of man's arrival and growing influence.

AREAS AND MAPS

The systematic survey of Scotland is based on a division into a grid of 19 arbitrary Areas (Fig. 3). Each Area is based loosely on the pattern of double-page areas used in the larger road atlases available, in particular the *Collins Road Atlas, Britain*. The object is to provide total coverage of the land areas and islands of Scotland,

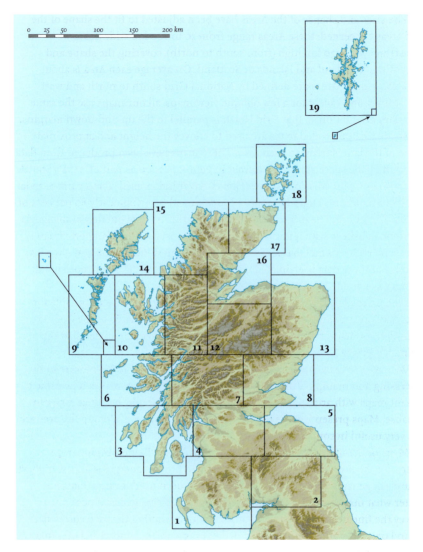

FIG 3. Division of Scotland into 19 Areas.

allowing the reader to navigate easily from place to place. At the beginning of each Area chapter, a location map explains the relationship between the Area and its neighbours. Ordnance Survey (OS) National Grid references are provided for the edges of the Area, in kilometres east and north of the arbitrary National Grid origin some 80 km west of the Isles of Scilly, southwest England.

The sizes and shapes of the Areas have been adjusted to fit the shape of the land areas concerned: these Areas range from 50 to 100 km wide (from west to east) and 70 to 130 km high (from south to north), covering the shape and form of the mainland and islands of Scotland. On average each Area is about 100 × 100 km. All Areas are defined by National Grid south to north and west to east lines, and except for a few oblique view maps, all our maps use the same boundary orientation so that Grid North is parallel to the up-and-down margins.

Shaded, colour-coded maps are used to convey the height and approximate shape of the land surface in each Area. These maps have been produced from data collected by the space shuttle *Endeavour* in February 2000 as part of NASA's Shuttle Radar Topographic Mission (SRTM). This 11-day mission used stereo pairs of radar images to build up a Digital Elevation Model (DEM) covering nearly 80 per cent of the Earth's surface. The original dataset used in this book is publicly available via the SRTM website (www2.jpl.nasa.gov/srtm) and consists of pixels, approximately 90 × 90 m, each of which has an associated elevation value. The absolute vertical accuracy of these data is estimated to be ± 16 m, whilst the absolute horizontal accuracy is ± 20 m.

Data on roads, railways, coastlines, town boundaries, rivers etc., suitable for reproduction at a scale of 1 : 200,000, have been made available by the Collins Bartholomew mapping agency. For further detail it is recommended that the Ordnance Survey Landranger (1 : 50,000) maps are used.

We have used ESRI ARC Geographic Information System (GIS) software in the processing and manipulating of the map data. This software makes it possible to present maps with artificial hill-shading, so that topography becomes easier to visualise. Maps presenting the directions and slope angles of sloping features are also very useful in some situations.

Many of the maps make use of a standard colour scheme, ranging from greens for the lowest ground through yellows to browns and greys for the highest ground. In general, the full range of colours has been used for each map, no matter what numerical range of heights is involved. This makes it possible to convey the fine detail of slopes and other features, whether the map covers flat ground or valleys and high peaks. To make it possible to compare between maps using this colour sequence, we have quoted the maximum elevation reached in each Area.

CHAPTER 2

Surface Modifications

THE LANDSCAPE CYCLE

IN CHAPTER 1, WE ILLUSTRATED our use of the word *landscape* to indicate an area a few kilometres to many kilometres across that is distinctive in appearance and origin. We have also found the word *landform* useful for smaller features of landscapes formed by distinctive surface processes during the modification of the landscape surface. In this chapter, we shall be examining further some aspects of certain of these landforms.

Our developing understanding of the larger workings of the Earth has shown us that although surface modifications are almost always apparent, the Earth's crust and its surface have been subject to continual movements generated *within* the Earth. Earthquakes and volcanoes are obvious signs of these internal movements. Any landscape is the result of the interplay between these contrasting internal and external systems, as illustrated using the cycle diagrams (Figs 4, 5). These illustrate the two systems in usefully different ways.

DIGITAL MAPS, SLOPES AND DOWNSLOPE MOVEMENT

We explained in Chapter 1 that our primary information about the shapes and patterns of Scottish landscapes comes from the use of the digital elevation datasets that are now available. Most people are familiar with the representation of elevation information on maps, using colour shading, or contours representing lines of specified elevation on the surfaces. The GIS software that we have used is a powerful tool for presenting topography in these ways. The same software makes it possible to represent topography using a *hill-shade* approach,

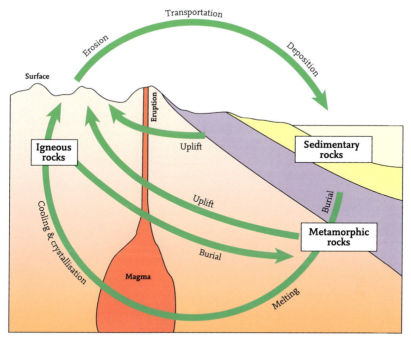

FIG 4. Diagram illustrating the processes of movement occurring within the outer layers of the Earth's crust, and how these relate to the processes and features of the Earth's surface and atmosphere.

which portrays topography using a shadowing effect, as estimated by an artificial light source with a specific orientation and elevation angle. The effects can appear similar to those produced by *hachuring*, as used in early Ordnance Survey maps, although hachure shading owed much to the eye of the individual draughtsman.

As outlined in Chapter 1, our maps of Scotland are based on digital elevation data where areas are divided into large numbers of small square unit areas (pixels), arranged in a rectangular grid. The elevation above sea level of each of the pixels is recorded in the database, and much of our data are based on a pixel size of 90 × 90 m. Although this resolution is adequate to provide information on larger landforms, we have to accept that many smaller landforms will be invisible if the pixel size is similar in area to, or larger than, the landform.

Digital elevation data can be directly represented on a map using colour shading or contours. It is also possible to define slopes by measuring changes of elevation within clusters of neighbouring pixels, allowing each pixel to be assigned a local slope value and converting the simple grid of elevation

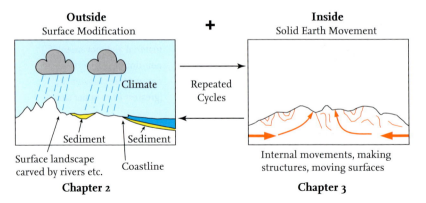

FIG 5. Landscapes are changed by surface modifications (Chapter 2) and solid Earth movements (Chapter 3).

measurements into a grid of differences in elevation, or slopes. These maps are sometimes referred to as 'first derivative' maps of the topography, because they represent changes of topography (local slopes) rather than the elevations themselves. Whatever the limitations of scale, there is no question that examining patterns of slope variation is a powerful way of studying the shapes of landscapes, and the Area chapters that follow make frequent use of maps of this sort.

We now consider the sorts of processes that are likely to give rise to various different features and patterns of slopes through time.

Slopes are likely to have a direct and profound influence on the way topography evolves through time, because any slope surface has the potential for downslope movement under gravity (Fig. 6). Movement will often require triggering, for example by earthquakes, freeze–thaw ice changes or even heavy rainfall.

Even more important in determining the amount of movement and the angle of slope that can occur is the nature of the materials making the slope. Bedrock of igneous or metamorphic origin, consisting mainly of coarse crystals of interlocking minerals, formed at high temperatures in the Earth, such as quartz, feldspar and other silicate minerals, is likely to produce a strong material in terms of its surface weathering behaviour. At the other extreme, certain sedimentary rocks, consisting of small particles of clay minerals separated from their neighbours by films of water, will be weak and strongly liable to downslope mass flow, tending to produce a distinctly lower slope angle.

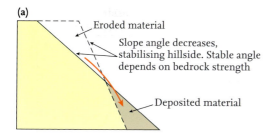
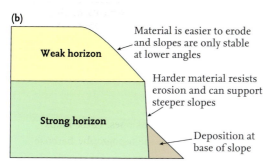

FIG 6. Models of downslope movement: (a) uniform material and movement; (b) non-uniform material and non-uniform movement (greatest from upper slope).

RIVER CATCHMENTS AND VALLEY PROCESSES

Looking back at the landscapes from Skye (Fig. 1), and excluding coastline considerations for the moment, the first step in analysing landscape shape or morphology, as just discussed, is to realise that most of the detailed features visible can be considered as combinations of different scales and combinations of slopes. Our survey of Scotland has confirmed for us that, under present-day climate conditions, rivers and streams are the fundamental agents forming and changing valleys and slopes. This is why we have designed our computer-based maps to display clearly the locations and shapes of these landforms.

We can demonstrate the widespread importance of these river-generated landforms by plotting the pattern of large river catchments across present-day Scotland (Fig. 7). This map further supports the claim that these river and stream agents are easily the most important agents in the modification by erosion of Scotland and its landscapes. This map has been compiled using data from the Scottish National River Flow Archive collected by the Environment Protection Agency. The areas of the larger river catchments are superimposed on an elevation-shaded map of most of Scotland. In the interests of clarity, only the larger catchments are shown, leaving clear a zone of land, up to some 40 km wide, around the coast and including the islands, where the catchments are smaller.

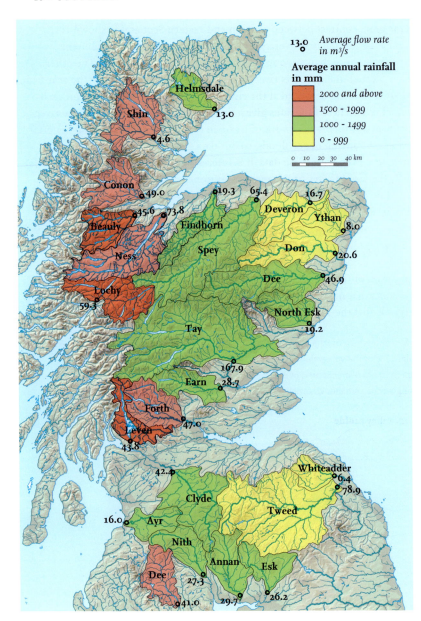

FIG 7. The larger river catchments of Scotland, based on the Scottish National River Flow Archive.

One great contrast between western and eastern Scotland is shown very clearly by the rainfall data averaged over the year and over the catchments, varying from more than 2000 mm to less than 1000 mm per year. The other variable plotted in Figure 7 is river flow rate (in m³/s), averaged over the year from the daily flow rates measured at the river gauge furthest downstream on each principal river. These flow rates give a first feel for the normal size of the river, but, of course, much of the work of rivers in eroding and transporting material is carried out during major floods, so our data give only limited grounds for comparison. Even with these data, it is interesting to see that the Tay (167.9 m³/s) is easily the largest river under most conditions, reflecting its large catchment area and its mid-range rainfall. It is interesting to note that the Thames and the Severn, in England and Wales, which both have large estuaries, have flow rates upstream from the tidal estuaries that are distinctly smaller (66 m³/s and 106 m³/s, respectively).

Some consideration can be given in our Area treatments to the shape and location of the different catchments, and to the bedrock materials and movements that may have been involved. Here the important general point that emerges is that the surface modification processes occurring in these river and

FIG 8. Comparison of valley cross-sections: (a) a simple valley created by channel incision in balance with the valley slope evolution; (b) a valley created by glacial incision and now occupied by a stream channel of similar water discharge to the earlier glacier, but now incising a much smaller channel.

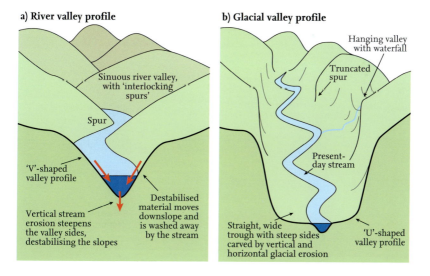

valley catchments in Scotland bear a unique responsibility for the changes taking place now in the landscapes that we want to understand better.

Valleys are bounded by boundary slopes that are inclined downwards towards the stream or river that flows along them. They can therefore be picked out on slope maps as pairs of areas of sloping pixels, providing clear evidence of the action of valley erosion, and the role of channel processes in the erosion of the catchment. Whereas downslope mass movement is a key component in removing material from the catchment, the incision and lowering of the river channel must also exert a control on the extent to which slope materials can be removed and transported down-channel and out of the catchment.

V-shaped cross-valley profiles in upland areas are commonly interpreted as the result of river or stream erosion by the valley channel. In contrast, U-shaped profiles are frequently interpreted as the products of glacial erosion (Fig. 8). It is generally accepted that most upland river valleys have a V-shaped profile, whereas upland valleys that have been occupied by glaciers tend to have U-shaped profiles. This can be readily understood in terms of the small eroding perimeter of a water-filled channel compared with the larger eroding perimeter of the much larger glacier channel, even though the discharge (in m^3/s) of rapidly flowing water or slowly moving ice down the valleys may have been similar under the two climatic regimes.

Another climate-related factor should be mentioned at this point. Under periglacial (near-glacial) conditions, freeze–thaw processes, particularly within the surface blanket, will often keep the blanket materials in a state of frequent

FIG 9. Dendritic channel pattern growth. This shows three phases in the development of a computer-based erosional model, in which valley erosion from the southern edge of a study area proceeds by headward erosion of each valley which is randomly free to choose its erosion direction. The map model was provided by Dimitri Lague and was based on the work of A. Crave and P. Davy.

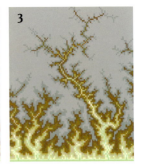

FIG 10. Other landforms typical of river catchments, including channels of different geometries, flood plains and river terraces.

A) Bedrock channel

B) Incised sinuous channel

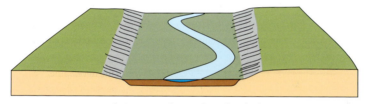

C) Sinuous channel in flood plain

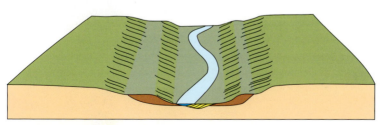

D) Sinuous channel, flood plain and terraces

downslope movement. The degree to which this happens is likely to have a profound influence on the evolution of valley-slope and channel systems.

The catchment map (Fig. 7) shows clearly the dendritic patterns developed by all river and stream drainage systems, and it is these patterns (Fig. 9) that make the recognition of valleys so easy on our slope maps.

In the lower reaches of channel systems, other landforms develop that are typical of deposition of sediment being carried down the system (Fig. 10). This may influence the sinuosity of the channels, so that only slightly sinuous channels, often carrying rather coarse gravel or sandy sediment, may be replaced downstream by meandering (highly sinuous) channels that flow between banks of muddy sediment. Flood plains of relatively fine-grained sediment are increasingly the obvious landforms low down in river systems, and these are typically very flat extensive plains. Terraces often represent fragments of former flood plains left at a higher level as the active channel has cut down to a lower elevation.

SEA COASTS

A special slope consideration is raised by the landscapes of Figure 1, and frequently in other parts of Scotland also. This occurs where a change of sea level has initiated the formation of new coastal landforms, sometimes largely erosional and sometimes depositional (Fig. 11).

Erosion of a coastal slope has similarities to the erosion of river or stream valley slopes, except that coastal slopes are caused by mass downslope movement towards sites of sea-cliff erosion. A very different situation occurs where sea-level changes initiate the deposition of sediment to form coastal flats, with very flat overall slopes, and patterns of coastal sediment bars, sediment flats and salt-marshes. Sediment supply is obviously a key factor in the growth of potentially extensive landforms and landscapes, often with distinctive landforms and very flat surfaces or zero-angle overall slopes.

a) Coastal erosion along 'hard' coastlines – cliffs and wave-cut platforms

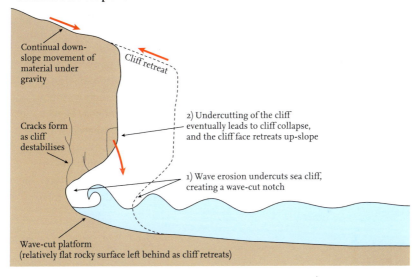

b) Coastal deposition – beaches, spits and coastal flats

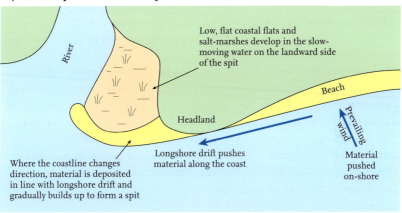

FIG 11. Coastal slopes: erosion and deposition; a) 'vertical profile' and b) 'plan view'.

CHAPTER 3

Movements of the Earth from Within

EARTH-SURFACE MOVEMENTS DUE TO PLATE TECTONICS

TO UNDERSTAND THE CHANGES AND MOVEMENTS affecting the appearance of the landscape on large scales we need to review current understanding of some geological systems, especially *plate tectonics*. Many of the widespread changes that have created landscapes over long periods of time can now be understood using this discovery.

Knowledge of the processes causing the movement of large areas of the Earth's surface (10–1000 km length scale) has been revolutionised by scientific advances made over the last 50 years. During this time, scientists have become convinced that the whole of the Earth's surface consists of an outer shell of interlocking *tectonic plates* (Fig. 12). The word *tectonic* refers to processes that have built features of the Earth's crust (Greek: *tekt*, a builder). The worldwide plate pattern is confusingly irregular – particularly when seen on a flat map – and it is easier to visualise the plates in terms of an interlocking arrangement of panels on the Earth's spherical surface, broadly like the panels forming the skin of a traditional leather football.

Tectonic plates are features of the lithosphere, the name given to the ~125 km-thick outer shell of the Earth, distinguished from the material below by the strength of its materials (Greek: *lithos*, stone). The strength depends upon the composition of the material and also upon its temperature and pressure, both of which tend to increase with depth below the Earth's surface. In contrast to the mechanically strong lithosphere, the underlying material is weaker and known as the asthenosphere (Greek: *asthenos*, no-strength). Note that in Figure 13 the crustal

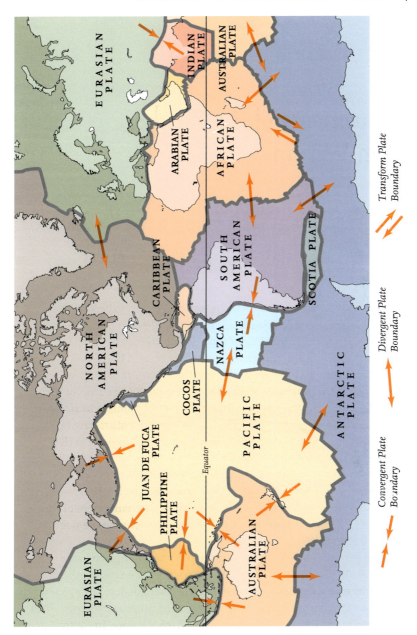

FIG 12. World map showing the present pattern of the largest lithosphere plates.

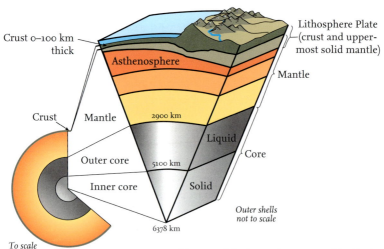

FIG 13. Diagram of the internal structure of the Earth.

and outer mantle layers are shown with exaggerated thickness, so that they are visible.

Much of the strength difference between the lithosphere and the asthenosphere depends on the temperature difference between them. The lithosphere plates are cooler than the underlying material, so they behave in a more rigid way when forces are generated within the Earth. The asthenosphere is hotter and behaves in a more plastic way, capable of deforming without fracturing and, to some extent, of 'flowing'. Because of this difference in mechanical properties and the complex internal forces present, the lithosphere plates can move relative to the material below. To visualise the motion of the plates, we can use the idea of lithospheric plates floating on top of the asthenosphere.

The pattern of earthquake activity and actively unstable mountain belts corresponds very well with the pattern of the tectonic plates now recognised. The largest plates (Fig. 12) clearly mark relatively rigid and stable areas of the lithosphere, with interiors that do not experience as much disturbance as their edges. Plates move relative to each other along *plate boundaries*, in various ways that will be described below. The plate patterns have been located by investigating distinctive markers within the plates and at their edges, allowing the relative rates of movement between neighbouring plates to be calculated. These rates are very slow, rarely exceeding a few centimetres per year, but over the millions of years of geological time they can account for thousands of kilometres of relative movement.

It has proved much easier to measure plate movements than to work out what has been causing them. However, the general belief today is that the plates move in response to a number of different forces. Circulation (convection) within the mantle is driven by temperature and density differences, but other forces are also at play. Where plates diverge, warm material rises from within the Earth to fill the surface gap, and, being warmer, it may also be elevated above the rest of the plate, providing a pushing force to move the plate across the surface of the Earth. At convergent boundaries, cold, older material sinks into the asthenosphere, providing a pulling force that drags the rest of the plate along behind it. Deep within the Earth, the sinking material melts and is ultimately recycled and brought back to the surface to continue the process.

Knowledge of how tectonic plates interact provides the key to understanding the movement history of the Earth's crust. However, most people are much more familiar with the geographical patterns of land and sea, which do not coincide with the distribution of tectonic plates (Fig. 12). From the point of view of landscapes and scenery, coastlines are always going to be key features because they define the limits of the land; we make no attempt in this book to consider submarine scenery in detail.

The upper part of the lithosphere is called the *crust* (Fig. 13). Whereas the distinction between the lithosphere and the asthenosphere is based upon mechanical properties related to temperature and pressure (see above), the distinction between the crust and the lower part of the lithosphere is based upon composition. Broadly speaking, there are two types of crust that can form the upper part of the lithosphere: *continental* and *oceanic*. An individual tectonic plate may include just one or both kinds of crust.

Continental crust underlies land areas and also many of the areas covered by shallow seas. Geophysical work shows that this crust is typically about 30 km thick, but may be 80–90 km thick below some high plateaus and mountain ranges. The highest mountains in Britain are barely noticeable on a scale diagram comparing crustal thicknesses (Fig. 14). Continental crust is made of rather less dense materials than the oceanic crust, or the mantle, and this lightness is the reason why land surfaces and shallow sea floors are elevated compared to the deep oceans. Much of the continental crust is very old (up to 3–4 billion years), having formed early in the Earth's life when lighter material separated from denser materials within the Earth and rose to the surface.

Oceanic crust forms the floors of the deep oceans, typically 4 or 5 km below sea level. It is generally 5–10 km thick and is distinctly more dense than continental crust. Oceanic crust only forms land where volcanic material has been supplied to it in great quantity (as in the case of Iceland), or where other

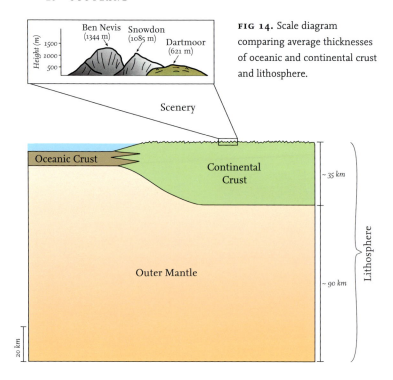

FIG 14. Scale diagram comparing average thicknesses of oceanic and continental crust and lithosphere.

important local forces in the crust have caused it to rise (as is the case in parts of Cyprus). Oceanic crust is generally relatively young (only 0–200 million years old), because its greater density and lower elevation ensures that it is generally *subducted* and destroyed at plate boundaries that are *convergent* (see below).

Figure 12 shows the major pattern of tectonic plates on the Earth today. The Mercator projection of this map distorts shapes, particularly in polar regions, but we can see that there are seven very large plates, identified by the main areas located on their surfaces. The Pacific plate lacks continental crust entirely, whereas the other six main plates each contain a large continent (Eurasia, North America, Australia, South America, Africa and Antarctica) as well as oceanic crust. There are a number of other middle-sized plates (e.g. Arabia and India) and large numbers of micro-plates, not shown on the world map.

Figures 12 and 15 also identify the different types of plate boundary, which are distinguished according to the relative motion between the two plates. *Convergent* plate boundaries involve movement of the plates from each side towards the suture (or central zone) of the boundary. Because the plates are moving towards each other, they become squashed together in the boundary zone. Sometimes

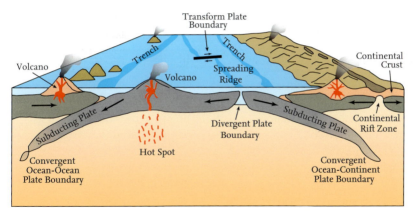

FIG 15. Diagram (not to scale) illustrating the movement processes of plates.

one plate moves below the other in a process called *subduction*, which often results in a deep ocean trench and a zone of mountains and/or volcanoes, as well as earthquake activity (Fig. 15). The earthquakes that happened off Indonesia in December 2004 and off Japan in March 2011 were two of the strongest known since records began. Both seized world attention because of the horrifying loss of life cause by the tsunami waves they generated. Both were the result of sudden lithosphere movements of several metres on faults in the convergent subduction zones where the Australian and Pacific plates have been moving under the Eurasian plate (Fig. 12).

In other cases the plate boundary is *divergent*, where the neighbouring plates move apart and new material from deeper within the Earth rises to fill the space created. New oceanic crust is created by the arrival and cooling of hot volcanic material from below. The Mid-Atlantic Ridge running through Iceland is one of the examples nearest to Britain of this sort of plate boundary, and volcanic ash-cloud activity there caused widespread disruption to air transport during 2010.

Other plate boundaries, sometimes called *transform* boundaries, mainly involve movement parallel to the plate edges. The Californian coast zone is the classic example but there are many others, such as the transform boundary between the African and Antarctic plates. In some areas, plate movement is at an oblique angle to the suture and there are components of divergence or convergence as well as movement parallel to the boundary.

Britain today sits in the stable interior of the western Eurasian plate, almost equidistant from the divergent Mid-Atlantic Ridge boundary to the west and the complex convergent boundary to the south where Spain and northwest Africa are colliding. In its earlier history the crust of Britain has been subjected to very direct plate boundary activity. The results of convergent activity in Devonian and Carboniferous times (between 416 and 299 million years ago) are visible at the surface in southwest England, and in Ordovician to Devonian times (between 490 and 360 million years ago) in Wales, northwest England and Scotland (see Chapter 4).

Present-day plate boundaries are often picked out by the location of earthquakes, as described above. Mention should also be made at this point of the importance of volcanoes and igneous bedrock in providing information about movements within the upper levels of the Earth. Highly sophisticated analytical work has illuminated the whole subject of the chemical and mineral evolution of igneous material as it evolves and moves in the crust. For the purposes of this book, a very simple twofold division of igneous rocks into *felsic* and *mafic* will be sufficient.

Felsic igneous rocks tend to be light-coloured and of relatively low density, containing the minerals quartz and feldspar. Typical types are granite, syenite (coarsely crystalline) and rhyolite (finely crystalline). Continental crust consists of felsic and mafic igneous rocks, as well as sedimentary and metamorphic rocks.

Mafic igneous rocks tend to be darker-coloured and of relatively high density, containing feldspar and dark minerals rich in magnesium and/or iron, such as augite or hornblende. Typical types are gabbros (coarsely crystalline), andesites and basalts (finely crystalline). Oceanic crust is dominated by mafic igneous materials.

MAKING LOCAL MEASUREMENTS OF EARTH SURFACE MOVEMENTS

We have been considering the large movement systems that originate within the Earth. There are also more local movement systems operating on the Earth's surface, which are linked to a very variable degree to the large-scale movements of plate tectonics. To explore this complex linkage further, it will be helpful to look now at different processes that may combine to cause particular local movements.

Tectonic plates are defined by their rigidity, so there is relatively little horizontal movement between points within the same plate, compared to the deformation seen in plate boundary zones. This extreme deformation may involve folding and fracturing of the rock materials, addition of new material from below, or absorption of material into the interior during subduction.

Nonetheless, deformation is not restricted solely to plate boundaries and does occur within the plates, although to a lesser extent. In some cases, major structures that originally formed along a plate boundary can become incorporated into the interior of a plate when prolonged collision causes two plates to join. The Caledonian convergent boundary that extended across

Scotland (see Chapter 4) provides an excellent example of movements that occurred hundreds of millions of years ago, but also contains many examples of structures formed in later movements. These structures have often been reactivated long after they first formed in order to accommodate forces along the new plate boundary via deformation within the plate. Conversely, changes of internal stress patterns can sometimes lead to the splitting of a plate into two, forming a new, initially divergent plate boundary. Many of the oil- and gas-containing features of the North Sea floor (Fig. 2) originated when a belt of divergent rift faults formed across a previously intact plate.

It needs to be stressed that the patterns of deformation (fracturing and folding) due to these plate motions occur at a wide range of different scales, from centimetres to thousands of kilometres. Sometimes they are visible at the scale of an entire plate boundary, such as the enormous Himalayan mountain chain that marks the collision of India with Asia.

The effects of features as large as plate boundaries on landscapes persist over hundreds of millions of years, long after the most active movement has ceased. For example, parts of southwestern England, Wales and the Scottish Highlands are underlain by bedrocks that were formed in convergent boundary zones of the past. The tin and lead mines of Cornwall owe their existence to a 300-million-year-old convergent plate boundary, where an ocean was destroyed as two plates converged and continents collided. The convergence released molten rock that rose in the crust and gradually cooled to form granite, whilst metals were precipitated in the surrounding crust as 'lodes' containing tin and lead (see Chapter 4).

Mapping the patterns of bedrock exposed at the surface often reveals folds and faults that provide key information about the movements that have taken place during the past (Fig. 16). Figure 17 provides a key to some of the terms commonly used to classify these structures, as a step towards understanding the sorts of movement patterns that they represent. In broad terms, folds tend to indicate some form of local convergent movement, though they may be the result of larger movement patterns of a different kind. Normal faults tend to indicate divergent or stretching movements, at least locally, whereas reverse and strike-slip faults tend to indicate convergence. Two broad types of fold are distinguished: *synclines* are U-shaped downfolds, while *anticlines* are the opposite – A-shaped upfolds.

Further mapping of folds and faults often reveals complex patterns of changing movements. A complex example is shown in Figure 18. Divergent movements in an area of crust produced plastic deformation in the warmer lower crust, and faulting into a number of discrete blocks in the colder, more brittle upper crust. This was then followed by an episode of convergent

FIG 16. Outcrop in the Atacama Desert, Chile, showing a very regularly bedded succession of mudstones, formed originally as horizontally layered deposits in a lake. Since their deposition the mudstones have been tilted. They have also been fractured during an earthquake, resulting in a step, or normal fault (see Fig. 17), that is particularly clear because it has cut through a white layer in the deposits. An outcrop such as this makes it possible to measure the local movements that have taken place in this material after it was deposited. (© Nicholas Branson)

movement that resulted in closing up the upper crustal blocks and further flow in the plastic lower crust, causing crustal thickening and mountain building at the surface.

VERTICAL CRUSTAL MOVEMENTS

The movement of lithospheric plates, as described above, is the main cause of horizontal convergent and divergent movements affecting thousands of kilometres of the Earth's surface. As shown in Figures 16 to 18, horizontal movements are generally accompanied by vertical movements of local crustal surfaces. Some of these could have produced very large scenic features, such as a mountain belt or a rift valley. In this book we are primarily concerned with scenic features at a more local scale, so we now consider various other processes that may contribute to the creation of vertical crustal movements.

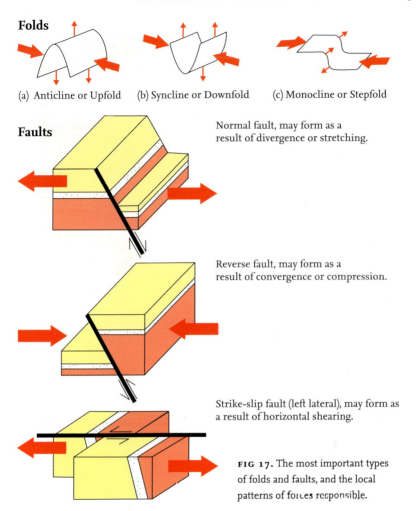

FIG 17. The most important types of folds and faults, and the local patterns of forces responsible.

Vertical crustal movement linked to erosion or deposition

Addition or subtraction of material to the surface of the Earth is happening all the time as sediment is deposited or solid material is eroded. The discipline of *sedimentology* is concerned with the wide range of different processes that are involved in the erosion, transport and deposition of material, whether the primary agent of movement is water, ice, mud or wind. An important point is that few of these sedimentary processes relate directly to the large tectonic movements of the Earth's crust that we have discussed above. Landscape is often

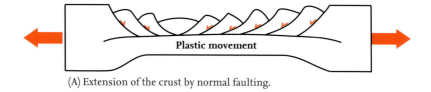

(A) Extension of the crust by normal faulting.

(B) Onset of compression with inversion of normal faults.

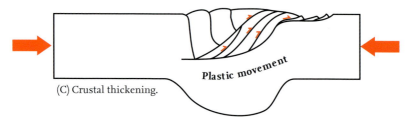

(C) Crustal thickening.

FIG 18. Example of a cross-section through the crust, showing how a divergent movement pattern (A) may be modified by later convergent movements (B and C).

produced by erosion of thick sedimentary deposits that formed in sedimentary basins where material eroded from the surrounding uplands accumulated. One of the characteristic features of these thick deposits is their layered appearance – as, for example, in the Torridonian Sandstones of northwestern Scotland (see Chapter 4). Layering varies from millimetre-scale laminations produced by very small fluctuations in depositional processes, to sheets hundreds of metres thick that extend across an entire sedimentary basin. These thicker sheets are often so distinctive that they are named and mapped as separate geological units representing significant changes in the local environment at the time they were deposited.

Vertical crustal movements due to loading or unloading

In addition to the direct raising or lowering of the surface by erosion or deposition, there is a secondary effect due to the unloading or loading of the crust that may take some thousands of years to produce significant effects. As mentioned above, we can visualise the lithosphere as 'floating' on the asthenosphere like a boat floating in water. Loading or unloading the surface of the Earth by deposition or erosion will therefore lower or raise the scenery, just as a boat will sit lower or higher in the water depending on its load.

An example of such loading has been the build-up of ice sheets during the Ice Age. The weight of these build-ups depressed the Earth's surface in the areas involved, and when the ice melted the Earth's surface rose again. Western Scotland provides an example of an area that has been rising because of 'rebound' since the ice of the Ice Age disappeared on melting.

A second example of this is the lowering of the area around the Mississippi Delta, loaded by sediment eroded from the more central and northern parts of North America. The Delta region, including New Orleans, is doomed to sink continually as the Mississippi River deposits sediment around its mouth, increasing the crustal load there.

Conversely, unloading of the Earth's surface will cause it to rise. Recent theoretical work on the River Severn suggests that unloading of the crust by erosion may have played a role in raising the Cotswold Hills to the east and an equivalent range of hills in the Welsh Borders.

Vertical movements due to thermal expansion or contraction

Changes in the temperature of the crust and lithosphere are an inevitable result of many of the processes active within the Earth, because they often involve the transfer of heat. In particular, rising plumes of hot material in the Earth's mantle, often independent of the plate boundaries, are now widely recognised as an explanation for various areas of intense volcanic activity (for example beneath Iceland today). These plumes are often referred to as 'hot spots' (Fig. 15). Heating and cooling leads to expansion or contraction of the lithosphere and can cause the surface to rise or sink, at least locally.

An example of this is the way that Britain was tilted downwards to the east about 60 million years ago. At about this time, eastern North America moved away from western Europe as the North American and Eurasian plates diverged. The divergence resulted in large volumes of hot material from deep within the Earth being brought to the surface and added to the crust of western Britain. It is believed that the heating and expansion of the crustal rocks in the west has elevated them above the rocks to the east, giving an eastward tilt to the rock layers and exposing the oldest rocks in the west and the youngest ones in the east.

THE CHALLENGE OF MEASURING CRUSTAL MOVEMENTS

Having just reviewed some of the processes that may cause movements of the Earth's surface, it is useful to consider the practical difficulties of how such movements are measured.

For present-day applications, it seems natural to regard sea level as a datum against which vertical landscape movements can be measured, as long as we remember to allow for tidal and storm variations. However, much work has demonstrated that global sea level has changed rapidly and frequently through time, due to climate fluctuations affecting the size of the polar icecaps and changing the total amount of liquid water present in the oceans and seas (see Chapter 5). It has also been shown that plate tectonic movements can have an important effect on global sea level by changing the size and shape of ocean basins.

Attempts have been made to develop charts showing how sea level, generalised for the whole world, has varied through time. However, it has proved very difficult to distinguish a worldwide signal from local variations, and the dating of the changes is often too uncertain to allow confident correlation between areas.

In sedimentary basins, estimates of vertical movements have been made using the thicknesses of sediment layers accumulating over different time intervals in different depths of water. In areas of mountain building, amounts of vertical uplift have been estimated using certain indicator minerals that show the rates of cooling that rocks have experienced as they were brought up to the surface. However, both these approaches are only really possible in areas that have been subjected to movements of the Earth's crust that are large and continuous enough to dominate completely other possible sources of error.

Local movements are also difficult to estimate, although fold and/or fault patterns may allow a simple measure in some cases. Over short present-day periods of time it has proved to be possible to detect vertical movement patterns using satellite imagery. Movement of sediment across the Earth's surface by rivers or sea currents can be estimated if mineral grains in the sediment can be tracked back to the areas from which they have come. In the detailed consideration of landscapes in this book, we have to rely on using the widest possible range of types of evidence, carefully distinguishing the times and scales involved. Even then, we are often left with probable movement suggestions rather than certainties.

CHAPTER 4

Episodes in the Bedrock History of Scotland

Chapters 2 and 3 have introduced the idea that natural landscapes are the results of combinations of surface modification (Chapter 2) and internal movements (Chapter 3). The responses of the Earth's surface to these combinations have depended on the bedrock present locally on the surface at each stage. It is now time, therefore, to turn specifically to Scotland, to summarise the distribution and history of its bedrock.

The mapping of the bedrock of Scotland has been a heroic task that started over 200 years ago. Most of the systematic work has been carried out by the British Geological Survey, and is now available on different scales, forming a monument to the efforts of many remarkable people and the Survey itself (Fig. 19). For the generalising approach of this book much of this work has had to be simplified.

Scotland's geological history is unusually long and varied for a country of its size. One reason for this is that present-day Scotland is the result of the convergence or movement together of at least five different areas of crust, often referred to as *terranes* (Fig. 20). These terranes are fragments of continental crust that have been carried together by plate tectonic movements that resulted eventually in the construction of crustal Scotland, as we find it now.

Although most of the surface modifications and internal movements have overlapped in time and space, it helps to pick out discrete episodes in summarising aspects of Scotland's history. The first nine of these episodes are represented in the bedrock record and are outlined in the rest of this chapter. Episodes 10–12 are mainly represented in the record of recent surface modifications, and they are described in Chapter 5. All 12 episodes have been placed in chronological order in Figure 21 (where Episode 1 is the oldest and 12 the most recent) using the International Stratigraphy Chart 2009, which

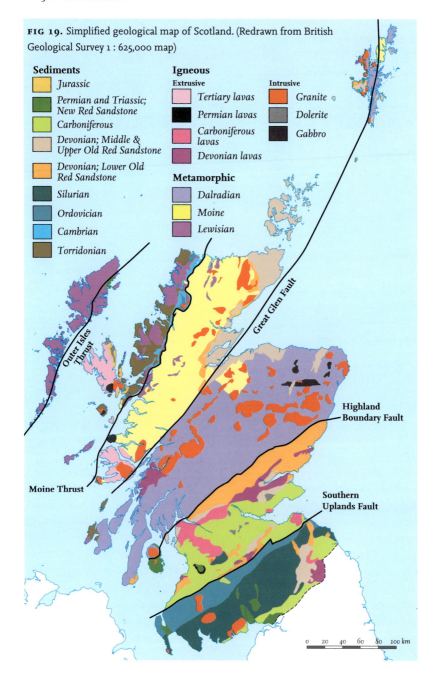

FIG 19. Simplified geological map of Scotland. (Redrawn from British Geological Survey 1 : 625,000 map)

provides an accepted standard for the names used in dividing and describing geological time (see www.stratigraphy.org).

We provide a 'Timeline' as part of the description of the geology of each of our Areas. These timelines are designed to summarise the time sequence of events that is represented in or near each Area, using the standard International Stratigraphic divisions. Standard colours are used for the divisions and ages. If part of the stratigraphic record is absent, the division is not coloured.

The bedrock episodes can be grouped as follows:
(1) Pre-Caledonian Greenland-margin episodes (Episodes 1–3)
(2) Caledonian mountain-building episodes (Episodes 4–6)
(3) Post-Caledonian episodes (Episodes 7–9)

The distribution of these groups of rocks is shown in Figure 22, and the episodes involved in their formation are described below.

PRE-CALEDONIAN GREENLAND-MARGIN EPISODES

Episode 1: formation of the Lewisian Complex

Rocks of the Lewisian Complex are very largely restricted to the Hebridean terrane, where they make up almost all of the bedrock of the Outer Hebrides, and much of the bedrock of the mainland. They also occur occasionally in the neighbouring part of the Northern Highland terrane, where they became involved in the much younger Caledonian movement history. The Lewisian Complex takes its name from the largest and northernmost of the islands of the Outer Hebrides.

The Lewisian Complex consists of metamorphic rocks (typically coarsely crystalline gneisses) that formed by alteration of earlier rocks when high temperatures and/or pressures peaked during movements at deep levels within the Earth's crust. The great interest of these metamorphic rocks is that they can provide information about the conditions deep within the crust when these movements were taking place. Unlike igneous rocks that formed by crystallisation from completely melted rock material, metamorphic rocks have involved changes in rocks that were at least partly solid, so they preserve information about features present before, as well as conditions during, the metamorphism. In most cases, the minerals now present are stable at present-day surface temperatures and pressures, are large in crystal size, and interlock with neighbouring crystals, so the rocks are resistant to surface weathering compared with many other rock types.

FIG 20. The five terranes of Scotland. (After Trewin 2002)

FIG 21 (RIGHT). Episodes in Scotland's geological history. The age scale is not linear and has been deliberately chosen so that younger episodes are given greater space than older ones, because they are usually known in greater detail. The chart indicates the ages covered by the 12 episodes, and the dominant processes represented by them. (Redrawn from International Stratigraphy Chart 2009, www.stratigraphy.org)

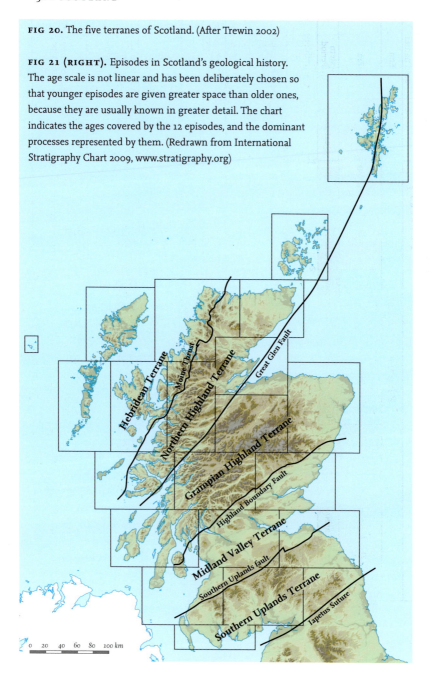

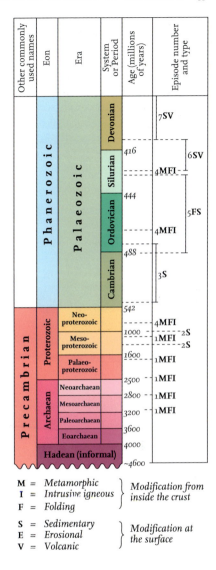

M = Metamorphic
I = Intrusive igneous   } Modification from inside the crust
F = Folding

S = Sedimentary
E = Erosional   } Modification at the surface
V = Volcanic

One of the most important research tools applied to the Lewisian rocks has been the dating of the various mineral components, using the fact that some of them contain radioactive materials that have been steadily changing since they were first trapped when the minerals formed. The amount of change gives a measure of the time over which it has been taking place. New analytical methods have led to increasingly accurate and reliable figures. As this work has continued, it has become clear that the Lewisian is truly a 'complex', made up of many distinct volumes of crust, each preserving certain episodes of movement and rock alteration. Many of the folds or fractures mapped in the Lewisian have a northwest/southeast trend, almost at right angles to the Moine Thrust Zone and the associated folds and fractures that form the margin of the Hebridean terrane. However, mapping of these structures has shown that the movement and alteration of the Lewisian occurred in a number of phases with different compression and shearing directions. The evidence is too fragmentary to allow identification of the boundaries of tectonic plates similar to those that can be identified in younger bedrock areas. This is hardly surprising, because these are some of the earliest movement events recognised anywhere on the surface of the whole Earth, representing glimpses of early crustal activity that has escaped reworking or obliteration in more recent episodes.

Important phases of activity and mineral alteration have been recognised in the Lewisian Complex, some in the Archaean (3.2 and 2.8 billion years ago), generally named Scourian and Inverian. Other rocks were formed and/or altered in the Proterozoic (2.4, 1.7 and 1.1 billion years ago) and are named Laxfordian. The Archaean phases are older than any other for which there is evidence in Britain. Most of the rocks altered in these phases were originally igneous but some were sedimentary, and all had actually been formed as rocks even earlier. It is clear from the minerals present that some phases involved crust being moved downwards to considerable depths – several tens of kilometres below the surface – although before the next episode (described below) the rocks had been moved back upwards and were exposed at the surface.

Surface modification of the Lewisian during the Tertiary and the Ice Age has carved it into typical 'knock-and-lochan' topography, in which the land surface consists of hillocks of exposed rock tens to hundreds of metres across (called *knocks*, from the Gaelic *cnoc*, a small, rocky hill), separated by water and bog-filled hollows (*lochans*) which often pick out folds and linear fractures in the bedrock (Fig. 23). This wild knock-and-lochan landscape was once thought to represent the first formed surface of the Earth, but it is now realised that the surface shapes of the landscape are very much younger, and that the metamorphic alterations and movements, although very old, were preceded by even earlier episodes.

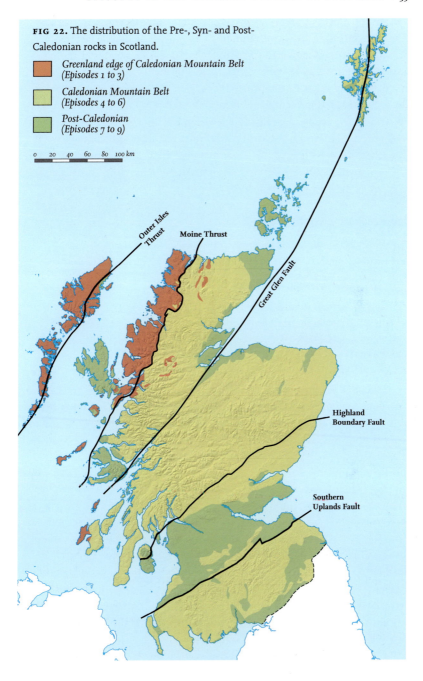

FIG 22. The distribution of the Pre-, Syn- and Post-Caledonian rocks in Scotland.

- Greenland edge of Caledonian Mountain Belt (Episodes 1 to 3)
- Caledonian Mountain Belt (Episodes 4 to 6)
- Post-Caledonian (Episodes 7 to 9)

FIG 23. Aerial oblique view of Suilven (731 m), carved from Neoproterozoic Torridonian Sandstones resting unconformably on the knock-and-lochan topography of the Lewisian Complex. (© Adrian Warren/lastrefuge.co.uk)

Episode 2: formation of the Torridonian Sandstones

Mountains and slopes made of uniform but well-layered successions of Torridonian Sandstones, often tens to hundreds of metres thick, provide some highly characteristic elements of the Hebridean terrane (Fig. 23). The layers are generally rather flat-lying, except in the folded and faulted bedrock of the Moine Thrust Zone where the Torridonian has been deformed along the eastern terrane boundary. Careful examination of the layering shows that it generally reflects episodes in the life of Torridonian rivers, which occasionally flooded and deposited sandy or gravelly river bars, often with muddy tops that have weathered to pick out the layers . Although much of the Torridonian was deposited by rivers, some of it accumulated in lakes or in the sea.

At least two different episodes of deposition are represented in the Torridonian Sandstones, and these have been dated, using radiometric methods, as Mesoproterozoic and Neoproterozoic (1.2 and 1.0 – 0.95 billion years ago respectively: Fig. 21). These two episodes left thick successions of sediment in the crustal record: up to 2 km in the Mesoproterozoic and up to 5 km in the Neoproterozoic. Thicknesses as great as these imply the downward movement of certain areas (basins) of the Earth's surface close to areas where erosion due to upward movement was producing large quantities of sediment. In other words, although the Torridonian Sandstones are the result of modification by surface processes, these processes must have been linked to important vertical movements of the crust, due to forces acting within the Earth.

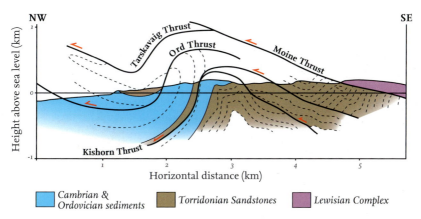

FIG 24. Cross-section through the Ord window of Southern Skye, showing the folded and fractured structure of the bedrock below the Moine Thrust.

The contact between the flat-lying layering of the Torridonian and the underlying Lewisian Complex is an unconformity that formed when the Torridonian sediments were deposited onto topography of valleys and hills (often hundreds of metres in relief) that had been carved in the Lewisian Complex. This unconformity, although preserving local Proterozoic hills and valleys, is relatively flat-lying overall, showing that widespread vertical movements – rather than significant folding or tilting – must have been involved.

The western and eastern margins of the present-day Atlantic Ocean were close to one another within a 'super'-continent when the Torridonian sediments were accumulating. It seems likely that much of the sediment was derived from upland areas whose crust is now in Greenland or eastern Canada.

Episode 3: Cambrian and Ordovician sedimentation

A rather uniform succession of sediments of Cambrian and Ordovician age occurs more or less continuously along a strip from Skye, in the south, to the north coast of the Scottish mainland (Figs 19, 20, 22: our 'Greenland edge'). This succession was deposited unconformably on the eroded rocks of the Lewisian Complex and the Torridonian Sandstones. These Cambrian and Ordovician sediments only occur in the Hebridean terrane, and their usually gentle tilt is evidence of the lack of later movements, although they have been folded and fractured in the Moine Thrust Zone along the terrane's edge (Fig. 24).

Where most fully developed, this sedimentary succession is about 1 km in thickness and consists of a lower unit of quartzites (up to 100 m thick) that forms a greyish-white cap on some mountains and weathers to produce distinctive angular scree and boulder fields. Above this is a thin unit of mudstones, fractured and folded by subsequent movements on the Moine Thrust, overlain by a thick succession of limestones which, according to the fossil evidence contained within them, span the time interval from early Cambrian to early Ordovician (Fig. 21). In the present-day landscape, these limestones often produce swallow holes and caves formed by solution of the limestone's fracture joints, as well as unusually lush grass wherever there is significant soil development.

The whole of this succession appears to have formed on the edge of a sea, and the occurrence of similar sediments on both sides of the present-day North Atlantic, a much more recent feature of the Earth's surface, suggests a widespread uniformity in the coastal environments at this time. It is believed that these deposits formed due to surface modification involving global sea-level change, with no clear evidence of local movements due to processes deeper within the Earth.

CALEDONIAN MOUNTAIN-BUILDING EPISODES

The Latin adjective *Caledonian* is widely used to indicate Scottish-ness, and is used in geology for the important phase of mountain building that dominated earth movements and surface modification in Scotland between Ordovician and Devonian times. Evidence of similar movements and modifications during the same time periods is found along the east coast of the USA, Canada and Greenland, and through Ireland, Norway, Sweden and Spitsbergen. The terranes now recognised in Scotland have been mentioned above and shown in Figure 20. Distinct areas of continental crust, some thousands of kilometres across, others much smaller, rode on plates (Chapter 3) that moved independently and came together at different stages over Ordovician, Silurian and Devonian times to create the final assemblage of crustal fragments now present in Scotland. The main crustal fragments and their plates and intervening oceans are tracked in summary in Figure 25.

Episode 4: making the core of the Caledonian mountains

The core of the Caledonian mountain belt is represented by the metamorphic bedrock that forms most of the Northern Highland and Grampian Highland terranes (Fig. 20). The metamorphism of the originally largely sedimentary rocks occurred under the high pressures and temperatures that reflect their deep burial when compressive movements caused thickening of the crust and mountain uplift at the surface.

For many years a distinction has been drawn between the Moine and Dalradian supergroups in the mapping of the metamorphic core of the

Caledonian mountain belt (Figs 19 and 20). The Moine Supergroup was named after a stretch of moorland on the north coast. It forms most of the Northern Highland terrane and may be present also in part of the Grampian Highland Terrane (Fig. 19). In contrast, the Dalradian Supergroup contains a greater variety of metamorphic rock types that have made it possible to trace distinctive subdivisions across most of the rest of the Grampian Highland terrane and even into Shetland. The name Dalradian has many historic roots and, in a geological sense it simply indicates association with the Scottish Highlands and parts of Ireland. There is general agreement that the original (pre-metamorphism) sediments of the Moine are older than those of the Dalradian, but the mapping

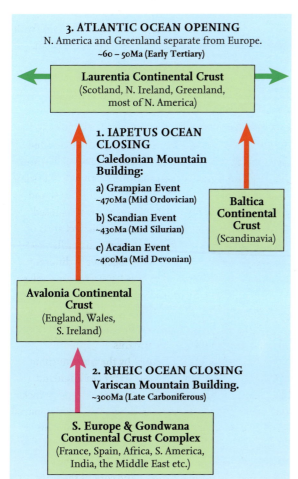

FIG 25. Diagram showing major plate-scale ocean closings and openings, with compressive events on the plate margins that generated events during the Caledonian and later Variscan mountain building. Ma (mega-annum) = million years ago.

of any boundary between them is still very arbitrary, and is not important in our review of landscapes across Scotland.

The dominant bedrock of both these supergroups is metamorphic. In other words, the bedrock has been altered but not melted, during the growth of new minerals under the high temperatures and/or pressures generated by compressive movements and thickening of the crust. The original rocks of the Moine and Dalradian were mostly formed as sediments, mainly muds and sands but also occasionally lime-rich sediments. These sediments have now been transformed into schists (also called pelites; originally mudstones) and psammites (originally sandstones).

Knowledge of the age of the original rocks and the age of their alteration depends on sophisticated analysis of the decay of radioactive mineral components. The Moine Supergroup appears to have been deposited in the Neoproterozoic (about 1000 – 900 million years ago), so it was being formed at the same time as part of the Torridonian succession, although horizontal movements have brought them closer since they formed. Today, the Moine contains evidence of at least three different episodes of mineral alteration, the first around 850 million years ago (Knoydartian), the second 470 million years ago (Grampian; mid-Ordovician) and the last roughly 430 million years ago (Scandian; mid-Silurian), each resulting from phases of movement in the Earth's crust where the rocks were moved, folded and fractured (Fig. 21). The Grampian and Scandian episodes are usefully distinguished as important phases in building the core of the Caledonian mountain belt. A further phase, the Acadian (mid-Devonian, 400 million years ago), is more clearly seen in other areas, showing that the movement pattern along the mountain belt involved many distinct continental fragments with different movement histories (Fig. 25). Much later, in the Mesozoic and Cenozoic, this belt was split by the plate divergence that formed the Atlantic Ocean, explaining why today there are other fragments of the Caledonian belt in Canada, Greenland and Scandinavia.

The Dalradian Supergroup was originally a succession of sediments more varied in type than the Moine. This has allowed the mapping of distinctive rock types across the country, revealing a complex pattern of folds (some upright, others over-folded) and fracture surfaces, themselves often folded after their original formation. These were formed by complex, multi-phase movements which occurred during a general convergence of the crust in a northwest/southeast direction. Radioactive dating indicates that much of this movement took place 470 million years ago, in the same Grampian episode that also deformed the Moine. It is estimated that the crustal rocks of the northern part of the Grampian Highland terrane were uplifted by some 25–35 km during this event, creating a major mountain range. Note that, despite such large amounts of uplift being indicated by research on the pressures that cause the metamorphism, mountains themselves never reach heights above sea level of this magnitude. The present height of Mount Everest is about 9 km, and this is thought to be some indication of the maximum height to which mountains can be lifted, given the powers of erosion that can be generated in present-day steep and high mountain belts. The mountains being measured in planets and moons may be bigger because of the different gravitational forces present.

Igneous intrusions were also formed during the Caledonian episodes, as heat from the compression produced molten magma that rose in the deforming crust, cooled and solidified, most commonly forming granites. These igneous volumes were emplaced both during and after the various phases of Caledonian movement. Where they have been exposed by erosion, they have given rise to differences in the material properties of the bedrock that have locally influenced the present-day landscapes.

The Great Glen Fault is one of the most obvious features of the landscape when Scotland is viewed from a satellite in space. Unlike the complex forms of the coastline and the river valleys, it represents a simple, straight or perhaps very slightly curved, vertical fracture cutting the crust (Figs 19, 20, 22). This major feature separating the Northern Highland and Grampian Highland terranes, and bisecting the Caledonian core, is now thought to have been part of a system of fractures that formed first in the Scandian phase (mid-Silurian, 430 million years ago) due to compressive continental movements that involved a strong enough oblique component to produce sliding parallel to the bedrock fabric of folds and faults generated by the general compression. A recent estimate of the amount of strike-slip sliding between Laurentia and Baltica (Fig. 25) during this phase is that it was about 1200 km, although this total movement was distributed between numerous faults. In the simple analysis of fault mechanics in Chapter 3 (Fig. 17), a clear distinction was drawn between reverse faulting, resulting from convergence or compression, and strike-slip faulting, resulting from shearing. The present belief is that the Great Glen, and other similar faults, formed as a result of a combination of compression and shearing, sometimes referred to as oblique-slip, or *transpression*.

Episode 5: formation of the Lower Palaeozoic of the Southern Uplands terrane
Strongly folded, fractured and altered Ordovician and Silurian bedrock predominates in the Southern Uplands terrane. The commonest material is mudstone, often altered to slate. Altered sandstones are also common, with lesser amounts of altered limestone and volcanic material (Fig. 19). In the present

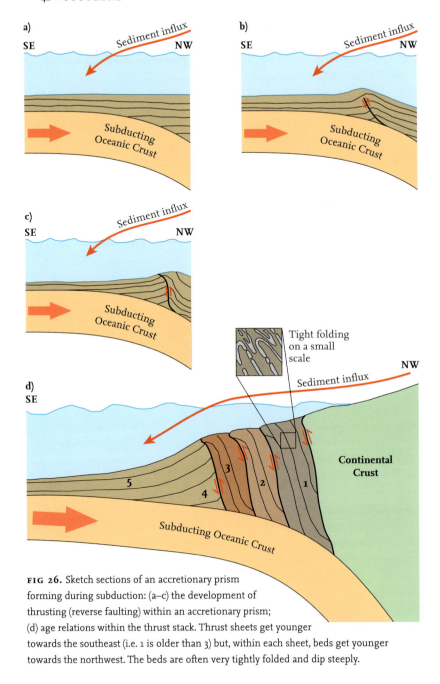

FIG 26. Sketch sections of an accretionary prism forming during subduction: (a–c) the development of thrusting (reverse faulting) within an accretionary prism; (d) age relations within the thrust stack. Thrust sheets get younger towards the southeast (i.e. 1 is older than 3) but, within each sheet, beds get younger towards the northwest. The beds are often very tightly folded and dip steeply.

landscapes, much of this material has been weathered and covered to some degree with Ice Age deposits, so good exposures of the sediments are rare and the hills of the Southern Uplands are generally more rounded and less rocky than those of the Highlands.

It is thought that these sediments first formed as an *accretionary prism*, created when ocean crust in the southeast was subducted (see Chapter 3) beneath the deforming continent to the northwest, now represented by the Highlands. As subduction continued, the newly deposited sediments were folded and scraped up into a number of slices that were made of younger and younger ocean floor sediment as the movement continued (Fig. 26). How much of the Southern Uplands formed as one of these accretionary prisms is uncertain, but it is clear that the setting was marginal to the main Caledonian mountains that lay to the north. The oceanic crust was subducted along a line (locally called the Iapetus Suture: see Fig. 20) that lay to the southeast of the Southern Uplands, roughly along the present Scotland–England border.

Episode 6: formation of the Lower Old Red Sandstone

Old Red Sandstone is the name commonly given to the red sandstones, mudstones and conglomerates that underlie rocks of Carboniferous age. The Old Red rests unconformably on older rocks in all of the Scottish terranes except the Hebridean, where it is absent (Figs 19, 20). Successions of this bedrock have been classified as Lower, Middle and Upper Old Red Sandstone, depending on their fossil content and spatial relationships. Episode 6 concerns only the deposition of the Lower Old Red Sandstone.

Although fossil evidence for dating the Lower Old Red Sandstone is not common, the primitive fish and plant fossils that do occur indicate that it was deposited during the late Silurian and early Devonian, about 420 – 400 million years ago (Fig. 21). The weathering properties of these rocks are such that, in their present-day erosional landscapes, the conglomerates (with their associated lavas) have generally resisted erosion, tending to produce distinct ridges and steep slopes.

The processes of surface modification that deposited the Lower Old Red Sandstone took place largely on land, in rivers and lakes, with small amounts of sediment transported locally by the wind. Great thicknesses of lava are also important, particularly in the Midland Valley, Grampian Highlands and the Cheviot area of the Southern Uplands. The andesitic composition of these lavas suggests they were formed by internal Earth movements related to the plate subduction associated with Episode 5, and they are the earliest Scottish rocks to have yielded reliable measurements of their magnetism at the time of their formation. This information has been used to show that Scotland was located

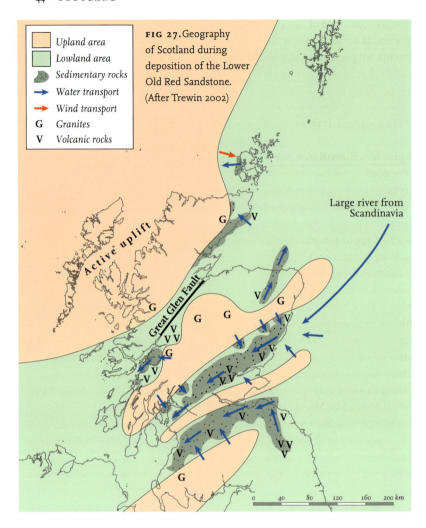

FIG 27. Geography of Scotland during deposition of the Lower Old Red Sandstone. (After Trewin 2002)

roughly 20 degrees south of the equator at this time, and it is believed that the Scottish terranes had moved into approximately their present-day positions, relative to one another, by the end of this episode (Fig. 25).

It seems likely that many of the late Silurian and early Devonian sediments and igneous rocks accumulated in distinct subsiding basins, separated by a series of northeast/southwest-trending uplifting areas that formed during the later phases of the Caledonian mountain building. Although much of the sediment in these basins was derived locally from these actively moving uplands, there is evidence that some of it was transported here by large rivers flowing from other areas of active movement in Scandinavia. The fact that the Lower Old Red sediments are predominantly non-marine in nature shows that most of the crustal surface of Scotland had been raised above sea level by this time (Fig. 27).

POST-CALEDONIAN EPISODES

Episode 7: formation of the middle to late Devonian, Carboniferous and Permian

It is convenient to group together as one episode the deposition of the Middle and Upper Old Red Sandstone (Devonian), the rocks of the Carboniferous and those of the Permian. The total time period represented by these units extends from about 395 to 290 million years ago, by which time Scotland had moved north to equatorial latitudes. The rocks of this episode consist largely of mudstones and sandstones, deposited by rivers in lakes, on coasts and in shallow seas. They vary considerably in age and extent, lying on the eroded top of the deformed Caledonian bedrock and often reaching thicknesses of many kilometres.

Although there is plenty of evidence of internal earth movements during this episode, their intensity and regional geography indicates a change from the strongly compressive regime associated with the Caledonian mountain building and the closing of the Iapetus Ocean (Episodes 4 to 6). By the mid-Devonian, extension had begun through much of Scotland, resulting in the formation of subsiding basins. The Middle Old Red Sandstone formed in a particularly large basin often referred to as the Orcadian Lake Basin (Fig. 28). This extensional tectonic regime continued to characterise Scotland during much of the Carboniferous.

During the Devonian and Permian, sandy, wind-blown dune fields and evaporating groundwater conditions existed at times when local deserts developed under arid climatic conditions. The Carboniferous by contrast lacks evidence of such arid climates: river mouths were often deltaic, and the regular movement of river channels deposited distinctive cycles in the sedimentary succession, consisting of vertical changes in sediment type – most obviously between sheets of sandstone and mudstone. Limestones are also sometimes dominant where sources of sand and mud were absent. Coal-forming conditions developed repeatedly during the Carboniferous, particularly in parts of what is now the Midland Valley, and hydrocarbon-bearing mudstones were briefly but vigorously exploited west of Edinburgh. Both these had an important influence on economic and social development both locally and nationally. Carboniferous limestones, ironstones and certain sandstones have been economically important as well, at least in local terms.

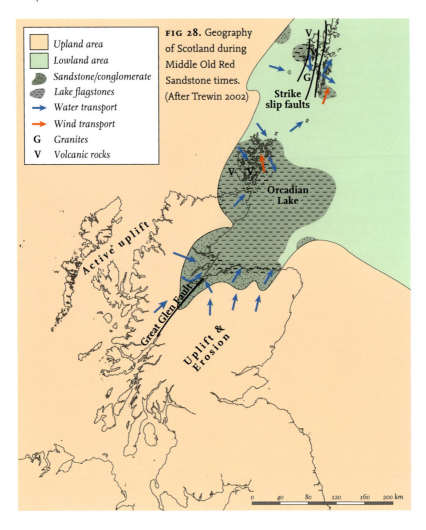

FIG 28. Geography of Scotland during Middle Old Red Sandstone times. (After Trewin 2002)

Legend:
- Upland area
- Lowland area
- Sandstone/conglomerate
- Lake flagstones
- Water transport
- Wind transport
- G Granites
- V Volcanic rocks

Because of their economic significance, many of the Carboniferous deposits formed in this episode have been studied in great detail: tracing individual marker beds and attempting to date them by painstaking analysis of the fossil fauna and flora contained within them. This work has revealed that the Carboniferous sediments were deposited in large numbers of subsiding basins, usually only a few kilometres or tens of kilometres across (Fig. 29). These basins formed due to vertical movements of the Earth's crust along faults, the continued activity of which caused thickening and thinning of the sediments as they accumulated.

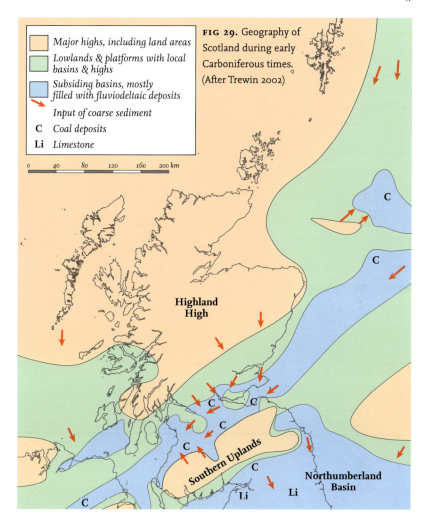

FIG 29. Geography of Scotland during early Carboniferous times. (After Trewin 2002.)

As well as sedimentation, this episode also involved considerable Carboniferous igneous activity, creating volcanoes and extensive lava fields and injecting large bodies of molten rock into the crust. This igneous bedrock has had a profound effect on the present-day landscape of the Midland Valley, and also on parts of the Southern Uplands. The weathering and erosion of the landscape has preferentially picked out the igneous bedrock because it is generally more resistant than the neighbouring sediments.

The Variscan mountain building (Fig. 25) is clearly represented in southwestern

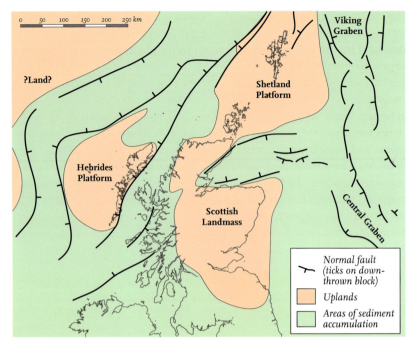

FIG 30. Geography of Scotland and its surroundings during the Jurassic.

England and southern Ireland. In Scotland, it appears to be represented only by a change from Carboniferous deltaic sedimentation to undoubtedly freshwater or aeolian sedimentation in New Red Sandstone times, ushering in the Mesozoic.

Episode 8: Mesozoic sedimentation

There are only relatively small volumes of Mesozoic sediment preserved as bedrock within the land area of modern-day Scotland, but large offshore areas of the sea bed are underlain by sediment of this age. The simple explanation for this is that the approximate map-shape of present-day Scotland was already becoming established by the beginning of the Mesozoic, resulting in extensive erosion of much of today's landmass, followed by deposition in areas that are still offshore. Reconstructions of the geography of Jurassic times, say 175 million years ago, show an upland area roughly the shape of present-day eastern and northern Scotland. This area was surrounded by basins along the Hebridean and Atlantic margins to the west and by the North Sea to the east, into which sediments accumulated (Fig. 30). Conditions varied between the areas of accumulation, but this broad pattern continued from the Triassic, through Jurassic and Cretaceous times.

The sandstones and mudstones of the Triassic are often red due to oxidisation of their iron minerals, indicating a dry, desert-like climate. Conditions at this time were influenced partly by the global climate, but also by the general pattern of plate movement which, by the end of the Triassic, saw Scotland at about 30 degrees north – equivalent to the present-day latitude of the Canary Islands.

In Jurassic times, where river deltas fed into shallow seas, a wide variety of rock types was deposited: mudstones, sandstones and limestones, along with rare ironstones and coals. Organic material – largely algal – formed locally in some of the muddy seas and was particularly abundant in the case of the Late Jurassic Kimmeridge Clay. This unit has been the main 'source rock' for the North Sea hydrocarbons that have had such a critical influence on the British economy over the last 40 years. Key points in the trapping and preservation of the hydrocarbons are the presence of sandstone with a suitable porosity, and earth movements that have subsequently stretched the crust, faulting it to seal the hydrocarbon reservoirs. Meanwhile, fault-related Jurassic landslide deposits are a spectacular feature of outcrops on one stretch of the east coast of the northern Highlands (see Areas 16 and 17), while in some parts of the Hebrides Jurassic sandstones have provided resistant bedrock that has influenced the development of the landscape.

Cretaceous bedrock is very rare on land in Scotland and is generally only preserved as isolated fragments in areas of Tertiary volcanism, where sheets of lava have protected the Cretaceous rocks from the erosion that has removed them elsewhere. Small amounts of sandstone and chalk (the Late Cretaceous algal limestone that is such a dominant feature of the landscape of southern England and northern France) are preserved in some of the volcanic centres, but do not tend to influence landscapes on a scale that can be considered in this book. On the other hand, the offshore record of the Late Cretaceous around Scotland is much more complete, and the lack of mud and sand (derived from the erosion of land-based bedrock) in these deposits suggests that Scotland had been eroded down to a largely flat landscape by this time.

Episode 9: Tertiary volcanism

About 60 million years ago, in the earliest Tertiary, a dramatic episode of igneous activity took place along the western seaboard of mainland Britain. The resulting bedrock has played a major role in forming features of the landscape of the western Hebridean, Northern Highland and Midland Valley terranes. Successions of lava flows formed volcanic lava fields tens to hundreds of metres thick in many areas of the Inner Hebrides and northern Ireland. Distinct fields have been dated

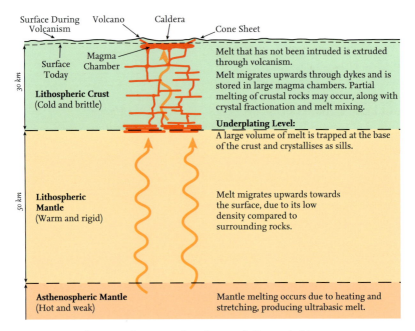

FIG 31. General pattern of processes thought to underlie a typical igneous centre.

around Eigg and Muck at 60.5 million years old, around Skye and Canna at 58 million years old and around Mull and Morvern at between 58.5 and 55 million years old. The layered ('stepped') landscapes eroded in the bedrock of these lava fields are striking, and are due primarily to differences in erosional resistance between the lower and upper parts of each lava flow.

Even more striking are the centres of volcanic activity and igneous intrusion that developed in a scatter of localities shortly after the lava fields formed (Fig. 31). The coarsely crystalline intrusive rocks of these centres dominate the landscapes of their surroundings, because of the resistance of this material to erosion. The eroded remains of these ancient igneous centres now form the remarkable Cuillin and the Red Hills of Skye, the mountains of Rum, the hills of the Ardnamurchan peninsula and the main mountains of Mull and Arran, not to mention the islands of St Kilda and Ailsa Craig.

In wider geographical terms, these Tertiary igneous activities, along with the associated uplift and erosion, were responses to the tectonic plate divergence movements that created the Atlantic Ocean, with additional igneous input related to 'hot-spot' activity in east Greenland, Iceland, the Faroes, western Scotland and northern Ireland.

CHAPTER 5

Later Surface Modifications

THE PREVIOUS CHAPTER dealt with nine episodes recorded in the bedrock of Scotland. This chapter deals with three more recent episodes (Episodes 10–12; Fig. 21) which have modified the surface, removing bedrock and adding soft material to the surface blanket.

SURFACE-MODIFICATION EPISODES

Episode 10: Tertiary landscape erosion
Dating of the lavas extruded in Episode 9 suggests that Tertiary igneous activity in Scotland lasted for only about 5 million years and finished about 55 million years ago. This was followed by more than 50 million years of Tertiary and Quaternary landscape erosion (Fig. 21), during which time the main valleys of present-day Scotland increasingly approached their present shape and size.

Sedimentary bedrock of Tertiary age (Palaeogene and Neogene) is very largely absent on land in Scotland, even where volcanic and other igneous bedrock is present. This suggests that the crust below the present land area of Scotland was moving upwards and was subjected to net erosion during most of the Tertiary. Part of the evidence for this is the large thickness of Tertiary sandstones and mudstones that are found offshore to the east, north and west of Scotland, as shown by extensive oil exploration.

The valleys and mountains of Scotland, along with the lochs, sea lochs and offshore rock basins, have all been shaped by this erosion, principally by Tertiary rivers but also by more recent glacial ice (Episode 11). The present-day drainage pattern in Scotland (see Chapter 2) represents the latest phase in the evolution of this erosional system, and provides clues to the way it may have developed over the past 55 million years.

Episode 11: the Ice Age

During the nineteenth century, it became generally accepted that much of Britain had been subjected to glaciation by ice sheets and valley glaciers. Since then, this distinctive episode in the history of the British landscape has been referred to as the Ice Age, broadly equivalent to the Quaternary period of the internationally accepted series of time divisions (Fig. 21).

Over the last few years of geological research, one of the most far-reaching developments has been the establishment of the detailed record of fluctuating climate changes that have occurred during the Ice Age. A key step in this advance was the realisation that various indicators (often called *proxies*) of climate change can be measured at very high time resolution in successions of sediment or ice. The first of these successions to be tackled covered only the last few thousand years, but further work has now provided estimates of global temperature extending back several million years.

One of the best climate indicators has turned out to be variations in the ratios of oxygen isotopes (oxygen-16 versus oxygen-18), as recorded by microfossils that have been deposited over time on deep ocean floors. When alive, these organisms floated in the surface waters, where their skeletons incorporated the chemistry of the ocean water – including the relative amounts of oxygen-16 and oxygen-18. During cold climatic periods (*glacials*) water evaporating from the oceans may fall as snow on land and may be incorporated within ice sheets. Because oxygen-16 is lighter than oxygen-18 it evaporates more easily, so during cold periods the newly formed ice sheets tend to be rich in oxygen-16, relative to the oceans. The ratio of oxygen isotopes in the world's oceans, as recorded by microfossils, can therefore be used to distinguish glacial and interglacial periods. Other useful indicators of ancient climate have come from measuring the chemical properties of ice cores, which preserve a record of the atmospheric oxygen composition, to complement the oceanic data from sediment cores.

Ratios of the isotopes of oxygen have turned out to provide one of the most important indicators of climate change, because they depend principally on ocean temperature and the amount of water locked up in the world's ice sheets. There are, however, numerous other factors that can affect the ratios in ice and sediment cores, so interpretation of the data is rarely straightforward.

Figure 32 shows corrected oxygen isotope ratios as an indicator of temperature over the last 3.3 million years. The numbers on the vertical axis are expressed as $\delta^{18}O$ values (pronounced 'delta 18 O'), which compare the oxygen-18/oxygen-16 ratios in a given sample to those in an internationally accepted standard. The greater the proportion of heavy oxygen-18 in a sample the larger the $\delta^{18}O$ value and, as described above, the lower the corresponding

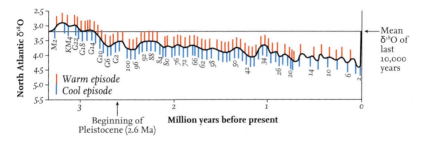

FIG 32. Oxygen isotope ratios track the more than 100 climate fluctuations over the last 3.3 million years. Warm episodes (red lines above the curve) alternate with cold episodes (blue lines below the curve). These have been used as the basis for numbering the global oxygen isotope stages, as shown.

ocean temperature. For this reason, the vertical axis on Figure 32 is plotted with the numbers decreasing upwards, so that warmer temperatures are at the top of the figure and cooler ones at the bottom. The pattern shown in Figure 32 is of an overall cooling trend with, in detail, a remarkable series of over 100 warm and cool periods or oscillations. These alternations have been numbered, for ease of communication by the scientific community, with even numbers for the cold periods and odd numbers for the warm periods.

Our next step involves looking in greater detail over roughly the last 400,000 years (Fig. 33). Over this period, there has been a distinctive pattern of increasingly highly developed 100,000-year-long cold stages, separated by 10,000-year-long warmer stages. This temperature curve (also calculated from isotope ratios) is saw-toothed in shape, representing long periods of cooling followed by rapid warming events. The most recent of the four glacial episodes covered in this diagram (the Devensian) has left abundant fresh evidence on the landscapes of Scotland and obliterated most of the evidence of the earlier ones. In this important respect, the Scottish evidence differs strongly from that of southern England, where the much earlier Anglian glacial episode has left abundant evidence of ice as far south as London. This is because later glaciations, such as the Devensian, did not reach so far south. Not surprisingly, the older evidence in southern England is not as fresh as that of the younger glaciation in Scotland.

An even closer look at the last of these cold-to-warm changes (Fig. 34, black line) allows us to appreciate better the glaciation which has been responsible for much of the recent modification of Scottish landscapes. Starting with the Ipswichian interglacial, the Greenland curve shows fluctuations in the oxygen isotope ratios that were frequent and short-lived, though generally implying

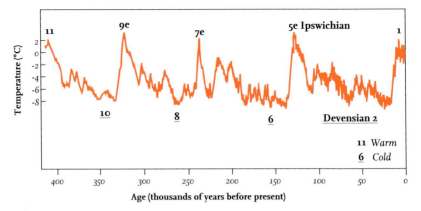

FIG 33. Isotopic temperature of the atmosphere changing through the last 400,000 years, measured from ice cores taken from Vostok, Antarctica.

increasingly cool conditions. This part of the record is helping to define the Devensian glaciation and shows clearly the Late Glacial Maximum (LGM) at between about 30,000 and 20,000 years ago. Following this, the beginning of the Holocene warm period (about 10,000 years ago) is also clear.

The link between oxygen isotopes, temperature and sea level becomes clear if we compare oxygen isotope ratios from the Greenland ice (Fig. 34, black line) with sea-level data from tropical reefs in Papua New Guinea (Fig. 34, red line). The data show how colder climates are generally associated with lower sea levels, reflecting

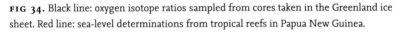

FIG 34. Black line: oxygen isotope ratios sampled from cores taken in the Greenland ice sheet. Red line: sea-level determinations from tropical reefs in Papua New Guinea.

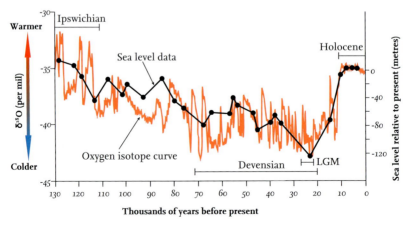

the locking up of oxygen-16-rich water in land-based ice sheets during these colder times.

At its maximum extent the Devensian ice sheet covered the whole of Scotland, including the western and northern islands. It also covered most of Wales and northern England and extended as far south as the Midlands, the Bristol Channel and the Wash. Maintaining a thickness of many hundreds of metres, it joined Norwegian ice on the Norwegian side of the northern North Sea (Figs 35, 36).

FIG 35. One estimate of the maximum extent of the Devensian ice sheet, with generalised ice-flow directions. At a later stage the Scottish and Norwegian ice became separated.

FIG 36 (BELOW). West-to-east generalised cross-section at the maximum extent of the Devensian ice sheet.

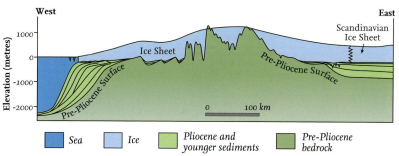

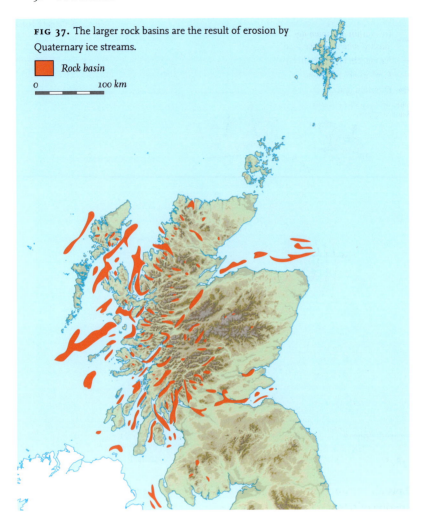

FIG 37. The larger rock basins are the result of erosion by Quaternary ice streams.

There is abundant local evidence in Scotland of the modification of valleys by glaciers and ice streams, which deepened and opened out the valley profiles, removing spurs and side ridges, to produce classic U-shaped glacial troughs. These troughs are very different from the V-shaped cross-sections and sinuous forms typical of river erosion (see Fig. 8, Chapter 2). This modification work is likely to have taken place in every one of the Ice Age glacial stages that occurred in Scotland, and the same processes have also been responsible for the elongate rock basins now recognised in many offshore areas (Fig. 37).

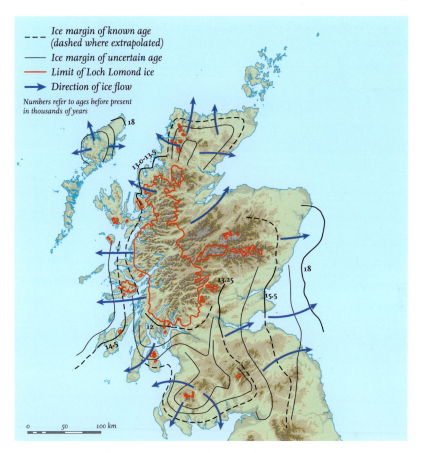

FIG 38. Shrinking of the main Scottish ice sheet over the last 18,000 years.

Episode 12: since the Devensian Late Glacial Maximum

The period of rather more than 20,000 years since the Late Glacial Maximum represents one of the most recent phases of intense landscape evolution (Fig. 38). Because this was a period when ice cover was generally decreasing, local evidence is often preserved that would have been destroyed during a major phase of advancing ice. The last 10,000 years is often referred to as either the Holocene or the Flandrian Interglacial, the latter name emphasising that the ice may well return.

The record of climate change since the Late Glacial Maximum has been greatly illuminated by the same use of oxygen isotopes as described above for Episode 11. One important advantage in working on these recent times is that it is possible to seek additional, independent information for the ages of samples.

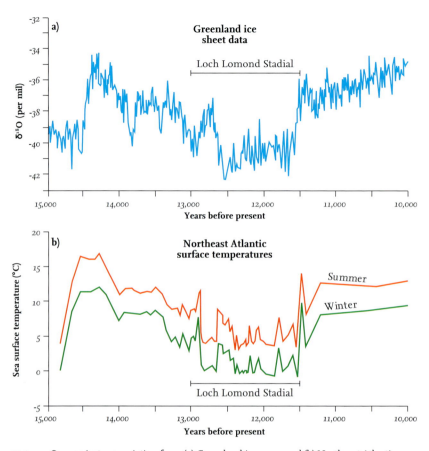

FIG 39. Oxygen isotope variation from (a) Greenland ice cores and (b) Northeast Atlantic sea-surface temperatures, both over the time period from 15,000 to 10,000 years BP (before present).

Some of this dating may be based on comparison of plant remains, particularly pollen from cores extracted by drilling into lake beds or peat-rich wetlands. Other dates come from the analysis of radioactive carbon, whose rapid decay rate makes it a powerful tool in dating material that is so relatively young.

Although the dominant feature of global climate change over the past 20,000 years has been the general warming trend, detailed research has established a complex pattern of climatic fluctuations. In Scotland, the most important of these fluctuations is the Younger Dryas cold phase, also known as the Loch Lomond Stadial (Fig. 39). During this time, between about 13,000 and 11,500 years ago, the generally retreating ice re-advanced to form an icecap covering much of the western Highlands (Fig. 38, red line). The local effects of this Loch Lomond Advance are particularly clear within the area of western Scotland where moraines were pushed forward.

SEA-LEVEL CHANGE

In Areas with coastlines, some of the freshest features of the landscape have formed since the Late Glacial Maximum as a result of changes in sea level. Two different mechanisms have combined to produce these changes:

(1) Worldwide ocean-volume changes of the water occupying the world's ocean basins. These have been the direct result of the locking-up or releasing of water from land-based ice sheets as they grow or shrink due to climate fluctuations. The water itself may also have expanded or contracted as its temperature changed. These worldwide processes are often grouped together as *eustatic*.
(2) Solid Earth local movements which have resulted in the local raising or lowering of the ground surface relative to the level of the sea. These movements were responses to changes in the local temperature or stress pattern within the Earth. Ice-sheet melting unloaded the crust of the Earth locally, resulting in uplift, while ice-sheet growth loaded the crust, resulting in subsidence. These effects are often referred to as *isostatic* adjustments of local sea level (see Chapters 2 and 3).

Some parts of the world, for example many tropical areas, have been free of ice since before the Late Glacial Maximum and so have avoided any solid Earth movements associated with loading and unloading by ice. Records of changing sea level from these areas can therefore be used to estimate worldwide (eustatic) changes in the volume of the world's oceans since the Late Glacial Maximum. Figure 40 shows that eustatic sea level has risen by about 120 m over the past 18,000 years, beginning with a slow, steady rise until about 12,000 years ago, followed by a rapid increase until about 6,000 years ago, and then another slow, steady phase up to the present day.

Curves of local sea-level change for any area can be estimated (relative to the present) by recognising and dating various features that indicate elevations in ancient coastal profiles. These features, preserved in the rocks either above or below the present sea level, include former erosional cliff lines, wave-cut platforms and ancient tidal, estuarine or freshwater deposits. The similarity or otherwise of such curves to the eustatic curve (Fig. 40) depends on whether the areas in question have been subjected to any localised solid Earth movements, such as ice loading or unloading.

Two examples of British sea-level curves, relative to the present, illustrate how the local uplift and subsidence history varies for different coastal areas around Britain. In the Thames Estuary, local evidence shows that a rise of some 40 m has taken place through time over the last 10,000 years, at first very rapidly but then more slowly between about 6,000 years ago and the present (Fig. 41, red circles). Modelling of the processes involved, incorporating estimates of eustatic (global) sea-level change and local solid Earth movements, gives a fairly good match to the observational data (Fig. 41, black line).

Our second example of relative sea-level change comes from the upper River Forth and is quite different. It shows that there has been a *fall* of relative sea level of about 50 m over the past 15,000 years, so that former coastline features are now visible well above the present-day coast (Fig. 42, red circles). This type of curve is common in Scotland and, given the ~120 m worldwide rise in sea level shown in Figure 40, it is clear that the crust of the Forth region must have been subjected to significant uplift (~170 m) in order to produce the curve shown in Figure 42. This uplift is largely the result of *isostatic rebound* due to unloading of the crust as the ice retreated.

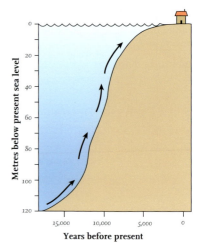

FIG 40. Generalised change of worldwide (eustatic) sea level over the past 18,000 years. (After Van Andel 1994, Fig. 4.11)

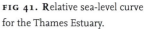

FIG 41. Relative sea-level curve for the Thames Estuary.

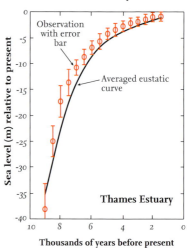

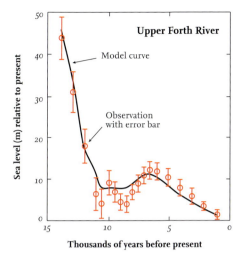

FIG 42. Relative sea-level curve for the upper River Forth at Arnprior.

In some curves, as with the upper Forth, oscillations in the curve represent changes in the rates at which the two mechanisms of change were operating. Such changes may leave characteristic coastline features in the landscape, which will be considered in the Area descriptions.

At larger scales, it is useful to consider average rates of crustal movement over a given time period, which can then be plotted as contour maps. The contours shown on Figure 43 are based on estimates of local elevation changes averaged over roughly the last 5,000 years, attempting also to allow for the effects of eustatic sea-level variations. Additional support for this approach comes from data from tide-gauge studies, collected over the last 200 years, which show some consistency with this pattern.

Although our two local studies in the Thames region and the upper Forth (Figs 41, 42) involve a rather longer timescale than the regional analysis (Fig. 43), all three studies highlight the clear contrast between crustal movements in southeastern England and those in western and central Scotland. These variations have been produced by differences in ice-sheet thickness and extent during the last (Devensian) glacial.

The distinctive rise of the land of Scotland relative to sea level lends itself to another approach to the study of sea-level change. Figure 44 shows a plot of the elevations and gradients of various old shoreline features that are now above present-day sea level across Scotland and northern England. These old shoreline features have clearly been uplifted, and those further inland have generally risen more than those near to the present-day coast, so that they now form a dome-like structure. This dome is broadly centred on Rannoch Moor, which was one of Scotland's main ice centres during the last glaciation. We can therefore usefully identify a Rannoch Rebound Dome as an active feature of local Earth movement, resulting from unloading of the crust of western Scotland in response as the Devensian ice melted.

FIG 43. General trends of crustal movement, relative to sea level, averaged over the last 5000 years.

FIG 44 (BELOW). The elevations and gradients of various old shoreline features along a horseshoe-shaped traverse across northern Britain, suggesting the Rannoch Rebound Dome.

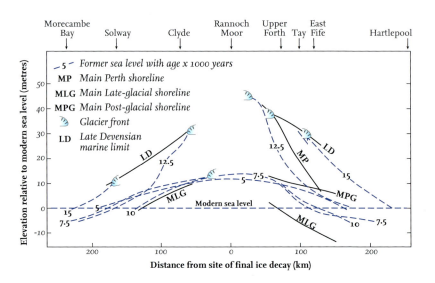

CHAPTER 6

Area 1: Galloway

AREA 1 EXTENDS FROM AYR in the northwest down to Dumfries in the southeast (Fig. 45). It lies mainly within the western half of the Southern Uplands, a terrain of rolling hills, bounded to the west by the Firth of Clyde and its numerous sandy bays. The Southern Uplands Fault crosses the northern half of the Area, separating the Southern Uplands from the generally lower-lying ground of the Midland Valley, with its volcanic hills and important coal reserves (Fig. 46).

People have inhabited this Area for thousands of years, and it was an important gateway between England and Ireland. There are many remains of human occupation dating from prehistoric times to the present day, ranging

FIG 45. Location map for Area 1.

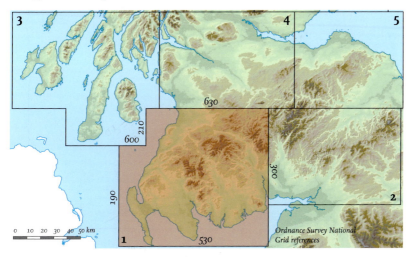

FIG 46. Natural and man-made features of Area 1.

from Mesolithic fish traps to medieval burghs and castles. Another interesting feature of Area 1 is the unusual place names, particularly in the Southern Uplands themselves, where Old Norse, Gaelic and Celtic influences can be seen. Examples are the Rig of the Jarkness and the Dungeon of Buchan.

STORIES FROM THE BEDROCK

Geologically speaking, Area 1 lies mainly within the Southern Uplands terrane, sandwiched between the Iapetus Suture in the south and the Southern Uplands Fault in the north (see Fig. 20, Chapter 4). The bedrock of the Southern Uplands (Figs 47, 48) is mostly altered Ordovician and Silurian sedimentary rocks, deposited between 490 and 420 million years ago on the floor of the Iapetus Ocean (see Chapters 1–5). The sediments which make up this bedrock were swept off a nearby continental shelf and down the continental slope in

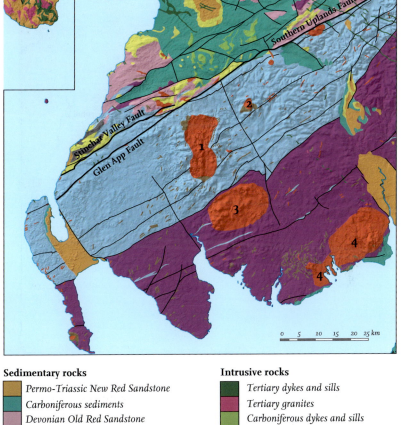

Sedimentary rocks
- Permo-Triassic New Red Sandstone
- Carboniferous sediments
- Devonian Old Red Sandstone
- Silurian sediments
- Ordovician sediments

Extrusive rocks
- Palaeozoic lava and tuff

/ Major fault
/ Fault

Intrusive rocks
- Tertiary dykes and sills
- Tertiary granites
- Carboniferous dykes and sills
- Devonian gabbros and basic dykes
- Devonian granites and felsic dykes
- Cambro-Ordovician ophiolite

1 Loch Doon granite
2 Cairnsmore of Carsphairn granite
3 Cairnsmore of Fleet granite
4 Dalbeatie-Criffel granite

FIG 47. Simplified geology and hill-shaded topography for Area 1.

turbid (muddy, cloudy) currents – underwater avalanches, more dense than the surrounding sea water – that were probably earthquake-triggered. On reaching the flat ocean floor, the entrained sediments in each avalanche gradually settled – coarse sands first, followed by fine sand, and then the much slower

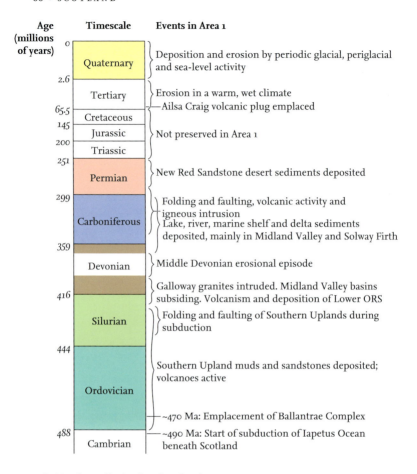

FIG 48. Timeline of bedrock and surface-layer events in Area 1.

deposition of clay and mud. In this way, each turbid current resulted in a graded bed, from coarse-grained at the bottom to fine-grained at the top, and as the process repeated itself many times, a thick sequence of such beds built up. Small amounts of limestone were also deposited, along with volcanic material such as pale ash layers. Graptolites – small, now-extinct marine animals – are common in the fine-grained sediments of the Southern Uplands. Their rapid evolutionary changes of form mean they have become very useful time markers for determining the relative ages of different sedimentary beds, especially when combined with studies of the folds and faults, in reconstructing the origins of the Southern Uplands.

Prior to the Caledonian mountain building, the crustal foundations of Scotland and England were separated by the Iapetus Ocean. Around 490 million years ago, this ocean began to be destroyed by subduction: oceanic crust moved down into the mantle beneath the Grampian Highlands, and then beneath the Midland Valley (see Chapter 4). A small fragment of this oceanic crust escaped subduction, being instead thrust up onto the margin of Scotland, to be 'welded' onto the Midland Valley by around 470 million years ago. Today, this small but intensively studied area of complexly interfolded rock units outcrops around Ballantrae, the so-called the Ballantrae Complex. Rocks characteristic of the deep sea and oceanic crust are found – sediments such as black shale and chert, basalt lavas with pillow structures, ash, sheets of dykes and upper mantle rocks. The latter originated at depths of up to 40 km in the Earth's crust, and are today coarse-grained (mafic) gabbros and serpentinite.

The main deformation of the Southern Uplands terrane occurred during the later stages of the Caledonian mountain building, between the mid-Ordovician and the early Devonian. As oceanic crust continued to be subducted, the sediments which today make up the Southern Uplands were scraped off the ocean floor along a series of thrust faults and stacked up in a pile against the edge of the Midland Valley (Fig. 28). During this deformation, the sediments became tightly folded and weakly metamorphosed: fine-grained mudstone and siltstone became slate, while cement within sandstones recrystallised to produce a tough, hard rock (greywacke). Today, bedding in the Southern Uplands is aligned in a general northeast/southwest direction and dips very steeply to the southeast, and northeast/southwest faults divide the region into numerous fault blocks.

By the start of the Devonian (around 415 million years ago), the major deformation of the Southern Uplands had ceased and Scotland and England were welded along the Iapetus Suture. It was around this time that the major granite bodies of the Southern Uplands (Fig. 47) were emplaced: partial melting at the base of the thickened crust produced liquid magma, which then rose up into the upper crust where it slowly solidified to form coarse-grained igneous bodies (plutons). As the overlying rocks were subsequently removed by erosion, three major plutons were revealed in the Southern Uplands. The most northerly of these is the hourglass-shaped Loch Doon intrusion, said to be one of the finest examples in Scotland of a concentrically zoned pluton: the interior of the body is silica-rich (felsic) granite, separated from the outer silica-poor grey granodiorite which makes up most of the body by a transition zone. Similar well-developed concentric zonation is seen in the eastern half of the Criffel–Dalbeattie body on the south coast, although overall this body is much less compositionally evolved (i.e. it has a lower silica content) than the other Southern Uplands granites.

FIG 49. Cairnsmore of Fleet, 711 m (10 km east of Newton Stewart), viewed from the southeast. This mountain landscape has been created by erosion of the Fleet granite intrusion. (© Lorne Gill, Scottish Natural Heritage)

It is also the most deformed: originally oval, its western part has been distorted southwards by complex faulting. Porphyrite dykes and sills commonly surround the main intrusion (e.g. at Black Stockarton Moor), made up of large crystals embedded in a fine, glassy groundmass. Between the two, the roughly oval Fleet pluton was intruded around 390 million years ago (Devonian) into a broad ductile shear zone, making it the youngest reliably dated Caledonian pluton in mainland Scotland (Fig. 49). It is also the most evolved of the Southern Uplands intrusions, consisting entirely of granite, and is the only intrusion whose magmas were sourced wholly from the melting of metamorphosed sediments (rather than igneous rocks). Because of both its young age and its evolved composition, this pluton has more in common with the Lake District and Northern Ireland granites than with those of Scotland, and it has been suggested that these areas shared a magma source.

As these hot granite bodies were emplaced, their heat baked the surrounding rocks, creating an encircling metamorphosed zone (an *aureole*) 1 km or, in the case of the Criffel–Dalbeattie intrusion, even 2 km wide. These aureoles are often rich in mineral veins, deposited by hot circulating fluids released by the crystallising granite. Gold, silver, copper, lead and zinc are common, particularly around the Fleet intrusion, and over 60 copper and iron-rich carbonate veins have been located northwest of the Criffel–Dalbeattie pluton.

Volcanic vents active during the early Devonian are also present in the area, although they are generally poorly preserved. An exception is the large vent at Shoulder o' Craig, 17 km southwest of Castle Douglas, on the Dee estuary. The headland here is principally made up of a vent-filling intrusion breccia, which consists of Silurian sandstone and siltstone clasts within a basalt (mafic) matrix. Both vent rock and country rock are cut by very potassium-rich dykes, indicating a magma source deep within the mantle. These dykes often have irregular shapes, and one dyke in the area is known as the 'Loch Ness Monster' due to its particularly bizarre outcrop pattern. On a regional scale, this area presents a bit of a conundrum, as volcanic vents, mantle-derived dykes and granite plutons, i.e. igneous rocks from all depths within the crust, were intruded around the same time (between around 415 and 400 million years ago, earliest Devonian), and are now seen at the same level of erosion.

Further north, the late Silurian and early Devonian was the time when a series of basins first began to develop in what would become the Midland Valley, as crustal tension caused movement on the Highland Boundary and Southern Uplands faults. At this time (around 420 to 400 million years ago), Scotland lay in the interior of a large continent some 20 degrees south of the equator, and in this environment the new Caledonian mountains were eroded rapidly because soil-binding plant cover had not yet evolved. Rivers and streams washed the sediment into the developing Midland Valley basins, forming coarse conglomerates, red sandstones and mudstones, collectively called the Lower Old Red Sandstone. Volcanic rocks (associated with crustal extension) are common in the upper 600 m of the Lower Old Red Sandstone, where lava sheets (predominantly andesite) are intercalated with river and lake sediments, mostly sandstones. Today, principal outcrops include a 400 m-thick lava pile underlying the Carrick Hills and a 600 m-thick lava pile in the Dalmellington area (20 and 30 km east of Girvan, respectively).

The Carrick Hills lava pile is particularly well exposed along the coast around Dunure (10 km southwest of Ayr). This coastal section has been studied for over a century in an attempt to unravel the complex relationships between the lava and intervening sediment; the upper and lower surfaces of andesite (mafic) sheets are often very irregular, with bulbous, finger-like protrusions that extend upwards and downwards into the sediment, or have become detached completely, forming zones of lava pillows. In places, lava engulfs patches of sediment; elsewhere, the lava is surrounded by sediment. The andesite sheets are generally well jointed, and these joints are often filled with hardened sandstone. Despite these contorted relationships, lamination in the sandstones is generally intact, save for a small zone near the contact. Such irregular contacts are thought to result from the sills being intruded into wet, unconsolidated sediment; as hot magma was emplaced, it vaporised water at the magma–sediment contact, fluidising the sediment in a narrow zone next to the contact. This vapour and its entrained sediment then flowed away along the hot contact surface, offering very little resistance to the magma and allowing bulbous protrusions to form. Likewise, the liquid magma could not push directly against the wet host sediment, and so this sediment remains largely undeformed, except at the contact zone. After intrusion, large amounts of water vapour were trapped in sediment enclaves and at contact zones. As the andesite then cooled, it contracted and cracked, often resulting in a sudden decrease of pressure in the sediment. This led to explosive boiling of the water, fluidising the sediment and blasting it along the fractures and cooling joints. Vesicles (cavities formed by gas bubbles) are also very common in the lavas, generally now infilled by minerals such as quartz, agate or chalcedony precipitated by circulating groundwaters.

By the middle Devonian (400 to 385 million years ago), further earth movements resulted in uplift and erosion of much of the sediment laid down in early Devonian times, and some of the underlying Ordovician and Silurian. The main granite bodies probably became exposed at the surface during this time, as evidenced by the clasts of Criffel–Dalbeattie granite found in Upper Old Red Sandstone deposits in Area 2 to the east. These late Devonian deposits are rare in Area 1, only outcropping near Dalmellington in a thin strip north of the Southern Uplands Fault.

The Caledonian Mountains had been largely eroded by the start of the Carboniferous, around 360 million years ago, although the Southern Uplands still formed a considerable upland area. Throughout the following 60 million years of the Carboniferous, deposition occurred mostly in the lowlands of the Midland Valley and the Solway Firth basins in marine or coastal-plain environments. Sea levels varied, resulting in the deposition of limestones, sandstones, mudstones and coal, often arranged in 'cycles' of varying layers, as shallow seas and river estuaries gave way repeatedly to swampy forests. Towards the end of the deposition of the Lower Carboniferous, the Southern Uplands had been sufficiently lowered by erosion to be breached by the sea along what is today Nithsdale, and the Midland Valley and Solway Firth basins were linked. Coal deposits were laid down under swampy conditions in the Carboniferous, and are today found around Sanquhar and Thornhill and in the larger Ayr Basin. These sedimentary basins were defined by numerous northwest-trending normal faults. The Carboniferous was also a time of renewed igneous activity, after the quiet of the mid- and late Devonian. This activity was associated with faulting and basin formation, and continued intermittently for some 100 million years until mid-Permian times. Today, lavas, volcanic plugs and sills from this time underlie much of the high ground in the

Midland Valley. Hot fluids associated with this igneous activity resulted in mineral veins forming, and in many cases these have been economically important for the region. Gold, silver and lead have been mined for centuries from the well-known mining district around the Lowther Hills and Leadhills (20 km north of Thornhill, Fig. 46). Leadhills has been designated a Site of Special Scientific Interest (SSSI) because of the variety of rare lead minerals present. Lead smelting in the Leadhills area has left its mark on the countryside, in the form of old tips, abandoned machinery and poisoned vegetation.

By the end of the Carboniferous, Scotland had drifted northwards from the equator and the climate changed from tropical to arid. Throughout the Permian (between 300 and 250 million years ago), Scotland had a desert climate in which the red sandstones and conglomerates of the New Red Sandstone were deposited, often on top of Carboniferous rocks as sedimentary basins continued to subside. Today, significant outcrops of Permian sediments are found between Loch Ryan and Luce Bay (near Stranraer), in the southern and central parts of Nithsdale and east of Ayr.

During the Mesozoic, sea levels were at times up to 300 m higher than today, and shallow-water sediments are likely to have been deposited at least in the

FIG 50. South end of Ailsa Craig. The highest point of the island is 338 m above sea level. The term 'Paddy's Milestone' has been applied, because the island is a marker by sea between the Clyde ports and those of Ireland. The paddle steamer *Waverley* is close to the shore, which is fringed by a raised beach marking the recent uplift of the island relative to sea level. (© David Law)

Midland Valley. However, no Mesozoic rocks are preserved today, showing that, overall, the last 250 million years have been a time of net erosion in Area 1, as in much of Scotland.

The youngest bedrock in this Area underlies the small but remarkable island of Ailsa Craig, some 15 km northwest of Girvan (Fig. 50). The island is the deeply eroded remains of a volcanic plug, emplaced at the start of the Tertiary (around 60 million years ago) into gently dipping Permo-Triassic rocks. The intrusion is a fine-grained granite, whose unusual minerals give the rock a characteristic bluish colour. Columnar jointing is very prominent around the island, as are quarries from which the rock has been extracted to manufacture the famous polished curling stones (or 'ailsas').

MAKING THE LANDSCAPE

In early Tertiary times, sea-floor spreading in the North Atlantic was accompanied not only by the eruption of lavas in the Tertiary Volcanic Province (including the intrusion of the Ailsa Craig microgranite), but by widespread uplift across much of the Scottish mainland. The Southern Uplands and Highlands were once again uplifted, while the Midland Valley, lying on the periphery of these two blocks, became relatively lowered. The uplift, and the more modest episodic uplift events of the later Tertiary, were accompanied by vigorous denudation, often concentrated along lines of geological weakness such as faults and softer sedimentary units. In the generally warm, wet climate of the Tertiary, the intervening phases of tectonic stability were times of deep bedrock weathering that enhanced the pre-existing relief, widening valley floors and basins and resulting in the development or extension of erosion surfaces. In this way, the main landscape features seen today were initiated during the Tertiary: an erosion surface between 400 and 600 m in elevation developed across the Southern Uplands, dissected by numerous river valleys. The final form of the Southern Uplands owes much to glacial erosion, but the Tertiary erosion surface is still apparent as the smooth, rounded hills tend to be at uniform heights at approximately this elevation. The projecting hills of the Southern Uplands tend to be underlain by more resistant material, which would have formed topographic features during the Tertiary before being moulded by glaciers. Examples are the higher hills of the Lowther Hills or Leadhills (in places over 750 m high), which tend to be made of tougher and more resistant quartzites and thick beds of grit, whereas the thinner greywackes and shales have been weathered into gentler rolling hills. Further west, the highest hills of the Southern Uplands are found around the Loch Doon granite, although they are

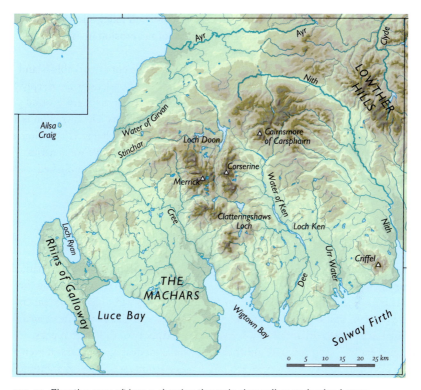

FIG 51. Elevation map of Area 1, showing the main river valleys and upland areas.

not underlain by the granite itself. This will be examined later, when looking at the effects of glacial erosion on the landscape.

The rolling hills of the Southern Uplands are interrupted by the broad valleys of the rivers Cree, Dee and Nith, which flow roughly southeast off the high ground into the Solway Firth (Fig. 51). Another prominent area of low ground oriented roughly northwest to southeast has been flooded by Loch Ryan and Luce Bay, and therefore separates the Rhins peninsula from the mainland. It is obvious in Figures 47 and 51 that the river valleys of the Cree and Dee are aligned roughly parallel to large northwest/southeast-trending faults, and it seems likely therefore that the more easily weathered rocks in the fault zone provided a relatively easy pathway for river erosion, probably as early as the Tertiary and certainly more recently. It is also clear from Figure 47 that Luce Bay–Loch Ryan and Nithsdale are in part underlain by Devonian to Permian sedimentary rocks. These rocks are softer than the surrounding Ordovician and Silurian rocks, and have been more extensively weathered to form the low ground seen today. In effect, the Nith

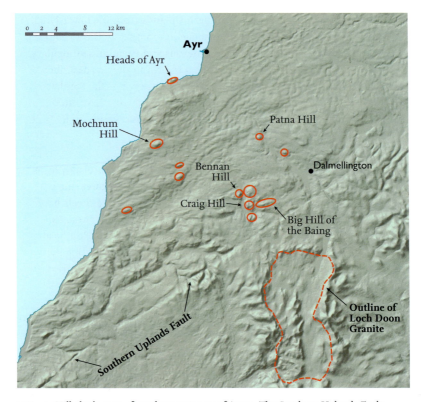

FIG 52. Hill-shade map of southwestern part of Area 1. The Southern Uplands Fault shows up well, as do other erosional and depositional features due to glaciation. Note the drumlins north and west of Patna Hill.

is once again flowing down what would have been a valley at least as far back as Carboniferous times, when a sedimentary basin became established running at right angles to the northeast/southwest-trending major faults, such as the Southern Uplands faults and the general folding of bedrock.

The fault which is most obvious in the landscape is the large Southern Uplands Fault. River and stream valleys have been preferentially eroded along the fault over much of its length. The fault is particularly prominent at its southwestern end (Fig. 52), where it splits into two (the southern Glen App Fault and northern Stinchar Valley Fault: Fig. 47). Preferential weathering along the Glen App Fault has resulted in the remarkably steep-sided, linear valley of Glen App, whilst the more curved line of the Stinchar Valley Fault has been excavated and now underlies Stinchar Valley. In broader terms, the Southern Uplands Fault separates the generally higher, hillier ground of the Southern Uplands from the lower-lying, flatter ground of the Midland Valley. This change in topography is not, however, generally clear-cut across the fault, as Carboniferous and Permian sedimentary rocks infiltrate into the Southern Uplands along the Nith valley, as described above, whilst igneous rocks are relatively common just north of the Southern Uplands Fault within the Midland Valley and, as described later, have often resisted erosion to form hills comparable to those found just south of the fault.

Glacial landscape development

Whilst the broad outlines of the present Scottish landscape had probably been established by the end of the Tertiary, its detailed configuration owes much to events of the Quaternary period. During the last million years, ice sheets have repeatedly expanded to cover much of Scotland, including Area 1. These ice sheets flowed radially outwards from centres in the Highlands and Southern Uplands and were powerful agents of erosion and deposition, moulding the uplands, scraping sediments from the lowlands and locally depositing great thicknesses of boulder clay (*till*).

The most recent glacial episode, the Devensian, reached its coldest about 25,000 to 20,000 years ago, when an ice sheet centred on the Western Highlands and Southern Uplands had expanded to cover most of Scotland and all of Area 1. The broad pattern of ice flow during this time is shown in Figure 53: the thickest ice was centred on the Southern Uplands, and it flowed radially outwards from an ice divide that extended from Merrick in the west to the Lowther Hills in the east. Ice flowing northwards into the Midland Valley came up against southwards-flowing Highland ice, forcing ice to flow east and west across the low ground of central Scotland.

Landscape modification by glacial erosion

Glacial erosion has played an important role in creating the final shape of the landscape seen today. Most of Area 1 was extensively ice-scoured throughout the course of the Pleistocene glaciations, and the land surface present at the end of the Tertiary became heavily modified. Glacial erosion in this Area is most obvious in the uplands, which have been extensively ice-scoured. The mountains around the Loch Doon and Carsphairn igneous intrusions have an, albeit very rounded, Alpine form, with corries, rounded arêtes and intervening glacial troughs. These large-scale landforms were produced over the course of multiple glaciations, in particular by local valley and cirque glaciers during early and late phases of glaciation. The intensity of glacial erosion, at least during the Devensian glaciation, decreased eastwards towards the Lowther Hills, where more localised

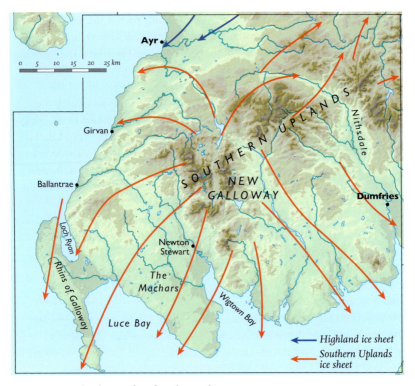

FIG 53. Generalised map of ice flow during the Devensian.

erosion took place: powerful ice streams continued to deepen the main valleys, but the intervening ridges and plateau were relatively unmodified. The corries that are relatively common in this southwestern part of the Southern Uplands are largely absent from the northeastern Southern Uplands. This could reflect a difference in climate from west to east, with the glaciers of the warmer, wetter southwest flowing much more vigorously, and hence eroding more than those of the colder, drier northeast, where the ice was frozen directly onto the rock and was therefore unable to scour deeply.

It is often the case in Scotland that, where granite intrusions are present in the bedrock, they are visible in the landscape because they form topographic highs. The relationship does not, however, seem to be so clear-cut in Galloway, where the different granite bodies have responded differently to both Tertiary and glacial erosion. The Cairnsmore of Fleet and Dalbeattie bodies do seem to be loosely associated with topographic highs: round, smoothed hills in the case of the Fleet body, and some of the only elevated ground on the south coast in the case of the

Dalbeattie body (Figs 47, 51). However, in both cases only part of the intrusion seems to have resisted erosion to form elevated ground: the western half of the Fleet body and the southeastern margin of the Dalbeattie. Elsewhere, the elevation of the land is not discernibly different to that underlain by the surrounding Palaeozoic metamorphics. However, a contrast is seen in the 'texture' of the land, with those areas underlain by granite or granodiorite having a much more 'smoothed' appearance, probably reflecting the more uniform nature of the rock, and its response to erosion, than the surrounding folded Silurian rocks. Likewise, the Carsphairn intrusion underlies the large hill of Cairnsmore of Carsphairn, with its knock-and-lochan topography and craggy faces. Again, however, there is no change in topography at the contact between the pluton and the surrounding rock, and the area north and east is almost equally as mountainous.

Something very different is associated with the Loch Doon granite. This area formed the centre of accumulation for the local icecap during the Devensian glaciation, and likely earlier, with glaciers moving outwards onto lower ground with an approximately radial pattern of flow. As such, it has been subject to intense glacial erosion, both under an extensive icecap during the glacial maximum and by local valley glaciers during early and late phases of glaciation. It is obvious from Figure 52 that the Loch Doon pluton itself has resisted this erosion much less than the baked Ordovician sediments which surround it. These tough hornfels (baked sediments) today underlie the distinctive elevated ridge of peaks which almost completely surrounds the Loch Doon pluton. These hills include the Rhins of Kells, with Corserine (814 m) on the eastern flank and Merrick on the western flank (Fig. 51), which at 843 m elevation is the highest point in Scotland south of the Highlands. The view from the summit of Merrick is exceptional, from Ben Cruachan northeast of Oban, across to the Paps of Jura and then south across the Isle of Man and the Lake District to Snowdonia. The granodiorite which makes up much of the Loch Doon pluton has a tendency to form the low boggy ground between these hills, averaging around 300 m elevation. Glacial rock basins have been gouged out of this granodiorite, and today they are flooded to form the numerous small lochs which are seen within the boundaries of the intrusion, such as Loch Enoch. Meanwhile, the granite which forms the centre of the intrusion is obviously more resistant than the granodiorite, and underlies a ridge of high ground including the hills of Craiglee, Hoodens and Mulwarchar (692 m).

Throughout these uplands, bare, scoured rock is relatively common, particularly around the Loch Doon and Carsphairn area, although the jagged peaks and cliffs common in the Highlands are mostly absent. Where present, this bare rock provides an interesting contrast to the otherwise rolling moorland.

One particular craggy outcrop southwest of Loch Enoch has been named the 'Grey Man of Merrick', because of its resemblance to a man's face when seen from the side. Another interesting feature is the so-called 'Devil's Bowling Green' on Craignaw, a remarkably flat, smooth glaciated rock surface strewn with rounded boulders.

Elsewhere in Area 1, the ground is much lower-lying, and the effects of glacial erosion are not so obvious. This ground, already low at the end of the Tertiary, has been further lowered and smoothed by the passage of ice. Where hills are present, they tend to have been rounded by ice scouring, and often have a streamlined shape. An excellent example is the island of Ailsa Craig (Fig. 50). Although the island has been considerably modified by subsequent marine action (which produced its precipitous cliffs, discussed below), its overall shape is round, but elongated from north to south, reflecting southerly ice flow. The granite has clearly resisted erosion much more effectively than the soft Permo-Triassic sandstones into which it was intruded. Ailsa Craig was positioned in the path of many different ice streams during the Devensian glaciation, and these ice streams carried blocks of Ailsa Craig microgranite in the direction they were flowing. As the microgranite has a very distinctive composition, these blocks are easy to identify, and they have proved very useful in tracing flow directions of the last ice sheet across Britain. Indeed, the Ailsa Craig boulder train is one of the most famous and largest in the British Isles, extending south across the Irish Sea and parts of England and Wales as far as Pembroke, and westwards to Ireland.

North of the Southern Uplands Fault, the relatively soft sedimentary bedrock of Devonian to Permian age has generally been heavily weathered and eroded by the passage of ice, forming a low-lying landscape. However, the sedimentary units are punctuated by horizons of lava and numerous plugs of fine-grained igneous rock, only the largest of which are shown in Figure 47. As a result, the generally low-lying landscape is frequently interrupted by rounded hills, underlain by the more resistant units. This is well illustrated in the Straiton area (20 km northeast of Girvan), where the craggy hill tops of Bennan Hill and Craig Hill are underlain by more resistant Devonian lavas, with Devonian sediments underlying the gentler slopes of the surrounding area. Likewise, Mochrum Hill (Fig. 52), near Maybole, is underlain by the eroded remains of a large Devonian volcanic vent, around 1 km in diameter. The vent is filled with agglomerate (coarse angular blocks of volcanic material), which has resisted erosion to form the prominent, rounded hill, whilst the surrounding Lower Old Red Sandstone is much softer and lower-lying. The sandstone in this area is feldspar-rich, and has weathered to produce particularly fine arable soils. Younger volcanic rocks are also common, such as the Permian, agglomerate-filled volcanic neck underlying Patna Hill, just northeast of Patna. There are more than 20 such vents in the

Patna–Dalmellington area, many of which are responsible for small topographic features. As these intrusions are often basaltic (mafic), they have weathered to produce nutrient-rich soils, the so-called 'Green Hills' of Ayrshire.

In places, prominent hard bands within the sedimentary rocks are also associated with rounded, glacially scoured hills. An example is the 'Big Hill of the Baing' southeast of Straiton (20 km northeast of Girvan), an elongated, faulted ridge of Ordovician boulder conglomerate. More extensive outcrops of this conglomerate occur in the Girvan–Ballantrae area, where, along with the Ballantrae Complex, they underlie higher, hillier ground than the softer rocks further south.

Landscape modification by glacial deposition
Much of Area 1 is relatively low-lying, and here the effects of glacial erosion are more subtle than in the high ground of the Southern Uplands: the ground level was lowered, pre-existing Tertiary valleys were deepened and the low hills were moulded and streamlined. Equally important in the formation of today's landscape in these lowland areas was glacial deposition: on deglaciation, great thicknesses of till were deposited and today glacial till, sand and gravel mantles much of the lowlands. These deposits have a range of surface forms, including eskers, kames, outwash terraces and, in particular, drumlins.

Drumlin swarms are important landscape features throughout the lowlands of this Area, tending to broadly correspond with the arrows on Figure 53. They mantle much of the Rhins of Galloway, the Machars, the Glenluce, Ballantrae and Girvan districts and Nithsdale. They also make up much of the land surface of the Midland Valley, being responsible for the rather intriguing, 'hummocky' texture that is so characteristic when viewed from the air, or on a simple hill-shade map (Fig. 52). The drumlin swarms in these areas produce a distinctive landscape of low hills, typically around 30 m high and 300 m long, all oriented in the same direction and with similar shapes – blunt at one end and tapered at the other, rather like an egg. This streamlined shape is produced by deposition at the base of a flowing glacier: drumlins often have a core of rock or glacial till, and as sediment-laden ice flows over these obstructions, material is deposited downstream of the core, where it is relatively sheltered from ice erosion. As this process repeats itself, a streamlined mound is gradually produced, with a tapered end pointing downstream and a blunt end pointing upstream. One is aware of the whaleback shape of the drumlins that make up these swarms from the ground, but an aerial view allows the best appreciation of their three-dimensional streamlined form. Excellent examples are seen, for example, around Newton Stewart and in the New Galloway district. Smaller swarms are also present in the uplands.

The broad Carsphairn Valley cuts across some of the highest ground of the Southern Uplands, with the Loch Doon hills to the southwest and the Cairnsmore hills to the northeast. Reconstructions of former ice-flow directions in the valley indicate that, during the Late Glacial Maximum, a northeast/southwest ice divide was located across its central part, passing from Cairnsgarroch summit through Craig of Knockgray to the Cairnsmore Hills. The thickest and most extensive till deposits present in the Carsphairn Valley are found around the area of this ice divide, which seems somewhat contradictory. Horizontal ice flow is minimal at ice divides, and the till cannot therefore have been deposited when the divide existed, so the source and age of this till is an interesting question. The answer seems to be that the till was deposited during or before the glacial maximum, during the growth of the Late Devensian ice sheet. At the start of the Late Devensian glaciation, ice would have initially accumulated in the corries and trough heads northeast and southwest of the Carsphairn Valley. As the glaciation advanced, these glaciers expanded and finally converged in the valley bottom, and as their flow was impeded till would have been deposited. During the subsequent glacial maximum, the preservation of this till beneath great thicknesses of ice is likely due to its location under the ice divide, as although the ice sheet expanded and thickened, the slow rates of ice movement meant the ice had little erosive power here.

This till, deposited during the growth of the Late Devensian ice sheet and preserved under the ice during the glacial maximum, was then remoulded during a late stage of glaciation into a set of interesting landforms – *rogen*, or *ribbed*, moraine, which consists of sinuous, 20 m-high, elongated ridges that run perpendicular to the valley axis. The mechanism by which these till ridges formed, perpendicular to the down-valley direction of Devensian ice flow, is another interesting point. A likely scenario is that the rogen moraines represent ridges of sediment produced by thrusting (by compression) or fracturing (by extension) at the base of the ice sheet. For this to happen, the flow speed of the lower part of the ice must have varied downstream: a sudden speeding-up would produce fracturing by extension; a sudden slowing-down, such as upstream of an obstacle, would produce thrusting by compression. This would have been most likely to happen during a late stage of ice-sheet deglaciation, when faster, more concentrated flow occurred within the main valleys. The most recent episode recorded by this till involved the drumlinisation of the rogen moraine, as the original landforms became elongated down-valley to varying degrees.

Important amounts of sediment were also deposited by sediment-charged meltwaters flowing out from retreating glaciers, referred to as glaciofluvial deposits, and present in a variety of forms. Sediment may accumulate in channels, ponds and lakes trapped between lobes of glacier ice or between a glacier and the valley side. Where such sediment has a ridge or mound form, it is termed a *kame*; where it is a flat-topped mound, it is termed a *kame terrace*, and is likely to have been deposited in a lake. When sub-glacial meltwater drains through tunnels, the sub-glacial stream may deposit sediment as a surface stream would, but confined to the tunnel. The result is a long sinuous ridge of gravel, termed an *esker*. *Outwash plains* often build up downstream of the melting glacier, large plains of poorly sorted, stratified sediment deposited by braided streams. Sequences of terraces are often seen in these plains, formed by river incision. *Kettle holes* are also common features, formed by blocks of ice that become buried in outwash sediment, and then melt to leave behind a depression. Many of these kettles have been infilled with sediments, particularly peat, during the post-glacial times, but some are still visible today as small isolated lakes or deep water-filled depressions in boggy areas that were once the low-lying outwash plains.

A famous example of 'kame-and-kettle topography' is found in Nithsdale, north of Dumfries. Particularly on the eastern side of the valley, there are many short, linear glaciofluvial ridges separated by depressions and hollows. The relative relief between ridge crest and depression is usually between 8 and 25 m, and the ridges are relatively short, with very few being over 500 m long. The extensive gravel pit at Kilblane, for example, is developed in three such kame ridges. The coarse sediment that makes up these ridges, and other linear kame ridges in this part of Nithsdale, was probably deposited in meltwater channels that flowed between ice-cored ridges parallel to the ice margin. As the ice ridges melted, the sediment-filled channels became inverted to produce the kames seen today. Kame terraces are also seen on both sides of the Nith, with the best developed just east of Duncow (8 km north of Dumfries) at an altitude of around 55 m. Further north, in the mid-part of the Nith valley (south of Thornhill), a similar kame-and-kettle topography is seen. The glaciofluvial deposits of Nithsdale account for the rather large number of sand and gravel pits seen just north of Dumfries, now often flooded. Glaciofluvial deposits are relatively common elsewhere in Areas 1 and 2, such as in many of the valleys on the south side of the Southern Uplands and in the area around Stranraer.

The mapping of glaciofluvial deposits in the Nith Valley has allowed the reconstruction of the pattern of glaciofluvial drainage which developed during a late stage of deglaciation. The result shows a narrow marginal zone of ice-cored ridges and troughs in the north, feeding meltwater and sediments to the ice front north of Dumfries. This ice front is marked by a terminal moraine across the Nith valley, which is crossed by the River Nith in a gorge in Dumfries. Further southeast, the drainage fed outwash systems in the Lochar Water and Nith valleys. Today, this outwash plain underlies much of the uniformly flat surface southwest of Dumfries.

A closer look at Late Devensian ice-flow directions

The broad ice-flow pattern shown in Figure 53 is useful, but presents a highly generalised picture; in reality, ice-flow directions over the course of the Late Devensian were somewhat more complicated. The large number of streamlined glacial deposits found throughout Area 1, particularly in the lowlands, has allowed a much more detailed reconstruction of Devensian ice flow. A recent study looked in detail at the glacial features present in the western part of Area 1, in particular at drumlins, erratic trains and glacial striae. It was found that several generations of these features can often be seen superimposed on one another, recording multiple passages of ice from different ice centres. These changing flow directions are summarised in Figure 54, and record the changing relative strengths of the Southern Uplands and Highlands ice centres.

Some of the earliest features in the western Southern Uplands indicate that ice from the Highlands was initially dominant during the Late Devensian, when it streamed southwards from the Firth of Clyde and crossed the Glenluce lowlands, producing north/south lineations. This Highland ice was then replaced over much of Area 1 by Southern Uplands ice, as shown by a southwest-oriented flow set running across Glenluce and the southern Rhins. A similar story is recorded by till deposits in the southern Midland Valley, around the margins of the Southern Uplands. For example, a vertical section cut by the River Nith at Nith Bridge, just south of Cumnock, reveals three tills deposited during the Late Devensian and separated by glaciofluvial sands and gravels. These tills have been carefully studied, and the bottom two were both found to have been deposited by Highland ice, which probably flowed across central Ayrshire from the Firth of Clyde area. The topmost till, by contrast, was deposited by ice originating in the Southern Uplands. There were, therefore, at least two distinctive phases of ice movement across central Ayrshire, with an initial advance of Highland ice being succeeded by Southern Uplands ice. The evidence at Nith Bridge matches similar evidence found across the southern Midland Valley, and the story indicated by streamlined landforms further southwest. It seems, therefore, that Highland ice initially expanded to encroach on the Southern Uplands, and that it was only as glaciation progressed that Southern Uplands ice became more dominant in Area 1. Further south, another major ice centre was established in the Lake District, and converging drift lineations at the tip of the Machars peninsula mark the confluence of this and Southern Uplands ice.

At the coldest stage of the last glaciation, around 20,000 years ago, Highland ice one again played a role – an ice stream flowed out from the Highlands and along the western seaboard of Area 1. As the ice moved down the Firth of Clyde, it scraped marine deposits off the sea bed and re-deposited them further south.

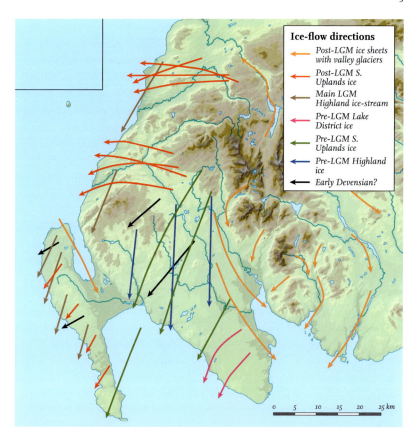

FIG 54. More detailed examination of local ice-flow directions during the Devensian (LGM is the Late Glacial Maximum that occurred late in the Devensian). After Salt and Evans, 2004

These shelly deposits are found, for example, on top of a 10 m-high shore platform around the Mull of Galloway. The Highlands ice sheet also brought glacial erratics of the distinctive Ailsa Craig microgranite and Arran granite southwards, found today throughout the Rhins peninsula.

Following the glacial maximum, climate began to warm, and both the Southern Uplands and Highland ice centres contracted. Some time after Highland ice had retreated from the western seaboard, a phase of local ice expansion interrupted the general waning, and Southern Uplands ice once again flowed across the western part of Area 1. For much of the western, lowland parts of this Area, this would be the last time they were ice-covered, and the ice sheet left behind the extensive drumlin swarms described above. This Southern

Uplands ice flowed southwestwards across the Rhins of Galloway, bringing with it erratics of Loch Doon granite. It also flowed roughly westwards across the Ballantrae and Girvan districts. In the Ballantrae area, flow was somewhat valley-contained, showing that the ice sheet was much thinner than it had been during the glacial maximum. Further north around Girvan, the lineations are particularly notable for their cross-cutting relationships, probably produced by the slight shifting in the main ice-dispersal centre with time.

The most recent flow set was also produced during the waning of the Southern Uplands ice sheet, again during a minor re-advance. This time, valley glaciers radiated out from a Southern Uplands dispersal centre located around Merrick, down valleys such as Nithsdale, Glenluce and northwards into the Midland Valley. Again, erratic trains from distinct granite outcrops around the Galloway area provide useful trackers, along with moraine ridges and drumlins. A local surge of Highland ice down Loch Ryan also occurred at this time, and a prominent moraine at the head of Loch Ryan (the Stranraer moraine) marks the outer limit of this re-advance.

Pollen and beetle records indicate that temperatures in Area 1 may have risen to as warm as present by around 13,000 years ago, by which time southwest Scotland must have been completely deglaciated. Temperatures then fell sharply around 12,000 years ago, culminating in the Loch Lomond Stadial. This climatic deterioration was accompanied by the return of glaciers to parts of the Southern Uplands, although these glaciers were of very limited extent, generally being confined to the highest corries. Where glaciers developed, they bulldozed earlier till deposits into moraine ridges. A fine example of one such moraine is seen at Loch Dungeon, just southeast of Corserine. Steep cliffs of Silurian sediments rise from the southeast shore of the loch, and a subsidiary corrie of Corserine opens out on the northwest shore. A glacier emerged from this corrie, and its terminus is marked by a large terminal moraine to the west of the loch and by a shallow area within the loch itself.

Even in unglaciated upland areas, ice growth often caused extensive frost shattering. The scree and loose rock this produced is still visible today, particularly on summits and upper slopes, and has often been modified by subsequent flow to form a series of lobes and sheets. Elsewhere in the lowlands, the cold climate of the Loch Lomond Stadial made itself felt through the development of permafrost, as evidenced today by features such as ice wedge casts, seen most commonly in gravel pits. Evidence for periglacial disturbance and movement of the soil (solifluction) is also widespread on lowland slopes, usually affecting 1–2 m depth of soil, though in the valley floors of the Southern Uplands, great thicknesses of solifluction deposits have accumulated.

Post-glacial landscape development

At the end of the Loch Lomond Stadial, a temperature rise of around 7 °C occurred within just 700 years, marking the start of the current Flandrian (or Holocene) period. Although the effects of glaciation still dominate much of the landscape, in the 10,000 years since the disappearance of the last glaciers the land surface has been slowly adjusting to non-glacial conditions. These changes are particularly evident in areas of high relief, where glacial retreat exposed a bare rock landscape with over-steepened slopes. Soon after deglaciation, this landscape began adjusting to the new conditions, with rock falls, debris flows and reworking of glacial sediments. As the landscape re-equilibrated and soils and stabilising vegetation became established, it seems that these processes almost stopped, as shown by the vegetated, relict nature of most of the talus slopes, debris cones and alluvial fans in this Area.

Today, Area 1 is notable for its variety of river types and sizes, reflecting contrasts in relief and catchment size throughout the Area. Most of the main rivers originate in the high ground of the Southern Uplands and drain southwards, including the Nith, Cree and Dee (Fig. 51). The upland tributaries of these rivers are akin to mountain torrents, becoming wandering gravel-bed rivers in their middle reaches as the relief becomes more subdued. Most of the major rivers have highly sinuous, meandering courses in their lower reaches, and drain into silty estuaries in the Solway Firth (Fig. 55). The River Ayr, in the Midland Valley, has one of the most meandering courses in this Area, as it weaves across a flat lowland strewn with glacial deposits. Many of the lower reaches of the watercourses in this Area have been embanked to prevent flooding of adjacent land, and some of the smaller rivers show signs of having been straightened in the past.

The first vegetation to become established early in the Holocene was a juniper-dominated community, followed by birch and hazel around 9000 years ago, and then by oak and elm during the middle Holocene. Pine forest was present in the Galloway Hills, but was never the dominant species in this Area. From around 5000 years ago, human activity first began to have a significant impact on the landscape, primarily through forest clearance to make way for agriculture. There is evidence that woodland began to be progressively replaced by peat around 5000 years ago, and that by around 4200 years ago forest cover had essentially disappeared from the Area, replaced by blanket mire. This deforestation is thought to have led to enhanced soil erosion, with an increase in slope failure, debris flow activity and river incision. Peat has been the most widespread soil type in Area 1 since around 4000 years ago, in the form of blanket bog (including the internationally important Silver Flowe Bog in the low ground of the Loch Doon intrusion), or drier heather-covered slopes.

FIG 55. Tidal marshes showing typical, highly sinuous channels, where the wavelength of the channels cut in the muddy sediments reflects the tidal discharges involved. (© Patricia & Angus Macdonald/ Aerographica/ Scottish Natural Heritage)

More recently, damming is another way in which humans have significantly altered parts of Area 1, flooding valleys to create reservoirs. The Galloway hydroelectric scheme was built between 1930 and 1936, and was the first of its kind in Scotland. Although small compared to some of the later Highland schemes, it is a model of unobtrusive and ecologically sensitive hydroelectric engineering, and is studied by engineers from around the world. Making use of water principally stored in Loch Doon, Clatteringshaws Loch and Loch Ken, the scheme includes eight dams, 12 km of tunnels, aqueducts and pipelines together with six power stations along 130 km of river. Whilst Loch Doon is on the site of a natural loch, damming has increased the water level by some 9 m, submerging various small islands. Before the Loch Doon dam was built, Loch Doon Castle, a thirteenth-century castle originally located on an island in the centre of the loch, was moved, stone by stone, to the adjacent bank where it now stands. Elsewhere, dam building flooded valleys, thereby significantly altering the landscape. Such reservoirs include Clatteringshaws Loch and Loch Ken on the Water of Ken. Loch Ken is now a major nature reserve and a breeding ground for many varieties of wild birds.

Man has also altered the landscape by mining and quarrying activities, particularly prevalent in the Midland Valley where large opencast coal workings are still operational today in places, such as east of Patna. Recent clean-up efforts have greatly reduced the impact of colliery tips (bings) on the landscape, such as northeast of Girvan, where they have been landscaped and forested. Local stone has also been quarried for building stone, roadstone and crushed rock aggregate. An important source of building stone is the area around Mauchline, from which the attractive orange-red Permian sandstone has been extracted. Stone from this area has been widely used throughout the UK and Ireland, and even shipped to the USA. The granites have also been economically important for the region – the Glasgow and Liverpool docks, for example, were constructed using Criffel–Dalbeattie granite. Glacial sands, silts and gravels have also frequently been quarried, often leaving their mark on the landscape with flooded gravel pits.

Today, the Area is generally very wet and mild, as the North Atlantic Drift maintains higher temperatures than those found on the east coast. Indeed, plants normally associated with more southerly latitudes are found on the Rhins, along with dolphins and basking sharks off the coast. Much of the Southern Uplands in this Area lie within the Galloway Forest Park, managed by the Forestry Commission, and as well as rolling moorland, conifer plantations are common on the shallow, poor soils. The main river valleys (such as the Urr, Dee, Cree and Nith) provide a contrast to this rolling moorland, providing much of the good arable land of the Southern Uplands.

The formation of the coastline

As described in Chapter 5, sea level in much of Scotland has not been constant, but has risen and fallen according to the interplay between global sea level and the elevation of the land. Global sea level decreases during an ice age, as water is locked up within the ice, and rises again as this ice melts. Meanwhile, during glacials, the crust becomes depressed locally under ice sheets, sinking into the mantle, and slowly rebounds once this ice has melted. The sea level at the coast at any one time therefore depends on the interplay between these two effects, and in the past sea level in Area 1 has been both higher and lower than at present. When sea level has remained constant for long enough, shorelines formed – marked today by erosional features such as rock-cut platforms backed by cliffs, or by beach deposits. Where subsequent uplift has outstripped global sea-level rise, these shorelines now take the form of raised beaches, raised deltas, raised estuarine deposits (known in Scotland as carse), and raised rock platforms and cliffs. Good examples of these features are found in this Area. Shore platforms are relatively common on stretches of rocky coastline, and are particularly well developed, for example, between the Heads of Ayr and Turnberry and around Ballantrae. In the latter area, numerous small caves and gullies often delineate the foot of the cliff, and occasional raised sea stacks rest on the raised platform. Further south, a shore platform can be traced around most of the Mull of Galloway at approximately 10 m above present sea level, and deposits of glacial till on top of it show that it predates the Devensian glaciation. In places, several shorelines are present, such as some 8 km southwest of Girvan, where two old shorelines give the skyline a stepped profile. These shorelines occur as a series of benches, commonly cut into boulder clay. Mafic, dolerite dykes have been etched out by the sea during the formation of each of these shorelines, and today stand as raised sea stacks.

In the lower-lying coastal areas, past increases in sea level involved the flooding of sometimes large patches of land. For example, along the Ayrshire coast the late glacial sea was nearly 30 m higher than at present, and so the sea would have come several kilometres inland from its present position. Along the Solway coast in the south of the Area, large sections of the present shore are backed by raised estuarine deposits of silt and clay, which provide valuable records of this sea-level change over the last 15,000 years. Good examples occur flanking the heads of the Cree and Fleet estuaries, which in this area lie between 7 and 10 m above present sea level.

The sediments within cores taken from the carselands flanking the Cree estuary have been analysed and dated, and have proved very useful in reconstructing the sea-level history of the Solway Firth, as summarised in Figure 56. These deposits show that sea level rose to cover this area by around 9600 years ago, followed by a rise to the so-called Main Post-glacial Shoreline by 6500 years ago, when sea levels were between 7 and 10 m above present and some 9 m of estuarine deposits were laid down in the Cree area. Sea level then fell from the uppermost carse surface to its present level as the land continued to rebound, whilst worldwide sea volume changed very little.

The large-scale shape of the coastline is controlled by a number of factors, many of which are in turn related to one another. Rising sea levels cause valleys to become flooded, forming bays and islands, whilst the location of these valleys often reflects rock type (i.e. hardness) and structure (both the presence of jointing within a rock unit and lines of weakness, such as faults). Climate and tidal energy

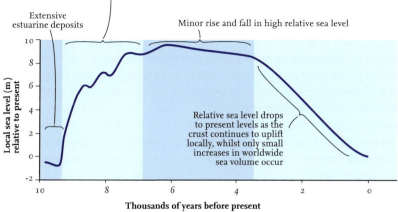

FIG 56. Sea-level curve for the Solway Firth. (Data from Smith *et al.* 2003, Transactions of the Royal Society of Edinburgh: Earth Sciences, 93, 301–31)

also play an important role, controlling wave energy environments and terrestrial processes, such as sediment supply. The amount of sediment supply to a coast of course depends on the availability of that sediment, and in this regard glaciation has been very important. At the end of the Devensian, great volumes of glacial debris were deposited on the continental shelf. As sea level recovered to present levels, this sediment was reworked and moved towards the shore, to form the basis of our present beach and sand-dune systems. Today, where sediment supply is abundant, the coastline is currently advancing seawards, whilst in areas where sediment supply is in decline, the coastline is usually retreating through erosion. Humans, also, can have an impact – for example through building, quarrying, constructing sea defences and trampling of stabilising vegetation.

The number of large bays is one of the more obvious features of the coastal strip of Area 1. The main ones are Loch Ryan and Luce Bay, which together define the Rhins of Galloway, and Wigtown Bay further east. Numerous smaller bays are present along the south coast, including the Water of Fleet and Kirkcudbright Bay on the southeast side of Wigtown Bay. In general, these bays are located in the lower-lying ground of this Area, and therefore do not reflect a large difference in rock strength between headland and bay. Instead, they seem to roughly coincide with the large northwest/southeast faults shown in Figure 47, and with the outlets of major rivers. The exception is the Loch Ryan–Luce Bay pair, which may have been the site of a Tertiary river, now partially flooded by the sea.

Igneous rocks underlie some of the more prominent headlands on the west coast of Area 1, such as the Carboniferous vent rocks that make up the Heads of Ayr, a prominent headland some 6 km southwest of Ayr. The vent has been intruded into a colourful mix of Early Carboniferous sediments, including limestone, grey-green shales and red and green sandstones. Ash erupted from the Heads of Ayr vent is thought to underlie the knoll on which Greenan Castle has been built, around a kilometre up the shore towards Ayr. Where Silurian and Ordovician sedimentary rocks have been cut by cliff sections, the result is often rather impressive because of the exposed folding within the bedrock. Particularly spectacular 'textbook' examples of rock folds and other structures are found on the Machars peninsula, for example at Back Bay, just south of Monreith on the west coast, and around the Isle of Whithorn in the southeast. The fold structures at Back Bay not only illustrate two fold generations with a second set of folds superimposed on a first, but represent one of the most dramatic large-scale exposures of major re-folded folds in the UK.

Perhaps some of the most dramatic coastal scenery in Area 1 is found on the island of Ailsa Craig (Fig. 50). Despite being only 1.2 km wide, the island is nearly surrounded by 340 m-high cliffs. The height of these cliffs reflects the exposed nature of the island to marine erosion, the strength and resistance of the bedrock to this erosion, and also the topographic high left behind here after the retreat of the last glaciers. For the most part, the foot of these cliffs is now between 5 and 10 m above sea level, and so marks a raised shoreline. A distinctive triangular raised beach is located on the eastern side of the island, fringed by storm ridges and an associated spit. These landform features highlight the importance of prevailing wind and storm direction, as they were caused by the westerly winds and waves since post-glacial times: sediment is deposited on the sheltered side of the island. The importance of exposure is also seen on the Rhins of Galloway, where the exposed western coast is generally rugged with steep cliffs and occasional inlets, in contrast to the calmer eastern coast with its sandy beaches.

South of the Southern Uplands Fault, the coast is generally rocky, with low cliffs and only small local beaches or small stretches of shingle. Cliffs are particularly well developed along the exposed western coast of the Rhins, reaching a maximum of 120 m in height near Dunman. This cliff line is largely inactive now, having been raised clear of wave action by crustal uplift. On the north coast of the Solway Firth in particular, the rocky coastline is punctuated by a number of large bays, generally river estuaries (see above). The more sheltered conditions within these bays and the ample sediment supply have allowed wide expanses of sand-flat, mud-flat and salt-marsh to accumulate, and together the flats and marshes of the Solway Firth provide one of the largest continuous areas of intertidal habitat in Britain. Remnants of formerly more extensive lowland peat bogs are developed on raised estuarine sediments. These include the nationally important Lochar Moss and Moss of Cree.

Beaches are generally more common and extensive in this Area than in the Highlands of Scotland. The main reason for this is the relative abundance of sediment, primarily glacial sediment laid down on the near-shore shelf during the Devensian glaciation, and then driven onshore during the Flandrian sea-level rise, where it became stranded as sea levels fell again across the region. The relatively mild winds and waves experienced by the lowlands then meant that this abundant sediment source has remained fairly stable, and many of the beaches in this Area are still accreting today, rather than eroding. Old dune deposits are relatively common on the coastal strip south of Troon on the north edge of the Area, and sands were formerly worked from pits in these dune sands northwest of Monkton. Now, most of the dune deposits on the coast around Ayr are covered by golf courses.

Large expanses of tidal sand-flats are found along the southern coast of Area 1, and at low tide many kilometres of sand are exposed, such as at Mersehead Sands (20 km south of Dumfries). Further inland, the reworking of raised beach deposits and other sandy sediments by the wind has, in some coastal locations, produced extensive spreads of sand dunes, now for the most part anchored by coarse grass or forestry. The largest beach-dune system in southwest Scotland is found at the head of Luce Bay, home to a complex array of dune-related landforms, and still actively accreting today. The entire peninsula of the Rhins acts as a huge breakwater from the currents of the North Channel, creating the relatively calm waters of Loch Ryan and Luce Bay.

Salt-marshes are typically developed on low, raised beaches of sand or shingle and display a complex topography of pans, creeks and terraces. The salt-marshes of the Cree estuary in Wigtown Bay are particularly well developed, sandwiched between extensive sand-flats seawards and reed-swamps and emerged estuarine deposits (carse) landwards. The extensive carse deposits of the Cree estuary show that sedimentation has prevailed here over most of the last 10,000 years, despite changing sea levels. The estuary is well sheltered by Burrow Head to the south, and this has produced a largely unidirectional wave climate in which sediment is brought into the bay, with little subsequent removal. It appears that this system still operates, since many of the sand-flat and salt-marsh systems are accreting today. The presence of Sellafield-derived radionuclides attached to the sediment in the Cree and Water of Fleet sandbanks confirms the Outer Solway as a major sediment source, whilst important amounts of mud within the Cree mouth itself suggest a more fluvial source, further enhanced by active reworking of sediment from the carse deposits.

CHAPTER 7

Area 2: Southern Borders

AREA 2 COVERS THE CENTRAL PART of the Southern Uplands, sandwiched between Areas 1 (Galloway) and 5 (Edinburgh) (Fig. 57). It straddles the southern part of the English–Scottish border, extending from Annandale and Moffatdale in the west to the Cheviot Hills in the east (Fig. 58). The discussion provided here is restricted to features on the Scottish side of the border.

In the northern half of the Area, the River Teviot drains the relatively low-lying ground of Teviotdale, which in turn feeds into the larger Tweed Basin of

FIG 57. Location map for Area 2.

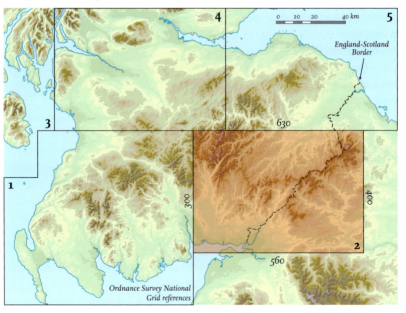

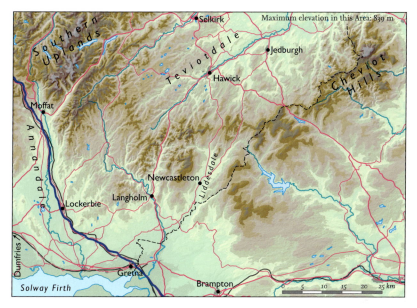

FIG 58. Natural and man-made features of Area 2.

Area 5 (Chapter 2, Fig. 7). Teviotdale is bounded to the east by the Cheviot Hills and to the west by the Moffat Hills of the Southern Uplands. These rounded hills reach heights of over 800 m, and form a broad region of elevated ground which dominates the landscape in the northwestern part of this Area. The Solway Firth with its adjacent low-lying plains is the main feature of the southwestern corner of Area 2, along with the broad valleys of the Annan and Esk, which penetrate northwards into the hills of the Southern Uplands.

STORIES FROM THE BEDROCK

Area 2 is principally made up of hard Ordovician and Silurian sediments, which are also the oldest rocks in the Area (Figs 59, 60). These sandstones (greywackes), siltstones and shales were deposited between around 490 and 420 million years ago on the floor of the extensive Iapetus Ocean that, during this time, formed an Atlantic-scale ocean with Scotland and England on opposite margins. Around 490 million years ago, this ocean began to become smaller, as oceanic crust became subducted beneath the Grampian Highlands, and the Ordovician and Silurian sediments were scraped off the ocean floor and stacked up in a pile

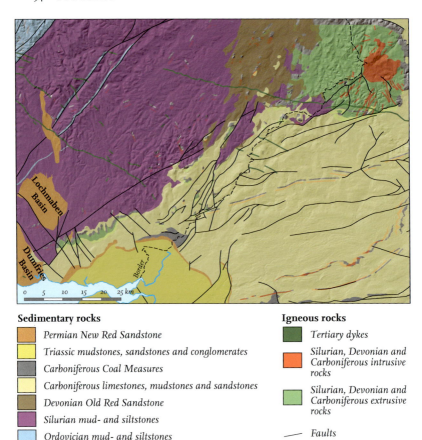

Sedimentary rocks
- Permian New Red Sandstone
- Triassic mudstones, sandstones and conglomerates
- Carboniferous Coal Measures
- Carboniferous limestones, mudstones and sandstones
- Devonian Old Red Sandstone
- Silurian mud- and siltstones
- Ordovician mud- and siltstones

Igneous rocks
- Tertiary dykes
- Silurian, Devonian and Carboniferous intrusive rocks
- Silurian, Devonian and Carboniferous extrusive rocks
- Faults

FIG 59. Simplified geology and hill-shaded topography for Area 2.

against the Midland Valley (Fig. 28). This deformation created a fold system across the uplands of this Area, with the fold axes trending northeast to southwest. Superimposed on this larger structure are countless minor parallel folds, which give a 'grain' to the oldest bedrock of the Area. During these movements, the sediments were altered to brittle sandstones and slates.

By the Devonian (around 410 million years ago), the major uplift and deformation of the Southern Uplands had ceased and the crustal materials of what are now Scotland and England became 'welded' along the Iapetus Suture. The mountainous ground of the Southern Uplands then began to be eroded, and large rivers flowed across the Area, depositing sandstones, siltstones and occasional conglomerates on lower-lying plains fringing the mountains.

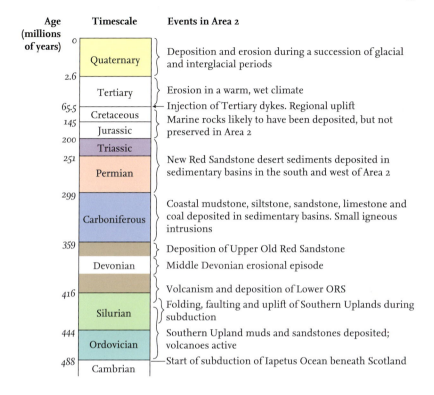

FIG 60. Timeline of bedrock and surface-layer events in Area 2.

This Area lay in the interior of a large continent, and sediments accumulated on river flood plains where oxidising conditions led to the deposits being stained with red iron oxide. These Devonian sediments were deposited on the eroded surface of older, deformed Silurian and Ordovician rocks. This surface was far from uniform – in places, it had a relief of elevation of over 100 m. As a result, the thickness of the Devonian sediments varies from place to place, in part reflecting the fact that these river sediments were filling hollows in the topography. These deposits, collectively termed the Old Red Sandstone, today underlie a sizeable area just west of the Cheviot Hills.

The early Devonian was also a time of igneous activity, and Devonian igneous rocks are often associated with interesting landscape features in Area 2. The largest area underlain by Devonian igneous bedrock is the Cheviot Hills in the northeast. Here, great thicknesses of sub-horizontal lava flows (predominantly mafic andesite) rest unconformably on Silurian marine sediments. This lava was extruded from an igneous centre that today straddles the border between Scotland and England. The centre experienced several stages of igneous activity: an initially explosive volcano was followed by a large out-pouring of lava, which today, after erosion, covers around 600 km^2 of the Earth's surface. This large area of lava was then intruded at depth by felsic granite, which after millions of years of erosion has been exhumed and today underlies the highest part of the Cheviot Hills, over the border in England. Elsewhere in the Area, much smaller Devonian volcanic vents and intrusions are relatively common.

By the start of the Carboniferous, around 360 million years ago, the Caledonian Mountains had been largely eroded, although the Southern Uplands still formed a considerable upland area. Throughout the following 60 million years of the Carboniferous, deposition in this Area occurred mostly in the lowlands of the Solway Firth Basin and along the border with England. Marine and coastal plain environments dominated, although varying relative sea levels resulted in the deposition of a variety of sediments, including limestones, sandstones, mudstones and coal. The Carboniferous sediments near Glencartholm, just south of Langholm (Fig. 58), contain one of the richest Carboniferous fish faunas in Great Britain, and indeed in the world. The site is remarkable for the number of species of fish discovered, around 35, several of which are unique to the site. Some Carboniferous to Permian-aged igneous rocks are also found in this Area, generally in the form of small intrusions of coarser-grained rock.

By the end of the Carboniferous, Scotland had drifted northwards from the equator and the climate became more arid. Throughout the Permian (between 290 and 250 million years ago), red desert siltstones, sandstones and conglomerates were again deposited by winds and rivers. Fossils are not particularly common, but at Locharbriggs, just northeast of Dumfries, numerous reptile footprints have been discovered, generally heading in a southwards direction (very possibly towards the nearest source of water, in the Solway Firth Basin). The hot and arid climate of the Permian continued into the Triassic, and boulders, pebbles and sands continued to be washed and blown from the higher ground of the Southern Uplands down into sedimentary basins in the south and west of Area 2. These Triassic units tend to be mostly red, yellow and brown mottled sandstones, and comprise the Sherwood Sandstone Group. Together, both Permian and Triassic units make up the New Red Sandstone Supergroup.

In this Area, the New Red Sandstone was deposited in a series of basins, preserved in what are today the valleys of Nithsdale and the lower part of Annandale. These basins generally have a north-northwest/south-southeast trend, broadly perpendicular to the regional Caledonian trend. The Dumfries and Lochmaben basins are fault-bounded, and gravity studies suggest that Permian strata in these basins reach thicknesses of over 1000 m. They are flanked to the south by the much larger Solway Firth Basin, whose axis overlies the Iapetus Suture. The basement of this large basin is made up of tightly folded Ordovician and Silurian strata, overlain by up to 6 km of Devonian to Lower Jurassic fill.

No Mesozoic rocks are preserved in Area 2, although they would certainly have been present once: by the end of the Cretaceous, the sea had risen to cover all but the highest topography then present in this Area, and marine sediments would have been deposited during this time. However, during subsequent uplift and erosion all these younger rocks were washed away, such that during the last ~230 million years this Area has been subject to net erosion. The youngest bedrock present in this Area consists of Tertiary dykes, which despite being very small can be responsible for distinct walls in some landscapes. These dykes are long, thin intrusions of igneous rock, injected from igneous centres in western Scotland, such as Mull, around 60 million years ago.

MAKING THE LANDSCAPE

Tertiary erosion

In early Tertiary times, widespread uplift occurred across much of Scotland, particularly in the west. The Southern Uplands were again uplifted, and, in the warm, wet climate of the time, the result was vigorous weathering and erosion. As in the rest of Scotland, this weathering initiated some of the largest-scale landscape features seen today: the main upland and lowland areas became either defined or enhanced, and most of the main river valleys were initiated. Although there is not an exact correlation, bedrock has obviously played a role in determining the characteristic of the landscape – the high ground of the Southern Uplands is underlain by relatively hard Silurian strata, whilst the softer Devonian to Triassic rocks underlie generally lower ground. The bedrock of the Cheviot igneous centre has also resisted erosion, forming the Cheviot Hills (Fig. 61).

The Southern Uplands would have been a relatively high table land at the start of the Tertiary. The subsequent erosion cut into this plateau, carving out valleys and watersheds which today define the hills. Although glacial erosion has been very important in creating the ultimate shape of the landscape, the remnants of this plateau surface are still visible in the flat or rounded hill tops, which all lie at similar elevations.

In places, weathering has clearly been concentrated along lines of geological weakness, such as faults and softer sedimentary units. The remarkably linear

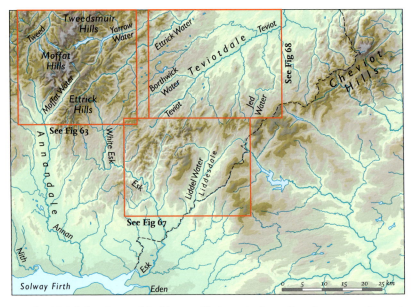

FIG 61. Digital elevation model of Area 2 with the main river valleys shown, as well as main upland areas. Sub-areas discussed in later maps are indicated by rectangles with red borders.

valley of Moffat Water, for example, coincides with a large Caledonian fault and a thin band of softer Ordovician shale. Likewise, the major valley of Annandale appears to have been eroded in the softer Permian sedimentary rocks, whilst the thin band of Silurian rocks separating the Permian of Dumfries and Lochmaben is obviously more elevated. The main rivers in Area 2 are the Tweed, Annan, Esk, Ettrick, Yarrow and Teviot, and the sources of all but the last lie in the higher hills in the northwest of the Area. Many of these rivers flow along northeast/southwest-trending valleys, parallel to the underlying folded strata, the water having taken advantage of either faults or weaker bands within the succession. Another important valley is found in the southern part of the Area: Liddesdale runs approximately northeast to southwest, with Liddel Water defining the Scottish–English boundary for several kilometres before joining the Esk. The development of this valley, too, appears to have been influenced by the underlying geology, as its location coincides with an area of heavily faulted and soft Carboniferous sedimentary rocks.

Evidence that the Solway Firth area acted as a basin for sedimentation in Permian and Triassic times has been outlined above. It seems very likely that it was acting as a river valley during Tertiary times.

Landscape development during the Quaternary glacials

The final form of the landscapes in Area 2, as in the rest of Scotland, owes much to the action of ice and ice meltwater. During the last 2 million years, ice sheets have repeatedly expanded to cover much of Scotland. These ice sheets flowed radially outwards from centres in the Highlands, the Southern Uplands and the Lake District, and were powerful agents of erosion and deposition.

The most recent glacial stage reached its coldest in the Late Glacial Maximum about 20,000 years ago, at which time Area 2 was overrun by Southern Uplands ice flowing roughly eastwards across the Area from an ice divide located over the outer Solway Firth (Fig. 62). This flow is recorded by west/east-oriented drumlins along the low ground adjacent to the Solway Firth, and by a beautifully preserved array of ice-streamlined ridges along the Teviot valley. This flow direction must have been influenced by the presence of a strong ice dispersal centre in the Lake District that deflected the Southern Uplands ice to flow eastwards along the inner Solway Firth. Ice also accumulated in the Moffat Hills in the northwest of this Area, and a small but independent ice centre, powerful enough to withstand the pressure of the main ice mass, was present in the Cheviot Hills.

After the glacial maximum, the Lake District ice centre decreased in size and strength and Southern Uplands ice became dominant throughout the region. In the northeastern half of the Area, ice continued to flow roughly northeastwards down Teviotdale, but in the southwestern half, flow directions were reversed: drumlins and glacial striae indicate that ice flowed from the uplands around Moffat southwestwards down into the Solway Firth. As deglaciation continued, ice flow became valley-contained, and a final flow phase is recorded by north-northeast/south-southwest-oriented drumlins in the lowlands around the Solway Firth. Mapping of glacial deposits west of Annan and north of Gretna shows that ice then receded up the Solway Firth, as the Solway glacier retreated.

As mentioned above, the Cheviot Hills acted as a small but independent centre of ice accumulation and glacier dispersion during the Devensian glaciation. During this time, Cheviot ice flowed radially outwards from the centre, shielding the higher parts of the massif, particularly those above about 300 m, from the ice from the Solway Firth and Tweed basins. The lower peripheral hills, meanwhile, were overwhelmed and smoothed by this ice, and blocks of bedrock from the Tweed and Solway areas were deposited by the ice up to altitudes of around 300 m. Above this level in the central parts of the massif, soft, deeply rotten bedrock is relatively common and there are tors, erosional relics, over the border in England. These areas have clearly been glaciated, as they are often overlain by till, and yet they have survived erosion. Perhaps at the centre of Cheviot ice dispersal, the preservation favoured net deposition rather than erosion.

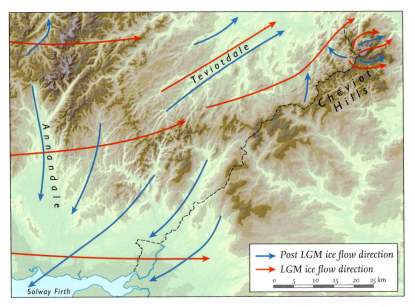

FIG 62. Ice flow in Area 2 at different times during the Devensian (LGM is Late Glacial Maximum).

The brief return to glacial conditions which occurred during the Loch Lomond Stadial (around 13,000 to 11,500 years ago; see Fig. 39) had only a limited effect in this Area. Glaciers returned only to the highest ground, such as around Broad Law, but even here the largest was only a few kilometres long. The position of these glaciers is clearly represented by terminal moraines – ridges of glacial till bulldozed by the Loch Lomond Stadial glaciers. Good examples are found, for example, at Loch Skene (Fig. 63), where a series of terminal moraines records fluctuations in glacier growth during retreat. The terminus of one ice lobe from this time has been located at the head of the Grey Mare's Tail waterfall, at an altitude of around 450 m. Another terminal moraine forms a prominent ridge some 250 m long that runs parallel to the northeastern side of the loch ('the Causey'). Indeed, Loch Skene owes its presence to these moraines, which effectively dam the loch outlet.

Glacial modification of the uplands

Glacial erosion has played an important role in creating the final shape of the landscape. Most of Area 2 was extensively ice-scoured throughout the course of the Quaternary glaciations, and the land surface present at the end of the Tertiary

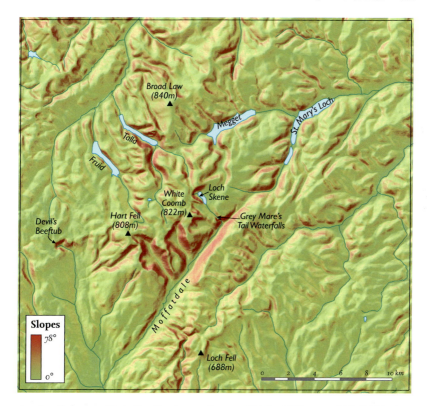

FIG 63. Slope map illustrating the steeper slopes and highest hills around Moffatdale (located on Fig. 61).

became heavily modified. In the uplands, moving ice lowered the valley bottoms and smoothed the mountains, creating the high broad hills seen today. This erosion was not as intense as that to which the western Southern Uplands were subjected, and whilst the main valleys were deepened by powerful ice streams, the intervening ridges and plateaus escaped deep scouring. In general, the uplands of this Area therefore lack the 'Alpine' form seen in the Highlands of Scotland: corries, arêtes and troughs are not as common nor, when present, as pronounced (Fig. 63). However, several good examples are seen, such as the Devil's Beeftub at the head of the River Annan (Fig. 64). This deep, rough corrie was excavated into the greywacke bedrock of the region over the course of numerous glaciations, although it is much less perfectly formed than those found in the granite uplands of the western Southern Uplands. Its unusual name derives from its use as a hiding place for cattle rustled by the Border Reivers (raiders) of the thirteenth to sixteenth centuries.

FIG 64. Looking northeast with the A701 road in the foreground and the Devil's Beeftub to the right just beyond the road, 8 km north of Moffat. (© Patricia & Angus Macdonald/Aerographica/Scottish Natural Heritage)

FIG 65. Looking southwest along the fault zone of Moffatdale. The car park for the Grey Mare's Tail waterfall is in the foreground. (© Lorne Gill, Scottish Natural Heritage)

During the growth and retreat of the ice sheets, glaciers occupied the major valleys of this Area. Rather than the widespread erosion that might be expected under an ice sheet, these glaciers caused enhanced erosion along valley bottoms, lowering the valleys and often creating the U-shaped profile typical of glacial erosion, with relatively flat valley bottoms and steep valley sides. Examples of glacially eroded valleys in this Area can be seen throughout the uplands, although perhaps the best example is Moffatdale (Fig. 65). Its straight profile appears to be because it has excavated along a major southwest/northeast-trending fault from Moffat to St Mary's Loch. The shatter belt associated with the fault seems to have been easily eroded by ice to become one of the major trunk valleys draining the Moffat Hills.

Numerous tributary glaciers would have flowed into the Moffatdale glacier, such as that coming from the cirque now occupied by Loch Skene. Because of its greater ice discharge, the trunk Moffatdale glacier had greater erosive capability than its tributary glaciers, and so Moffatdale was eroded more rapidly than the side valleys. With time, the bottom of the main valley became lower than the elevation of several of the tributary valleys, and on deglaciation these side valleys were left 'stranded' above the main valley bottom, creating so-called *hanging valleys*. Tail Burn, which joins Moffat Water via the Grey Mare's Tail waterfall, is a classic example of a hanging valley, in this case over 200 m above the valley floor. Tail Burn has eroded into the valley wall of Moffatdale, creating a series of fast-moving chutes and cascading waterfalls. The detailed form of the falls is controlled by the underlying geology: the flow is at right angles to the layering in the underlying Silurian, and this layering has been picked out by water erosion.

Where glacial erosion was particularly intense, such as at the junction of two important glaciers, localised scouring has created glacial basins – scoured hollows in the valley bottom. St Mary's Loch, the largest natural loch in the Scottish Borders and some 40 m deep, occupies such a basin, carved out by glaciers spilling out of the Moffat and Megget Hills before travelling on down the Yarrow valley (Fig. 66). The much smaller Loch of the Lowes lies at the southern end of St Mary's Loch. Once part of St Mary's, it has been cut off from the main body of water by alluvial sediments deposited by local burns.

Further south, closer to the border with England, the importance of bedrock on the final form of the landscape, particularly its response to glacial erosion, is apparent. Carboniferous sedimentary bedrock does underlie some important regions of high ground, such as immediately northwest of Liddesdale and along the border south of the Cheviot Hills. However, these hills have notably smoother, broader and more rounded profiles than hills of equivalent elevation developed in Silurian bedrock. This is apparent in a closer look at the high ground immediately northwest of Liddesdale (Fig. 67).

FIG 66. Looking northeast up Moffatdale towards the area where St Mary's Loch is hidden in the hills. The Birkhill Cottage in the centre was lived in by Charles Lapworth when he collected fossil graptolites from Dobb's Linn, the first branch valley this side of the cottage, establishing an international standard for these Ordovician and Silurian fossils. (© Lorne Gill, Scottish Natural Heritage)

In valleys overridden by ice moving from the west, it has been suggested that the greatest modification to the cross-profile of the valleys has resulted from the deposition of till on the lee sides, relative to ice movement. A characteristic Southern Uplands valley therefore might have a thick covering of boulder clay on its southwestern side, whilst on the northeastern side successive craggy hillsides mark the outcrop of harder layers (such as just beyond Melrose, ascending Gala Water). Several instances of this can indeed be seen in the Southern Uplands of this Area (Fig. 68).

On a smaller scale, the cold climate of post-glacial times and the Loch Lomond Stadial resulted in frost shattering in unglaciated upland areas. The scree and loose rock this produced is still visible today, particularly on summits and upper slopes, and has often been modified by subsequent flow to form series of lobes and sheets.

Glacial modification of the lowlands

Much of Area 2 is low-lying, and glacial erosion in these regions has produced a very different landscape to the broad, rounded hills of the Southern Uplands and the Cheviots with their deep glacial valleys. Already low by the start of glacial times, the ground has been further lowered, scoured and smoothed by the passage of ice.

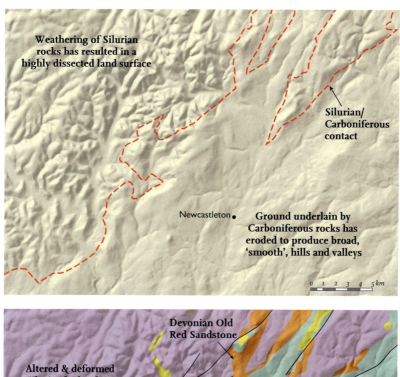
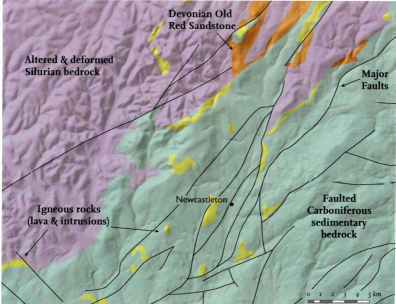

FIG 67. Comparison of topography developed on Silurian and Carboniferous bedrock around Liddesdale (located on Fig. 61).

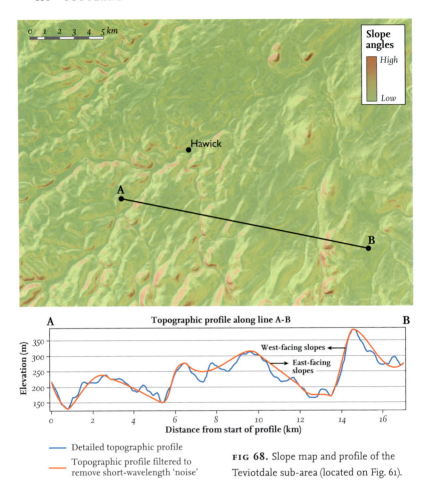

FIG 68. Slope map and profile of the Teviotdale sub-area (located on Fig. 61).

During the Late Glacial Maximum, a large ice stream flowed along the Tweed drainage basin, of which Teviotdale is the upper portion. Ice streams are local areas of fast-flowing ice that move at much greater velocity than the surrounding ice sheet. At its maximum, the Tweed ice stream would have drained some 3500 km² of the last British ice sheet, flowing from its onset zone between the Lammermuir and Cheviot Hills around the level of Hawick, northeastwards to the North Sea. The fast-flowing ice was particularly erosive, and moulded the underlying ground surface into parallel ridges that are today characteristic of the Tweed Basin and Teviotdale (see also Fig. 111, Area 5). At the upper end of the ice stream, in the hilly country around Selkirk and Hawick, these ridges have been created by glacial erosion: the ridges and intervening hollows tend to have been scoured out of the underlying, highly folded, bedrock. Glacial erosion is not only obvious in ridge shape and orientation, but also in the smooth and polished nature of any exposed rock bosses and the presence of northeast-trending striations on the bedrock surfaces. The depressions and basins found between the ridges have generally developed, since deglaciation, into a series of basin mires rich in biodiversity.

In some cases, the upstream ends of the ice-sculpted ridges are formed by a resistant bedrock hill that has produced a 'crag-and-tail' geometry. Such isolated hills are a typical feature of the eastern half of Area 2, and tend to be underlain by harder igneous material, such as horizons of lava or plugs of fine-grained igneous rock. Good examples are Rubers Law, some 9 km southwest of Jedburgh, and the prominent Maiden's Paps, 10 km south of Hawick. The former is a volcanic neck plugged with mafic basalt, which has clearly withstood erosion more than the surrounding sedimentary rocks and lavas. Likewise, the Paps are made up of a group of roughly circular plugs of basalt intruded into much softer Carboniferous sandstones and siltstones. Area 5 (Edinburgh) also contains good examples of this landscape effect.

Further down, the ice stream moulded glacial deposits into drumlins, creating a distinctive landscape of low, egg-shaped hills. This is the upstream end of the large drumlin field stretching from Hawick, in this Area, down to Berwick-upon-Tweed on the English coast. At the margins of the ice stream, the transition from fast-flowing to slow-flowing ice is obvious in the abrupt transition from streamlined to non-streamlined ground, seen for example on the flanks of the Cheviot Hills. Drumlins are common on the site of former ice streams, and so they are present in many of the other valley bottoms of this Area, particularly in the lowlands. Drumlin fields are also present and well developed around the Solway coastline, and indeed detailed mapping in this region has shown several generations of superimposed drumlins, which in turn record changing ice directions in the Area as the Devensian glaciation progressed (Fig. 62)

Glacial deposition has been an important modifier of the landscape in other ways too. On deglaciation, great thicknesses of till were deposited, and today glacial till, sand and gravel mantles much of the lower-lying valleys and hills of Area 2, as well as the valley sides of the uplands. Glaciofluvial deposits, sediments laid down by glacial meltwater, are also common in the lowlands of this Area. A large outwash plain, for example, is present in the southwestern corner of Area 2, in the lower part of Nithsdale, and underlies much of the uniformly flat land surface. Glaciofluvial deposits are also abundant in the lower reaches of Annandale. These features have been dated to around 15,000 years old, which suggests that by this time these lowland areas at least were deglaciated.

Post-glacial landscape development

At the end of the Devensian glaciation, the newly deglaciated landscape was very susceptible to erosion: glacial drift mantled much of the land, whilst in the uplands several slopes had been over-steepened by glacial erosion. Since deglaciation, large amounts of glacial material have been reworked, brought down from the uplands to be deposited lower down the stream or river system, or out at sea. As a result of this, thick river deposits – reworked glacial deposits – tend to be present in valley bottoms, causing these to be relatively flat and wide. Rivers have often begun down-cutting into these alluvial deposits, and river terraces, too, are common. These processes would have been most active shortly after deglaciation; as the landscape re-equilibrated and soils and vegetation became established, they began to have a stabilising effect on the landscape.

Today, most of the main rivers of this Area originate in the high ground of the Southern Uplands. The upland tributaries of these rivers are akin to mountain torrents, surrounded by moorland and conifer plantations. In their middle reaches, wandering gravel-bed rivers are more common, as the relief becomes more subdued. The rivers at these slightly lower elevations are flanked by pastoral regions, with grassy or heathery rounded hills and occasional woods. In their lower reaches, most of the major rivers have sinuous, meandering courses as they wander across relatively flat flood plains, through a region of pasture and arable land.

After deglaciation, vegetation recolonised the land. First, this was in the form of small shrubs, giving way by the mid-Holocene to a forest of oak and ash. In Area 2, this forest would have covered all but the highest hills of the Cheviots and the Southern Uplands. From around 5000 years onwards, human activity began to have a significant impact on the landscape, primarily through forest clearance to make way for agriculture: by around 4200 years ago, forest cover had essentially disappeared from the Area. Today, Area 2 is mostly pastoral, with rolling hills of grass and heather. Conifer plantations are also common, mostly planted within the last 150 years and frequently clothing hills to their summits. Only the northeastern corner of this Area provides good arable land, and it is extremely good – some of the most fertile in Scotland.

More recently, man has significantly altered several valleys in Area 2 by damming to create reservoirs. These were built to supply the nearby capital with drinking water: Edinburgh requires some 200 million litres of water a day, and the majority of this is sourced in the Southern Uplands of Area 2. The three largest storage reservoirs are the Megget, Talla and Fruid Reservoirs. The Talla, which supplies some 45 million litres a day, is the oldest, completed in 1899. It is topped up with inflow from the Fruid Reservoir, built in 1967. During the 1970s, Edinburgh's water consumption grew to the point where additional supplies were needed, and so the Megget Reservoir was built, completed in 1983. Much of the Megget valley had to be flooded to create this reservoir, and farms, houses and a historic ruin had to be moved from the valley bottom. The reservoir is retained by the largest earth dam in Scotland, and supplies over 100 million litres of water a day. It takes around 18 hours for this water to pass through 40 km of underground pipes, propelled only by gravity, to reach water treatment works in and around Edinburgh.

The formation of the coastline

The Solway Firth is the fourth-largest estuary in Britain and one of the least industrialised and most natural large estuaries in Europe. Area 2 covers the northern shore of the inner firth, where the coast is relatively flat and low-lying, with little exposed bedrock. Instead, it is characterised onshore by low raised beach cliffs, sand dunes and beaches. Perhaps most characteristic, however, is the intertidal zone, with its wide expanses of sand-flat, mud-flat and salt-marsh. To the east of Rockcliff, in particular, vast tracts of intertidal sand-flat exist, particularly visible at low tide. These are separated by constantly shifting tidal channels and sandbanks, and are considerably more extensive than elsewhere in Scotland. Salt-marshes of the Area tend to be developed on low, raised beaches of sand or shingle and display a complex topography of pans, creeks and terraces. Although some have been lost to land claim, especially fine examples are found at Caerlaverock, where growth of a 1 km-wide swathe of marsh has been recorded in just 140 years. The sub-tidal sandbanks and intertidal flats of the Solway Firth together form one of the largest continuous areas of active sedimentation in the country. It is therefore considered to be of international importance as an estuarine habitat, and the majority of it is now protected.

The nature of the coastline in this Area reflects a number of factors. One of the obvious requirements for the development of such extensive beaches and sand-flats is an adequate supply of sediment and, as is the case in much of Scotland, this sediment is glacial in origin: at the end of the Devensian, vast volumes of glacial debris were deposited not only over the land but also in the Solway Firth. As described in Chapter 5, sea level in much of Scotland has not been constant, but has risen and fallen over time according to the interplay between worldwide ocean volume changes and local solid Earth movements of the land. The coast of Area 2 is generally low-lying, and the higher sea levels that occurred in this Area some 7000 years ago flooded the region adjacent to today's coastline (Fig. 69). During this period of higher sea level, glacial sediment was reworked and driven onshore, where it became stranded as sea levels fell again across the region. Much of the present coastline is therefore backed by

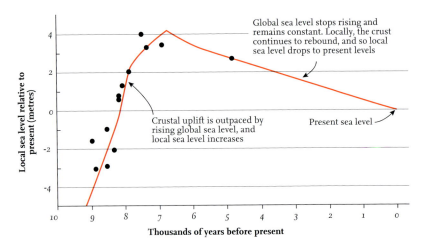

FIG 69. Relative sea-level curve for the inner Solway Firth, covering the last 10,000 years, comparing data points based on radiocarbon dating of coastal sediments with a geophysical model (red line).

extensive raised estuarine sediments of silt and clay. Raised beach deposits are also common, and in some coastal locations these, and other sandy sediments, have been reworked by the wind to produce extensive spreads of sand dunes, now for the most part anchored by coarse grass or forestry. Offshore, the floor of the inner Solway Firth is still today made up of coarse glacial sands, overlying Triassic sandstones. This sediment is the primary material supplying the intertidal sand-flats and beaches of the zone, as rivers entering the Solway Firth do not bring any appreciable amount of fresh sediment.

It is not enough, however, to have a good supply of sediment. The wind and wave environment needs to be sufficiently mild for this sediment to remain in the region. Such sheltered conditions prevail in the inner Solway Firth of this Area: Ireland and the Isle of Man shield the firth from the full force of the Atlantic, whilst its relatively shallow depth (it is generally less than 20 m deep) means that waves are limited in the size they can attain. This, in addition to the generally mild winds, has meant that the abundant glacial sediment has remained fairly stable, and many of the beaches in this Area are still growing today. As well as sheltered conditions and an abundant sediment supply, the development of the Solway tidal flats requires a large tidal amplitude. Estuaries tend to experience larger tidal ranges than elsewhere, due to their narrowness and the funnelling effect this produces. The spring tidal range for the inner Solway Firth is over 8 m, and this has allowed the extensive tidal flats to develop.

CHAPTER 8

Area 3: Jura to Arran

AREA 3 COVERS THE SOUTHERN HALF of Argyll, including the large islands and peninsulas of Jura, Islay, Colonsay, Bute, Knapdale (with Kintyre as its southern continuation) and Cowal, as well as the Isle of Arran (Figs 70, 71). Only 12 km separates the coast of Northern Ireland from the southern tip of Kintyre, the remarkable peninsula that runs north to south across the Area. Indeed, the proximity of the various islands and peninsulas of southwest Scotland to the coast of Ireland has led to many cultural links, not least the arrival of the Christian faith in Scotland from Ireland. Archaeological relics are locally abundant in Area 3, and provide evidence of early and varied cultural development.

STORIES FROM THE BEDROCK

Area 3 lies predominantly within the Grampian Highland terrane (Fig. 20), and as such the majority of the bedrock is made up of the eroded roots of the Caledonian mountains. The present-day distribution of bedrock lithologies at the surface is illustrated in Figure 72, and the main events in the formation of the bedrock are shown in Figure 73.

The oldest rocks in this Area are Precambrian (Proterozoic) gneisses, visible at the surface in the southern third of the Rhinns peninsula of western Islay (Fig. 71). Originally igneous rocks, these 1800-million-year-old gneisses have been subjected to many phases of folding and alteration. Today they are hard, dark-green- and pink-banded rocks which appear to represent a fragment of crust formed and deformed in Palaeoproterozoic times. Bedrock bodies that may have similar origins are found in Northern Ireland, and may underlie a large portion of the Grampian Highlands. Overlying the Rhinns gneisses are deformed and altered sandstones

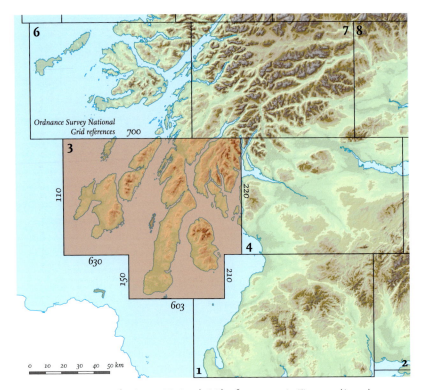

FIG 70. Location map for Area 3. National Grid references as in Figure 45 (Area 1).

and mudstones, which today make up the bedrock of Oronsay, Colonsay and the northern half of the Rhinns peninsula. A similar unit outcrops east of the Gruinart Fault on Islay. The ages of these sandy units are very uncertain, and both have been correlated at different times with Torridonian, Moine or Dalradian rocks. In Figure 72 these units are marked as Neoproterozoic sandstone.

Most of this Area is underlain by a varied group of metamorphic rocks, collectively mapped as the Dalradian Supergroup. Most of these rocks originated as sediments deposited on the edge of the Iapetus Ocean between 750 and 480 million years ago. During Caledonian mountain building, the sediments and numerous interspersed igneous layers were folded and faulted as continents collided. As the crust thickened, they became buried up to depths of 20 km beneath the Caledonian mountain chain, where temperatures reached 600 °C. These high temperatures and pressures caused general alteration of the rocks: 'clean' sandstones were altered to white quartzites, mudstones to slates and schists.

AREA 3: JURA TO ARRAN · 113

FIG 71. Natural and man-made features of Area 3.

The oldest Dalradian sediments in this Area are made up of a succession of black altered mudstones, lime-rich schists and quartzites, which today outcrop in a roughly north/south-trending band across central Islay. Overlying these rocks and outcropping in northern Islay is an interesting unit, composed largely of glacial sediments (called *tillites*) deposited by late Proterozoic ice sheets during what may have been a near-global glaciation (following 'Snowball Earth' ideas). Limestone (or marble) beds are also common in northern Islay, and these cap the glacial sediments. This limestone succession has also been well studied by geologists because it contains some of the best-preserved stromatolites in Britain. These laminated domes were built by calcifying algae, and are some of the earliest fossils found in the UK. Following the deposition of the limestones, shallow seas laid down coastal sands, which today form the hard quartzites that make up most of Jura and parts of Islay. A distinctive unit of carbonates, thick lavas and sills occurs next in the succession, outcropping today in northern Knapdale. Some

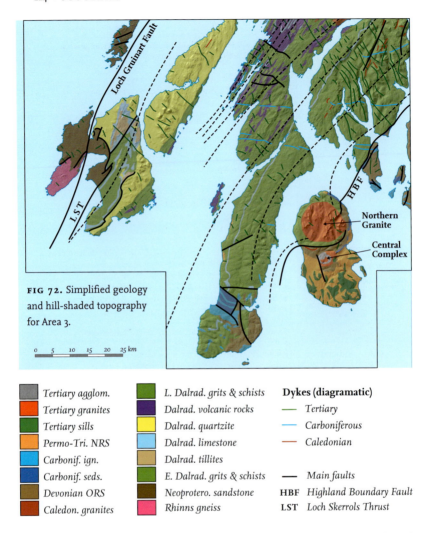

FIG 72. Simplified geology and hill-shaded topography for Area 3.

Tertiary agglom.	L. Dalrad. grits & schists	**Dykes (diagrammatic)**
Tertiary granites	Dalrad. volcanic rocks	—— Tertiary
Tertiary sills	Dalrad. quartzite	—— Carboniferous
Permo-Tri. NRS	Dalrad. limestone	—— Caledonian
Carbonif. ign.	Dalrad. tillites	
Carbonif. seds.	E. Dalrad. grits & schists	—— Main faults
Devonian ORS	Neoprotero. sandstone	**HBF** Highland Boundary Fault
Caledon. granites	Rhinns gneiss	**LST** Loch Skerrols Thrust

of the lavas were erupted underwater, and the pillow-lava structures produced are still locally visible. The youngest Dalradian rocks in this Area stretch across Kintyre, north Arran, Bute and Cowal, and consist of slates, schists, quartzites and grits that are often more deformed and altered than the older Dalradian rocks further north.

During the Caledonian mountain building, the Dalradian rocks were moved by compressive forces acting in a general northwest-to-southeast direction, resulting in folds and faults trending northeast to southwest. The main Dalradian

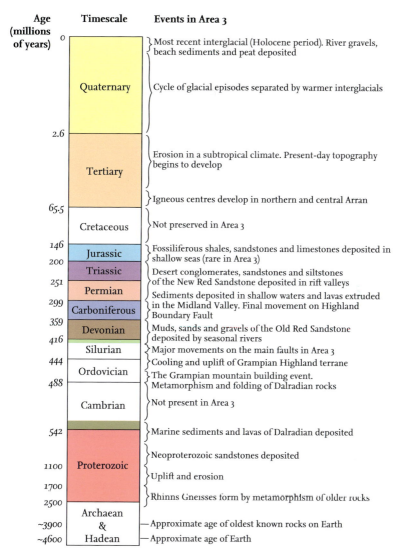

FIG 73. Timeline of bedrock and surface-layer events in Area 3.

faults in Area 3 are shown in Figure 74, while Figure 75 shows a generalised cross-section through the Dalradian succession. In the northwest, the Jura quartzites formed a rigid block between the Islay Anticline (upfold) and the Loch Awe Syncline (downfold), the latter being made up of several smaller folds. Further

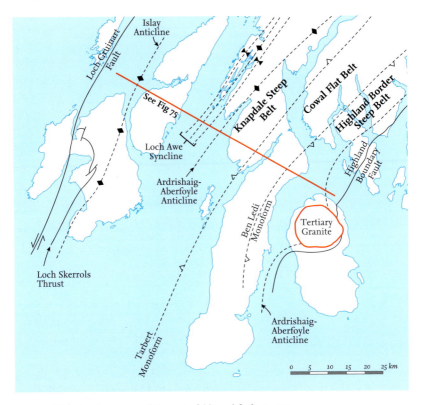

FIG 74. Map showing some of the main folds and faults in Area 3.

southeast, the crustal structures become more complex: the large Ardrishaig–Aberfoyle Anticline (upfold), formed in an early folding event, has been arched over to form the Cowal Anticline (upfold). Subsequent deformation has flattened out the centre of this upfold, so that today a region of flat-lying beds (the Cowal Flat Beds) is separated from rocks to the northwest and southeast by two monoclines (folds with only one steep limb). Because of this structure, layers in the Dalradian bedrock are near vertical throughout the so-called Knapdale Steep Belt. Further southeast in the Flat Belt of Cowal and Kintyre, bedrock layering is much less steeply inclined, rising to vertical again adjacent to the Highland Boundary Fault. In Arran, flat layering has been locally steepened by the much later (early Tertiary) intrusion of the North Arran granite.

These old Caledonian rocks are separated from the younger rocks of the Midland Valley by the Highland Boundary Fault Zone, a roughly 400-million-year-old fault zone which crosses Bute and Arran in this Area. Other important

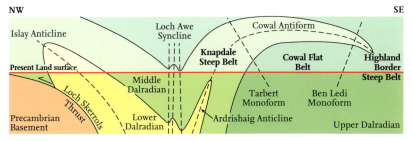

FIG 75. Cross-section through the main fold belts of Area 3. Located on Fig. 74.

Caledonian faults are the Loch Skerrols Thrust, thought to be a southern extension of the Moine Thrust, and the Loch Gruinart Fault.

The next important episode in this Area occurred in the late Silurian and early Devonian (between around 420 and 400 million years ago), when a basin formed across Kintyre and Arran. Flash floods and ephemeral rivers brought sediment from the eroding Caledonian mountains into this basin, filling it with mudstones, sandstones and conglomerates, along with some lavas and volcanic ash. Bedrock formed during this episode is generally referred to as the Lower Old Red Sandstone, and today it outcrops in southern Kintyre and central Arran. During the mid-Devonian, a phase of uplift resulted in erosion of much of the Lower Old Red Sandstone in this Area.

The deposition of the Upper Old Red Sandstone followed, during the late Devonian and early Carboniferous, with the accumulation of river and wind deposits. Today, these sandstones and conglomerates outcrop in the southern half of Bute and in northeastern Arran. Scotland then drifted northwards throughout the Carboniferous and, as it approached warm, tropical latitudes, a marked change in conditions occurred. Deltaic environments became predominant, with river and coastal sands, coals and lagoonal muds accumulating around and on delta-top coastal shelves. The sea periodically invaded, leaving lime-rich sediments, sometimes rich in shelly fossils. Today, these deposits are found dotted around southern Kintyre, Bute and Arran. The Carboniferous was also a time of extensive volcanism, with the formation of thick accumulations of lava and volcanic centres in the Midland Valley. The remnants of this lava today form the bedrock of the southern tip of Bute, around Machrihanish in southern Kintyre, and the island of Little Cumbrae.

During the Permian and Triassic, Scotland's northerly movement had placed it once again at desert latitudes, this time north of the equator, and it lay in the interior of a large continent. As in the Devonian, coarse breccias, gravels and sandstones accumulated (the New Red Sandstone), sourced from local hills and typically with red pigments due to the oxidising desert conditions. In this Area, the most spectacular outcrops are on Arran, where well-preserved giant cross-bedding is evidence of the existence and movement of desert sand dunes. Seismic studies suggest that there are great thicknesses of New Red Sandstone offshore – over 1000 m in the Firth of Clyde and up to 2500 m southwest of Islay. During the remainder of the Mesozoic the sea encroached on much of this Area, depositing shallow marine sediments. However, subsequent erosion means that Jurassic and Cretaceous sediments are rare on land today, although they are still present offshore southwest of Islay and in the southern part of the Sound of Jura.

Tertiary bedrock episodes

At the start of the Tertiary (about 60 million years ago), Greenland and North America began to move away from northwest Scotland along a zone now occupied by the North Atlantic Ocean. Widespread volcanism accompanied this crustal rifting, and numerous localised centres of igneous activity developed across western Scotland. Two such centres are found on Arran, probably at least in part due to the island's location extending across the Highland Boundary Fault Zone (Fig. 74), which would have provided a relatively easy pathway to the surface for rising magma.

The oldest Tertiary rock on Arran is the so-called 'Northern Granite' that underlies most of northern Arran (Fig. 76). In reality, this body consists of two separate intrusions, an older 'Outer Granite', and a younger 'Inner Granite'. The final emplacement of the cylindrical, plug-like body of the Outer Granite probably occurred when the granite was nearly solid, as it pushed up the overlying Dalradian rocks by some 3 km, causing the surrounding older rocks to be sheared and altered. The Inner Granite was then intruded into the Outer Granite by ring-faulting and block subsidence. Such large granite intrusions were emplaced in the other Scottish Tertiary igneous centres, but these centres differed from Arran in that, after emplacement, they were then intruded by large numbers of mafic (gabbroic) ring dykes that all but obliterated the original uplifted granite plug. This did not happen in northern Arran, which, along with its superb exposure, is what makes the Outer Granite particularly special.

Igneous activity then moved south to central Arran, where another igneous centre (the Central Ring Complex) and associated volcanoes developed (Fig. 72). A large explosive eruption occurred soon after igneous activity began here, during which large volumes of magma were expelled from the underlying chamber. Overlying surface rocks subsided by about 1 km into the newly created void, resulting in a circular surface depression (or caldera) nearly 5 km in diameter. Wall rocks collapsed into this caldera, including Tertiary lavas, which probably

FIG 76. Mountains eroded in the North Arran granite. Cir Mhor is in the centre, Goatfell (874 m) is to the right. (© Patricia & Angus Macdonald/Aerographica/Scottish Natural Heritage)

covered much of Arran in the early Tertiary, along with large blocks of Mesozoic sediments (collectively marked as an area of 'agglomerate' on Fig. 72).

Dykes and sills are present throughout the Area, representing an even more widespread product of Tertiary igneous activity. The dykes tend to be oriented roughly northwest to southeast, aligned with the stress field created during crustal stretching. Several distinct 'swarms' of these dykes occur in this Area: the Islay Jura swarm, the Mull swarm (extending southeast from Mull across northern Knapdale and Cowal) and the Arran swarm. The south coast of Arran is claimed to provide one of the best examples of a swarm in the world – around 200 well-exposed dykes are found along roughly 5 km of coastline, representing stretching that extended the crust by about 10 per cent. Textbook examples of dyke intrusion features can be seen along this shoreline. As well as flowing along steep fissures cross-cutting the older bedrock, molten rock has often been forced sideways between bedrock layers to produce sills (Fig. 77). Many such sills were intruded into the New Red Sandstones of southern Arran, some of dark, mafic dolerite, others of lighter, felsic quartz-rich rock. Arran has subsequently been slightly tilted, so that many of these sills are inclined.

FIG 77. Drumadoon Sill, western Arran. (© Patricia & Angus Macdonald/Aerographica/ Scottish Natural Heritage)

MAKING THE LANDSCAPE

Tertiary landscape evolution

At the start of the Tertiary, local uplift combined with lower global sea levels meant that most of this Area would have lain above sea level. In the warm, wet climate of the Tertiary, this exposed land surface was subject to extensive erosion, washing away most of the Mesozoic bedrock and cutting down into the underlying basement. The paths of the Tertiary rivers were largely defined by the structure of the underlying bedrock – the Caledonian folds and faults and associated bedrock contrasts (Fig. 74). A large river flowed, for example, parallel to the folds in the north of the Area, eroding a river valley that has since been glacially deepened and flooded by the sea to form the Sound of Jura. By the end of the Tertiary, the main valleys separating the islands and peninsulas of this Area would have been in place.

Whilst most of Area 3 was subject to the same weathering conditions throughout the Tertiary, different bedrock responded differently to this erosion: softer bedrock weathered more easily and therefore more extensively than harder bedrock, and this contrast can be seen in the landforms present today. Much of this Area is underlain by metamorphosed Dalradian rocks, which on the whole

FIG 78. The Isle of Gigha in the foreground, looking northwest across the Sound of Jura towards the Paps of Jura. (© Patricia & Angus Macdonald/Aerographica)

are fairly hard and resistant to erosion, so that much of this Area is relatively elevated. However, as described above, the Dalradian Supergroup is made up of several different rock types, which have weathered to produce a variety of landscapes. Some of the toughest Dalradian rocks are the quartzites which make up most of Jura and parts of Islay, and which tend to have resisted erosion to form high and hilly terrain. The quartzites were deposited as pure quartz sands, which were then toughened by quartz cement during the burial. Jura, for example, is much more rough and mountainous than most of Islay, culminating in the famous Paps of Jura, three distinctive mountains between 730 and 785 m high (Figs 78 to 80). The quartzite bands on Islay also underlie high moorland and rounded hills, in contrast to the low-lying, fertile landscape of much of the rest of the island, a result of the more extensive weathering of the softer sandstones, limestones, graphitic schists and slates. The number of inhabitants on these islands directly reflects the differing landscapes: some 3000 people live on Islay, while Jura is home to only about 200.

Another good example of differential weathering between individual units of the Dalradian is seen on Knapdale. The Dalradian here has been subject to complex folding (Fig. 75), and today the bedrock is made up of hard bands of metamorphosed sandstone and volcanic rock separated by softer bands of

FIG 79. Sunset on the Paps of Jura. (© Patricia & Angus Macdonald/Aerographica)

limestone and phyllite. Streams tend to have exploited the softer units, so that these underlie valleys, with the harder bodies underlying the intervening ridges of higher ground. Banding in the Dalradian is generally oriented northeast to southwest (Fig. 74) and so this weathering has produced a strong northeast/southwest grain to the landscape. Whilst this lineation is most prominent in Knapdale, where layering in the Dalradian is almost vertical (Fig. 75), it is also present to a certain extent throughout the Area. Carradale Water in eastern Kintyre, for example, gets to within 2 km of the coast before being diverted by a southwest valley, and then travels southwestwards parallel to the coast for nearly 10 km, finally making it to the sea at Carradale Bay (Fig. 71).

On the whole, Dalradian metamorphic rocks are generally harder and more resistant to erosion than younger sedimentary rocks, as shown in southern Kintyre. The high ground forming the southern tip of Kintyre (the Mull of Kintyre) is separated from the equally high backbone of the rest of Kintyre by a broad area of low-lying, flat ground (Fig. 85). This area of lower-lying ground corresponds almost exactly to the areas where Carboniferous deposits outcrop (Fig. 72), and these have weathered much more easily than the Upper Dalradian schists to the north and south. A change in topography between Dalradian schists and younger sediments is also obvious on Bute, which has been bisected

FIG 80. Looking northeast, with the tilted Dalradian strata of east central Islay in the foreground and the Paps of Jura in the background. (© Patricia & Angus Macdonald/Aerographica)

FIG 81. Looking northeast across the Isle of Bute along the line of the Highland Boundary Fault towards Rothesay. Note the raised cliffs on the coastal slopes to left and right. (© Patricia & Angus Macdonald/Aerographica)

by the Highland Boundary Fault. North of the fault, the harder Dalradian schists underlie bare, rounded uplands, whose thin, acid soils mean it is largely uncultivated, apart from extensive forestry plantations. Meanwhile, the softer Old Red Sandstone south of the fault has produced a lower, dissected plateau of rounded hills with highly cultivated fertile soils. Along the fault itself, erosion has picked out the softer fractured rocks and formed a valley, today partially flooded to form Rothesay and Scalpsie Bays, and Lochs Fad and Quien (Fig. 81).

In general, the igneous rocks emplaced during the Tertiary are some of the hardest rock types in this Area. Arran's Northern Granite, for example, seems to be responsible for the shape of the northern half of the island – Tertiary rivers would have been deflected around the resistant granite body, eroding river valleys that today separate the island from the mainland, whilst the granite itself became a marked topographic feature. The central Arran igneous complex, by contrast, has almost no surface expression. These contrasting landscapes, despite similar igneous settings, are due to the amount of uplift associated with the two centres. The intrusion of the Northern Granite caused intense, localised uplift, and the intruding magma pushed the overlying Dalradian rocks up by around 3 km. During the early Tertiary, the uplifted dome of Dalradian rocks (probably with an overlying volcanic complex) was eroded away, exposing the granitic rocks beneath by around 50 million years ago. These hard granites resisted subsequent erosion to form rather rugged mountains, culminating in the peak of Goat Fell at 874 m. Meanwhile, the central volcano was not uplifted nearly as high as the northern volcano, and so less rock was eroded away during the Tertiary: erosion has only lowered the land surface to the level of the caldera, rather than down to the solidified remnants of magma chamber beneath the volcano. These caldera rocks are a fragmented mix of lava, ash and Mesozoic sediments, a mix which has weathered relatively easily to form low, gentle hills.

Igneous rocks elsewhere in the Area also tend to underlie distinctive landscape features. Southern Arran is made up of slightly tilted, alternating layers of igneous sills and sedimentary rocks, and the softer sedimentary rocks have been preferentially eroded away, leaving the sills standing proud. Today, sills underlie most of the hills in southern Arran, often forming steep 'steps' in the landscape such as in the hills above Whiting Bay. Where streams cross from igneous to sedimentary bedrock, the contrasting strength of the two rock types has resulted in the formation of waterfalls – the softer rock is eroded away whilst the sill remains, forming a step in the stream bed. Such waterfalls abound in southern Arran. Carboniferous igneous rocks, whilst not voluminous in this Area, also tend to form distinctive landscape features. For example, some of Bute's most rugged terrain is found at its southern tip, where a patch of hard Carboniferous basalts has produced a wild landscape of near-horizontal plateaus separated by steep scarps. Meanwhile, Davaar Island, at the mouth of Campbeltown Bay in southern Kintyre, is a small island surrounded by sea cliffs, composed of a plug of igneous rock.

Glacial landscape evolution

Climate cooled dramatically around 2 million years ago, and since then Scotland has undergone repeated glaciations during which ice sheets advanced and covered this Area. The last major glaciation (the Devensian) reached its climax between 25,000 and 20,000 years ago, during which Scotland, including Area 3, was once again covered in thick ice sheets. After the Devensian Glacial Maximum, the climate began to warm and the ice sheets retreated, such that this Area was probably ice-free by around 13,000 years ago. The general warming trend was interrupted by a short period of cooling between 13,000 and 11,500 years ago, when the Loch Lomond Advance occurred (see Chapter 5). During this cold phase,

FIG 82. Reconstruction of Devensian ice-flow directions and Loch Lomond Advance limits.

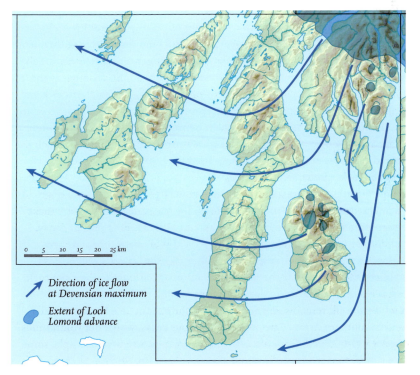

a large ice sheet returned to the Highlands, extending southwards as far as the northern Cowal peninsula, and mountain glaciers returned to northern Arran and eastern Cowal (Fig. 82).

During the Devensian, ice sheets and glaciers eroded deposits from previous glaciations, and so today the freshest small-scale glacial features (such as striae on bedrock surfaces, drumlins, moraine and glacial erratics) date from the most recent glaciation. The alignment and/or shape of these features can often be used to infer ice-flow direction, and so by surveying these glacial deposits and landforms a reconstruction of Devensian ice-flow directions can be made (as in Fig. 82). Blocks of northern Arran granite, for example, are found across Kintyre, indicating westwards ice flow, an observation that is corroborated by the east/west orientation of drumlins around Campbeltown in southern Kintyre. In general, Devensian ice flowed southwestwards from the Scottish Highlands across the eastern half of Area 3, before swinging to a northwesterly flow direction across the western half of the Area. This northerly deflection of the Highland ice was probably due to the presence of Southern Uplands and Irish ice masses in the south, which blocked the southerly movement of Highland ice. Meanwhile, Arran was high enough to develop its own ice dome, and ice flowed radially outwards from here to join the mainland flows.

A striking feature of Figure 82 is that Devensian ice appears to have flowed across rather than along glacially deepened valleys in much of the Area. For example, the ice stream that traversed Jura and Colonsay in a northwesterly direction crossed the Sound of Jura, a major submerged valley some 200 m deep, without any apparent deflection. Similarly, the ice movement from Arran to the west across Kintyre directly crossed the 180 m-deep Kilbrannan Sound. The implication is that these major ice erosional features (and by extension possibly others throughout the Area) were already in place before the Devensian, and that the last ice sheet had only minimal erosional impact. The glacial modification of this Area has therefore been a gradual process, occurring over the course of the repeated glaciations of the Quaternary, and, whilst most of our detailed information relating to glacial flow comes from the most recent ice sheets, these were not necessarily the most important in the glacial modification of the landscape.

Whilst Devensian ice appears to have run across the course of the major Tertiary valleys, it is obvious that during previous glaciations these valleys guided the course of several major ice drainage routes, at least for some of the time. Localised glacial scouring was therefore particularly intense along these valleys, and deep glacial troughs were gouged out. Today, these troughs have been flooded to form sea lochs and sounds, and therefore define the peninsulas and islands that characterise this Area.

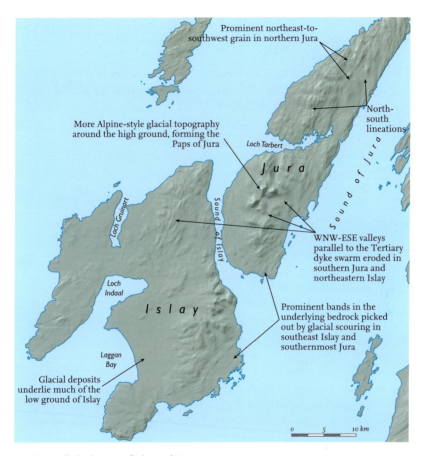

FIG 83. Hill-shade map of Islay and Jura.

Glacial scouring has greatly modified the landscape throughout the Area, and the parallel lines of ridges and valleys created by this scouring are easy to pick out on a simple hill-shade map. In general, these scour lines seem to run parallel to the underlying structure in the bedrock, as ice erosion took advantage of lines of weakness and softer rock units were preferentially eroded. An excellent example of the effect of scouring is seen on Jura, which became smoothed and moulded during repeated glaciations (Fig. 83). Parallel scour lines, defined by ridges and valleys, run along Jura in a northeast/southwest direction, as expected for an area underlain by Dalradian bedrock. Interestingly, two other prominent scour directions are visible, a set of roughly north/south-trending lineations in the northern part of the island, extending south as far as Loch Tarbert, and

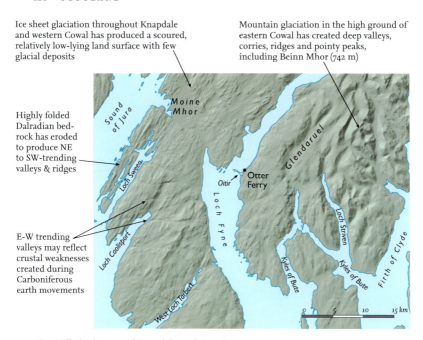

FIG 84. Hill-shade map of Knapdale and Cowal.

a set running roughly northwest/southeast, parallel to the flow direction of the Devensian ice sheet and particularly prominent around Loch Tarbert.

Most of the Area was overrun by the mainland ice sheet during the last glaciation, and probably during previous glaciations, and a typical product of the large-scale scouring which ensued is knock-and-lochan topography, where the land surface is made up of small rocky knolls and intervening hollows (now water-filled to form lochans, or peat-filled to form bogs). Such knock-and-lochan topography is found throughout northern Jura and Knapdale, as well as in small parts of southern Islay and western Cowal.

The landscape of Knapdale is particularly distinctive, made up of long, narrow parallel ridges and valleys, the latter often now flooded to form lochs (Fig. 84). This distinctive relief is due to the folded nature of the underlying Dalradian (Fig. 75), which has been folded to the extent that it is now made up of near-vertical parallel bands of epidiorite, schist, phyllite and limestone. Glacial erosion has both followed and exaggerated the Tertiary drainage system, creating the characteristic landscape seen today. Similar topography is seen along the southeastern coast of Islay (Fig. 83), where the Dalradian is also heavily folded, and extends into the western part of the Cowal peninsula. The long backbone of

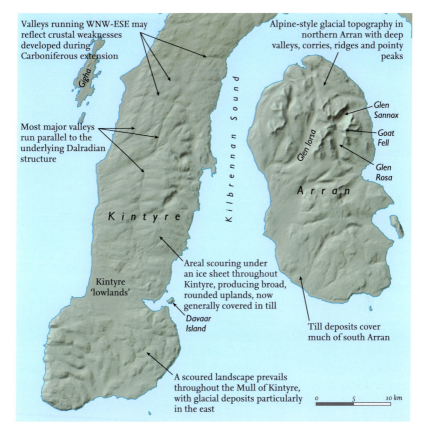

FIG 85. Hill-shade map of Kintyre and Arran.

the Kintyre peninsula, which lies within the Cowal Flat Belt, has been much less dissected than Knapdale, probably due to the lack of bedrock contrasts in the underlying Dalradian (Fig. 85).

Meanwhile, northern Arran and northern and eastern Cowal were areas of high ground by the end of the Tertiary, dissected by river valleys. These high areas acted as centres of ice accumulation, and so they were relatively protected from the indiscriminate scouring experienced by lower-lying areas, as the latter were overrun by the mainland ice sheet. These areas were also subject to mountain glaciation during the Loch Lomond Advance, and erosion by mountain glaciers has been particularly important in shaping the landscape. Glaciers flowed downhill, carving deeply into valley bottoms and sides and creating classic U-shaped valleys such as Glen Rosa and Glen Sannox in northern

Arran. Heads of valleys were gouged out to create deep rounded hollows (corries), ridges formed where two back-eroding corries met, and pyramid-shaped peaks developed where three or more corries met. Today, the valley sides of these upland areas tend to be steep and craggy, and glacial striations and polished rock surfaces are abundant.

On a smaller scale, glacial erosion has produced another distinctive feature of north Arran – tors. These craggy, wart-like outcrops of granite are generally found on the tops of ridges and hills, where they tend to be dissected by deep sub-horizontal and sub-vertical cracks, giving them a brick-wall appearance. Such jointing is common in granite, and is thought to form as the granite is exhumed: as the overlying rock is weathered away, less pressure is exerted on the underlying granite, which then expands and cracks along lines which are often parallel or perpendicular to valley floors and sides. Glacial plucking has taken advantage of these joints, reducing the ground level, block by block, and leaving only a few tors behind. On a larger scale, the position of gullies is often also controlled by jointing, or other vertical or sub-vertical lines of weakness such as faults or dykes. These gullies and chutes act as pathways for debris flows off steep mountainsides, and cones of debris are often present at their outlets.

Whilst glacial erosion has greatly modified the landscape, glacial deposition has also been important. This is most often in the form of till (a stony clay) laid down by melting glaciers, which today blankets the southern half of Kintyre and much of the low ground of Arran, central Islay, south Jura, Colonsay and Oronsay. Ridges of till (moraine) are common throughout Area 3, often forming distinctive landscape features. In northern Arran, for example, moraine deposited at the snouts of retreating glaciers makes up the hummocky ground of many of the valley floors today, such as Glen Rosa, as well as the foundation for the prehistoric fort of 'Bruce's Castle' in Glen Coy. A remarkable moraine ridge is found on the western side of the Paps of Jura, running from the foot of Beinn an Oir roughly 3.5 km northwest. This moraine formed at the junction of two glaciers, and has been described as the finest fossil medial moraine in the UK. It is made up of a series of parallel boulder belts, each belt up to 30 m wide and 2.5 m thick. The angular quartzite blocks probably came from Beinn an Oir, which would have stood above the ice as a nunatak during the waning of the Devensian ice sheet, around 15,000 years ago. Another glacial deposit which forms a particularly notable local landscape feature is the Oitir, which could easily be mistaken for a wave-formed coastal feature: it is a long spit, extending into Loch Fyne for some 2 km from Otter Ferry, in northwest Cowal (Fig. 84). It is thought to be the remnants of a terminal moraine complex that once extended across the loch, formed as the ice margin halted, or briefly re-advanced, during the waning of the

Devensian ice. Subsequent flooding of Loch Fyne has since turned the moraine into the remarkable spit seen today.

Another interesting glacial deposit is found near the Paps of Jura, at the foot of the scree slope on the eastern side of Beinn Shiantaidh, and said to be one of the best examples in Scotland of a 'rock glacier'. This lobate landform developed through the slow deformation of ice that formed in the scree during the Loch Lomond Advance, showing that there was permanently frozen ground at that time in this part of Scotland.

The formation of the coastline

Today, nowhere on land within this Area is more than about 10 km from the sea. The long coastline is very varied in nature, reflecting the underlying bedrock geology, the combined effects of Tertiary and glacial erosion, and recent sea-level changes.

The underlying bedrock has greatly influenced the shape and nature of the coastline on the broadest scale. In general, areas underlain by Dalradian rocks tend to have steeply inclined, rocky coastlines with numerous cliffs. The Mull of Kintyre, for example, is steep on all sides and, combined with the frequent sea fogs, this coastline has proved treacherous. Second World War planes litter the area, and it was also the site of the notorious Chinook crash in 1994. Meanwhile, where the coastline is underlain by softer sedimentary rocks the slope gradient is often somewhat gentler, as seen around southern Arran and parts of western Islay. In southern Arran, the contrasting resistance to wave erosion of sedimentary and igneous rocks is highlighted by the shape of the coastline, with most of the headlands, such as Kingscross Point and Brown Head, being underlain by the harder sills. Sills have also resisted erosion to form cliffs, such as at Holy Island, Pladda and Drumadoon. Meanwhile, as described above, the southern Arran coastline is world-famous for its dyke swarm in part because the dykes are so well exposed, having resisted erosion more than the intervening Triassic sandstone, so that today they form obvious clusters of walls, like features designed by humans to limit beach erosion.

The coast has only taken on its present form during the last 6000 years, as sea level has slowly approached its present level. During glacial periods, global sea level was lower by over 100 m because ice sheets locked up the world's fresh water. Global sea level then rose again during interglacials, as this ice melted and released its water. The level of the land has also varied, the crust sinking under the weight of the ice sheets which spread out from the Scottish Highlands, and rising up again when they melted. The crust was pushed down further where the ice was thicker, and so areas near the centre of the Scottish ice sheet (roughly

FIG 86. Dougarie Field, 2 km north of Machrie on the west coast of Arran, showing raised beach and cliff line, with small sea stacks and bays. (© Patricia & Angus Macdonald/ Aerographica/Scottish Natural Heritage)

centred on Rannoch Moor) have had further to rebound and are continuing to rise today, whilst areas near the periphery of the ice sheet finished uplifting several thousand years ago. This cycle of changing global sea level and changing local depression or rebound of the land occurred throughout the Pleistocene glaciations, resulting in times when sea level was both lower and higher than it is at present (see Chapter 5).

New coastlines were formed by these changing sea levels – platforms backed by cliffs were eroded into bedrock, caves and sea stacks were excavated into these cliffs, and beach deposits were laid down on the lower-angled slopes. Today, raised platforms and beaches are common throughout Area 3, providing evidence for periods of higher relative sea level in the past (Fig. 86).

The west coasts of Jura and northern Islay contain a particularly fine array of raised shore features, reputedly the best examples of raised shore platforms and shingle ridges in western Europe. Both the range of features and their extent and development are exceptional, and they provide a valuable record of past sea level that has greatly helped in the reconstruction of relative sea-level changes in western Scotland.

FIG 87. The High and the Low Rock Platforms on the northwest coast of Jura, north of Loch Tarbert. Numbers refer to coastal features shown in Figure 88. (© Patricia & Angus Macdonald/ Aerographica)

The oldest shorelines in this Area are two rock platforms, known as the High and the Low Rock Platforms. The High Rock Platform is particularly well developed north of Loch Tarbert on Jura (Fig. 87). It lies roughly 30–35 m above sea level, with an average width of 350 m, and is backed by 5–15 m-high cliffs. The Low Rock Platform is roughly horizontal, typically 100 m wide, and occurs in the intertidal area. It is well developed throughout southwestern Jura, and is also present in northwest Jura, northern Islay and Colonsay. The High and Low Rock Platforms have both been covered, in places, by glacial till, and the Low Rock Platform has also been locally ice-moulded. Both platforms must therefore have formed before the Late Devensian Glacial Maximum, probably during successive glacial periods.

The main shorelines present in northwestern Jura and northern Islay are summarised in Figure 88, and the graph in Figure 89 shows the associated changes in relative sea level over the past 15,000 years. After the Late Glacial Maximum (around 20,000 years ago), melting ice sheets caused a rapid rise in global sea level, whilst the crust had only just begun to rebound. Relative sea level reached its

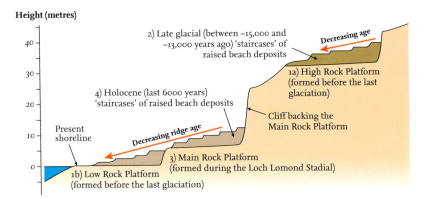

FIG 88. Interpretation of the shore profiles in northwestern Jura and northern Islay over the last 70,000 years.

maximum in this Area around 15,000 years ago, when it was 30–40 m higher than present (Fig. 89), flooding today's lowland coastal areas and lying just above the till-covered High Rock Platform. Crustal rebound then outpaced global sea-level changes, and relative sea level dropped. As it dropped, marine erosion of the till on the High Rock Platform resulted in the deposition of shingle ridges, which today form extensive 'staircases' of raised beach deposits throughout western Jura and northern Islay (Figs 87, 88). These deposits define two shorelines: an older, higher shoreline in northwest Jura and northern Islay (declining in altitude to the southwest, from 40 m at Corpach Bay to 25 m in northeast Islay), and a slightly younger and lower shoreline in southwest Jura (between 30 and 25 m above present sea level). It is thought that southwest Jura was ice-covered while the older shoreline formed in northwest Jura and Islay, and that the second shoreline formed shortly after the deglaciation of southwestern Jura.

During the Loch Lomond Stadial (about 13,000 to 11,500 years ago), the crust was once again depressed as ice returned to central Scotland. During the ensuing cold period, severe frost and wave action eroded the most prominent and extensive ancient shoreline in western Scotland, the Main Rock Platform (Fig. 88). This platform is commonly perhaps 20 m wide (reaching 150 m in places) and is generally backed by a former sea cliff 3 to 15 m high (reaching 100 m in northwestern Jura). Relics of marine erosion occur in these cliffs, for example sea stacks and caves. The platform has been uplifted and tilted by subsequent rebound, and today descends from an elevation of roughly 12 m at the head of Loch Fyne to 6 m in northern Jura, reaching sea level in northern Islay where it crosses the Low Rock Platform. Much of the road circling Arran has been built on

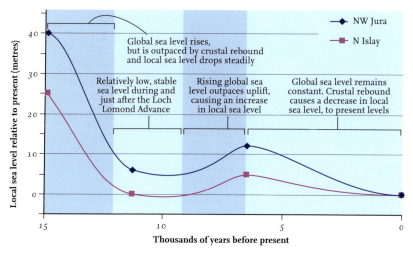

FIG 89. Relative sea-level changes over the last 15,000 years in northwestern Jura and northern Islay.

the relatively flat surface of the High Rock Platform, before it descends below sea level just south of the island.

Between 7000 and 6000 years ago, final melting of the North American and Scandinavian ice sheets caused a great increase in global sea level, and relative sea level in this Area once again rose. Since then, global sea level has remained more or less constant, whilst the crust has continued to uplift at an ever-decreasing rate (Fig. 89). Beach accumulations recording this relative fall in sea level are today found throughout western Jura, where they mantle the rock surfaces of the Main and Low Rock platforms. They generally take the form of extensive shingle ridge 'staircases', and the most spectacular suite occurs north of Inver in southwestern Jura, where 31 unvegetated beach ridges descend from an elevation of roughly 12 m to the modern beach.

On a much bigger scale, the net result of these changes in sea level is that the deeply scoured valleys eroded by ice streams during the Pleistocene glaciations became flooded by the sea. Today, these deep (up to 250 m), narrow channels and lochs define the numerous islands and peninsulas which make up Area 3. As Tertiary and glacial erosion tended to highlight the northeast-to-southwest 'grain' in the underlying Dalradian bedrock, the flooding of these valleys has produced islands and peninsulas with a northeast/southwest orientation, particularly throughout Knapdale. On a larger scale, the Kintyre peninsula and Jura are themselves oriented parallel to the Dalradian structure (Fig. 74). Exceptions to this pattern are found particularly in the vicinity of centres of ice accumulation, such as in the Cowal peninsula, where the main lochs radiate out southwards from old centres of ice accumulation.

Post-glacial landscape evolution
At the start of the Holocene, or Flandrian, period (around 11,500 years ago), the newly deglaciated landscape was unvegetated and covered with unconsolidated glacial debris. The drainage system had been greatly disrupted and over-steepened slopes were common. This relatively unstable landscape was very vulnerable to modification by surface processes, and the early Holocene was a period of readjustment to the new conditions. Landsliding occurred on over-steepened slopes, particularly throughout eastern Cowal, and the unconsolidated glacial debris which blanketed much of this Area was reworked.

Much of the glacial material present in the uplands of the Area was transported down to the lowlands by braided river systems typical of high sediment supply, which then deposited large quantities of sand and gravel on flood plains or at river outlets. At the coast, this coarse material has since been reworked by the sea to form cobble and gravel beaches, spits and tombolos (spits linking islands). At Auchalick Bay in western Cowal, for example, storm reworking of glacial deposits has produced a set of curved spits and beaches separating a complex system of pools. Tombolos are also common, for example at Asgog Bay and Glenan Bay in western Cowal, and connecting Davaar Island to Campbeltown Bay in southeastern Kintyre.

Most of the small bays in this Area contain boulders and coarse shingle – sandy beaches are rare and are generally only found in the sheltered mouths of rivers and streams, where a shallow offshore gradient allows sand to accumulate. The most important sandy beaches include Loch Gruinart in northwest Islay (in the form of intertidal sand-flats), Laggan Bay in southwest Islay and Machrihanish Bay in southern Kintyre. Where beaches are present, they are often backed by sand dunes. Salt-marshes are also rare, as they again require low-gradient coastlines and low-energy environments, although important examples are found fringing the Loch Gruinart sand-flats on Islay, at the head of Loch Crinan in northern Knapdale and at the head of Loch Ruel in Cowal. Both the Loch Crinan and the Loch Ruel areas are nationally important, as they show a complete succession from salt-marsh, through freshwater marsh and finally to woodland vegetation.

With the improving climate of the Holocene, vegetation recolonised the Area. Grasslands were succeeded by juniper and willow shrubs, and finally by forests, at least in the lowlands, which reached their maximum extent between 7500 and 5000 years ago. The development of vegetation and a soil cover stabilised the land surface, and the mid-Holocene was a time of relative landscape stability. From around 5000 years ago climate became slightly cooler and wetter, and humans began to have a marked impact on the landscape. Tree felling and burning greatly enhanced the rate of forest decline and its replacement by bog and heath, and grazing on upland areas has since kept vegetation cover to a minimum. Today, bog and heath cover much of this Area, including the impressive raised bog of Moine Mhor (Gaelic for 'Great Moss') in northern Knapdale, which has a very clear expression on Figure 84. On Islay, these peat deposits blanket much of the glacial till and are considered to be the secret behind the island's numerous single-malt whiskies. Conifer plantations are also characteristic of this Area, most of them planted between 1900 and the 1960s to fuel Scotland's growing timber trade.

CHAPTER 9

Area 4: Glasgow

AREA 4 EXTENDS RIGHT ACROSS the Midland Valley of Scotland, including part of the Grampian Highlands in the northwest and part of the Southern Uplands in the southeast (Fig. 90). The Area is in many ways centred on Glasgow, overwhelmingly Scotland's largest city. The city extends up and down the Clyde valley, and is surrounded on other sides, to an unusual degree, by ranges of high and empty hills. The most obvious of these

FIG 90. Location map for Area 4.

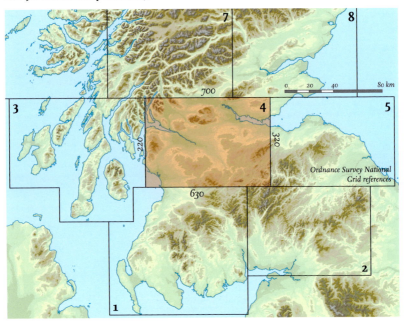

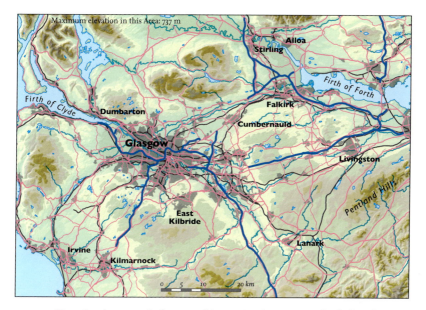

FIG 91. Natural and man-made features of Area 4. See also Figure 96 for further place names.

are the Campsie Fells to the north. Outside these encircling hills, there are other centres of population along and near the Ayrshire coast and along the Firth of Forth, and from Livingston towards Edinburgh in the east (Fig. 91).

The landscape lacks the grandeur of the Highlands, but contains an array of smaller-scale landscape features, resulting from episodes of igneous activity, the faulted edges of distinctive bedrock features and glacial landscape modification.

The Area has been the source of much of the coal of Scotland, which fuelled the Industrial Revolution and transformed the economics of the region. It is perhaps in this Area that the influence of geology and landscape on man is most apparent, and where man has also most changed the landscape.

STORIES FROM THE BEDROCK

The main bedrock types and ages in Area 4 are simplified in Figure 92, whilst a summary of the main events in the geological history of this Area is given in Figure 93.

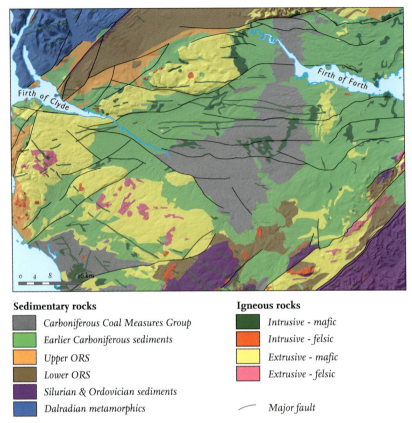

FIG 92. Simplified geology and hill-shaded topography for Area 4. Note the importance of igneous rocks in creating Glasgow's encircling hills.

Early episodes

The deep structure of the Midland Valley has been a matter of speculation for some time. The main bedrock cover ranges in age from Silurian to Permian in age, concealing an older 'basement' that was part of the northern continent of Laurentia, and which is now visible at the surface as the Laurentian Moine much further north in Scotland, as well as in Greenland, North America and Scandinavia (Fig. 94).

At the beginning of the Ordovician, around 490 million years ago, the Iapetus Ocean that extended southwards from the Laurentian margin began to close as the continental margin became a plate margin and active subduction began. The subduction involved consumption of much of the crust of the Iapetus Ocean

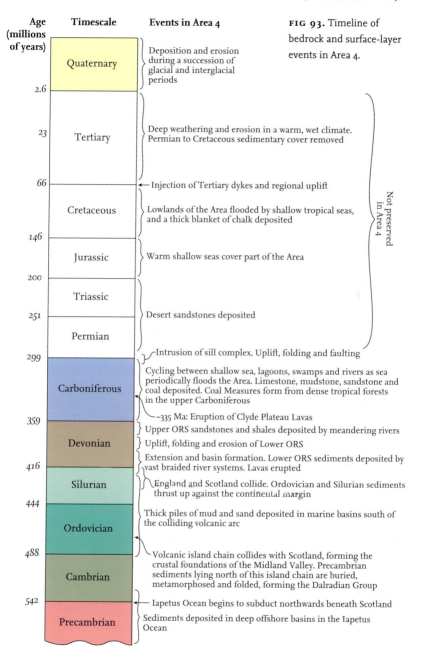

FIG 93. Timeline of bedrock and surface-layer events in Area 4.

floor, and the onset of Caledonian mountain building on the surface to the north (Chapter 4), as represented by the Grampian and Northern Highlands. Although most of the ocean floor moved downwards into the mantle, some small amounts were scraped up and thrust onto the continental margin, and remnants of this oceanic material can still be seen today along the Highland Border.

Around 470 million years ago, as subduction continued, a chain of volcanic islands collided with Laurentia, leading to one of the most significant tectonic phases of the Caledonian mountain building – the Grampian Event (see Fig. 25, Chapter 4). Much of the island chain was subducted, but relicts are preserved as the Highland Border Complex along the Highland Boundary Fault Zone. During this subduction, the Proterozoic and Lower Palaeozoic sediments that had been deposited north of the volcanic arc became deeply buried, where they were squeezed into large-scale folds and metamorphosed into the hard schists, slates and amphibolites of the Dalradian Supergroup. Today, these Dalradian rocks occur in the northwestern corner of Area 4, underlying most of the Loch Lomond and the Trossachs National Park.

The bedrock of the Southern Uplands formed at around this time, deposited as muds and sands between around 490 and 420 million years ago on the floor of the Iapetus Ocean, south of the volcanic island chain. Subduction continued, with ocean floor being pushed northwards beneath the newly created Midland Valley margin. As England began to collide with Scotland, around 430 million years ago, the Ordovician and Silurian sediments were scraped off the subducting ocean floor along a series of thrust faults and stacked up in a pile against the southern edge of the Midland Valley. The most important of these thrust faults is the Southern Uplands Fault, which defines the margin of the Midland Valley terrane. Further north, the collision of Scotland and England resulted in several kilometres of displacement along the Highland Boundary Fault Zone.

During continental collision and subduction, the sediment surface southeast of the Area emerged above sea level. Sediments deposited through this period record the changing environmental conditions, from relatively deep marine, to lagoons and then finally lakes. Some of the world's oldest known fossil fish have been found in Silurian rocks around Lesmahagow, 10 km southwest of Lanark, in Silurian rocks. They include primitive vertebrates (e.g. *Jamoytius kerwoodi*, named after the scientist J. Moy Thomas), as well as water scorpions up to 2 m long.

Formation of the Midland Valley Basin

During the mid- to late Silurian, late Caledonian strike-slip movement caused northeast/southwest-trending basins to begin forming within the larger Midland Valley, the northern (Strathmore) sub-basin and the southern (Lanark) sub-basin

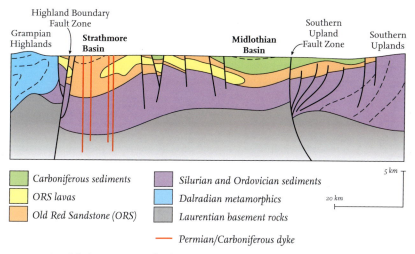

FIG 94. Simplified cross-section for the eastern part of the Midland Valley.

(see Fig. 27, Chapter 4). In the Strathmore sub-basin, between 1 and 4 km of Lower Old Red Sandstone, red sandstones, mudstones and conglomerates were deposited. By the early Devonian (around 410 million years ago), the periodic compression to which this Area had been subject for the previous 80 million years or so came to an end, and the Area began to undergo extension. The major faults, the Highland Boundary and Southern Uplands faults, became reactivated as normal faults, separating the subsiding, low-lying ground of the Midland Valley from mountain chains to the north and south (Fig. 94).

By this time, Scotland lay in the interior of a continent some 20 degrees south of the equator. Great braided rivers flowed from the Caledonian mountains into the Midland Valley basins, carrying with them large volumes of boulders, sand and gravel. Spectacularly coarse conglomerate beds, up to 2000 m in total thickness, were deposited in the Strathmore Basin, containing rounded boulders up to 1 m across in some localities. This Lower Old Red Sandstone provides some of the most direct evidence of the presence of high Caledonian mountains. As well as a range of sedimentary rocks, volcanic rocks are commonly intercalated with the river and lake sediments, particularly in its upper 600 m. Today, Lower Old Red Sandstone deposited in the Strathmore Basin occurs in a broad area adjacent to the Highland Boundary Fault in the north of the Midland Valley terrane. Laminated sandstones from this time are well exposed in the gorge at Finnich Glen, southwest of Killearn, some 20 km north of Glasgow. The Lower Old Red Sandstone of the Lanark Basin, in the south, is not as extensive, being present as isolated patches, now completely surrounded by younger rocks.

As well as individual lava flows within the mainly sedimentary successions, the Lower Old Red Sandstone contains more substantial amounts of igneous rocks. One such lava pile forms the Ochil Hills, in the northeast corner of this Area. The 2000 m-thick lava pile was part of a volcanic range of hills erupted in early Devonian times, when it helped to separate the Strathmore and the Lanark basins. As well as producing surface lava flows, igneous activity in the Devonian also resulted in material being intruded beneath the surface. Tinto Hill, some 10 km southeast of Lanark, is a prominent landscape feature at 707 m elevation, underlain by a tough fine-grained resistant red rock (felsite), dated at 412 million years old (earliest Devonian).

During the mid-Devonian (around 400 to 370 million years ago), the region was once again subject to movements, during which the Lower Old Red Sandstone deposits were compressed and folded and a large downfold further shaped the Strathmore Basin. Deposition had resumed by the late Devonian, at least in the Strathmore Basin, where around 1000 m of red-brown fluvial sandstones and shales (the Upper Old Red Sandstone) were laid down by large meandering rivers. These rivers rose in the Highlands and the Southern Uplands and carried material towards what is now the North Sea. Desert-like conditions persisted in these times of limited vegetation, as shown by the presence of wind-blown sand dunes in the sedimentary layers, and by the reddish brown colouration. The Upper Old Red deposits today underlie much of the coastal area north of Ardrossan, and inland in areas adjacent to Lower Old Red Sandstone. Sedimentary surfaces in these basins became lower, closer to sea level, as Devonian times passed into Carboniferous.

Carboniferous to Tertiary bedrock episodes

By the start of the Carboniferous, the mountains of the Highlands and Southern Uplands had been reduced by erosion to rolling hills. Britain lay in southern tropical latitudes, although northwards drift would take it to just north of the equator by the end of the period. The semi-arid environment of the Devonian gave way to more humid tropical conditions, before reverting to more arid conditions towards the end of the Carboniferous. Regional extension continued, with subsidence of the Midland Valley between the higher upland blocks of the Highlands and the Southern Uplands. Subsidence was not uniform – instead, blocks and basins formed, commonly oriented north-northeast and associated with downfolds. These blocks and basins controlled sediment accumulation, only thin and incomplete sedimentary sequences being deposited on the blocks, whilst thick and more complete successions accumulated in the basins. Further north, the area around Loch Lomond was a relatively stable region, remaining largely dry land when much of central Scotland was covered by sea.

Rivers again deposited sediment in the low-lying areas, and extensive spreads of Carboniferous strata today underlie large parts of the Midland Valley. Because of subsidence, these low-lying areas were periodically flooded by the sea to form lagoons or shallow arms of the sea. Indeed, cyclic sedimentation is a dominant feature of Carboniferous strata: river deltas grew out from river outlets, and the sedimentary succession tracks a deepening marine environment (limestone to mudstone) into which deltaic sand built out until the delta top lay above sea level and was colonised by swamp vegetation. Global sea-level changes also fluctuated during this time, due to the growth and melting of ice sheets far away from Britain, and interacted with more localised movement on the basin boundary faults and changes in local sediment input. Indeed, the Glasgow area was subjected throughout much of the Carboniferous to alternating cycles of flooding by the sea and re-emergence from the sea. As well as consisting of these cycles of sedimentation over time, Carboniferous successions are laterally variable, with sedimentation being periodically restricted by the eruption of lava barriers and changing of river patterns.

A major episode of volcanic activity in the Glasgow area interrupted this sedimentary sequence for around 5 million years. A major lava field around 1 km thick was formed, probably fed by dyke swarms, although large isolated volcanoes may also have been important, possibly some 5 km in diameter and rising to around 1 km above the surrounding plains. The thickest accumulation of these volcanic materials was in the Glasgow area, although a few flows reached as far south as Ardrossan and beyond. Together, these mostly mafic (basaltic) rocks are known as the Clyde Plateau lavas, and today they underlie the area between Greenock and Strathaven, 20 km southeast of Glasgow centre. The vents through which lava was erupted are also visible in some places, such as Dumbarton Rock, north of Glasgow.

Once volcanic activity ceased, weathering and erosion of the lava plateau began. The variable thickness of the lava flows meant that an uneven landscape was produced, which then largely controlled the distribution of land and sea during the remainder of the early Carboniferous. Eventually a shallow tropical sea encroached onto the whole plateau, and by around 330 million years ago most of the plateau became submerged. This shallow sea, akin to the modern-day Bahamas island platform, repeatedly flooded the landscape over the next 10 million years or so, resuming the cyclicity seen before the lava eruptions. Over millions of years, the constant switching from open shallow sea and coastal lagoons to swamp and river conditions, then back again, gave rise to repeating rock-layer cycles of limestone, mudstone, siltstone, sandstone, fossils soils such as *seatearths* and coal (Fig 93). Ironstone was formed under certain conditions, usually at the bottom of shallow-water lagoons.

Many creatures thrived in the Carboniferous seas and lagoons of the Area, and the fossil remains of these creatures, including sharks, corals, sponges and jellyfish, are particularly well preserved in the limestones of Ayrshire. Bearsden, some 8 km northwest of Glasgow centre, is one of the best and most important fossil shark sites in the world, and many significant discoveries have been made here in recent years. Several complete shark specimens have been found, sometimes so well preserved that even muscles and blood vessels can be seen.

In the second half of the Carboniferous period, the region lay near the northern edge of an extensive coastal plain that covered much of northwest Europe and probably extended far to the west. The Midland Valley was dominated at intervals by swamp and river environments that were periodically drowned by the sea. This was when the dense tropical forest covered large areas of the Midland Valley, giving rise to the economically important Coal Measures. Coal accumulated in three distinct low-lying basins in this Area, separated from one another by faulting and by higher ground underlain by older lavas. These subsequently formed the coalfields of central Scotland, Ayrshire and the Douglas valley.

Ongoing crustal extension in the Area continued to give rise to volcanic activity, and in late Carboniferous and very early Permian times, magma was intruded into cracks and between rock layers to form horizontal, inclined and vertically oriented sheets, sills and dykes. Together, these form a large sill complex. Each sill is anywhere between 25 and 170 m thick and may be linked by dykes, and the total thickness of intrusive rock may reach around 200 m. The complex underlies a very large area around the inner Firth of Forth, with dykes extending as far as the Outer Hebrides and the Central Graben of the North Sea. Excellent examples of these occur at Ardrossan and inland at Lugar, about 25 km east of Ayr. Columnar jointing is often present in the sills, and perhaps one of the best examples of regular jointing in Britain is found at Hillhouse Quarry in Dundonald, 7 km southwest of Kilmarnock.

By around 300 million years ago, all the world's continents had drifted together temporarily, forming the supercontinent of Pangaea. Despite Scotland's great distance at this time from active plate margins, the newly formed Carboniferous layers were gently tilted and folded, and in places new faults broke through the crust, often with an east/west orientation. Towards the end of the Carboniferous, Scotland had drifted north of the equator, and the great tropical forests, deltas and marine basins were replaced by inland river and desert conditions. Desert conditions continued through much of the Permian: sand blew across the desert landscape forming dunes, which built up to form sandstones hundreds of metres thick. Mesozoic rocks would certainly have been deposited in this Area, including a blanket of chalk deposited from warm Cretaceous seas. However, crustal uplift at the end of the Cretaceous raised the land above sea level, and much of the Mesozoic sedimentary rock was eroded away.

Almost from the time it was fully formed during the Permian, the Pangaea supercontinent began to drift apart, and new oceans started to form. By the start of the Tertiary, around 60 million years ago, the North Atlantic was beginning to open. This Area does not contain the more dramatic igneous centres of the Hebridean islands, but evidence of crustal tension and splitting is seen in the form of dyke intrusions across the Area. Good examples are seen at the coast, such as at Largs and Saltcoats, where they cut through softer sedimentary rocks. They tend to have been eroded less easily than the softer sedimentary rocks around them, and so often stand proud.

MAKING THE LANDSCAPE

Tertiary landscape modification

The Midland Valley has existed as an area of low-lying ground for much of the time since the Old Red Sandstone accumulated, sandwiched between upland areas to the north and south. However, the main valley systems of today's landscape are thought to have come into being during the Tertiary, an important time in the landscape history of much of Scotland. Western areas were uplifted during early Tertiary igneous activity, whilst the climate of the time was generally humid and warm, conducive to vigorous weathering which removed much of the Mesozoic cover of marine rocks, before beginning to dissect the underlying Permian, Carboniferous and Old Red Sandstone. As a result, the broad outlines of the present-day landscape are thought to have come into being during the Tertiary, although important features such as the valley occupied by Loch Lomond would be added later during the successive glaciations.

In general, this Area is relatively low-lying and flat (Fig. 95). Most of Scotland's mountains are underlain by hard basement rocks, which have resisted erosion well. These basement rocks are not visible in the Midland Valley, because they have been buried beneath softer basin-fill sedimentary rocks, which have been relatively easily weathered to produce broad valleys and gentle rolling hills

148 · SCOTLAND

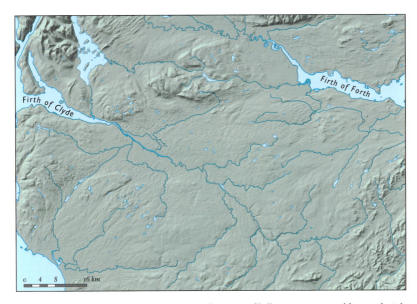

FIG 95. Hill-shade map for Area 4, showing location of hills, mountains and linear glacial landforms.

FIG 96. The main rivers of Area 4, and the Forth–Clyde canal.

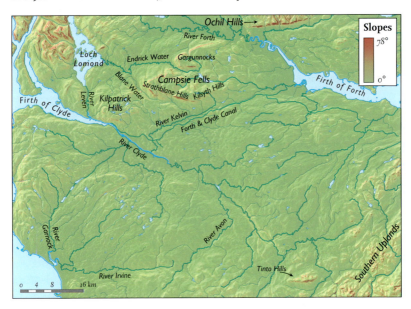

(Fig. 96). Meanwhile, the northwestern and southeastern corners of this Area are underlain by more resistant metamorphic rocks, which have formed the generally higher and more deeply dissected mountainous terrain of the Highlands and the Southern Uplands. The contact between these two very different generations of bedrock is sharply defined in both the north and the south by major fault lines: the Highland Boundary Fault in the northwest and the Southern Uplands Fault in the south. Today, an excellent view of the Highland Boundary Fault can be gained by looking northeastwards across Loch Lomond, as the fault crosses the loch's southern islands (Fig. 97).

Within the Midland Valley itself, differences in bedrock are responsible for the majority of the larger-scale topographic features. The Early Carboniferous Clyde Plateau lavas underlie much of the high ground around Glasgow and in Ayrshire, including the Campsie Fells, Kilpatrick Hills and Gargunnock Hills, rising to a height of around 580 m. On the northeastern edge of the Area, the Ochil Hills are also prominent, underlain by resistant Devonian lavas.

The importance of the strength and structure of the bedrock, even where sedimentary, is particularly well demonstrated in the north of this Area. In the Loch Ard Forest (just east of Loch Lomond) and in the Menteith Hills of Area 7, alternating beds of Devonian sandstones and conglomerates have weathered differentially to produce a ridged topography, with long, linear ridges underlain by the conglomerate, separated by intervening lower ground underlain by the softer sandstone.

Faults are perhaps responsible for fewer landscape features in the low grounds of this Area than they are in many other parts of Scotland, possibly due to the widespread glacial sedimentation that came later. However, there are several notable exceptions, where faults marked on Figure 92 are clearly associated with river valleys or scarps. Perhaps the most dramatic example of this is the Ochil Fault, where the undulating plateau of the Ochil Hills abruptly ends in a remarkably steep, linear escarpment, dropping to the relatively flat, low-lying plain of Clackmannan. This escarpment is considered by many to be one of the finest examples of a fault line in the country. Another fine example of a fault-controlled scarp occurs along the southwestern margin of the Campsie Fells. Where scarps define the edges of lava plateaus, as at the faulted contacts described above, terracing is often visible. This 'trap' landscape is common in areas underlain by lava plateaus, and is described more fully in Chapter 15 (Area 10, Skye). Few valleys follow faults in this Area, unlike in many other parts of Scotland. A notable exception is the prominent valley running southwest from Barrhead, about 11 km southwest of Glasgow centre.

FIG 97. Looking northeastwards across the island of Inchcailloch, to Balmaha, on the far shore of Loch Lomond. The ridges on the island and beyond Balmaha mark thick units of Lower Old Red Sandstone resting tilted to the right, against Dalradian Supergroup metamorphic rocks along the Highland Boundary Fault Zone. (© Patricia & Angus Macdonald/Aerographica/Scottish Natural Heritage)

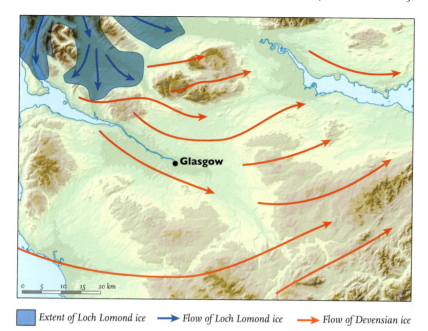

FIG 98. The general directions of Devensian ice movement, and the extent of ice advance during the Loch Lomond Stadial.

Glacial landscape modification

Whilst the broad landscape features seen today – the main upland and lowland areas and the large valleys – were in place by the end of the Tertiary, the finer details of today's landscape were created largely during the glaciations of the last 2 million years. As described in Chapter 5, the climate alternated between glacials and interglacials five or six times during the last 750,000 years. During the more intense glacials, ice sheets covered all of this Area, whilst during the periodic less cold episodes, smaller mountain glaciers probably ceased to exist even in the mountainous regions.

During the last glaciation, the Devensian, glaciers expanded out from the southwest Highlands some time after about 30,000 years ago, reaching their Late Glacial Maximum extent around 22,000 years ago. Ice extended southwards from the Highlands and Loch Lomond across the Midland Valley and along the Firth of Clyde, which at that time was a river valley, rather than a sea loch or estuary, because sea level was so low. Shortly after this, ice from the Southern Uplands ice centre expanded northwards across the southern and central parts of the Area, forcing Highland ice eastwards across Ayrshire (Fig. 98). The competition between these northern and southern ice masses is reflected today in the character of the glacial deposits in central and southern Ayrshire, where glacial deposits with erratics carried by glaciers from the Highlands are overlain by deposits derived from the Southern Uplands. All in all, the Devensian ice sheet buried the local landscape to a depth of more than 1000 m, and even the higher ground in the northwest and southeast of this Area would have been largely covered by ice.

Each successive glaciation not only helped shape the landscape, but also removed most of the deposits of earlier glaciations. Many of the glacial deposits seen today therefore date from the last glacial, the Devensian (around 30,000 to 11,500 years ago). This Area is however known to contain a few crucial sites where pre-Devensian deposits exist. These include peats, whose pollen content can provide clues about the pre-Devensian climate, as well as the bones of large mammals. In the lower Clyde, for example, mammoth, woolly rhinoceros and reindeer bones have been found, indicating cold, non-glacial conditions similar to those of the present-day Arctic.

In the higher ground of this Area, particularly in the Highlands and Southern Uplands, the cumulative effects of the Quaternary glaciations dramatically affected the landscape. River valleys were deepened and widened, and new valleys were often carved, altering the pre-glacial drainage system. Loch Lomond itself was gouged out over the course of multiple glaciations, cutting across the regional geological structure and dissecting river valleys. The lower parts of the Clyde and Kelvin valleys were also greatly deepened, forming rock basins that descend to over 70 m below present sea level. Further east, ice was channelled through the existing Forth Valley at Stirling, resulting in vigorous erosion under the fast-moving ice stream, particularly where the ice was funnelled between the Ochils and the high ground to the south and west of Stirling, where a rock basin some 200 m deep was gouged out.

Deposition, crag and tail, drumlins

Within the Midland Valley itself, glacial erosion is only responsible for landforms in the higher ground, for example the volcanic hills such as the Campsie Fells. Here, ice erosion created a distinctive knock-and-lochan topography, described further in Areas 10 and 14, of small irregular hills and enclosed basins, and on the higher slopes mafic basalt lavas produced scarps. Elsewhere, massive volumes of sediment were deposited beneath the Devensian ice, mostly in the form of till, a chaotic mix of boulders, gravel, sand and clay. As such, the dominant Devensian landscape modification in the Midland Valley was glacial deposition, and all but the tops of the volcanic hills were smothered in a blanket of till.

As ice flowed over this till it was often moulded into distinctive low, elongated, egg-shaped hills, or drumlins, which today cover most of the lower

FIG 99. Drumlins just north of Glasgow. (© Patricia & Angus Macdonald/ Aerographica/Scottish Natural Heritage)

ground of this Area. Drumlins vary greatly in size and form, from tens of metres to several kilometres in length. Much smaller, irregular till hillocks are also common, generally formed between or on the lower slopes of drumlins. By far the most impressive and dense clustering of drumlins in central Scotland is within the Clyde Valley around Glasgow and in the lowlands to the east (Fig. 99). Within the city of Glasgow itself, curving street patterns often follow the layout of the drumlin swarm, such as in Maryhill and Mosspark, whilst the university buildings stand on drumlin crests. Drumlin orientations document vigorous easterly flow of Highland ice across the region from an ice centre located over the mountains and sea lochs of Cowal (Area 3) into the Firth of Forth. The Glasgow area also contains excellent examples of superimposed drumlins, where later smaller drumlins have been carved on top of previous, larger 'megadrumlins'. The orientation of these later drumlins suggests that, as ice thinned towards the end of the Late Glacial Maximum, the main trajectory of ice movement became northwest to southeast, up the Clyde Valley.

The Irvine district lay far enough south to feel the force of Southern Uplands ice, and here there are two prominent sets of drumlin and crag-and-tail directions – an earlier east/west trend overprinted by a later north/south trend. This is similar to trends seen in central Ayrshire, and is thought to represent a deflection of Highland ice by the radially draining Southern Uplands ice, shortly after the Late Glacial Maximum.

As well as drumlins, Area 4 contains excellent examples of crag-and-tail hills, particularly in the east of the Area just south of the Forth. These formed where more resistant volcanic plugs or sills protected weaker sedimentary rocks on their lee sides from the full force of the glaciers. Examples include Loudon Hill in Ayrshire and the Necropolis in Glasgow. Other prominent hills in the lowlands of this Area are often underlain by igneous intrusions, such as the isolated hill of Dumgoyne (427 m) on the edge of the Campsie Fells, and the hill on which Stirling Castle sits.

Melting ice: meltwater channels, glaciofluvial deposits and dams

As climate warmed after the Late Glacial Maximum, the ice sheet covering this Area began to melt, and the Midland Valley gradually emerged from beneath its ice cover. Highland glaciers retreated towards the northwest, so that the Clyde estuary remained blocked by ice at a time when the ice in the Clyde Valley had melted. These glaciers acted as dams, creating lakes in the middle and lower Clyde Valley and in the valleys of the Avon Water and the River Kelvin.

The melting ice released vast quantities of meltwater, which flowed to the east through the Kelvin Valley into the Forth, toward the south into the ice-dammed lakes within the Clyde Valley, and to the northeast through a gap in the Campsie Fells into the Forth lowlands. These meltwaters had great erosive power, and in places cut into the bedrock to form deep channels. As the meltwater source then disappeared, the channels were left, now often forming dry valleys. Exceptionally well-developed meltwater channels can today be seen on the southern slopes of the Kilsyth Hills, on the hillside between the Kelvin Valley and the Clyde Valley, and on the north side of Tinto Hill. The largest meltwater channel is at the eastern end of the Kelvin Valley, forming the watershed between this valley and the Forth Valley (between western and eastern Scotland). Deep tunnel valleys run along the foot of the Ochil Hills and down the axis of the Firth of Forth, and were probably also cut by glacial meltwater moving under water pressure below the ice.

On lower ground, meltwaters deposited large amounts of sand and gravel, and the glacial deposits in many of the valleys of this Area, such as the Kelvin and Leven valleys, are covered by thick sequences of glaciofluvial mounds (*kames*), ridges (*eskers*) and terraces. Perhaps the most spectacular are the Carstairs Kames,

FIG 100. Carstairs Kames, a few kilometres east of Lanark, formed by sub-glacial and ice-front river action. (© Patricia & Angus Macdonald/Aerographica/Scottish Natural Heritage)

a few kilometres east of Lanark (Fig. 100). These are a series of esker ridges that formed as part of the major glacial drainage system directed northeast towards the Firth of Forth, although the extent of the landforms has been significantly reduced by sand and gravel quarrying. Large thicknesses of sand and gravel are also present in the Darvel area, mostly as flat-topped glaciofluvial terraces along the bases of the Irvine and Avon valleys. These were deposited in temporary lakes, formed as ice sheets in this area wasted westwards along the Irvine Valley, and today they account for a considerable sand and gravel resource that is still quarried. During the last stages of ice wastage, around and east of Glasgow, an extensive kame landscape also contains kettle holes (water-filled hollows once filled by blocks of ice), indicating that the ice became stagnant and disintegrated *in situ* in the base of the Kelvin Valley.

The weight of the main Late Devensian ice sheet had depressed the Earth's crust beneath it. At the same time, global sea level had been lowered by more than 100 m as a significant volume of water was locked up in continental ice sheets. As Scottish ice receded, rebound of the land surface at first failed to keep up with the worldwide rise in sea level resulting from the melting of the ice sheets, and sea level in Area 4 was around 30–40 m higher than at present. The sea first entered the Glasgow area from the Lochwinnock Gap (southwest of Glasgow), causing marine shorelines to form around Glasgow and as far west as Kilpatrick. With further retreat of the ice margin to the west, the sea entered the Firth of Clyde from the south and formed a large embayment in the Paisley area, whilst further north, Loch Lomond was temporarily turned into a sea loch. Thick beds of estuarine clays and silts were deposited during this time of higher relative sea level, the so-called Clyde Beds, containing cold-water sea shells. The sea also flooded the lower-lying parts of the Ayrshire coast at this time, forming a large embayment between Ayr (Area 1) and Ardrossan, when the sea penetrated inland over 10 km up valleys such as the Irvine. Relative sea level then fell from this altitude as the land rebounded. The final stages of ice retreat were accompanied by the removal of the ice barrier across the Clyde estuary, allowing the ice-dammed lakes to drain.

Loch Lomond Stadial

The improvement in climate was briefly interrupted, some 13,000 to 11,500 years ago, by a brief cold period known as the Loch Lomond Stadial (see Chapter 5). An ice sheet once again developed over the western Highlands, moving southwards across the northern part of this Area down the valleys of Loch Lomond and Gareloch. Three large lobes extended out from this ice sheet – one down Loch Long and Gareloch, another down Loch Lomond, and a third down the Forth

Valley (the Menteith Glacier) (Fig. 98). Loch Lomond ice radiated out at its southern end, with separate flows heading towards the Leven and Endrick valleys. Beyond the ice limit, a large proglacial lake formed in the Blane and Endrick valleys, and this lake overflowed across the col between the Clyde and the Forth drainage systems to flow into and beneath the Forth Glacier lobe in the vicinity of Buchlyvie.

During movement across the Area this ice deformed its bed, reworking and degrading previous deposits. Following renewed warming, the icecap gradually wasted and its outlet glaciers retreated northwards. This retreat was not uninterrupted, however, and many glaciers oscillated at their margins, depositing moraines which can be seen as bouldery mounds scattered in the mountain glens. The largest of these moraines is found around the southern end of the glaciers, and clearly marks the limit of Loch Lomond ice. It is considered a classic example of a terminal moraine, formed at a glacier's snout. Along most of its length it forms a well-developed ridge of till, increasing in size across the Leven Valley, where it has since been partially dissected by meltwaters. Where it crosses the Endrick Valley it is rather different, being made up of a number of low-relief ridges of ice-deformed lake sediments and till. The height of these ridges, some 65 m above sea level, coincides with the highest level reached by a lake that formed beyond the ice. Around the Gartness area, the most complete moraine ridge runs roughly north/south several kilometres east of Drymen. Sediments on the western side of the moraine were heavily deformed by the advancing ice, whilst those on the east are relatively undisturbed.

The southern half of the Lake of Menteith lies within this Area, and it is scenically interesting. On the eastern side of the lake a series of ridges was thrust up by glacier ice, leaving a depression west of the ridges, today filled by the lake. This is an excellent example of a landform known as a *hill–hole pair*.

Elsewhere, outside regions directly influenced by ice, periglacial processes shaped the landscape. The summits of the hills in the southernmost part of the Glasgow and Ayrshire area are extensively covered in frost-shattered debris and deposits formed by the slow downslope movement of the soil (solifluction), which probably date in part from this time, and solifluction also affected the steeper slopes of the drumlins. On Tinto Hill, where the vegetation has been eroded, superb stone stripes are still actively forming today through freezing and thawing of the soil in winter.

This last glacial episode in Scotland's history also coincided with a period of relatively high and stable sea level, when the sea once again entered Loch Lomond, and frost weathering, sea ice and wave action combined to cut, or at least enhance, a prominent shore platform and backing cliff. This old raised shoreline is conspicuous along much of the coastline of the Firth of Clyde, in the Clyde estuary, south along the coast to Troon and inland around the southern shore of Loch Lomond. It is part of a feature known as the Main Rock Platform (see Fig. 88, Chapter 8), and it lies at an altitude of around 12 m at the southern end of Loch Lomond, descending to below sea level in Area 1. This gentle tilting came about later, as the Highlands had further to rebound on deglaciation than southern areas, which had been less depressed by ice. At the southern end of Loch Lomond, Loch Lomond Advance glacier deposits sit on top of the platform, showing that it was cut before the ice reached its maximum extent. Elsewhere, it is often overlain by post-glacial raised beach deposits, mainly of sand and gravel.

Post-glacial landscape modification

Between 7000 and 6000 years ago, final melting of the North American and Scandinavian ice sheets caused a great increase in global sea level, and relative sea level in this Area once again rose. Loch Lomond became a sea loch again, and large areas of low-lying coastline were drowned. In the Irvine area, the sea extended some 5 km inland, and sea level in the Paisley area was around 7 m higher than at present. Further east, the flooding of the Forth Valley resulted in the deposition of extensive carse deposits. Since then, global sea level has remained more or less constant, whilst the crust has continued to uplift at an ever-decreasing rate. This gradual emergence of the land has resulted in the formation of extensive raised-beach deposits. Around Prestwick and Irvine, for example, these extend some 4–5 km inland. Around the Forth, the raised-beach deposits take the form of a staircase of gently tilted raised beaches. Indeed, the western Forth Valley has one of the most important records of relative sea-level change in Scotland, with a sequence of buried beach and carse deposits. Back west, Loch Lomond became a freshwater loch once again, whilst sea shells and even the bones of stranded whales have been found some distance inland in the raised beach deposits laid down by these higher seas.

Holocene rivers

Following deglaciation, the main terrestrial modification of the landscape occurred through river activity, until man's arrival several thousand years ago. Extensive river incision took place on the hillside slopes, whilst alluvial infills are thick and extensive in the valley bottoms.

The last ice sheet had infilled the majority of the pre-existing river valleys with glacial deposits and, in some places, buried them completely. When the ice melted, rivers sometimes excavated entirely new valleys, leaving the old channels buried. The Clyde near Lanark, for example, cut a new post-glacial

FIG 101. Meanders and old channels of the River Clyde near its junction with the Medwin Water, known as the Meetings, 10 km east of Lanark. (© Patricia & Angus Macdonald/ Aerographica/Scottish Natural Heritage)

course through a narrow, 7 km-long rock gorge, producing distinctive sets of waterfalls. The Kelvin and Mouse also follow deep new post-glacial courses. Where the topography is less steep, post-glacial rivers have not been forced to excavate deep new channels, but instead have reworked the glacial deposits, meandering backwards and forwards across their flood plains until modern river engineering constrained their courses through canalisation and flood embankments. A good example of an actively meandering river which has not been subject to such major engineering works is the Clyde's junction with Medwin Water (Fig. 101). Former positions of the river are shown by the pattern of well-preserved abandoned channels and oxbow lakes on its flood plain, and the history of flood-plain activity is well documented for the last 150 years, on maps and air photographs. It is known, for example, that one bend in the upper part of the reach migrated some 280 m in 130 years, an average rate of over 2 m per year. The lower Endrick flood plain also provides excellent examples of cut-off channels, oxbow lakes and point bars, formed as the river has migrated laterally in recent times. The material it is reworking was mostly deposited as a delta around 6000 years ago, during the period of higher relative sea level described above.

This Area contains two large and important estuaries, the Clyde and the Forth. Both are glacially deepened basins, eroded over the course of many glaciations and then flooded during recent sea-level rises. Both have also played an important role in human history, and it is no coincidence that Scotland's two major cities lie on these important waterways. Both estuaries have been important sinks of glacial deposits since deglaciation, the shallow water depth of the Clyde being evident at low tide, when banks of mud and sand are exposed.

HUMAN INFLUENCE ON THE LANDSCAPE

Humans have had a great impact on the landscape of Area 4, perhaps more so than elsewhere in Scotland. This is mostly due to the relatively gentle topography of this Area and the higher proportion of good farmland than in much of Scotland. As described above, this topography is the result of many millennia of geological history. Also important are the great reserves of economically important rock types, mostly dating from the Carboniferous.

As in much of Scotland, one of the first effects of man's activity was deforestation. The low-lying ground of the Midland Valley has a gentle climate compared to the uplands to the north and south, and much of Area 4 would have been covered by forest. Once humans arrived, the majority of these trees were felled for wood and to create grazing for sheep.

Coal, limestone and ironstone have been extracted since at least medieval times, and were crucial for the industrial development of the Midland Valley. The importance of Carboniferous coal is hard to understate: it fired the Industrial Revolution, and allowed Glasgow to be transformed into the major city it is today. Fossil soils rich in aluminium (*seatearths*) found in association with the coal beds have also been of economic importance: the Ayrshire Bauxitic Clay found in the Dalry to Kilmarnock area, for example, is one of the highest-quality fireclays in the UK. The Clyde estuary has been crucial in the industrial development of Glasgow. Without the estuary, transport of goods away from the area would have been severely hampered. As a result, major efforts have been made since the mid eighteenth century to develop and maintain a deepwater channel for navigation.

Today, underground coal mining has ceased, but coal extraction continues through opencast working. Although opencast excavations are rather large and dramatic landscape features whilst active, they are backfilled once the accessible and economic coal reserve has been removed, the topsoil is replaced, and efforts are made to have the area restored to fit in with the surrounding landscape. Large modern quarries also exist for the extraction of Carboniferous igneous rocks, which tend to be strong and durable and good as aggregate for the construction industry. Unconsolidated materials, such as sand and gravel deposited by glacial meltwaters, have also frequently been exploited.

The extraction of these resources has left a legacy of mines, quarries and dumps. Some of the dumps form artificial hills, such as near Kirkintilloch, although in many places spoils have been largely removed for use as fill, or smoothed out and landscaped. In places, the collapse of old mine workings below ground has led to surface subsidence.

CHAPTER 10

Area 5: Edinburgh

AREA 5 STRADDLES THE ENGLISH–SCOTTISH BORDER and extends from Bamburgh and Holy Island in the southeast to Edinburgh (Scotland's dramatic capital) and Kirkcaldy in Fife in the northwest (Fig. 102). In the southeastern part of the Area the River Tweed drains the fairly flat, low-lying ground of the Tweed Basin, which is bounded to the south by the Cheviot Hills and to the northwest by the Lammermuir and Moorfoot Hills (part of the Southern Uplands). These rounded hills reach heights of between 500 and almost 750 m, forming a broad region of elevated ground which dominates the landscape in the central and southwestern parts of this Area (Fig. 103). North of the Southern Uplands is an area of generally low-lying ground, extending from North Berwick across to Edinburgh and northwards to Kirkcaldy. This is divided into two by the wide expanse of the Firth of Forth, and includes the coal-bearing Midlothian Basin (located on Fig. 106) as well as several isolated hills that are distinctive features of the landscape. Edinburgh itself is one of Scotland's earliest settlements, bounded on its northern side by the Firth of Forth and to the southwest by the Pentland Hills, which rise to heights of nearly 600 m, close to the edge of the city.

In terms of the history of science, this Area is notable for including several famous localities that played a key role in developing the way we think about the Earth today. In the late eighteenth century, during the period known as the Scottish Enlightenment, James Hutton (1726–97) became the central figure in a group of Edinburgh friends who examined the remarkable bedrock features in this Area and discussed interpretations for their origin. The result was a major advance in the understanding of processes operating in and on the Earth, laying the foundations for many developments in the earth sciences.

One of the most important localities examined by Hutton is Siccar Point, on a rugged part of the coast between Eyemouth and Dunbar. Storm erosion here has picked out a dramatic contrast between two rock types of different age, the layers

162 · SCOTLAND

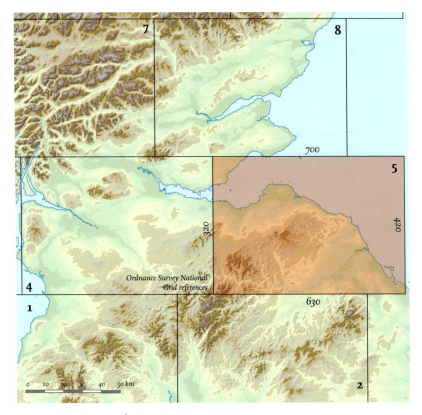

FIG 102. Location map for Area 5.

of which are inclined at very different angles to one another (Fig. 104). Hutton first visited this locality in 1788 and worked out the series of landscape-forming episodes shown in Figure 105.

Siccar Point is one of the best examples in Britain of an *angular unconformity*. At this locality, Hutton and his colleagues realised that the angular junction between two layered successions of sedimentary bedrock had important implications for understanding the processes that had been operating. They showed, for the first time, that the Earth's crust had experienced a succession of episodes during which bedrock had been formed by deposition of sediment, followed by movement (tilting) and surface erosion.

Such unconformities had previously been regarded as evidence that 'primary' materials, originating under unique conditions active when the Earth first formed, had been followed by younger 'secondary' materials (thought by some to

AREA 5: EDINBURGH · 163

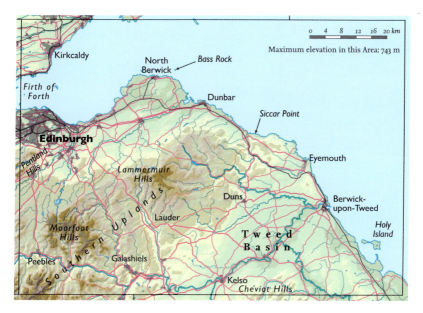

FIG 103. Natural and man-made features of Area 5.

FIG 104. Siccar Point, located in Figure 103, where James Hutton's unconformity shows near-vertical Silurian sandstones and mudstones that were tilted and eroded before the deposition of Upper Old Red Sandstone layers that now dip gently to the left. (© Lorne Gill, Scottish Natural Heritage)

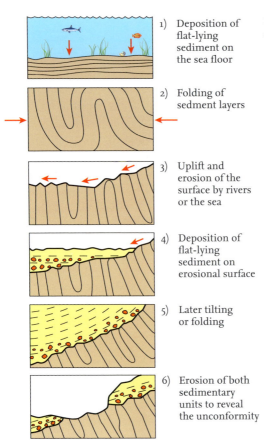

FIG 105. Diagram showing the episodes identified by Hutton from observations at angular unconformities such as that at Siccar Point.

be a result of the Old Testament flood). Hutton recognised that unconformities like this one are the result of cycles of Earth movement, erosion and deposition – like those shown in Figure 105 – which had happened as repeated episodes occurring many times in the Earth's history, and which are continuing today. He also realised that these processes are very slow, in human terms, and that a great deal of time must be required to form such landscape features. Hutton could see no evidence for any 'vestige of a beginning' in the natural record of what has since been called 'deep time'. This belief was in marked contrast to the traditional view at the time that the Earth was no more than a few thousand years old.

Hutton also advanced the understanding of many other Earth processes, for example the intrusion of igneous rocks, based upon his observations in this Area.

STORIES FROM THE BEDROCK

This Area straddles the Midland Valley and Southern Uplands terranes into which Scottish bedrock geology is generally divided (Chapter 4, Fig. 20). Figure 106 shows a simplified geological map of the Area, and Figure 107 provides a timeline highlighting the main geological and landscape-forming events.

The oldest bedrock in Area 5 forms the hills of the Southern Uplands, which are bounded to the northwest by the Lammermuir Fault, one end of a series of faults generally referred to as the Southern Uplands Fault System. The Southern Uplands bedrock itself is Ordovician to mid-Silurian in age (around 480 to 425 million years old) and originally formed from mud and sand deposits transported here by rivers and submarine flows from a highland region to the northwest. This material was deposited on a submarine plain at a time when crustal subduction (Chapter 3) was moving the oceanic crust of the Iapetus Ocean beneath the Southern Uplands terrane to the northwest. This movement deformed the newly deposited sediment, causing it to be faulted and tightly folded, squeezing out its water and gradually altering it to the mudstones, slates and sandstones that form the bedrock today. This Southern Uplands succession is now regarded as a classic example of the sorts of bedrock and structure produced by an episode of plate collision involving oceanic material on one side.

The next rocks to be deposited were mainly mudstones, sandstones and conglomerates, interspersed with volcanic lavas, ash and some igneous intrusions. These rocks underlie the Pentland Hills, the Cheviot Igneous Area and parts of the Southern Uplands and are often collectively referred to as the Lower Old Red Sandstone. They are of late Silurian to early Devonian age (about 425 to 405 million years old), although they are difficult to date accurately because the rare fossils within them are not good age indicators.

During the late Devonian and the Carboniferous (between 375 and 320 million years ago), a sequence of mudstones, sandstones, limestones and coals was laid down in the river deltas and shallow seas which covered this Area at that time. Today, this sedimentary sequence underlies most of the Tweed Basin and the Midland Valley, and in the latter it reaches thicknesses of up to 4 km, indicating that the Midland Valley was subsiding during this episode of deposition. Coal is found in both the Early and Late Carboniferous parts of the sequence, particularly in the Midlothian Basin. Elsewhere Carboniferous igneous activity created volcanoes now represented by, for example, Arthur's Seat and the Bass Rock, and intruded a number of scenically important igneous rocks, like the Whin Sill near Bamburgh in Northumberland.

166 · SCOTLAND

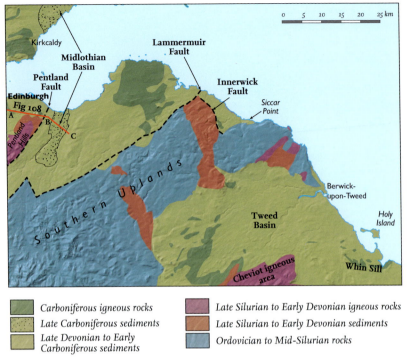

- Carboniferous igneous rocks
- Late Carboniferous sediments
- Late Devonian to Early Carboniferous sediments
- Late Silurian to Early Devonian igneous rocks
- Late Silurian to Early Devonian sediments
- Ordovician to Mid-Silurian rocks

FIG 106. Simplified geology and hill-shaded topography for Area 5.

After the formation of the Carboniferous succession, all of the bedrock in this Area was subjected to extensive folding, faulting and erosion, such that today the older Ordovician and Silurian rocks are mainly exposed in the central and southwestern parts of the Area, with the younger Devonian and Carboniferous strata to the southeast and northwest. On a smaller scale, folding and faulting have also brought older material to the surface in the Pentland and Cheviot Hills (Fig. 106).

MAKING THE LANDSCAPE

Early landscape evolution
The bedrock evolution of this Area was largely completed by the early Permian and, as shown in Figure 107, from this time until the late Cretaceous the region underwent a long period of net erosion, creating a landscape of generally low

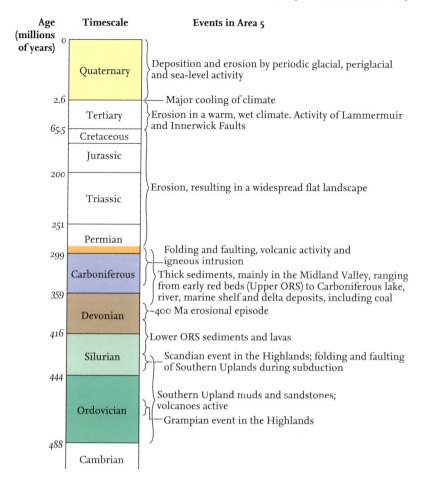

FIG 107. Timeline of bedrock and surface-layer events in Area 5.

relief. Most of the present-day scenery began to form later, during the Tertiary, when the climate was warm and wet. However, the very oldest landscape features in this Area date from a much earlier erosional episode and are found in the Southern Uplands around Lauder and Duns (Fig. 103). In these areas a number of ancient river valleys, carved into Ordovician and Silurian bedrock, were filled with sediments some 400 million years old. They formed distinctive basins, filled with Lower Old Red Sandstone (late Silurian to early Devonian) sediments that cut across the Ordovician to Silurian rocks of the Southern Uplands (Fig. 106).

By the Tertiary, activity on the Lammermuir and Innerwick faults (Fig. 106) raised the Southern Uplands block, creating a distinctive hill-front overlooking the Midland Valley to the northwest. Intense erosion of this elevated block under warm, wet climatic conditions established the ancestor of the present drainage system, carving early valley networks and dissecting the Southern Uplands landscape. In comparison with the Late Devonian and Early Carboniferous sediments in the Tweed Basin and the Midland Valley, the older rocks of the Southern Uplands are more resistant to erosion, and this has contributed to their greater elevation today.

Meanwhile, the Tweed Basin and Midlothian Valley have generally weathered and been eroded recessively to form broad areas of low relief, interspersed with ridges of higher ground formed by occasional more resistant units, such as the Carboniferous Fell Sandstone. Tertiary erosion in these areas also began to pick out isolated outcrops of hardwearing Carboniferous igneous rocks, such as those around North Berwick and between Kelso and Galashiels, many of which form prominent hills today. In the far southeast of this Area, around Bamburgh, a series of igneous sheets and dykes known as the Whin Sill has resisted erosion to form a number of ridges running inland from the prominent platform upon which Bamburgh Castle is built.

Another example of differential weathering and erosion, beginning in Tertiary times, can be seen to the east of Edinburgh, where a distinct north/south downfold in the Carboniferous strata has created the Midlothian Basin, extending all the way across the Firth of Forth to the area northeast of Kirkcaldy (Fig. 108). The rocks at the centre of the downfold are soft, coal-bearing sediments, while those in the eastern limb are harder-wearing sandstones and limestones. The early river system in this region – ancestors of the present-day North and South Esk – took advantage of the softer rocks, while the sandstones and limestones weathered prominently to form a broad ridge, clearly visible on the slope map (Fig. 109) and known fancifully as the Roman Camp ridge. The coal-bearing units in the Midlothian Basin have played an important role in the human and economic development of this Area.

To the west of the Midlothian Basin, Late Silurian to Early Devonian (Lower Old Red Sandstone) igneous rocks have also resisted landscape erosion to form Blackford Hill and the Braid Hills, with their golf courses, immediately south of Edinburgh. Similar rocks are responsible for the attractive double-crested range of the Pentland Hills, a little further south again. This range of hills is bounded to the southeast by the Pentland Fault (Figs 106, 108, 109), roughly parallel to the A702 road, and creating a sharp contrast in the bedrock that has given the Pentlands their distinctive linear southern margin, rising some 400 m above the

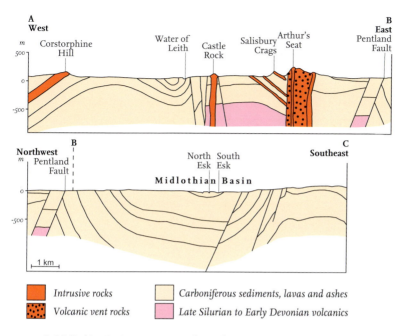

FIG 108. Midlothian Basin cross-section, located on Fig. 106.

Carboniferous units and very obvious as one approaches Edinburgh by road from the south.

To the north of the Pentlands, in the Edinburgh area, a number of other hills and ridges are formed by resistant Carboniferous igneous rocks, many of which are the relicts of ancient volcanoes. These rocks now form some of the most famous landscape features of this Area, creating the prominent outcrops upon which Edinburgh's earliest settlements were built. Within Edinburgh itself, examples include Arthur's Seat, the Salisbury Crags, Calton Hill and Castle Rock. Similar outcrops further east include the spectacular Bass Rock, North Berwick Law, Traprain Law and the Garleton Hills. We will return to these localities later in the chapter.

Finally, at the very southern margin of this Area, the high ground of the Cheviot felsic igneous area (Fig. 106) is underlain by Late Silurian to Early Devonian lavas, along with granites that intruded the lavas after their extrusion. As with the Pentlands, the strong resistance of these igneous rocks to later erosion is the main reason for the existence of the Cheviot Hills, which now overlook the lower, more easily eroded ground of the Tweed Basin to the north.

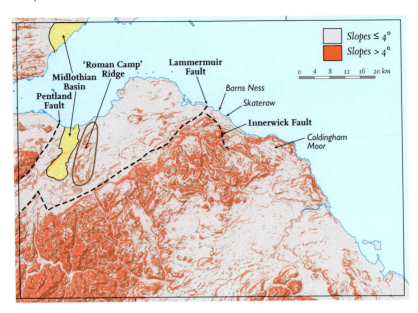

FIG 109. Slope map of Area 5, showing slopes greater than 4 degrees in red.

Glacial landscape evolution

Around 2.6 million years ago, Britain's highly fluctuating climate entered the first of the series of cold periods that became severe enough eventually to produce widespread glaciations (see Fig. 32, Chapter 5). There appear then to have been glacial and interglacial episodes. Because younger glacial cycles tend to rework the deposits of older glaciations, it is generally not possible to recognise landscape features from individual early glacial episodes. However, cumulatively, these repeated glaciations and deglaciations have played a highly significant role in creating the landscape that we know today.

The most recent, Devensian, glaciation reached its greatest extent between 30,000 and 20,000 years ago (the Late Glacial Maximum). Because the deposits of this glaciation have not been largely destroyed by subsequent glacial events, the Late Devensian situation is, on the whole, better understood than any of the earlier glaciations. The extent of the ice at the height of the Late Devensian is indicated in Chapter 5 (Fig. 35), and the processes active then and during the deglaciation that followed provide us with some understanding of how the landscape has evolved during the Ice Age as a whole (Pleistocene and Holocene, the last 2.6 million years).

During the Late Devensian glacial, Area 5 was completely covered by ice, with

AREA 5: EDINBURGH • 171

FIG 110. Southeastern part of Area 5, showing the drumlin field in and around the Tweed Basin.

FIG 111. Landscape some 6 km west of Coldstream, looking southwest and showing drumlins formed with long axes parallel to bedrock ridges. (© Patricia & Angus Macdonald/Aerographica/Scottish Natural Heritage)

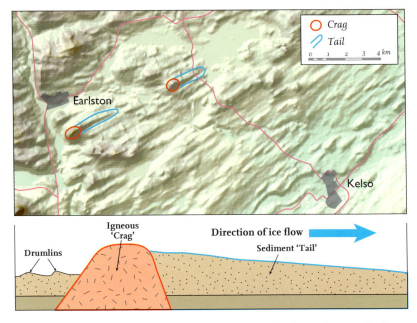

FIG 112. Small area between Earlston and Kelso showing drumlins and crag-and-tail landforms, and a profile showing how an igneous crag can result in the formation of a tail.

glaciers in the Southern Uplands flowing into the Forth and Tweed basins. The pattern of ice flow is reflected in a remarkable array of linear, ice-streamlined ridges, beautifully preserved in the central part of the Tweed Basin and clearly visible in Figures 110 and 111. In the area around Kelso these ridges trend approximately northeastwards, curving gently to the east as they near the present-day coast, where the ice flow was probably deflected to some extent by the harder rocks of the Southern Uplands. In some cases, the upstream ends of the ice-sculpted ridges are formed by a resistant (often igneous) bedrock hill that has produced a crag-and-tail geometry, as shown in Figure 112.

Further north a number of similar crag-and-tail features can be found, the most famous of which is Edinburgh's Castle Rock (the crag) and the adjoining Royal Mile (the tail). The Castle Rock itself is the remains of a Carboniferous volcano, eroded by ice flowing from west to east. Because of the direction of ice flow, Castle Rock presents sheer cliffs some 80 m high to the north, south and west while the Royal Mile, underlain by sedimentary material that has been shielded from glacial erosion, slopes away gently to the east (Fig. 113). This sculpting by the ice made Castle Rock very easy to defend, and a fortified settlement was

FIG 113. In the foreground is Edinburgh Castle, built on the columnar jointed bedrock of a Carboniferous volcanic vent. Leading from the castle down to Holyrood Palace, in the distance, is the Royal Mile, built on the 'tail' of sediment left by the main ice flow towards the east. To the left is Waverley Station, built on the low ground formerly occupied by the Nor Loch, and behind that is the Carboniferous igneous bedrock massif of Calton Hill. (© Patricia & Angus Macdonald/Aerographica/Scottish Natural Heritage)

FIG 114. Edinburgh Castle, the Royal Mile and Waverley Station are in the left foreground of the photograph. In the middle distance the Carboniferous sill of Salisbury Crags is clearly visible. Behind the sill, Arthur's Seat has been eroded from bedrock formed in the vent of the Arthur's Seat volcano. To the left and right of the Arthur's Seat summit are the Carboniferous sediments into which the vent was intruded. (Reproduced by permission of the British Geological Survey. © NERC. All rights reserved)

established here as early as 850 BC. The only strategic drawback of this location was the difficulty of obtaining water, as the jointed igneous bedrock is an extremely poor aquifer – a weakness which was exploited during times of siege.

About 1.6 km to the east of Castle Rock is Arthur's Seat, another extinct Carboniferous volcano and a very famous Edinburgh landmark. As shown in Figure 114, glacial erosion has removed most of the original volcanic cone to expose the hardwearing agglomerate in the volcanic pipe. This has resisted erosion better than the surrounding rocks to form the summit of Arthur's Seat, today 251 m above sea level and offering superb views across the city to the west.

Between Arthur's Seat and Castle Rock are the Salisbury Crags, the glaciated remains of a Carboniferous sill, which today forms cliffs up to nearly 50 m high. They are composed of mafic igneous rocks that have shielded the rocks to the east from glacial erosion, to form yet another crag-and-tail feature. The 'tail' in this case descends gently towards Arthur's Seat and is clearly visible in the cross-section in Figure 108.

The Salisbury Crags include another of James Hutton's famous localities, known as 'Hutton's Section'. In this part of the cliff, the sill includes chunks of

FIG 115. The Bass Rock with its gannet colony. (© Patricia & Angus Macdonald/ Aerographica)

sedimentary rock, entrained in the magma as it was injected into the Carboniferous sediments. Hutton's studies and careful sketches here convinced him that the sill material must have been injected in a molten state under pressure into the older sediments. This argues against another theory popular at the time, that all crystalline rocks had formed by precipitation from a 'primordial sea'.

Elsewhere in this Area other volcanoes, very similar to those in and around Edinburgh, have been eroded by the ice to produce famous landmarks such as the Bass Rock, just off the coast from North Berwick (Fig. 115), and North Berwick Law.

In the region to the southeast of Edinburgh, ice flowing roughly northeastwards along the Southern Uplands hill-front eroded material around the Lammermuir Fault, exploiting ancient southwest/northeast-trending folds in the bedrock and resulting in the hill-front retreating southeastwards. This scarp retreat began in pre-glacial times, but probably intensified during the Ice Age. The result is that, today, the Southern Uplands hill-front is roughly parallel to, but almost 3 km south of, the Lammermuir Fault, while the fault itself has very little expression in the topography. This effect can be seen on the slope map (Fig. 109), which clearly picks out the steep ground of the present Southern Uplands hill-front and also shows the line of the Lammermuir Fault to the north.

Another large and important landform in this Area that was significantly modified by glacial erosion is the Firth of Forth. This large estuary must in part owe its existence to ice-sheet modification (particularly deepening) of the Forth

Valley. This valley formed one of the main routes taken by the ice as it flowed from the Highlands towards what is now the North Sea. A number of deep glacial basins have been identified in the Firth of Forth. During the Ice Age, ice has advanced into this valley on many occasions, each time carving into the landscape and then retreating to leave large quantities of unconsolidated sediment. During the warm interglacial phases, this relatively soft, ice-laid sediment was rapidly removed by meltwater rivers, so that by the next cold phase the glaciers were once again carving into the bedrock. This repeated cycle provides a very efficient method of eroding the landscape, so that the Forth Valley is both wide and deep today.

At a smaller scale, a number of glacial features not related to ice scouring have been preserved, running roughly parallel to the coast between Siccar Point and Eyemouth (Fig. 103). These features include ridges or *eskers*, interpreted as the deposits of meltwater flowing in tunnels beneath ice, and valleys, interpreted as meltwater channels carved by glacial streams at the margins of the ice.

Factors involved in changing sea levels have been discussed in Chapter 5. It was pointed out that during the whole of the Ice Age, the total volume of water in the Earth's oceans and seas varied, depending on how much water was locked up as frozen water in ice sheets and glaciers. The larger the amount of ice, the lower the Earth's free seawater volume would be, and the lower worldwide sea levels would tend to be. However, build-up of ice on land would cause a local lowering of the land surface in ice-covered regions, as the solid Earth responded to the loading by internal flowage of rock materials within the deeper Earth. At times of maximum glaciation, worldwide sea level would be low, and local bedrock surfaces in ice-rich areas would also be low because of the ice loading. When ice sheets were melting, worldwide sea level would tend to rise, and local bedrock surfaces would tend to rise because of the unloading.

Post-glacial landscape evolution

Figure 116 shows a plot of sea-level change for the upper Forth area, relative to present sea level, over the last 17,000 years. This shows that 17,000 years ago, local Firth of Forth sea level was some 80 m higher than today, *relative to present sea level*, showing that large areas of the present coastal zone were flooded by the sea.

At the same time, 17,000 years ago, the volume of water in the Earth's oceans and seas was so much less than at times of no ice sheets, that worldwide sea levels would have been some 120 m lower *relative to a reference point at the centre of the Earth*. As a crude estimate, this seems to imply that in the Firth of Forth area the Earth's bedrock surface has risen by 80 m plus 120 m, a total of 200 m, relative to the reference point at the centre of the Earth, due to the loss of Scottish ice-load over this period.

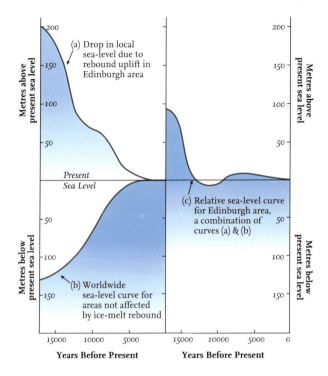

FIG 116. Uplift and subsidence curves for Edinburgh. The combination of (a) decreasing local sea level due to rebound uplift and (b) global sea-level rise results in (c) the relative Edinburgh sea-level curve.

When the ice retreated, it left a covering blanket of ice-laid material, now found mainly on the lower valley slopes due to erosion and downslope transport since the Late Devensian glaciation. This material has since been dissected and reworked by powerful meltwater streams, which carved terraces and flood plains as their channels switched back and forth. As described above, sea level, relative to its present level, was higher at the end of the last glaciation (Fig. 116), so the earliest post-glacial terraces are now found some distance inland, for example at Neidpath Castle on the Tweed, just upstream from Peebles. As relative sea level dropped due to crustal rebound, terrace and flood-plain erosion and deposition moved to lower elevations, closer to the present-day coastline. Most recently, over the past few thousand years, the River Tweed has reworked soft sediments to construct a large flood plain in the middle of the Tweed Basin, distinctive on the slope map (Fig. 109) because of its flatness.

Since the end of the Devensian glaciation, many of the rivers in this Area have incised up to 30 m through the ice-laid surface blanket and into the bedrock, developing sinuous, meandering courses on the post-glacial drumlin and crag-and-tail surface. As is usually the case, the size of the meanders varies with the

FIG 117. Drainage map showing average flow rates for main rivers.

average flow rate of the rivers: the present-day Tweed has large meanders and a high average flow rate, while the White Adder, for example, has much smaller meanders and a significantly lower flow rate (Fig. 117).

The general orientation of the present-day drainage network has been strongly influenced by the ancient southwest/northeast bedrock fabric, particularly in the Southern Uplands, where the majority of slopes face either northwest or southeast. Further north, much of the natural pattern of earlier drainage is obscured by the Firth of Forth, which represents the lower part of a large ancient river system that has been flooded by the post-glacial sea-level rise to produce a large estuary. Only very minor rivers drain into the firth from its Fife (northern) coastline, and even its longer southerly coastline is crossed only by the small river systems that drain the Lothians (the Water of Leith, Esk and Tyne: Fig. 117). These smaller river valleys have been formed by strong incision into a relatively weak blanket of ice-laid sediments, and many of the rivers have now cut downwards into the bedrock. In many cases valley sides are steep, and the lack of degradation of the soft material that makes up these banks (for instance at the Dean Bridge on the Water of Leith and near Penicuik on the North Esk) implies that they are very young. It seems likely, therefore, that this incision has happened over the last few thousand years, as the crust rose rapidly (Fig. 117).

At Craigforth, 45 km west of the western margin of Area 6 and above the River Forth's tidal limit, the river has an average flow rate of 47 m^3/s, making it one of the two main drainage conduits flowing across Area 5. The other is the River Tweed, with an average flow rate at Norham of 78.9 m^3/s (Fig. 117). Given that the Forth and Tweed represent similar-sized river systems, it is intriguing to note the contrast between the present-day size of the Forth estuary (~1600 km^2) and that of the Tweed (~2 km^2). This is probably due to a combination of factors: the size of the Tweed estuary is strongly constrained by the bedrock to the north and south of Tweedmouth, and the ice stream that fed the Forth Valley, which flowed from the large West Highland ice sheet, was probably more vigorous than the stream that flowed down the Tweed Valley, fed by the smaller Southern Uplands ice field. The Forth Valley's proximity to the centre of the thicker West Highland ice must also have caused greater crustal uplift on melting, resulting in more intense erosion of the Forth Valley in recent times.

The large size of the Forth estuary was very important to the early development of settlement in Scotland, providing relatively easy access to the interior as well as a benign environment for the growth of its capital.

CHAPTER 11

Area 6: Mull

MOST OF AREA 6 IS OCCUPIED BY SEA (Fig. 118). In the west, the large islands of Tiree and Coll are the first landscape features facing into the Atlantic. The even larger island of Mull and the peninsula of Ardnamurchan occupy the centre of the Area, whereas further east the continuous mainland of Highland Scotland, from Morvern in the north to the area around Oban, is breached by Loch Linnhe, marking the line of the Great Glen Fault Zone (Fig. 119).

Like other Areas that include parts of the Northern Highland terrane, this Area contains evidence of a history of varied crustal movements and surface modifications that extends over a longer period of geological time than that covered in any other part of Britain.

STORIES FROM THE BEDROCK

The Lewisian Complex is the oldest unit of bedrock mapped in Britain. In Area 6 it forms the islands of Tiree and Coll (Fig. 120), and part of the small island of Iona, off southwestern Mull (Fig. 121). The bedrock of the complex consists mainly of granites and other igneous rocks that solidified and were altered as distinct crustal units with different movement histories, involving recrystallisation of minerals in episodes between 3.1 and 1.1 billion years ago (Fig. 122). Locally schists and marble are also present, showing that surface modification involving deposition of sediment also took place. Some of the marble, for example from quarries on Tiree and Iona, has been used as ornamental stone.

Much of the crustal movement that took place during the long period of formation and alteration of the Lewisian Complex resulted in the development of a number of areas of mountain landscapes with distinctly different ages. Material from these landscapes was transported by rivers, deposited and altered

AREA 6: MULL · 181

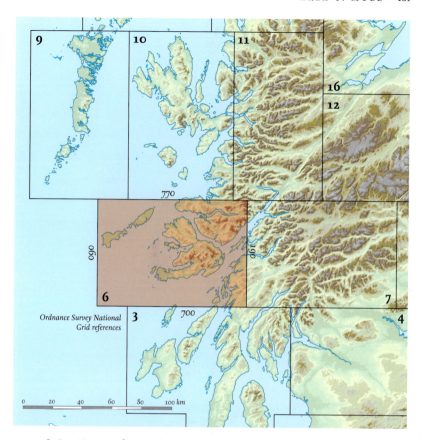

FIG 118. Location map for Area 6.

to be preserved as conglomerates, sandstones and mudstones, generally grouped as parts of the Torridonian unit, dating from about 1 billion years ago. Today, in Area 6, this Torridonian unit makes up part of the island of Iona, and other small patches exist in Mull.

During roughly the same period, between 1 billion and 870 million years ago, sandstones and mudstones, now preserved in other parts of the Area, were being deposited and altered by folding, burial and heating to form what is now mapped as the Moine Supergroup. Episodes of movement occurred at about 830, 460 and 430 million years ago, the two later (Grampian and Scandian) events being regarded as parts of the Caledonian episode. In Area 6, the Caledonian movements resulted in folding about axes that now trend north/south, evidence for convergence in what is now a west-to-east direction, In Ardnamurchan

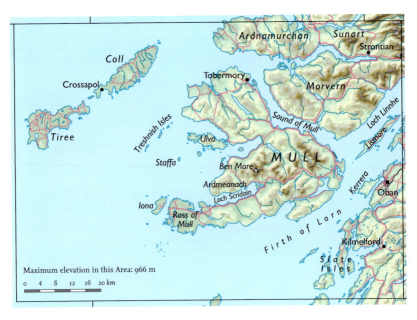

FIG 119. Natural and man-made features of Area 6.

and the centre of the Morvern peninsula, these Moine rocks were relatively undeformed, and the ghost traces of ripples and other forms of original sedimentary layering are visible locally.

To the southeast of the Great Glen Fault the bedrock is part of the Grampian terrane (Chapter 4, Fig. 20), in which the bedrock of the Dalradian Supergroup was deformed and altered in younger movement episodes than those just summarised for the Northern Highland terrane. This bedrock accumulated between 850 and 500 million years ago as a varied group of marine sediments (muds, silts, sands and lime-rich sediments), along with basic lavas. It was deformed (Fig. 27), with predominantly northeast/southwest folding trends, and heated mainly during the early Caledonian movements known as the Grampian movements, dating from about 470 million years ago. The main lithologies now visible include limestones, which make up the island of Lismore at the mouth of Loch Linnhe, graphitic schists and quartzite, which make up Scarba and the islands and coastal strip southwest of Oban, and epidiorites, which is a term used locally for the altered mafic lavas.

The next bedrock episode recorded in this Area resulted in the deposition of the Lower Old Red Sandstone of late Silurian and early Devonian age, the extrusion of large quantities of lavas, and the emplacement of granites. The

FIG 120. The Island of Coll, showing the knock-and-lochan topography of this Lewisian landscape, looking southwestwards, with Tiree in the distance. (© Patricia & Angus Macdonald/Aerographica)

Lower Old Red Sandstone mainly outcrops around Oban and on the island of Kerrera, visible below a cover of lavas. The sediments appear to have formed on river flood plains and in lakes, and fossils of primitive fishes have been found.

During this episode pressure and temperatures within the Caledonian mountains became high enough for crustal rocks, such as the Lewisian Complex, to begin to melt. As the melt was rich in silica, volumes of this relatively low-density liquid formed and rose gradually through the crust. This melt then cooled slowly within the crust, producing relatively uniform, coarse-grained granite bodies. After many tens of millions of years of erosion these granites have been exhumed and today form the bedrock around Strontian, around Kilmelford and at the western end of the Ross of Mull. The Ross of Mull granite only covers an area of about 30 km², and half of this is under the sea, but it is remarkable for the clear examples it displays of the process of *stoping*. This process involved the fracturing and engulfing by rising granite magma of discrete chunks of the solid pre-existing rock, in this case chunks of the Moine Supergroup. The Ross of Mull granite also has one of the best-developed contact metamorphic zones, or *aureoles*, seen around Highland granites. In this zone, the Moine material has been baked into a hard contact schist. Meanwhile, the Strontian granite is famous for the mineralised Carboniferous dykes which dissect it near the town of Strontian. These veins were mined for lead, silver and zinc ores between 1722 and 1904, but

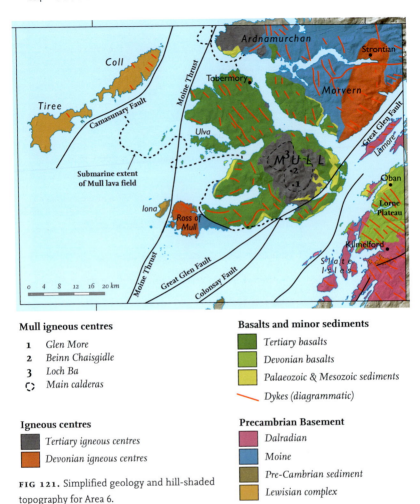

FIG 121. Simplified geology and hill-shaded topography for Area 6.

Mull igneous centres

1. Glen More
2. Beinn Chaisgidle
3. Loch Ba
◌ Main calderas

Igneous centres

- Tertiary igneous centres
- Devonian igneous centres

Basalts and minor sediments

- Tertiary basalts
- Devonian basalts
- Palaeozoic & Mesozoic sediments
- Dykes (diagrammatic)

Precambrian Basement

- Dalradian
- Moine
- Pre-Cambrian sediment
- Lewisian complex

are best known for the discovery of the mineral strontianite in 1791. It was from this mineral that the element strontium was isolated for the first time in 1808.

During these late Silurian to early Devonian times (around 410 million years ago), crustal melts reached the surface in several places, where they now form the mountains of Glencoe and Ben Nevis in Areas 7 and 11. In Area 6, mafic lavas were extruded above a thin cover of Lower Old Red Sandstone or directly onto the altered metamorphic rocks of the Dalradian Supergroup. The greatest extent of these lavas forms the Lorne Plateau, north, east and south of Oban.

AREA 6: MULL · 185

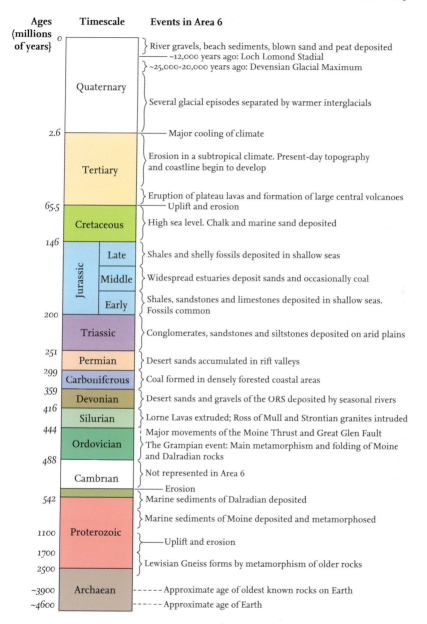

FIG 122. Timeline of bedrock and surface-layer events in Area 6.

FIG 123. The Treshnish Isles, west of Ulva, western Mull. (© Patricia & Angus Macdonald/Aerographica)

Carboniferous and Mesozoic sediments were certainly once more widespread across the Area, but have been removed by subsequent erosion or covered by Tertiary volcanic products. Today only small patches of Carboniferous and Mesozoic sediments are visible, generally along coastal strips. A small patch of Carboniferous, coal-bearing sediment outcrops on the south coast of the Morvern peninsula; Triassic sandstones and conglomerates occur in strips along the southern and southeastern coast of Mull; Jurassic shales and sandstones occur around the Ardnamurchan volcanic centre; Cretaceous greensands occur in Mull.

During the early Tertiary (Palaeogene), between 61 and 58 million years ago, a remarkable outpouring of volcanic lavas took place. This was an episode related to the still-continuing plate divergence that has resulted in the opening of the Atlantic and the increasing separation of what is now the crust of Scotland from that of Greenland. In this Area, up to 2 km of mafic lava flows were extruded. Today, Mull, its surrounding isles, and western Morvern, consist principally of the stepped (*trap*) topography left by erosion of these lavas, to form the present landscape.

FIG 124. MacCulloch's Tree at the western end of the Ardmeanach peninsula, western Mull. (Reproduced by permission of the British Geological Survey. © NERC. All rights reserved)

The first 1000 m of plateau basalts poured out from lines of fissure volcanoes, oriented northwest to southeast. Today these lavas outcrop throughout Morvern, and through north and west Mull (including the Treshnish Isles: Fig. 123), and are known as the Plateau Group. The Coire Gorm lavas, a sequence at least 250 m thick, overlie the Plateau Group lavas, but are only exposed today at the top of Ben More on Mull. On Ardnamurchan a similarly extensive plateau of lavas was built up, but only fragments remain.

Individual lava flows are commonly 10–15 m thick, and fossilised vegetation sometimes occurs between flows. A spectacular example is 'MacCulloch's Tree', a remarkably preserved fossil tree on the Ardmeanach peninsula of western Mull (Fig. 124). The vertical fossil conifer is a pipe-like cast, at least 1 m wide and 12 m tall, surrounded by columnar mafic lava that must have flowed around it while the tree was still alive. Well-preserved fossil leaves have been found at the Ross and Ardtun leaf beds at the mouth of Loch Scridain in southwestern Mull. The leaves were deposited in the peaceful waters of a lake during a quiet period before the next lava eruption.

After this main phase of lava eruption, volcanic activity became more centralised, and on Mull a further 1000 m-thick sequence of lavas erupted through the vents and craters of large, cone-shaped volcanoes. However, this lava pile has largely been removed by erosion and remnants are found today only in the central caldera and in southeastern Mull. On Ardnamurchan, smaller amounts of lava were erupted, along with explosive deposits. Finer-grained volcanic ash would have been blown clear of the vent, but lavas and coarser-grained agglomerate of pebble and cobble-sized blocks of rock remained within the confines of the crater, which may have been several kilometres wide. The presence of large areas of agglomerate on the peninsula (e.g. Maclean's Nose) is testament to both the size of the craters and the prolonged and violent nature of the eruptions.

Between and below these central volcanoes, magma chambers developed and felsic and mafic magmas were intruded into both the metamorphic basement and the Tertiary lavas (Fig. 125). Today these intrusions make up the central mountains of Mull and western Ardnamurchan, where they are mapped as features of the central complexes.

Within the complexes, centres of activity are defined by arcuate intrusions with cone sheets (relatively thin intrusions in the form of inverted cones with a common focus point at depth) and ring dykes (much wider, cylinder-like intrusions with near-vertical walls and cylindrical axes). The ring dykes seem to have formed when magma chambers were rapidly emptied during big eruptions, allowing the overlying crust to subside. Cone sheets seem to be a response to short-lived high-pressure episodes. The process of subsidence and

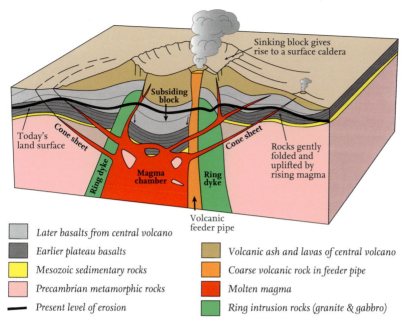

FIG 125. Diagrammatic reconstruction of the Mull Tertiary Igneous Centre, showing one phase in its volcanic history, and also the level of the present-day land surface.

intrusion happened many times over the lifetime of the Mull and Ardnamurchan complexes. On Mull it is estimated that the overlying crust subsided a total of about 1 km, and there are several hundred arcuate intrusions.

Overlapping centres record how the focus of magmatic activity moved over time, with the arcuate older intrusions being cross-cut by intrusions from younger centres. On Mull, the locus of intrusion moved in a northwesterly direction, from Glen More (Centre 1) through Beinn Chaisgidle (Centre 2) to, finally, Loch Ba (Centre 3) (Fig. 126). On Ardnamurchan, the movement was not so straightforward, with the first centre developing on Ben Hiant, the second several kilometres to the west, and the third northeast of the second. The third is by far the best developed, with large concentric structures (ring dykes) visible, the most perfectly formed being the so-called Great Eucrite, which is a near-continuous ring (Fig. 127).

The composition of the magma in both the Mull and Ardnamurchan centres changed in a complex way as the centres evolved. This resulted in intrusive sequences in which mafic and felsic magmas were intimately associated, and in some cases mixed. The Loch Ba ring dyke on Mull is a famous example of mixed intrusion in which 'toffee-like' inclusions and pillows of mafic material

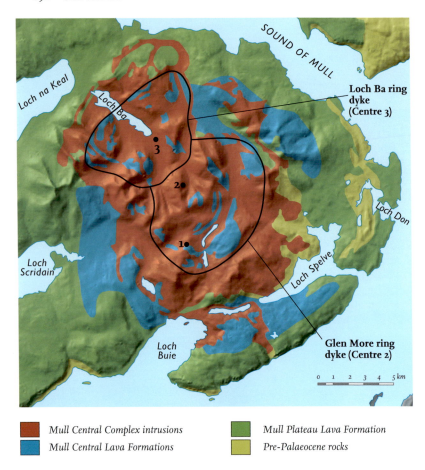

FIG 126. Hill-shaded map showing the overlapping of Centres 1–3 on Mull: (1) Glen More centre; (2) Beinn Chaisgidle centre (associated with Glen More ring dyke); (3) Loch Ba centre (associated with Loch Ba ring dyke).

occur in a felsic host. How such different types of magma became mingled, but not homogenised, is a great puzzle. One possible explanation is that during caldera collapse the magma chamber was compositionally layered with light felsic material floating on denser mafic material. Then, when the overlying crust collapsed into the chamber, the two magma types were violently intruded into the cylindrical ring dyke, in which cooling and solidification took place.

There are surprisingly large numbers of felsic intrusions at the surface on Mull, and for a while this puzzled geologists because the melt responsible for the

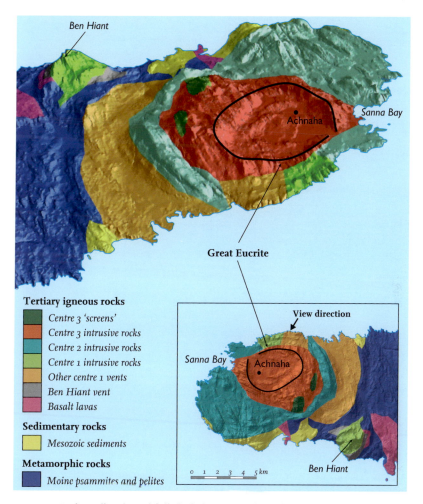

FIG 127. Geologically coloured, hill-shaded view over the Ardnamurchan peninsula, south to the top, to show the way the topography reflects the geological ring structure, particularly the bedrock of the Great Eucrite. The inset map shows the same area, north to the top.

intrusions is thought to have originated in the Earth's ultra-basic mantle, which would be unlikely to yield so much granitic material, even on partial melting. However, recent geophysical studies suggest that the granitic intrusions only form a 1–2 km-thick skin on top of a 6–13 km-thick mafic body. This can be explained in terms of fractional crystallisation within the magma chamber: as the magma cools, minerals crystallise out and sink to the bottom of the chamber, and the remaining magma changes in composition from an early ultra-mafic composition, via mafic to eventually felsic. This progression is seen at the western end of the Glen More ring dyke on Mull and in other areas.

Dykes and sills are common throughout Area 6. Dykes form when magma is intruded under pressure and steep cracks form in the crust, whilst sills form when the intrusions occur along cracks that form parallel to near-horizontal cracks in the bedrock, such as bedding or lava layering. Dyke swarms consist of large numbers of dykes parallel to one another, and the Mull regional dyke swarm is one of the largest in the Hebrides. It extends from Mull towards the northwest and southeast, where the Cleveland dyke in Northern England marks an intrusion distance of 400 km. This swarm is thought to be related to the collapse of the Centre 1 caldera, a remarkable illustration of the extent of the crustal forces involved in caldera collapse. Dykes were intruded throughout the Tertiary period of igneous activity, and their general northwest/southeast orientation indicates regional stretching of the crust perpendicular to this.

MAKING THE LANDSCAPE

When igneous activity ceased around 55 million years ago, erosion became the most active process in landscape change, and this was strongly influenced by the bedrock materials being eroded.

Erosion of local bedrock features

The trap, or stepped, topography is one of the most obvious signs of bedrock made of the Tertiary lava sequences. The tops and bottoms of most lava flows tend to have become more easily weathered than the inner parts of the flows, because the upper and lower margins had often cooled and shattered during the motion of the flow, and gas bubbles (vesicles) developed more readily in the upper margins. In addition, a time gap between successive eruptions has often allowed weathering, causing a soft, easily eroded soil horizon to develop. This means that erosion and weathering after the end of the volcanic activity tend to result in stepped or terraced hill slopes. An excellent example of this is the northern slope of Loch Scridain on Mull (Fig. 128).

Different lava flows in a succession often have slightly different compositions, and they may also have cooled at different rates. These differences may have been responsible for variations in the way the lavas have responded to later erosion and weathering. The lava flows that erupted early in the volcanic history of the

FIG 128. Trap topography in the mafic lava succession of Ardmeanach, western Mull, viewed northwards across Loch Scridain. (Reproduced by permission of the British Geological Survey. © NERC. All rights reserved)

Mull centre belong to the Staffa magma subtype, and appear to have assimilated large amounts of Moine and Lewisian rocks, resulting in felsic magmas. This magma was more viscous and slow-cooling than most of the lavas, and seems to have been more prone to develop columnar jointing.

Columnar jointing is famously seen in lavas on Staffa (Figs 129, 130), although many of the best-known examples photographed elsewhere in Scotland are in intrusive sills (for example, Salisbury Crags, Edinburgh, Area 5). When the hot molten igneous material flows against a surface of colder bedrock it cools and contracts, and a scatter of centres of contraction develops. As the molten material cools it starts to solidify, and cracks will tend to form perpendicular to lines connecting the shrinkage centres. These cracks propagate through the cooling material as it solidifies, producing the remarkable parallel columns of the classic examples.

In the east of the Area the coastal slopes and islands have a strong northeast/southwest trend parallel to the Great Glen Fault and the Caledonian Loch Awe Syncline (see Figs 74, 75, Chapter 8) and other structures in the Grampian terrane.

FIG 129. Aerial oblique view of Staffa, with Fingal's Cave at the nearest end. (© Patricia & Angus Macdonald/ Aerographica)

The distinctive Dalradian rock materials of marble (Lismore), slates (the Slate Islands of Seil, Easdale, Luing etc.) have picked out this trend, as well as creating smaller landform effects characteristic of their rock material.

In eastern Mull, the clearly developed circular ring folds formed by outward pressure from the main igneous centre has folded not only the Tertiary lavas but bedrock of Palaeozoic and Mesozoic ages, and subsequent erosion has picked out the ring trend in features now flooded to give form to the local lochs and their valleys.

In northern Mull and in the area of the Lorne Plateau lavas, east of Oban, the northwest/southeast trend of the Mull regional dyke swarm is evident from numerous valleys parallel to this direction, even though these tend to be relatively small features.

FIG 130. Columnar jointing on the Isle of Staffa (Fingal's Cave), showing the classic lower regularly jointed 'colonnade' and the upper irregular 'entablature'. (© Lorne Gill, Scottish Natural Heritage)

In the southwest of Mull, the Ross of Mull granite landscape is marked by the prominent sets of cooling joints that are typical of many granite outcrops generally. In the Ross, the spacing of the joints varies, and turret-like 'castellations' have often developed. This granite has been used as an ornamental stone, for example in the Albert Memorial in Kensington Gardens, London.

Tertiary erosion patterns

Sea level generally in the Tertiary was lower than today, and rivers flowed down valleys over much of the area now occupied by sea (Fig. 131). This part of Scotland was nearer to the equator, and its warm, humid climate produced deeper weathering of the bedrock. During this period, Lewisian, Moine and Dalradian bedrock was reduced to relatively low-lying, rounded hills. Most of the Mesozoic rocks were eroded, and the resulting sediment was transported away. The volcanic roots of the Mull and Ardnamurchan complexes, as well as the tops of the Devonian granite bodies, were exhumed. The originally 2200 m-thick basalt plateau was reduced to patches of stepped tableland covering an area of around 840 km^2.

The largest landforms, for example those that give the landscape its main areas of mountains, hills, slopes, lochs and islands, have in many cases been formed by erosion of the Tertiary igneous bed rock that has been described above. So they have clearly formed in the 55 million years since this igneous activity ceased. The amount of erosion involved in creating these landforms is so great that this Tertiary episode must be regarded as the major landscape modifier of the Area, even where no Tertiary igneous rocks are locally preserved. In the following section, examples of landforms are reviewed where the shape of the features has been influenced by structures such as layering, faults or dykes, and also by the resistance to erosion of the bedrock material present.

The effects of ice

It is not clear when the first ice sheets of the Ice Age developed in Britain, but work on the oxygen isotope record (see Fig. 32, Chapter 5) has shown that global periods of cooling alternated with warmer periods, on a roughly 50,000-year cycle, for much of the period from 3.5 to 0.5 million years ago. Since then, several cold-then-warm cycles have occurred, with a rather longer 100,000-year cycle. Most of the information that has been collected for Scotland relates to the last

FIG 131. Slope map of Area 6, showing slopes greater than 6 degrees in red, and also the offshore rock basins that help to define the main Tertiary drainage valleys.

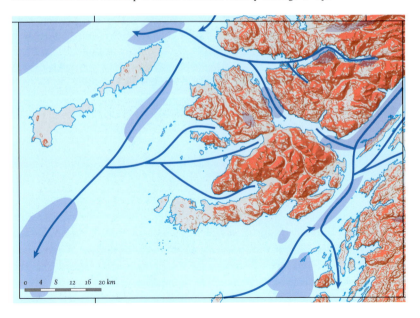

(Devensian) cold period (climaxing with the Late Glacial Maximum), which reached its maximum between about 30,000 and 15,000 years ago, and this was then followed by the important Loch Lomond Stadial between about 13,000 and 11,500 years ago. Devensian modification of the landscape has inevitably destroyed evidence of earlier glacial work, and attempts to consider the effects of earlier episodes are much more speculative.

During the Devensian, ice from the mainland flowed roughly westward across most of Area 6 (Fig. 132). Evidence of modification by ice will be summarised in a westward direction across Area 6.

Loch Linnhe and the Firth of Lorne appear to have been the sites of a large ice stream flowing southwesterly, parallel to the direction of the Great Glen Fault. This runs sub-parallel to the trend of the Caledonian Grampian folds in the Dalradian, and near parallel to the folding to the southeast of the Central Complex in Mull. So it appears that, in this case, the major ice stream moved parallel to topography already generated by earlier movements in the bedrock.

South of Oban, ice flow appears to have been guided by already existing topography, formed by folding, with its southwest/northeast trend and rock

FIG 132. General patterns of ice flow across Area 6 during the Late Glacial Maximum of the Late Devensian.

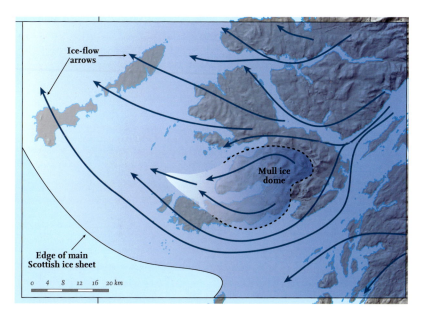

material contrasts in the underlying Dalradian bedrock. Where the Lorne plateau lavas cover this topography, ice seems to have flowed more westerly, influenced more directly by the location of the centre of the mainland ice sheet in the Rannoch area.

To the southeast, the main valleys, sea lochs and mountains of Morvern appear to have been formed by Tertiary river valley erosion, then eroded further as part of the Ice Age modification. There is little evidence that Ice Age modification caused major changes to the earlier valley pattern, and bedrock control is not obvious in the Mull lavas in western Morvern, the Moine in central Morvern, or the Strontian Granite complex in eastern Morvern.

In Ardnamurchan glacial striae on some of the Tertiary ring-dyke bedrock provides evidence for the northwesterly ice-flow directions marked on Figure 132, but the most striking features of the landscape are the ring dykes of the central complex which dominate the local topography, clearly indicating the contrast in erodibility of the different bedrock types.

Ben More on Mull is 966 m high and the only Munro (3000-foot (914.4 m) mountain) on the island (Fig. 133). It shows some evidence of erosion near the summit when it was emergent as a nunatak from a general ice sheet. However, there are a number of 700 m peaks that are composed largely of Mull Central Complex igneous intrusions, and there can be little doubt that this mountainous area was formed initially by Tertiary erosion followed by further development of the main valley systems by ice streams and glaciers. Important valleys have been eroded running northwest to southeast, including Loch Ba, and dykes, cone sheets and ring dykes locally run parallel to this direction. Southeast of the Central Complex further valley erosion has formed preferentially parallel to the arcuate axes of the folds that had formed in response to the expansion as the Central Complex grew in early Tertiary times.

The islands of Tiree and Coll extend for almost 40 km, with a typical width of some 5–6 km (Fig. 120). Their bedrock belongs predominantly to the Lewisian Complex, although Tertiary igneous intrusions are locally important. There are a few isolated hills exceeding 100 m in height but the topography generally is lower, although undulating. Much of this erosion may have been achieved by rivers, but the general appearance and setting suggests erosion by ocean waves.

Modification since the Devensian Late Glacial Maximum
The general retreat of ice after the Late Glacial Maximum was interrupted by some 1500 years of advance during the Loch Lomond Stadial, which has left evidence in the form of fresh moraines in many of the glaciated valleys of the mountainous parts of southeastern Mull. Since the disappearance of the glaciers,

large volumes of sediment left by the ice have been deposited in Mull's larger glens, such as Glen Forsa, and reworked into coastal areas.

During the worldwide Flandrian transgression, the rise of sea level flooded the lower parts of the river drainage systems that had formed during the Tertiary and been modified further during the Quaternary glaciations. This flooding means that today only immature headwaters of the drainage systems remain above sea level, and the system is still re-equilibrating. This explains the near absence of major rivers in the Area.

Peat deposits are now an important landscape feature in this Area. They have formed over the last 8000 years, as the climate has warmed, leading to accumulation of water in low-lying areas that are underlain by relatively impermeable rock. High rainfall and relatively cool temperatures have meant that soils have remained waterlogged, allowing peat to form because of the lack of breakdown of vegetation. It now covers extensive areas of undulating land, including slopes and mounds, some of which have been classified as raised bogs.

There are several internationally important raised bogs with patterned pool systems in this Area, such as Kentra Moss and Claish Moss, west and south of

FIG 133. The island of Eorsa and Loch na Keal, Mull, looking southeastwards, with Ben More behind. Note the trap lava landforms on the island and in the slopes of the mountains. (© Patricia & Angus Macdonald/Aerographica)

the western end of Loch Shiel in Sunart. Claish Moss is the largest of these; it is part of an extensive complex of valley-side mires lying between Beinn Resipol and Loch Shiel. Burns running to Loch Shiel divide the Moss into large sections of raised bog, each of which rises to a shallow dome shaped like a huge water droplet, elongated in a downstream direction. Of particular landform interest are the surface patterns of pools and ridges found on these domes, forming a concentric series of arcs apparently following the contours of the mire. The ridge-and-pool system has been a stable surface feature for around 5000 years, and the combination of this and the teardrop shape of individual raised bogs has given rise to the name *eccentric bogs*. Kentra Moss and Claish Moss are two of only three known eccentric bogs in the UK. The upper surface of a raised bog is independent of underlying topography, appearing to have grown independently and even to have diverted streams as it grew.

Quarrying by humans has influenced the landscape of this Area in some locations. Slate was quarried on the Slate Isles until the mid twentieth century, leaving large terraces and piles of quarry tailings as prominent landscape features. The hub of this work was Easdale, where the Scottish slate industry first began. Its slate was used to roof Glasgow Cathedral in the twelfth century, and the quarries continued to produce more slate than all the other Scottish quarries until surpassed by Ballachulish (Area 7) in the 1860s. Quarries were worked to depths of over 60 m, often with only a small wall left to protect the workings and workers from the sea. Today, many of these sea walls have been breached, leaving deep water-filled cuttings open to the sea.

Another site notable for the influence of quarrying is Glensanda, on the northern shore of Loch Linnhe. Here, one of the largest quarries in Europe occupies an entire granite mountain. Since the 1980s hard-rock aggregate has been produced at a rate of up to 6 million tonnes of granite per year, and including all the aggregate used for the British section of the Channel Tunnel lining.

Formation of the coastline

The high proportion of the Area occupied by sea, the large numbers of islands and the wide range of bedrock mean that the length of coastline and its variety are also exceptional. Mull, the largest of the islands, is separated into numerous 'wings' by sea lochs penetrating deep inland. Loch na Keal, for example, almost separates northern Mull from southern Mull. The strongly indented shape of the large Hebridean islands such as Mull, Islay, Skye and Lewis is a direct result of the flooding of the large landscape features formed by Tertiary valley erosion.

In Chapter 5, discussion of recent sea-level change has drawn a distinction between changes due to (1) worldwide volume change of ocean water, and (2) local solid Earth movements. In this Area, it seems clear that during times of thickest ice-sheet presence (the Late Glacial Maximum), crustal bedrock features now at the present-day sea level were lower (or nearer to the centre of the Earth). By 14,000 years ago enough ice had melted that the crust was rebounding, but sea level was still very much lower than the crustal rocks at present-day sea-level, so Mull, Iona and the Treshnish Islands were part of the mainland and most of the other islands would have been larger than they are today. Steadily rising sea levels since then, due to worldwide ocean volume changes, have turned Mull and areas of higher ground, or ancient peninsulas, into islands, so that glacial troughs such as the Sound of Mull (150 m deep) and the Firth of Lorne now separate Mull from the mainland.

Local evidence of episodes of bedrock erosion by the sea at levels higher than is possible with present-day sea level is almost continuous in this Area, demonstrating the importance of local solid Earth movement due to loading by ice, and subsequent rebound. Rock platforms, above present sea level and varying in width from 10 m to 150 m, are common, and are often backed by raised cliffs. Bedrock lithology obviously tends to control the local form of these platforms and cliffs. Limestone and quartzite generally have narrower platforms and larger raised cliffs, indicating their greater resistance to erosion than bedrock of lesser erosional strength. Deformational features such as cleavage and jointing also influence these relative effects. Caves are common at the bases of raised cliffs, and there are several striking examples of raised arches eroded along faults near the tips of narrow headlands. The natural arch below Gylen castle on Kerrera, Clach Toll near Port Appin, and the Dog Stone near Oban are examples of these features.

Rock platforms are particularly well developed around Oban and eastern Mull: the islands of Lismore, Kerrera and Shuna are entirely surrounded by rock platforms. Smaller islands have often been completely planed off at the level of the platform, and Frank Lockwood's Island southeast of Mull is an example of this. The level of this major erosional surface varies from about 4 m above present-day sea level in western Mull to about 11 m in Oban. The westerly tilt of the surface presumably reflects the greater loading and stronger rebound in the east. Extrapolation of this surface westwards suggests that in western Mull and at Fingal's Cave in Staffa, the same surface may be present, although at an even lower level, locally below present sea level.

Fingal's Cave on the Isle of Staffa (Figs 129, 130) is one of the UK's most famous caves. The origins of its spectacular columnar jointing have been discussed above. The bedrock consists of a basement volcanic ash bedrock overlain by columns of the Staffa magma type that form the faces and walls of the principal caves of the south end of the island. Overlying the columnar basalt is a slaggy layer that has not been eroded so readily. Fingal's Cave itself penetrates some 80 m into the bedrock with its roof some 20 m above the waves. It became internationally famous after a visit by Sir Joseph Banks (1743–1820), en route to Iceland on one of his natural history expeditions. Since then it has been the inspiration for musicians, artists and writers, most notably remembered for Mendelssohn's *Hebrides Overture*.

The recent flooding of the Flandrian worldwide sea-level rise is clearly represented in every feature of the coastlines of the Area. The effects are particularly critical in a few key parts of the Area where the precise configuration of land and sea have produced dramatic present-day configurations, with strong tides and treacherous channels. One notorious channel is south of Lunga, only some 200 m wide and scoured by the 'Grey Dog' tidal race that reaches 4.5 m/s (8.8 knots) at full flood. A few kilometres to the southwest, the narrow Gulf of Corryvreckan, between the islands of Jura and Scarba, is reputed to be the home of the third-largest whirlpool in the world. Strong Atlantic tidal currents and an unusual underwater topography conspire to produce a particularly intense tidal race in the Corryvreckan channel. As the flood tide enters the strait between the two islands, similar speeds of up to 4.5 m/s are reached as it meets a variety of sea-bed features including a deep hole and an underwater pinnacle only some 30 m below the surface. These features combine to create whirlpools, standing waves and a variety of other surface effects. The writer George Orwell and his son were briefly shipwrecked near the whirlpool when crossing the gulf during his a on Jura in 1947.

Bedrock contrasts have often resulted in differences in coastal features. At the western end of the Ardmeanach peninsula in Mull, great thicknesses of Tertiary lavas (with trap topography: Fig. 128) are underlain by Moine granulites and psammites with a distinctive rhomboidal jointing pattern which has produced coast chasms, sea stacks, cliffs and arches that are collectively known as 'The Wilderness'. On the Ross of Mull, the coast is characterised by long promontories and inlets with white sandy bays, shaped by the roughly north/south fabric of the metamorphic rocks. Meanwhile, sandy bays have often formed where sedimentary bedrock occurs underneath igneous cover. An example is Carsaig Bay, on the south coast of the Ross of Mull, where Mesozoic bedrock sediments have been eroded into an amphitheatre backed by 215 m-high basalt cliffs: the whole area is crisscrossed by a large number of sills and dykes, which have often weathered prominently compared with the sediments surrounding them and look like walls going out to sea. Large cannonball concretions, similar to those on Skye, occur in the cliffs at the back of the bay, and fossils are common.

Dykes have often eroded differentially. Where they intrude sedimentary rocks, they tend to be more resistant to erosion. This is the case on Lismore, where differential erosion has generally left dykes as headlands, and as stacks projecting from cliff walls seawards. The opposite is observed in some other areas, where the intrusions have eroded away more than the host rock. Marine erosion has often taken advantage of lines of weakness, provided by dykes or fault planes, so that, despite being only 1 or 2 metres wide, Tertiary dykes have been responsible for much larger caverns.

Beaches are not common in the Area, apart from on Coll and Tiree, where numerous white, sweeping beaches are separated by low cliffs of hummocky gneiss of the Lewisian Complex, with countless small reefs and skerries (Fig. 120). This occurrence of beaches seems to reflect the western location and the high winds of these islands. Their extreme wave exposure is combined with a shallow shore gradient, which provides a surround of high sediment supply and accumulation.

Inland from the large sandy beaches on Coll and Tiree, sand accumulates, trapped by vegetation and the low cliffs and hummocks of gneiss. Wide expanses of *machair*, or dune pastures of rich lime sand are a major feature of the Isles (Fig. 134), and are more fully discussed in our chapter on the southern Outer Hebrides (Area 9). Large dunes have also accumulated locally. The largest dunes in Britain are claimed to be those at Crossapol on Coll, where individual dunes exceed 35 m in height. Smaller dune areas occur on the exposed tips of the Ross of Mull and Ardnamurchan.

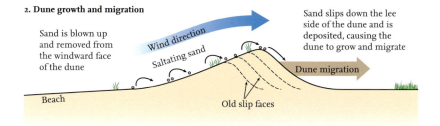

FIG 134. Diagram showing how dunes may be initiated and grow during wind transport of the sand, and the role of vegetation.

CHAPTER 12

Area 7: Rannoch

THE LANDSCAPE OF AREA 7 consists largely of mountains, deep valleys and extensive moors (Fig. 135). The Area contains many of the classic localities of the southwestern part of the Grampian Highlands, such as Glencoe, Rannoch Moor, Schiehallion, Ben Cruachan, the Arrochar Alps and the Trossachs (Fig. 136).

FIG 135. Location map for Area 7.

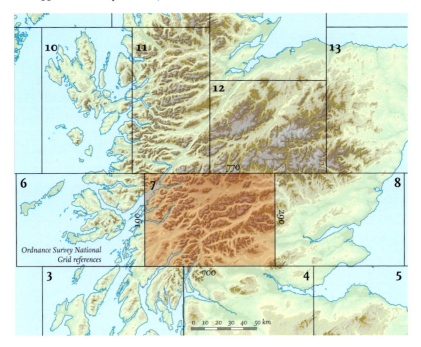

STORIES FROM THE BEDROCK

Caledonian mountain-building events

Most of the bedrock of this Area was formed, moved and modified during the plate convergence that resulted in the building of the Caledonian mountains (Chapter 4). The metamorphic rocks of the Dalradian Supergroup form the predominant metamorphic basement of Area 7, with the bedrock northwest of the Great Glen Fault now assigned to the metamorphic Moine Supergroup (Fig. 137). All these metamorphic rocks formed originally as sediments along with some igneous rocks, during the Neoproterozoic (Fig. 138). The sediments were mainly muds and sands, and more rarely limestones, and they accumulated to thicknesses of many kilometres, indicating important movements of the crust with some sinking and thick sediment accumulation, on the one hand, and other areas of uplift and erosion, on the other hand.

The compressional movements of the Caledonian mountain building folded and thickened the crust, uplifted its surface and subjected the deeper rocks to high temperatures and pressures, converting them into metamorphic rocks. The oldest of these rocks in the Grampians are those mapped as part of the Moine

FIG 136. Natural and man-made features of Area 7.

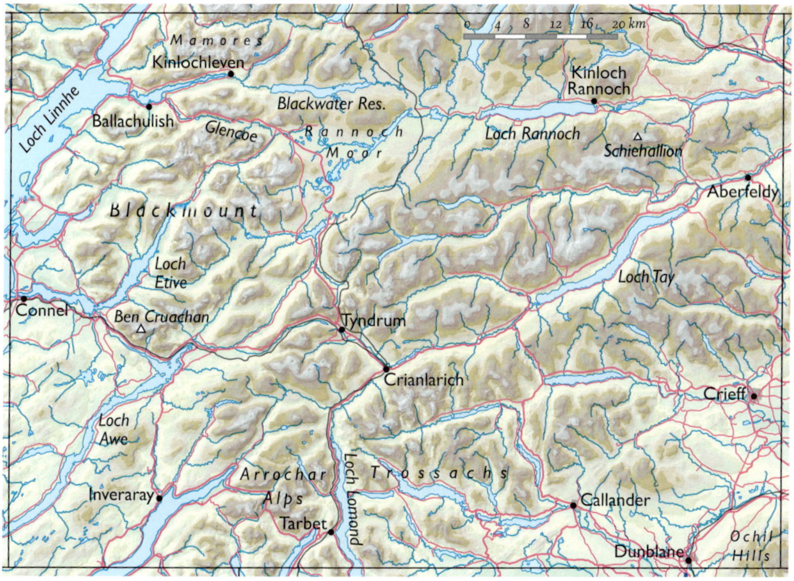

Maximum elevation in this Area: 1210 m

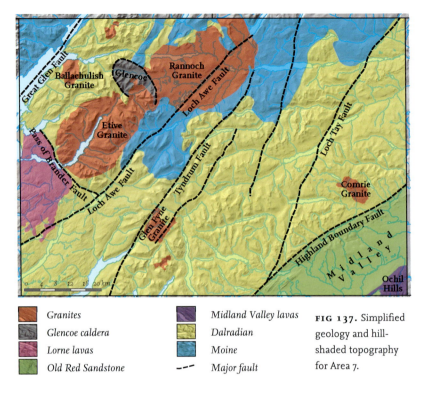

	Granites		Midland Valley lavas
	Glencoe caldera		Dalradian
	Lorne lavas		Moine
	Old Red Sandstone	- - -	Major fault

FIG 137. Simplified geology and hill-shaded topography for Area 7.

Supergroup, with outcrops to the north and west in the form of rather massive metamorphic rocks, rich in quartz and feldspar. Overlying these rocks through Area 7 are more varied rocks of the Dalradian Supergroup, consisting largely of metamorphic schists and slates along with quartzites and occasional marbles. Slate quarries were once plentiful, in particular around Ballachulish, where the black slates played a key role in the roofing of some of the rapidly expanding cities of Victorian Britain. Igneous rock also intruded the Dalradian sequence, mostly basic sills, and these have been deformed and metamorphosed along with their surrounding sediments. The fold and fault structures in these supergroups are similar to those across the rest of the Highlands, with fold axes and faults often oriented approximately northeast to southwest (see Chapter 4). Local cross-folds, as near Schiehallion (Fig. 144), show that movement patterns were often strongly oblique to the dominant overall convergence, suggesting squeezing out of the material along the dominant fold axes. Another special movement pattern occurs in the southeast of the Area where Dalradian rocks have been moved into a flat belt, the overturned limb of a large fold (Fig. 26, Chapter 4; and Area 3, Jura).

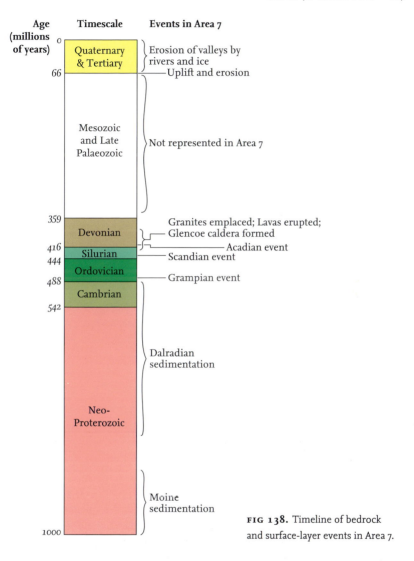

FIG 138. Timeline of bedrock and surface-layer events in Area 7.

As shown in Figure 25 (Chapter 4), dating of phases of new mineral growth in the metamorphic rocks, along with work on the surrounding non-metamorphic sedimentary rocks, has allowed the recognition of pulses of activity during the Caledonian mountain building. These pulses were the Grampian (around 470 million years ago, mid-Ordovician), the Scandian (around 430 million years ago, mid-Silurian) and the Acadian (around 400 million years ago, mid-Devonian), and they probably corresponded to phases of compressional movement in the Earth's crust.

The first of the phases, the Grampian, is likely to have seen the first uplift and erosion of the Caledonian mountain belt. Throughout the rest of the Ordovician and Silurian, regional uplift of the thickened crust and deep erosion led to the removal in places of up to 30 km of material from the surface of the crust. Most of the sediment produced by this erosion was transported into basins now below the North Sea and the Atlantic, and it is therefore not seen as bedrock in the land of Scotland today. The situation changed at the start of the Devonian, around 415 million years ago, when the crustal blocks now represented by the terranes of Scotland came together, and related crustal movements caused sedimentary basins to form in the Highlands and the Midland Valley (see Chapter 4). Throughout the Devonian, successions of sandstones and conglomerates accumulated thickly in these basins, and are now known as the Old Red Sandstone. Scotland lay just south of the equator at the time, and the river and desert-like, vegetation-poor environments gave the sediments their characteristic reddish colour. Today, the southeastern corner of Area 7, part of the Midland Valley terrane, contains these relatively soft sediments of the Old Red Sandstone. They are separated from the harder, more crystalline rocks of the Grampian Highland terrane by the Highland Boundary Fault, one of the major fault lines of Scotland (Fig. 137).

The convergence at the plate margin resulted in the closing of the Iapetus Ocean around 430 million years ago, as part of the Scandian phase, and was accompanied by a major change in the tectonic regime in Area 7. In the Grampian Highlands, strike-slip movement began along northeast/southwest-trending faults. This stage of the Caledonian mountain building was accompanied by a phase of magmatism, and the igneous rocks produced are an important part of the bedrock of this Area. The magma involved was generated beneath the crust, by partial melting of mantle rocks which had been hydrated by the underlying subduction zone of this convergent plate margin. Movement along crustal-scale faults, such as the Great Glen Fault, then triggered this melt to rise to upper crustal levels, with the faults acting as conduits. The result was the intrusion of large granite plutons in the Dalradian rocks, and in places volcanic eruptions at the surface.

The oldest of these granitic bodies in this Area are the Ballachulish and Rannoch Moor granites, intruded around 420 to 410 million years ago in the late Silurian or early Devonian. The Ballachulish granite occurs south of Loch Leven, and, despite its small size, it is notable for its superbly developed metamorphic surround. Other small granitic bodies in the Area are the Glen Fyne granite, famous for containing the greatest compositional variety of any British Caledonian intrusive complex, and the Comrie granite further east (Fig. 137). The next stage of magmatism in the Area involved volcanic eruptions at the surface, and thick sequences of lava flows and pyroclastic rocks accumulated. Three patches of these lavas outcrop in the Area today: the Lorne Plateau lavas and the Glencoe caldera rocks, both erupted between 420 and 415 million years ago, and the slightly younger lavas of the Ochil Hills in the Midland Valley terrane. The Lorne lavas consist of a 600 m-thick pile of andesite on top of a thin cover of Lower Old Red Sandstone, down-faulted up to 1 km into position along the Pass of Brander Fault. The Ochil Hills are made of a similar pile of mafic lava sheets, erupted after volcanism in the Grampian Highland terrane had ceased.

Calderas are volcanic structures that form when circular or elliptical areas of the crust, generally several kilometres across, subside, often during a succession of varied volcanic movement events. Subsidence takes place in response to changes in pressure in a chamber of more or less melted igneous material that underlies the caldera.

The volcanic rocks of Glencoe present an excellently preserved section through an ancient volcanic caldera that appears to have been active for perhaps 2–3 million years, in late Silurian or early Devonian times (perhaps between 420 and 410 million years ago). The 1200 m-thick sequence is made up of alternating layers of andesite sheets, thick deposits of lava and ash from explosive eruptions and sediments. The different stages in the development of the caldera are summarised in Figure 139, with Groups 1 to 7 labelling the main rock types preserved and visible in Glencoe, whose outcrop pattern is shown in Figure 140. Each eruption of the Glencoe volcano was accompanied by caldera collapse, as crustal blocks subsided into the void left by the volumes of magma displaced from inside the volcano. For the majority of the volcano's life, this subsidence happened in a piecemeal fashion, with small crustal blocks sinking independently along a set of faults more or less radial to the caldera margin. The so-called ring fault only developed during one of the final eruptions of the Glencoe volcano, a particularly massive eruption accompanied by wholesale subsidence along the encircling fault. None of the volcanic rocks from this cataclysmic eruption has been preserved, but the near-continuous elliptical ring fault surrounds the volcanic rocks of Glencoe, separating the down-faulted inner block of volcanic rocks from the undisturbed Dalradian basement outside. The numerous episodes of development and the form of the ring fault are clearly shown in Figures 139 and 140. Partly encircling the ring fracture is a ring intrusion – probably the remnants of a concentric vent, where magma was squeezed into the ring fault and solidified to form granite. Roughly 1 km of subsidence is thought to have occurred along the ring fault whilst it was active, compared to the previous ~800 m of subsidence by piecemeal block collapse.

The Etive Complex is the largest and youngest intrusive body in the Area, emplaced shortly after the Ballachulish and Rannoch Moor granites, and cutting across them. It is a classic ring complex centred on Glen Etive, composed of four broadly concentric intrusive units: the outer units are the oldest and most basic, giving way to younger more acidic inner units. One of the larger of these intrusions is the Cruachan granite, which invades the southeast side of the Glencoe caldera. The emplacement of the Etive Complex was accompanied by hot circulating groundwater which caused the mineralisation of numerous veins, in particular along the Tyndrum Fault zone. In recent times, these mineral veins were mined for gold and then lead. The similarities in age, location and chemistry of the Etive Complex, the Lorne lavas and the Glencoe caldera suggest that they are related to each other in some way. Whilst there is not enough evidence to say that the Lorne lavas and Glencoe are eruptive equivalents of the Etive Complex, it is very likely that the three sites represent different stages in the life of the same magmatic system.

One of the final phases of magmatism of the Etive Complex was the emplacement of the Etive dyke swarm, around 410 million years ago. This is the largest Caledonian dyke swarm in Britain and Ireland, with dyke intrusions occurring over an area greater than 100 × 20 km in a northeast/southwest-trending zone centred on the Etive Complex and Glencoe. This orientation is parallel to the Great Glen Fault and a set of smaller parallel faults, and the emplacement of the swarm was probably linked to movement along these faults. This dyke swarm is one of the last of the Caledonian episodes to be represented in the Grampian Highlands.

MAKING THE LANDSCAPE

River erosion

Erosion has been important in this Area, at least since the Ordovician–Silurian. Since that time uplift of the Earth's crust has occurred periodically, and great thicknesses of rocks have been removed by erosion at the surface, exposing the Moine and Dalradian rocks and the granites that once formed the roots of the Caledonian mountain chain. However, in terms of the mountains and valleys of the present-day landscape, the last 60 million years of erosion during the Tertiary have been the most important. It was during this time that the main river valleys developed. By the start of the Tertiary, Moine and Dalradian rocks were exposed at the Earth's surface in the form of a relatively low land surface of moderate relief. The drainage pattern at this time must have been influenced by southwest/

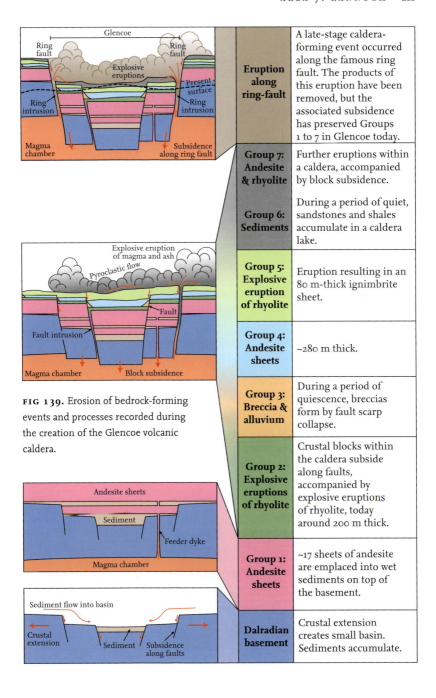

FIG 139. Erosion of bedrock-forming events and processes recorded during the creation of the Glencoe volcanic caldera.

	Eruption along ring-fault	A late-stage caldera-forming event occurred along the famous ring fault. The products of this eruption have been removed, but the associated subsidence has preserved Groups 1 to 7 in Glencoe today.
	Group 7: Andesite & rhyolite	Further eruptions within a caldera, accompanied by block subsidence.
	Group 6: Sediments	During a period of quiet, sandstones and shales accumulate in a caldera lake.
	Group 5: Explosive eruption of rhyolite	Eruption resulting in an 80 m-thick ignimbrite sheet.
	Group 4: Andesite sheets	~280 m thick.
	Group 3: Breccia & alluvium	During a period of quiescence, breccias form by fault scarp collapse.
	Group 2: Explosive eruptions of rhyolite	Crustal blocks within the caldera subside along faults, accompanied by explosive eruptions of rhyolite, today around 200 m thick.
	Group 1: Andesite sheets	~17 sheets of andesite are emplaced into wet sediments on top of the basement.
	Dalradian basement	Crustal extension creates small basin. Sediments accumulate.

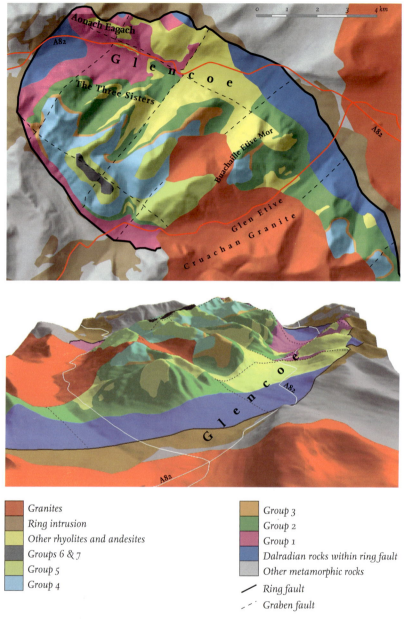

FIG 140. Simplified geological map and oblique view of Glencoe, using hill-shaded topography.

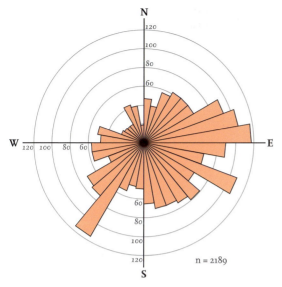

FIG 141. Diagram showing the orientation of the main valleys in Area 7. The orientations of downstream, 1 km-long lengths of the main valleys were measured using 10-degree groupings ('bins') of the measurements.

northeast-trending valleys, following the Caledonian folds and faults in the metamorphic rocks.

At the start of the Tertiary, Britain began to break away from North America as a new divergent plate boundary formed and the Atlantic Ocean started to develop. Associated with this, the crust of western Scotland was uplifted, giving a west-to-east downward tilt to the Scottish surface. This uplift combined with the warm, wet climate of the time to give vigorous down-cutting in the land surface, creating deep river valleys. As expected, many of these river valleys are oriented in a northeast-to-southwest direction, parallel to folding and faulting of the underlying Caledonian metamorphic rocks (Chapter 4). However, almost equally prominent are valleys trending west to east (Fig. 141), which may have developed as a result of the greater uplift in the west of the Area. The net result of this Tertiary erosion was that the surface of the Grampian Highlands became deeply dissected by river valleys, and the summits themselves became eroded downwards to their present heights of 700–1300 m. The exhumation of basement metamorphic rocks continued, and most of the volcanic rocks erupted during the late Silurian or early Devonian were removed from the Area. Only in Glencoe and Lorne were these volcanics preserved by the local subsidence they had undergone.

The landscape that developed throughout the Tertiary was, as ever, in part controlled by contrasts in the underlying bedrock. Perhaps the most obvious case of this is the difference in elevation and relief between the Grampian Highland

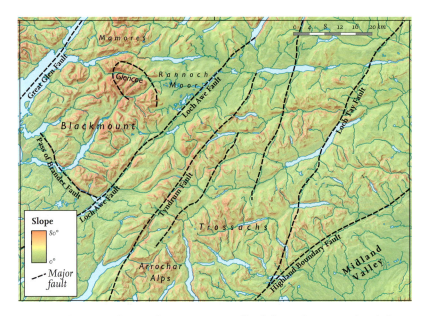

FIG 142. Slope map of Area 7, showing variation of local slope values across the whole Area. Note the flatness of the expanse of Rannoch Moor, and that many of the main faults occur at the edges of local areas of distinctive slope patterns.

terrane and the Midland Valley terrane: Moine, Dalradian and granites of the former have a relatively high resistance to erosion and so have remained as high ground, standing today as the Scottish Highlands. Meanwhile, the softer sediments of the Old Red Sandstone in the Midland Valley terrane have been more heavily eroded and form relatively low-lying, flat ground, apart from lavas in the sequence which now form the hillier Ochil area. The Highland Boundary Fault Zone between these two terranes is relatively obvious on the slope map, crossing the southeastern corner of the Area (Fig. 142).

Bedrock contrasts within the Grampian Highlands have also caused different areas to become lower-lying than others. A change in the landscape is visible across the Pass of Brander Fault in the west of the Area, with the Etive granite and Dalradian quartzite north of the fault having weathered much more prominently than the Lorne lavas to the south, so that there is a clear contrast across the fault from high mountainous ground to the northeast and the low-lying, relatively flat plateau to the southwest (Fig. 142). In general, areas underlain by granitic bodies tend to have resisted erosion more than areas underlain by Dalradian bedrock, meaning the granite intrusions tend to form higher ground,

FIG 143. Ben Cruachan, with Loch Awe and the high-level pump storage loch. (© Patricia & Angus Macdonald/Aerographica)

such as the very mountainous Blackmount, underlain by the Etive Complex, and Ben Cruachan (Fig. 143).

It is obvious from Figures 136 and 142 that Rannoch Moor is low and flat compared with other areas underlain by granite, and it may be that the glacial processes discussed below offer an explanation. As well as differences in elevation between areas underlain by metamorphic rocks and granite, the obvious northeast/southwest-trending valleys found in the metamorphic bedrocks tend to be absent in the granite, as these areas lack folds and many of the faults.

Even within the Dalradian metamorphic areas, bedrock contrasts have in many places been picked out by Tertiary valley erosion. Limestone layers within the succession tend to have weathered most recessively, forming relatively low-lying, verdant valleys. Dalradian schists also weather relatively recessively, giving low yet craggy topography, such as that found in the Arrochar Alps. By contrast, quartzites in the sequence tend to form prominent features, and pale quartzite mountains with interesting, rocky summits are common throughout the Area, such as the Pap of Glencoe at the western end of Glencoe. Dalradian metamorphosed mafic igneous rock have also resisted erosion to form smooth ridges of high ground running northeast to southwest around Loch Awe.

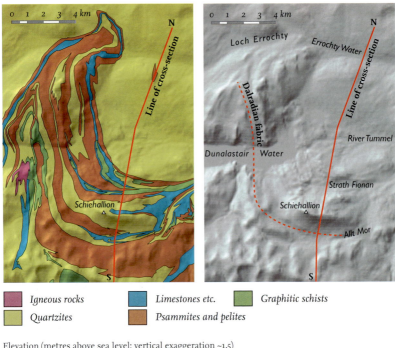

- Igneous rocks
- Quartzites
- Limestones etc.
- Psammites and pelites
- Graphitic schists

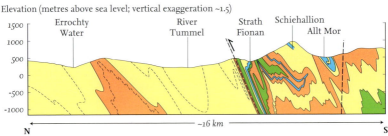

Simplified structural section showing younging direction. The apex of each red V points towards younger strata.

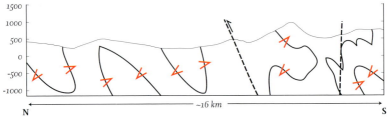

FIG 144. Geological and hill-shaded elevation maps of the Schiehallion area, with cross-sections drawn to illustrate the bedrock lithology and Caledonian fold and fault pattern.

FIG 145. Loch Rannoch and snow-clad Schiehallion, looking eastwards. (© Lorne Gill, Scottish Natural Heritage)

These variations in the resistance to erosion of different units of the Dalradian are clear in the area of the distinctive anticlinal cross-fold in the Dalradian, around Schiehallion, the shapely mountain some 6 km southeast of Kinloch Rannoch (Figs 144, 145). The high mountain ridge of Schiehallion is an erosional relict shaped locally by the presence of quartzite, which contrasts with the more variable and less resistant psammites, pelites and limestones to north and south. Similarly the north/south-trending limbs of the cross-fold are clear in the hill-shaded landscape, where they contrast with the west/east trends of the main river valleys of the Errochty, Tummel and Allt Mor.

Schiehallion's bulk, isolation and regular shape meant that it was selected, in 1774, as a suitable place in which to attempt a measurement of the mass of the Earth. The relative isolation from nearby mountains and its geometrically simple blade-like shape meant its volume and gravitational effect could be estimated with reasonable accuracy. The experiment itself was carried out by Nevil Maskelyne (1732–1811), the Astronomer Royal, by measuring the deflection of plumb lines. The results obtained were remarkably accurate, and helped support

FIG 146. Looking southwest up Upper Glen Lyon, from near Gallin, 17 km southwest of Kinloch Rannoch. (© Lorne Gill, Scottish Natural Heritage)

the new understanding of gravity and the density structure of the Earth. They also reflected new understanding of the importance of form in landscape. Indeed, the mathematician Charles Hutton (1737–1823), who published a further analytical study of Maskelyne's measurements, is also credited with the first use of land-surface contours as a way of representing landscape form.

Southwest of Kinloch Rannoch (and Schiehallion) is Glen Lyon, another example of one of the large west/east-trending valleys that has carved its way into the Dalradian bedrock (Fig. 146). The steepest slopes and cliff-bound outcrop areas correspond to Dalradian bedrock that is most resistant to erosion, but the width of the valley, often with an alluvial sediment-covered floor, is again evidence that this valley is likely to have been initially eroded during the Tertiary, before glacial processes came into operation.

Many of the larger faults mapped in Area 7, as a whole, have also been picked out by valley erosion, despite there not being an obvious bedrock contrast involved, and all of the following features can be seen clearly in Figure 137. The Great Glen Fault is the largest example, once the site of a major Tertiary valley and now occupied by Loch Linnhe. The Tyndrum Fault is also obvious in the landscape, particularly where it crosses the eastern side of Rannoch Moor and forms a linear feature occupied by streams and lochs. The course of the Loch Tay fault is particularly traceable where it has caused a dogleg in Loch Tay itself. Fold axes were also exploited, such as the Loch Awe syncline, now occupied by Loch Awe.

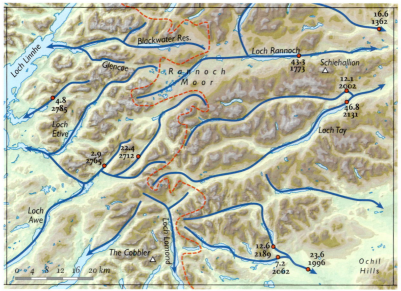

FIG 147. Main rivers/drainage systems of Area 7, with average flow rates and annual rainfall measurements at and above certain gauges.

- - - -   Drainage divide
●   Gauging station
2.9   Av. flow rate in m³/s
2765   Annual rainfall in mm

By the end of the Tertiary the landscape had taken on a form recognisable today. The drainage system has been subsequently altered somewhat by glacial erosion, but the main valleys and mountains seen today were in place before glacial times. One of the most remarkable features of this drainage system is the fact that the main Scottish divide between west-coast and east-coast drainage is located so close to the west coast. As shown in Figure 147, there are several places where the drainage divide comes within 20 km of the west coast, such as where it crosses the western side of Rannoch Moor. As a result of this, and the higher rainfall received in the west, river valleys draining westwards tend to be steeper and more erosive than those draining eastwards. They do not, however, have the catchment area required to form major rivers, and so the only rivers with sizeable flow rates in this Area are eastwards-flowing.

Erosion by ice

Around 2 million years ago, the Earth's climate was cooling generally. Since then Scotland has been undergoing repeated glaciations, during which ice sheets advanced and covered this Area. Each glacial episode modified the landscape, scouring valleys, eroding hill tops and generally removing many features created by previous glaciations. Because of this, it is the most recent glaciation that has left the freshest evidence, although previous glaciations have contributed important erosion and, to a lesser extent, deposition to the present landscape.

The last major glaciation, known as the Devensian glaciation (see Chapter 5), reached its climax (the Late Glacial Maximum) around 20,000 years ago. All of Scotland, including this Area, was covered in a thick ice sheet centred on Rannoch Moor, where the ice exceeded 1 km in thickness. This ice sheet began to decay about 20,000 years ago, only to return in this Area during the Loch Lomond Stadial (cold episode) around 13,000 years ago. The ice in this phase was not as widespread as at the Late Glacial Maximum of the Devensian, although in this Area an ice sheet again developed on Rannoch Moor, from where glaciers flowed radially downwards and outwards (Fig. 148). Unlike at the maximum of the Devensian, most of the larger hills in this Area would have stood out above the ice sheet during the Stadial, forming nunataks (using the term applied in Greenland).

During the repeated glaciations, ice streams generally followed the course of pre-existing Tertiary valleys, and the accompanying ice scouring continued the erosion that had begun in the Tertiary. Valleys became wider and deeper, often with steep sides, thereby taking on the classic U-shape of glacial valleys. The majority of the valleys in this Area have this profile today, only slightly altered by post-glacial processes. In places deep basins were carved into the bases of valleys, particularly where a sudden increase in ice thickness occurred due to the meeting of several glaciers or ice streams, as along Loch Linnhe.

An obvious effect of this glacial erosion was that the bedrock contrasts picked out by erosion during the Tertiary were further exaggerated. For example, the Lorne lavas today form a low-lying, heavily scoured rocky plateau, made up of craggy knolls surrounded by boggy ground. In contrast, Moine and Dalradian rocks, and most of the igneous rocks of the Grampian Highland terrane, formed mountains of higher elevation. On a smaller scale, layering in these metamorphic rocks, particularly the Dalradian, has been picked out by erosion, and folds in the sequence are often visible in the landscape, particularly for example in the Arrochar Alps, and already illustrated in the Schiehallion area (Fig. 144). Granites tend to form high ground, but with more rounded outlines than their metamorphic counterparts. Throughout the Area glacial corries, arêtes and horns abound, along with roches moutonées, glacial erratics and other signs of the passage of ice. Around Kinloch Rannoch glaciers of the Lomond Stadial have sliced through the lower end of ridges, forming steep cliffs above the valley – Craig Varr is an example, just north of Kinloch Rannoch and used as a rock-climbing venue for pupils from Rannoch School.

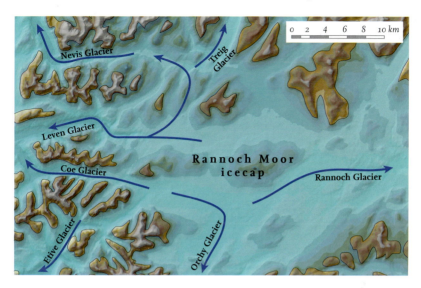

FIG 148. Reconstruction of the maximum distribution of ice in the Glencoe and Rannoch Moor areas during the Loch Lomond Stadial.

Glacial deposits are also common, with moraine occurring throughout the Area. Well-preserved kettle holes, left by the melting of ice blocks, are found in the Moss of Achnacree, just beyond the bridge over Loch Etive in a wide terrace of fluvioglacial sands and gravels.

We have already noted the unusual flatness of Rannoch Moor compared with other areas underlain by granite. The probable explanation for this combines several factors. Firstly, it has lain just east of the central Scottish east–west drainage divide since the start of the glaciation cycle. Its high elevation and the shallow gradient of any valleys dissecting it compared to their westwards-flowing equivalents would have encouraged the accumulation of a relatively thick ice sheet. Secondly, it is underlain by relatively homogeneous, hard granite, meaning that although it has been flattened by repeated ice ages it is still high, the average elevation being just over 300 m. The contact between the granite and Dalradian schists is obvious when approaching the moor from the south: near Achallader, the road makes a sweeping climb up to the Rannoch Moor plateau, crossing the geological contact.

Apart from the odd exception, an interesting feature around Rannoch Moor is the lack of any obvious correlation between bedrock and topography. In Figure 149a it is clear that the mountains of western Glencoe and the Mamores, to the north, have angular summits and narrow ridges separated by deep, steep-sided valleys. Meanwhile, further east, these same mountain belts become rounded and low, separated by broad, shallow valleys. This difference is probably due to different styles of glacial erosion. Figure 149b shows a reconstruction of the Loch Lomond ice sheet, with the relatively static Rannoch icecap giving way at the heads of the Leven–Blackwater and Glencoe valleys to fast-moving glaciers. The profile along the Leven–Blackwater valley shows a marked change in valley gradient where this crossover probably occurred (Fig. 149c). The thickness of ice on Rannoch Moor means hills on the moor itself or just adjacent to it will have been overridden by ice and subsequently smoothed and rounded. Once the ice became channelled into the fast-moving glaciers, the mountains between these glaciers emerged from the icecap to form nunataks. These nunataks were subject to erosion by small mountain glaciers and periglacial processes such as freeze–thaw shattering, which created the sharp ridges, pointed peaks and steep-sided valleys seen today.

The glacier which flowed down Glencoe during the Loch Lomond Stadial further deepened and steepened the valley, which is today some 16 km long with a valley floor less than 700 m wide. Its sides are vertical in places, and overall it provides an excellently exposed section through the volcanic caldera. The resultant outcrop pattern is shown in Figure 140, and the Groups labelled are described in more detail in Figure 139. The contacts between different units roughly follow hill contours, showing that the units are still relatively flat-lying, with the youngest units outcropping towards summits.

Glacial erosion appears to have exploited a number of structural weaknesses within the caldera. Perhaps most prominent are the southwest/northeast-trending valleys which seem to have developed along all but the northernmost graben fault. Bedrock contrasts also seem to have exerted some control on topography, as shown on the western face of Aonach Dubh, on the south side of Glencoe. Dalradian schists outcrop at either end of the valley, where they underlie relatively low-angled grassy slopes; above these at the western end of Glencoe are andesite sheets, which have withstood erosion much more to create a steeper, dark craggy hillside. Tops and bottoms of lava flows are easier to erode than the middles of flows, giving the hillside a banded, terraced appearance. On the south side of Glencoe the mountains are capped by thick rhyolite deposits, which have withstood erosion well to form massive buttresses of pale rock, lacking the terracing seen in the underlying andesite. These mountains are also the highest in

FIG 149 (OPPOSITE). Comparison of the landscapes of Rannoch Moor and Glencoe, using (a) hill-shade topographic mapping, (b) reconstruction of ice cover during the Loch Lomond Stadial and (c) reconstruction of vertical profile from Rannoch Moor down Glencoe.

AREA 7: RANNOCH • 223

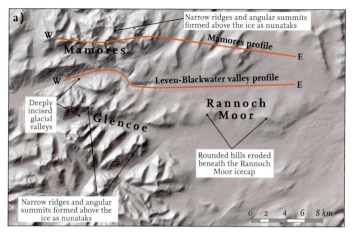

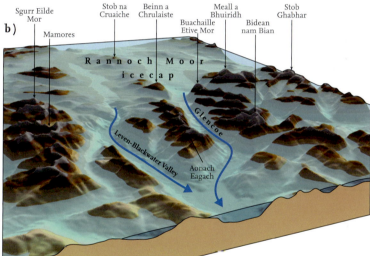

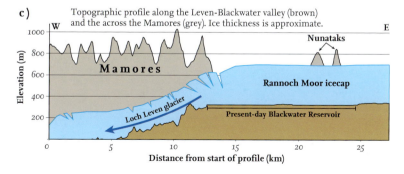

FIG 150. Looking westwards down Glencoe towards Lochs Leven and Linnhe, with the Three Sisters to the left and Aonach Eagach to the right. (© Adrian Warren/lastrefuge.co.uk)

the caldera. Capping Aonach Dubh, the three distinct felsic lava sheets of Group 2 (Fig. 139) can just be distinguished by colour variations. All three are very resistant to erosion and form the prominent, steep spurs of the Three Sisters of Glencoe (Figs 150, 151). The ring fault and numerous dykes crossing the centre tend to have weathered recessively compared to the surrounding rocks, and are responsible for at least some of the many gullies. An obvious spot from which to view the ring fault is at the western end of the glen near Loch Achtriochtan, where a prominent gully runs uphill towards the top of An t-Sron (Fig. 152). Meanwhile, a dyke is responsible for Ossian's Cave, high up on the eastern face of Aonach Dubh.

Post-glacial landscape evolution

The final phase in the evolution of the landscape in this Area occurred after the retreat of the glaciers. This retreat was followed by general crustal uplift, triggered by the removal of the weight of overlying ice (see Chapter 5). Accompanying this uplift, however, was sea-level rise, as large volumes of water re-entered the sea from the world's melting icecaps. The net effect of these changes is that in this Area the

FIG 151. The foreground is the eastern continuation of the Glencoe Aonach Eagach ridge. Beyond the Glencoe valley, in the middle distance to the right, are the three similar bluffs of the Three Sisters. Behind them, on the far skyline, is Bidean nam Bian (1150 m). (© Lorne Gill, Scottish Natural Heritage)

FIG 152. Photo from near the road in Glencoe, showing western outcrops of the ring fault. The right-hand part of the photo is the mountain of An t-Sron, composed of fault-related intrusions. The two diverging gullies forming the left-hand edge of the mountain are the result of the erosion of the late stage fault during the evolution of the ring fault system. The highest peak on the skyline is Stob Coire nam Beith, which is also traversed by the ring fault. (© Lorne Gill, Scottish Natural Heritage)

deep glacially scoured rock basins in the west became flooded by the sea, forming Loch Linnhe and Loch Etive amongst others. The lip of the rock basin now occupied by Loch Etive marks the point where the loch meets the sea, and is responsible for an impressive tidal race, popular with kayakers. The other numerous inland glacial rock basins also filled with water as the ice melted, leaving over-deepened hollows in which meltwater and rainwater collected. The resulting lochs vary in size from Loch Awe, the longest freshwater loch in Britain, to the innumerable small lochans that litter the surface of Rannoch Moor and the Lorne lava plateau.

In many places, valley sides had been over-steepened by the passage of ice, particularly where glaciers breached watersheds and therefore substantially lowered valley bottoms. Once the ice retreated, equilibrium was regained on these valley sides by means of landslides and slumps, sometimes on the scale of whole mountainsides. Landsliding was particularly common in the Arrochar Alps, and the distinctive shape of The Cobbler is thought to be caused by one such landslide. Slope failure is also responsible for the shape of Ben Vane, some 11 km northwest of Callander: a 7 m-high scarp just below the ridge crest marks the departure point for the slip, and a 500 m-long section of hillside below this has been deformed, resulting in a bulging valley side crisscrossed by up to 3 m-high uphill-facing scarps.

Although the climate warmed after the Loch Lomond Stadial, freeze–thaw processes continued, and continue today, on the higher peaks, causing rock to shatter and a layer of scree to blanket the majority of steeper hillsides. As the drainage system re-established itself, large volumes of glacial sediment were washed away, to be deposited as sand and gravel terraces such as those found around Loch Etive. Down-cutting into the bedrock has also occurred, and this is particularly prominent in areas underlain by Dalradian limestone bedrock. This limestone is easily dissolved, and streams have locally formed numerous potholes and sinks. An example of a limestone pavement occurs near Loch an Daimh, just to the north of Schiehallion.

Vegetation has recolonised the land since the retreat of the glaciers, with the growth of both pine and broadleaf forests. In areas underlain by limestone, lime-loving plants have thrived, such as rock rose, thyme, wild strawberry and many orchids. Many of the forested areas have now been lost, however, as throughout the Area an increase in rainfall and human-triggered deforestation about 6000 years ago combined to create large areas of blanket bog. One of the largest accumulations of peat in Europe is found on Rannoch Moor, where peat deposits up to 6 m deep, posed major difficulties to builders of roads and railways. Indeed, when the West Highland Line was built the tracks had to be floated on mattresses of tree roots, brushwood and thousands of tonnes of earth and ashes.

CHAPTER 13

Area 8: Dundee

THE GRAMPIAN HIGHLANDS occupy the northwestern corner of Area 8, extending northwards from the Highland Boundary Fault Zone, one of the main terrane boundaries of Scottish bedrock geology (Fig. 153). To the south of this boundary, the landscape of the Midland Valley meets the North Sea coast, and here the most obvious regional-scale features are the Tay estuary and the projecting headland of Fife Ness (Fig. 154).

The landscapes of the Grampian Highlands and Highland Border in Area 8 consist of mountains, hills and valleys similar in scale and form to those of the areas of metamorphic and igneous bedrock materials and Caledonian histories that extend across Scotland. In the Midland Valley part of Area 8, the influence on local landscapes of contrasts in bedrock, between sedimentary and igneous rocks, is even more clear.

The two largest cities of the Area, Perth and Dundee, owe their locations directly to their landscape settings. Each city has developed throughout its history in response to its setting: Perth as a gateway to the northern Grampian Highlands, and Dundee as a sheltered refuge for local and international trade by sea (Fig. 155).

STORIES FROM THE BEDROCK

The bedrock history of Scotland as a whole is summarised briefly in Chapter 4. Here the focus is on the bedrock of Area 8 (Figs 156, 157).

Dalradian Supergroup

Only the uppermost part of the Dalradian Supergroup succession of Scotland is visible as bedrock in Area 8. It was deposited as muds and sands, with occasional

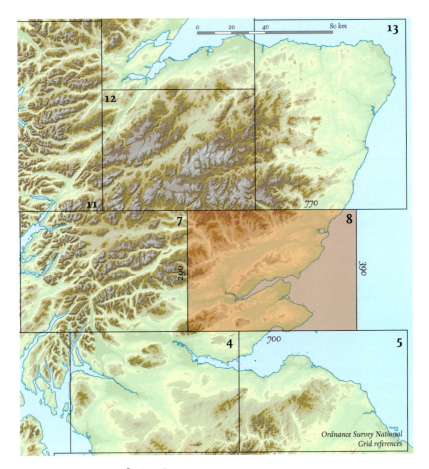

FIG 153. Location map for Area 8.

intervals with greater than normal proportions of lime- and/or quartz-rich grains. Deposition took place in a basin or basins that formed in the Neoproterozoic and lasted into the Lower Palaeozoic. The sediments were subsequently altered during Caledonian crustal folding, refolding and faulting movements, and became recrystrallised into metamorphic rocks. The most important of these Caledonian compressive movements shortened the crust in a northwest-to-southeast direction, as shown by the directions of the folds, indicating that the general inter-plate collision movement took place in that direction (see Chapter 4).

The processes of alteration or metamorphism of the bedrock into pelites (schists) and psammites, marbles etc. has been a special interest in this Area.

FIG 154. Natural and man-made features of Area 8.

Detailed studies have used knowledge of the properties of the minerals present to reconstruct the history of changes of pressure and temperature that took place as the crust became thickened during the Caledonian plate movements, compression and mountain building.

Highland Border: Ordovician

The Highland Border contains a clear linear feature, particularly in the central part of its traverse across the northern part of the land of Area 8. This can be seen well in Figure 154, which shows the elevation of the ground, and even better in Figure 158, where local patterns of slopes pick out linear edges, almost certainly faults, with remarkable clarity.

The Highland Boundary is one of the main faulted boundaries of Scotland that define the terranes of Caledonian collision (see Chapter 4). As well as the presence of linear faults, the Highland Boundary is often marked across Scotland by the presence of a fault-bounded strip of distinctive bedrock formally called the Highland Border Complex. This complex consists of highly fractured and altered rocks, including sediments perhaps ranging from Cambrian to early Silurian in age, metamorphic rocks and igneous rocks including mafic pillow lavas that may have been fragments of oceanic crust. Some of these bedrocks are now rich in the

FIG 155. Dundee, with the Tay road bridge across the estuary and the Grampian Highlands and Sidlaw Hills behind. (© Adrian Warren/lastrefuge.co.uk)

mineral serpentine, which has often also been altered to produce carbonate-rich rocks. The complex is notoriously poorly exposed. Even where the present-day rivers and their valleys have cut across the complex in Area 8, it has had to be identified by mapping the general geological pattern of the area, and its structure is difficult to map.

No matter how difficult it is to study, there is no doubt that the Highland Boundary preserves evidence of movement and bedrock alteration from at least early Ordovician to late Devonian times (well over 100 million years), and forms one of the most distinctive zones of landscape contrast in Scotland.

Caledonian intrusives

Areas of granite bedrock are much smaller and less common in Area 8 than they are further north and west in the Grampians, but there are discrete areas of this intrusive bedrock where granitic magma has risen upwards from deeper parts of the crust before solidifying. Most of this intrusion happened in late Silurian and early Devonian times.

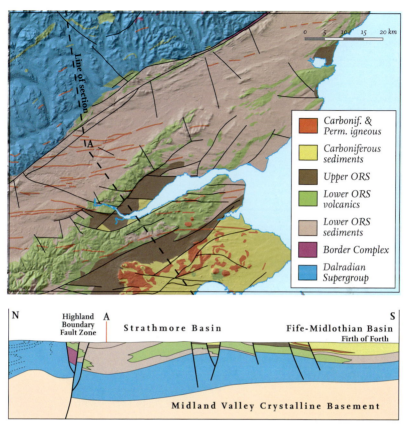

FIG 156. Simplified geology and hill-shaded topography for Area 8, with cross-section (2 × vertical exaggeration) along line marked.

Old Red Sandstone

The bedrock with the greatest extent in Area 8's landscape is the Old Red Sandstone, mostly of Devonian age. The Lower (or earlier) part of the Old Red Sandstone was deposited between about 420 and 400 million years ago, mainly during the Devonian period, but locally probably starting in the late Silurian. The deposits consisted of gravels, with sands and muds, largely transported by rivers and deposited on alluvial fans and on river flood plains. Some of this river-dominated scenery periodically contained local, relatively short-lived lakes, in which primitive vertebrates, invertebrates and plants became preserved. The Old Red Sandstone was generally formed as the deposits of rivers on land, making a striking contrast with the earlier, Proterozoic to Ordovician, sediments that

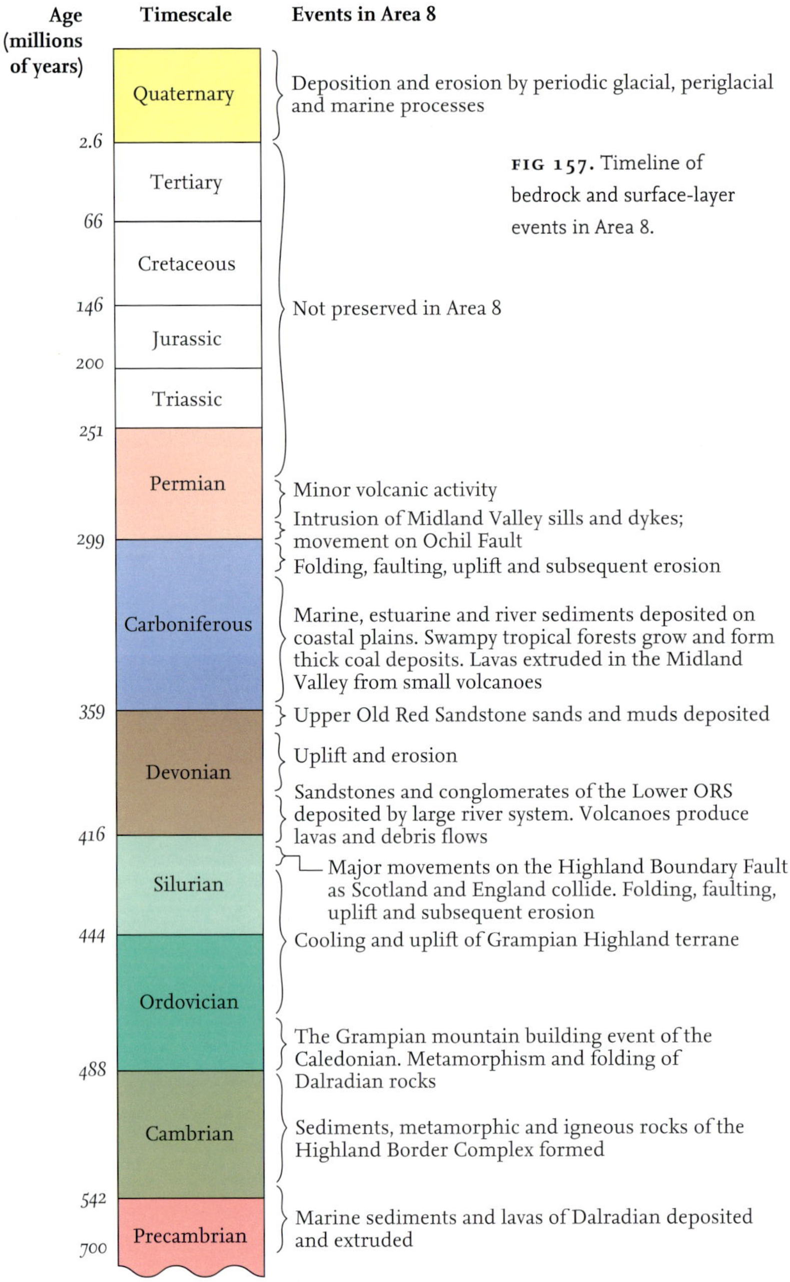

Age (millions of years)	Timescale	Events in Area 8
	Quaternary	Deposition and erosion by periodic glacial, periglacial and marine processes
2.6		
	Tertiary	
66		
	Cretaceous	
146		Not preserved in Area 8
	Jurassic	
200		
	Triassic	
251		
	Permian	Minor volcanic activity
		Intrusion of Midland Valley sills and dykes; movement on Ochil Fault
299		Folding, faulting, uplift and subsequent erosion
	Carboniferous	Marine, estuarine and river sediments deposited on coastal plains. Swampy tropical forests grow and form thick coal deposits. Lavas extruded in the Midland Valley from small volcanoes
359		Upper Old Red Sandstone sands and muds deposited
	Devonian	Uplift and erosion
		Sandstones and conglomerates of the Lower ORS deposited by large river system. Volcanoes produce lavas and debris flows
416		
	Silurian	Major movements on the Highland Boundary Fault as Scotland and England collide. Folding, faulting, uplift and subsequent erosion
444		Cooling and uplift of Grampian Highland terrane
	Ordovician	
		The Grampian mountain building event of the Caledonian. Metamorphism and folding of Dalradian rocks
488		
	Cambrian	Sediments, metamorphic and igneous rocks of the Highland Border Complex formed
542		
	Precambrian	Marine sediments and lavas of Dalradian deposited and extruded
700		

FIG 157. Timeline of bedrock and surface-layer events in Area 8.

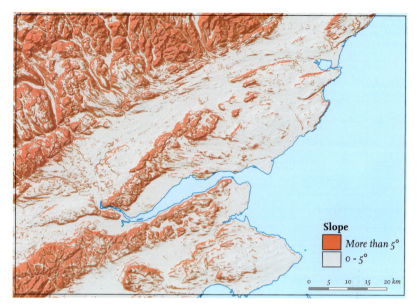

FIG 158. Slope map of Area 8, showing slopes greater than 5 degrees in red.

formed in seas. The deposition of the Old Red Sandstone provides evidence of the uplift of the land surface of the Area that occurred during the later part of the Caledonian mountain building. Later, after burial, the Lower Old Red Sandstone sediments became altered to conglomerates, sandstones and mudstones.

Igneous rocks are represented by large volumes of lava extruded periodically during the deposition of some parts of the Lower Old Red Sandstone of Area 8. Large volumes of lava, mainly of mafic composition, were erupted by volcanoes, although more felsic material also occurs (Fig. 159). The lavas have been weathered and eroded during the Tertiary and Quaternary to produce much of the topography of this part of the Midland Valley, particularly the Ochil and Sidlaw Hills and their extensions south of the Tay estuary and south of Montrose. These lava hills are characterised by rough landscapes with many small sloping features due to contrasts in the erodibility of the lavas, ashes and weathering horizons. In the Dundee area and elsewhere, intrusions in the form of pipes and sills mark places where igneous material passed upwards to higher levels where it was extruded to add to the successions of lavas. Because of their great resistance to erosion, these different igneous bodies now form hills in the landscape (Fig. 160).

The edges of some of the lava hill ranges are abrupt, and appear to have been formed by erosion of faulted margins; the Ochil southern margin fault, east of

FIG 159. Kinnoul Hill, near Perth, where the River Tay has cut through the Lower Old Red Sandstone lavas and intrusives of the Sidlaw Hills, and is crossed by the M90 motorway. (© Patricia & Angus Macdonald/Aerographica/Scottish Natural Heritage)

Stirling near the edge of Area 8, is one of the clearest. Bedrock of such different mechanical properties is very likely to fracture at boundaries when subject to crustal movements. Some authors have interpreted these volcanic rocks as parts of a large range of volcanoes that extended to include the bedrock of similar age and type in the southern parts of the Midland Valley. Estimates of the total thickness of often gently folded Lower Old Red Sandstone sediments and volcanics in the Area range between 2 and 4 km, providing evidence of crustal sinking movements on this sort of scale during this period.

Upper Old Red Sandstone is also present as mudstone and sandstone bedrock in Area 8, usually formed as muds and sands in rivers or transported locally across the river flood plains by the wind. In the cliffs north of Arbroath clean exposures of pebbly Upper Old Red Sandstone can be seen to have been deposited on an irregular, eroded surface of Lower Old Red Sandstone, showing that tilting earth movements and erosion occurred between the two Old Red Sandstone divisions (Fig. 161). Upper Old Red Sandstones at Dura Den, 10 km west of St Andrews, became famous in the nineteenth century for remarkable slabs covered with complete primitive, bone-scaled fishes, apparently killed in one or more river catastrophes and then carried triumphantly into many museums.

FIG 160. Dundee Law, formed by the resistance to erosion of an igneous intrusion formed during the Lower Old Red Sandstone lava extrusions. (© Patricia & Angus Macdonald/ Aerographica/ Scottish Natural Heritage)

Carboniferous sediments

Most of the southern half of Fife has sedimentary bedrock representing deposition through much of the Carboniferous period, some 360 to 310 million years ago. Mudstones, limestones, sandstones and coals are present, though not in the same total thickness or variety as the sediments of similar age that accumulated further south and west in the Midland Valley.

Compared with the Old Red Sandstone sediments, one of the distinctive features of the Carboniferous sediments is the way that they were deposited in cycles made up of regularly arranged layers, a few metres thick initially, of the muds, limey sediments, sands and swampy peats that became altered later into the mudstones, limestones, sandstones and coals that now make up the successions. The distinctive cycles were formed when rivers carried sediment into low, coastal ground and deposited it in deltas that then moved in location as they evolved with the passage of time. Understanding the way these deltas grew and formed the cycles has been the key to predicting where the different types of sediments, particularly the coals, were likely to have been deposited. These questions were of great importance to local economies when coal was still being mined.

Carboniferous and/or Permian igneous rocks

Igneous rocks formed as lavas within the succession of Carboniferous sediments, and also as intrusions associated with volcanoes, often forming sills extending

FIG 161. Sea cliffs north of Arbroath, showing the Upper Old Red Sandstone (coarse pebbly sandstones and conglomerates sloping 5 degrees to the right), forming the left-hand, upper part of the cliff. This pebbly material rests on an unconformity that is clearest in the centre of the photograph, where it slopes downwards to the left. The unconformity was an erosion surface cut in Devonian times across layers of the largely pebble-free Lower Old Red Sandstone, sloping 30 degrees down to the right. (© Lorne Gill, Scottish Natural Heritage)

over large areas. The remains of volcanic pipes and bedrock containing debris thrown out of volcanic craters form distinctive features, particularly when they have been eroded along present-day coastlines, for example in east Fife.

Most of these igneous rocks are of mafic composition, though they range from alkaline-rich to more quartz-rich in type, apparently depending on the level within the Earth's mantle from which the igneous liquid came, and the movement processes in the Earth that were taking place. Extensive sills locally dominate the topography, for example in the Lomond Hills of central Fife, some 20 km southeast of Perth.

MAKING THE LANDSCAPE

Tertiary erosion

There are no bedrock sediments younger than the Carboniferous within Area 8, but evidence gathered more widely across Scotland (Chapter 4) suggests that it was particularly after about 55 million years ago, during the early Tertiary, that Scotland

FIG 162. The Lomond Hills of central Fife, formed by erosion by eastward-moving ice sheets in a landscape underlain by Upper Old Red Sandstone and Carboniferous sediments intruded by igneous rocks. (© Patricia & Angus Macdonald/Aerographica/ Scottish Natural Heritage)

appeared as a land, recognisably similar to its present extent. It was at about this time that river erosion started to carve this land into the general pattern of hills, mountain valleys and lowlands that has evolved into the present landscape.

The erosion of large features of Area 8 is likely to have been proceeding during much of the 50 million years of the middle and later Tertiary. These would have included the large valleys, many of them trending roughly west to east, that traverse the Grampian Highlands, the Highland Border, the edges of the Lower Old Red lava hills (the Ochils and the Sidlaws) and the large igneous bodies of the Lomond Hills of Fife.

Ice Age modifications

It is now generally accepted (Chapter 5) that the Ice Age consisted of large numbers of episodes of cold climate separated by shorter episodes of relatively warmer climate. It is also accepted that the last (Devensian) of the cold episodes only came to an end about 10,000 years ago, after some 50,000 years in which much of northern Britain and its surroundings were covered by ice. In the case of Scotland, almost all of the evidence of modification of the landscape under ice, whether by erosion of bedrock or deposition of sediment, dates from this latest Devensian glacial episode.

Figure 158 clearly picks out the large, relatively flat-floored valleys, and locally the term *carse* is often used for these. Good examples are the great valley of Strathmore, and the central Fife valleys of the Devon, Earn and Eden. These contrast clearly with the neighbouring higher and more sloping ground, and although the contrast has been made even clearer by the covering of the valley floors by sediment since the ice departed, the margins of the high ground appear to have been sculpted by ice when wide ice streams occupied the large valleys in Devensian times (Fig. 162). In the high ground, the smaller valleys were eroded and became more U-shaped as the valley glaciers moved. When they retreated, they left sedimentary debris in the form of lateral, ground and terminal moraines. In the low ground, debris was widely distributed as ground-moraine, often shaped into drumlins. Near the sea, estuarine deposits provide local evidence of relative sea-level change.

The general easterly direction of ice flow across Area 8 can be seen in Figure 38 (Chapter 5), but local directions, particularly during the melting of the Devensian ice sheet, will have varied considerably, being influenced by the existing topography of the bedrock beneath the ice sheet. The slope map (Fig. 158) shows many examples of slopes that appear to represent local ice-flow directions. One clear example is the way the eastward movement of different ice sheets appears to have carved out the west face of the Lomond Hills and excavated the low ground occupied by Loch Leven, so well seen by travellers on the M90 motorway.

After the ice, sea-level changes

The present-day coastline of Area 8 contains many examples of former beaches and cliff lines that have formed since the local ice departed. They are now too high above sea level to have been formed by coastal processes active with the sea at its present-day level. Steps consisting of numerous raised beaches are particularly a feature of the coast of East Fife. For example, Kincraig Point near Elie, on the southern margin of Area 8 and some 20 km due south of St Andrews, is well known for the several clear raised coastlines that are visible there.

The history of relative sea-level change for the area south of Perth, covering the period from about 15,000 years ago to the present, is similar to that shown in Figure 42 (Chapter 5) for the upper Forth Valley. At the beginning of this period sea level was about 40 m higher, relative to the local landscape, than it is at present. This was about the time when fine-grained mud deposits, locally known as the Errol Beds, were being deposited, with fossils typical of cold sea conditions. These are preserved on land in many coastal and estuarine areas of Area 8, particularly around Errol, some 15 km east of Perth. The relative sea-level curve (Fig. 42) then shows a fall to near present-day levels some 10,000 years ago,

FIG 163. Tentsmuir Forest and Point, with the Tay estuary behind and Dundee to the left. The complex of coastal beaches, sand bars and spits is evidence of the active movement of sediment still taking place. The tree plantations of Tentsmuir have been growing on a large area of similar coastal sediments. (© Patricia & Angus Macdonald/Aerographica/ Scottish Natural Heritage)

rising again to reach some 7 m 6000 years ago, before falling to its present level. In Chapter 5, a very different curve was described from the Thames Estuary of southern England (Fig. 41). Whereas the Thames Estuary curve seems to result from a worldwide rise in sea level (relative to the Earth's centre) caused by an increase in the total water volume of the Earth's seas and oceans, the curves for Tayside and the upper Forth appear to represent uplift of the local landscape, relative to the Earth's centre, due to crust and mantle readjustment on loss of the weight of local ice sheets.

Measurements of these raised coastal features along coastlines have shown that they vary in height in a systematic way. Figure 44 (Chapter 5) summarises some of this information across a wide area of Scotland and northern England, and shows that old coastlines, dating from about 15,000, 12,500, 10,000 and 7500 years ago, have been recognised particularly in Areas 8 and 5 (Edinburgh). The old coastlines (for example the so-called Main Perth shoreline) slope strongly eastward, and this supports the idea of a Rannoch Rebound Dome (Chapter 5) that has been active since the last Devensian ice melted.

Striking evidence of the last melting of the Scottish ice sheets is the large amount of freshly transported sediment left on the landscape. Much of this was left on slopes and in river valleys, where it was particularly prone to movement down slopes, and as rivers evolved under conditions of changing freeze–thaw and rainfall climate at the landscape surface. Local studies are thus likely to show evidence of landsliding and slumping, as well as evidence of river channel instability and change of sediment load.

Coastlines are also particularly prone to changes in the distribution of sediment available. Area 8 contains many examples where the coastline has been building seawards, by a combination of beach and wind deposition – to produce the golf links that are so important to the development of many Scottish seaside resorts. The links that have achieved worldwide fame are those owned by the Royal and Ancient Club at St Andrews, occupying a series of regular coastal ridges built out as sand was supplied to the coastal bar that extends into the estuary of the River Eden.

Similar, but much larger, coastal build-outs, for example at Tentsmuir, further north in east Fife (Fig. 163), and at Budden and Barry, north of the Tay estuary, provide beautiful examples of the important sediment movement that has followed the glaciation of this part of Scotland.

CHAPTER 14

Area 9: Uists and Barra

AREA 9 COVERS THE SOUTHERN HALF of the Outer Isles or Western Isles chain, also known as the Outer Hebrides (Fig. 164). The Outer Isles form the northwestern edge of the British Isles, looking out across the Atlantic Ocean. The island group of St Kilda, some 70 km west of the northern end of North Uist, is also included within this Area (Fig. 165). The division in this book between the southern and northern parts of the Outer Isles is arbitrary; the northern part (Lewis and Harris) forms Area 14. The Uists and Barra have a much smaller human population, about 6000, compared with a total of about 20,000 in Lewis and Harris.

STORIES FROM THE BEDROCK

The Lewisian Complex

With the exception of the St Kilda group, all of the bedrock in Area 9 consists of metamorphic rocks belonging to the Lewisian Complex (Fig. 166). These rocks extend westwards well beyond the present day coastline, forming a shallow marine shelf some 60–70 km wide. To the east, the Lewisian bedrock is bounded by the Minch Fault, a large, deep structure with a long and complex history. This fault was active during Permian and Triassic times when the crustal rocks to its west were uplifted relative to those in the east, creating a basin into which Mesozoic sediments accumulated (Fig. 167; see also Area 14, Lewis and Harris). As a result, just offshore from the Outer Isles' eastern coastline, the Lewisian Complex is juxtaposed against the much younger sediments that immediately underlie the rest of the Minch.

The Lewisian Complex rocks are some of the oldest in Europe, preserving evidence of metamorphic events up to 3.2 billion years old. They are also quite

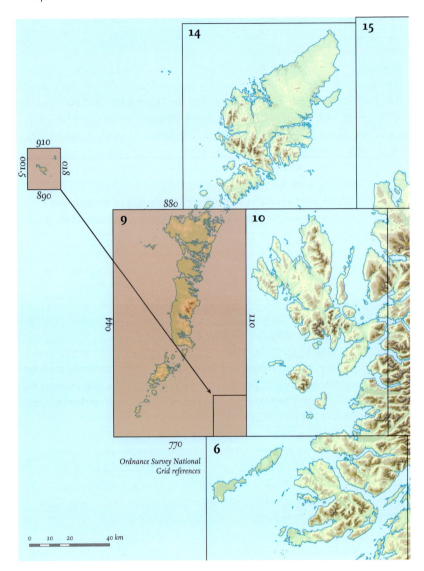

FIG 164. Location map for Area 9.

varied, due to differing degrees of metamorphism and variations in the original materials involved. Much of the pioneering work on the Lewisian Complex was first carried out in Area 15 (Cape Wrath) on the Scottish mainland, where it was realised that the rocks have been deformed and altered many times in numerous distinct episodes. These episodes have been detected and investigated by mapping detailed structures within the rocks, and by determining ages using radiometric dating techniques.

Subsequent work has shown that the history of the Outer Isles Lewisian has been similarly complex. In addition, research from further afield has made it clear that, both on the Scottish mainland and in the Outer Isles, the Lewisian has more in common with the metamorphic complexes of southeast Greenland than it does with the bedrock of the rest of Britain. It is now commonly accepted that the bedrock of Scotland and southeast Greenland was once part of a continuous area of continental crust, which only became divided when the Atlantic Ocean formed at this latitude some 60 million years ago.

In Area 9 it is possible to recognise two distinct episodes of tectonic and metamorphic activity in the Lewisian rocks – the Scourian and Laxfordian events. The earlier Scourian event took place between about 3.2 and 2.5 billion years ago and was responsible for the formation of the main elements of the Lewisian Banded Gneisses, involving extensive deformation and recrystallisation. This was followed by the intrusion of large volumes of mafic igneous material in the form of dolerite and basalt dykes and sills, often called the Younger Basic Suite in the Outer Hebrides, but generally considered to be part of the more widespread Scourie dyke swarm (see Area 15, Cape Wrath).

About 1.9 billion years ago, more metamorphic and igneous material was added to the existing Scourian rocks (perhaps by horizontal movements involving addition of volcanic crust) and the whole region was then metamorphosed again during the Laxfordian event (Fig. 167). The Laxfordian metamorphism significantly reworked the Scourian gneisses, and also metamorphosed the newly arrived rocks to form the meta-gabbros and meta-sediments shown in Figure 166. The Laxfordian event also destroyed or over-printed many of the earlier Scourian structures, creating most of the bedrock structures and textures that are visible in today's landscape.

The earth movements and metamorphism which took place during the Laxfordian event were also associated with movement on the Outer Isles Thrust (Fig. 166), a major fault system running along the eastern coastal fringes of North Uist, South Uist and Barra in this Area and also extending northwards into Area 14. The width of the fault zone widens to the north, from a belt about 3 km wide on the Isle of Barra to a band over 15 km wide in northeastern Lewis (Area 14), and the rocks within the fault zone are often heavily shattered and altered. There is evidence that the Outer Isles thrust was active again in late Caledonian (mid-Palaeozoic) times, at a broadly similar time to the Moine Thrust Zone on the Scottish mainland (see Fig. 22, Chapter 4). As we will see below, movement on this fault has had a significant impact on the scenery of Area 9.

Early Tertiary igneous activity on St Kilda

In geological and landscape terms, the remote and precipitous islands of St Kilda are very different from the rest of this Area. They are made up of a range of early Tertiary igneous intrusions, mainly mafic gabbros, dolerites and felsic granites, along with some igneous breccias. These rocks are the eroded relics of an igneous central complex comparable in structure, content and age to those of Skye (Area 10), Ardnamurchan and Mull (Area 6) and Arran (Area 3), all of which form part of a suite of igneous rocks associated with the separation of Greenland from Scotland and the opening of the North Atlantic Ocean (Chapter 4). The igneous complex on St Kilda was active between about 60 and 55 million years ago, and the solidified magma that now forms the islands was originally emplaced deep within the crust by intrusion into the surrounding Lewisian Gneisses. Broadly speaking, this magma was of two main types, the first (and oldest) of mafic gabbroic composition and dark in colour, the second of felsic granitic composition and pinkish/white in colour. The gabbroic rocks are today rather more abundant than the granites, forming the bedrock beneath all of Soay and Boreray and most of Hirta (Fig. 166). The granitic rocks are largely confined to the northeastern part of Hirta, where they underlie Oiseval (290 m) and Conachair (430 m), the latter being the highest point in the St Kilda island group.

As the igneous system on St Kilda evolved, the two different types of magma were brought into contact with one another, and magma mixing has produced a variety of rocks of intermediate composition and colour, most simply classified as diorites. At other times, the two types of magma seem to have been intruded into the surrounding rocks before homogeneous mixing could take place, resulting in some very striking black and white outcrops such as those exposed in the western part of Village Bay. This unambiguous evidence for the existence of so-called 'mixed magma intrusions' has turned out to be crucial to our understanding of other Tertiary volcanic sites throughout Scotland.

The final phase of igneous activity on St Kilda involved the intrusion of a suite of mafic basaltic dykes and sills which are now exposed in the felsic granite cliffs of eastern Hirta. These intrusions represent one of the best examples of a cone-sheet complex in the British Isles, radiating upwards and outwards from the top of a roughly 55-million-year-old magma chamber located northeast of Hirta (now offshore) and cross-cutting the slightly older Conachair granite in the process.

FIG 165. Natural and man-made features of Area 9.
Maximum elevation in this Area: 620 m

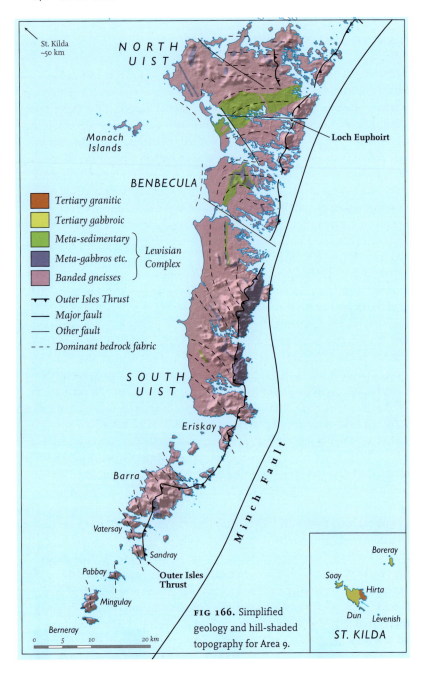

FIG 166. Simplified geology and hill-shaded topography for Area 9.

MAKING THE LANDSCAPE

The slope map (Fig. 168) and associated profile (Fig. 169) provide an excellent way of generalising the present-day topography in this Area, clearly highlighting the contrast between the generally flat western coastal fringes of the Outer Isles with their low hills, extensive beaches and tidal inlets, and the eastern coastlines, which are typically backed by steep hills hundreds of metres high. The hills in the east generally rise steeply out of the Minch and attain a maximum elevation of 620 m at Beinn Mhor on South Uist. To the west they descend quite abruptly to an uneven, but generally quite flat, rock platform which extends all the way to the western coastlines and then onwards to the edge of the continental shelf a further 60–70 km away.

The extent of glacial modification in this Area makes it rather difficult to unravel its early (pre-glacial) landscape history, but it is likely that a number of important, large-scale features were formed long before the Ice Age.

Consideration of the evolution of Scottish landscapes in general shows that many of the larger valleys, particularly in the west of the country, were formed by river erosion related to the uplift caused by the main phase of Tertiary igneous activity. The Jurassic palaeogeographic map in Chapter 4 (Fig. 30) shows that, prior to the Tertiary, the Inner Hebrides and much of the western mainland were submerged beneath the Minch Jurassic basin, as indicated by the presence of occasional marine sediments of Jurassic and Cretaceous age on, for example, the Isle of Skye (Area 10). The Outer Isles, on the other hand, were located to the west of the Minch Fault and formed part of the Hebridean Platform, which seems to have remained largely above sea level since at least Devonian times (see, e.g., Figs 27 and 30, Chapter 4). It is therefore likely that the drainage network here became established rather earlier than elsewhere in western Scotland, carrying eroded sediments westwards into the Rockall Trough and eastwards into the Minch Basin.

It is possible that the hilly ground down the eastern edge of the Outer Isles also began to form prior to the Tertiary, as erosion picked out contrasts in the altered bedrock along the ancient Outer Isles Thrust Zone. Because of the faulting, rocks in the east have been folded and fractured more than those in the west, creating numerous hard and soft bands along with some heavily altered fault rocks, often called *pseudotachylites*. The pseudotachylites consist of chunks of broken, friable gneiss that have been welded together by molten rock (now cooled to a black, glassy material) created by frictional heating in the fault zone. Over time these welded, massive rocks have resisted erosion better than the

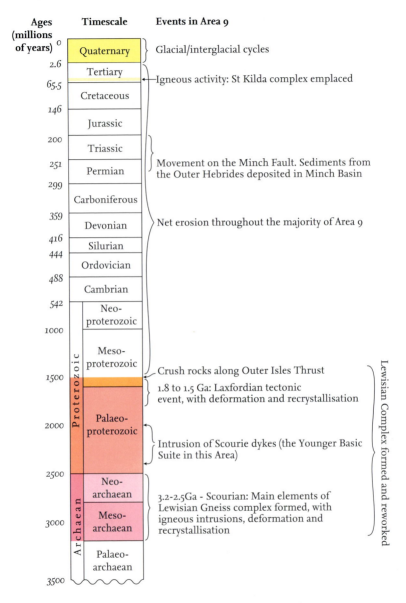

FIG 167. Timeline of bedrock and surface-layer events in Area 9. Ga is a standard abbreviation for thousand million (billion) years.

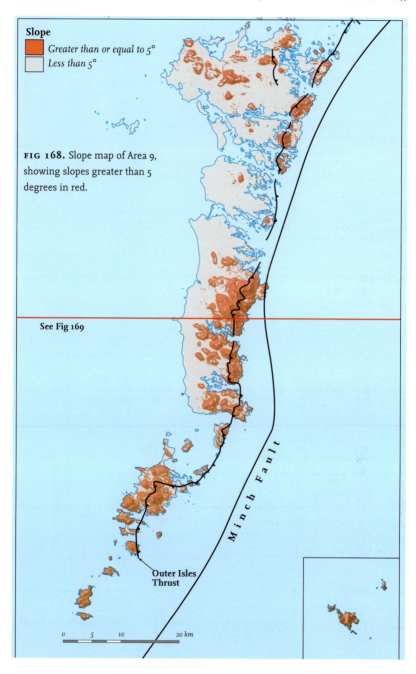

FIG 168. Slope map of Area 9, showing slopes greater than 5 degrees in red.

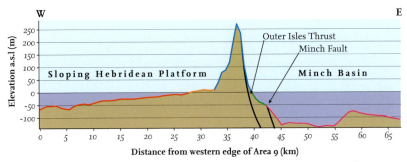

FIG 169. Bathymetry and topography along a west-to-east profile through South Uist, northing 830, located on Figure 168.

surrounding shattered gneisses, forming some prominent peaks and creating a more complex, hilly landscape in the east.

On South Uist, erosion has picked out the scarp of the Outer Isles Thrust itself to form a number of distinctive, triangular hills, including Beinn Mhor (620 m), Beinn Choradail (527 m) and Hecla (606 m). A little further up the coast on North Uist, the fault scarp can again be seen forming the eastern ridge of Eaval (347 m; Fig. 170), and a little to the north again the pseudotachylites are a feature of the prominent mountains of South Lee (281 m) and North Lee (251 m). Although all of these features have been heavily modified by more recent erosional processes – particularly glaciation – it is likely that differential weathering along the Outer Isles Thrust has been important in the landscape evolution of Area 9 for very much longer.

The Outer Isles Thrust is not the only bedrock feature to have influenced the landscape of Area 9: the location of the narrow strait separating Benbecula from South Uist and the position of Loch Euphoirt on North Uist both coincide very closely with bedrock faults on the geology map (Fig. 166). It is difficult to say exactly when these landscape features first began to form, but it is probable that the Tertiary rivers and streams here began by exploiting pre-existing weaknesses in the bedrock, most of which were later broadened and deepened by glacial erosion and some of which are today subject to further erosion by the Atlantic waves. The geology maps for Areas 9 (Uist and Barra) and 14 (Lewis and Harris) make it clear that bedrock structures have played an important role in dividing up the islands of the Outer Hebrides, and also in producing many of the Outer Isles' most dramatic valley and coastline features.

During the Tertiary, extensive igneous activity caused widespread uplift across western Scotland and also emplaced the igneous centre at St Kilda, which at the time probably formed a volcano in the middle of the Hebridean Platform. Once

FIG 170. View southeast across part of North Uist towards the isolated mountain of Eaval, whose summit ridge has been shaped by a fault of the Outer Isles Thrust Zone. (© Patricia & Angus Macdonald/Aerographica).

volcanic activity had ceased, this uplift combined with the warm, wet climate to create conditions of intense erosion (up to 2 km per million years), exposing the ancient Lewisian rocks and eventually exhuming the core of the St Kilda volcano. As erosion continued, the hard granites and gabbros of the St Kilda Complex resisted erosion more than the surrounding Lewisian gneisses to create prominent hills (Fig. 171). It is also possible that the two main valleys on Hirta date from this time: one drains roughly north-northwestwards into what is now Glen Bay and the other drains southeastwards into Village Bay, the location of the latter being largely controlled by two northwest/southeast-oriented faults that define its edges. Despite extensive subsequent modification, these two valleys are still visible today, and they can be traced offshore onto the Hebridean Platform, suggesting that they formed at a time when relative sea level was much lower than it is at present.

Continued erosion on the Hebridean Platform seems to have reduced the late Tertiary landscape of this Area to a largely flat plateau, studded with igneous hills like those of the St Kilda islands and perhaps with a hilly spine roughly coincident with the Outer Isles Thrust Zone. As the igneous activity associated with the opening of the North Atlantic moved away to the west, western Scotland experienced a small amount of thermal subsidence, which tilted the entire platform downwards by about 2 degrees to the west. It is this surface (modified, as always, by more recent processes) that forms the fairly flat ground in the west

FIG 171. The island of Hirta, St Kilda, from the southeast, looking into Village Bay with the Dun ridge to the left and Soay in the background. (© Adrian Warren/lastrefuge.co.uk)

of South Uist, Benbecula and North Uist (Figs 168, 169), sloping gently westwards from the hills along the Outer Isles Thrust and extending offshore all the way to the edge of the continental shelf, beyond St Kilda.

Glaciation

Since the onset of the Ice Age a little over 2 million years ago, Scotland has been subjected to repeated glacial and interglacial episodes that have extensively modified the pre-glacial landscapes. The glacial features in Area 9 include some of the most remarkable in this book, many of them located offshore on the gently tilted and recently submerged portion of the Hebridean Platform. Our understanding of these features has improved dramatically in recent years as our knowledge of the sea bed in this Area has increased, but there is still a lot that is not yet fully understood.

Figure 35 (Chapter 5) shows the maximum extent of the last (Devensian) ice sheet, when the icecap extended from the Scottish mainland across the Outer Hebrides and may have reached as far as the St Kilda archipelago. It is likely that previous glacial phases had a similar (or perhaps greater) ice extent but, as each

AREA 9: UISTS AND BARRA · 253

FIG 172. Ice movement directions across Area 9. Tails on the arrows indicate the areas from which the measurements were taken.

→ Direction of Late Devensian ice flow
--- Ice divide at Late Glacial Maximum

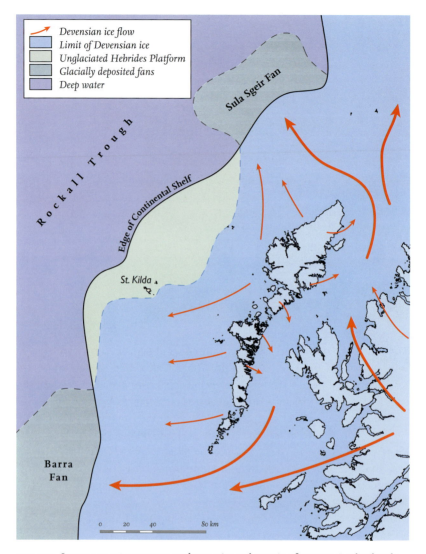

FIG 173. Ice movement patterns over the continental margin of western Scotland at the Devensian Late Glacial Maximum. (After Stoker *et al.* 1994)

successive glaciation has a tendency to rework the evidence of its predecessors, we know comparatively little about earlier glacial episodes. Nonetheless, there is very little doubt that the major glacially sculpted features in this Area have been carved not just by one glacial phase but by many.

FIG 174. View northwest across northern North Uist, showing the classic knock-and-lochan landscape and the coast in the distance. (© Patricia & Angus Macdonald/ Aerographica)

The vast majority of glacial striae on the Uists and Benbecula indicate eastwards-directed ice flow, suggesting that, during late Devensian times, an elongate ice sheet developed in this Area with its centre located at the western edge of the present-day island chain (Fig. 172). This ice sheet flowed eastwards into the Minch, where it met with westwards-flowing ice from the Scottish mainland, and it also flowed westwards across the Hebridean Platform towards St Kilda. Where the two ice streams met in the Minch they turned either to the north, rounding the northern tip of Lewis, or to the south, rounding Berneray and Mingulay, before both flowing more or less westwards to reach the edge of the continental shelf. Upon reaching deep water at the edge of the Hebridean Platform, these ice streams laid down two large deposits of glacial debris: the Sula Sgeir Fan and the Barra Fan (Fig. 173).

The Devensian ice flow transformed the landscapes of this Area. A deep glacial trough was carved into the Minch (see Fig. 37, Chapter 5), and many of the existing river valleys, such as the valley separating South Uist from Benbecula, were deepened and broadened. With the exception of the St Kilda archipelago and perhaps a few of the highest summits on South Uist (e.g. Beinn Mhor) virtually the whole of the Hebridean Platform was buried under ice, and much of it was scoured to create the knock-and-lochan topography that today characterises the flat ground of the western Outer Isles. The knocks are generally rounded, ice-sculpted mounds that are separated from one another by shallow, scoured depressions, often containing small lakes (the lochans). In the Outer Isles these lochans are very numerous, and they are often connected to one another by a complex network of small streams to create a very distinctive landscape (Figs 170, 174). This type of terrain is typical of glaciated areas underlain by Lewisian Gneiss, where the pattern of intense glacial erosion has been influenced by local variations in the degree of bedrock fracturing (due to joints, shear zones, faults etc.). Extensively fractured regions are generally excavated to form the hollows or lochans, while the more massive bodies of gneiss are able to resist ice abrasion to create the knocks.

Further to the west, on Hirta, the main island of the St Kilda group, valley glaciers developed in the two main valleys (mentioned above) and these were sculpted by the ice into more or less their present-day shapes. Moraine ridges from these glaciers have been identified at the western side of Village Bay, and the valley floor here is also covered in boulder clay, deposited when the ice retreated. Apart from this, however, there is relatively little evidence of glacial scouring on the rest of the archipelago, so it appears that St Kilda lay just beyond the edge of the main ice sheet and was never completely overtopped by the Late Devensian ice. The presence of occasional erratic blocks (material glacially transported from other locations) in some of the deposits at the eastern side of Village Bay suggests that St Kilda may have been overrun by ice during an earlier cold phase, when the ice extent was greater than during the Devensian, but the evidence for this is scant and the age of these deposits is unknown at present.

The position of St Kilda just beyond the limit of the Late Devensian ice makes the archipelago very unusual in Scotland: it is perhaps the only part of the entire country (with the exception of the highest mountain tops) that was not buried beneath an ice sheet at the height of the last glaciation. This is due, at least in part, to the islands being sheltered by the Outer Hebrides, which acted to deflect the ice flow from the Scottish mainland to the north and to the south, as shown in Figure 173. As a result, St Kilda managed to remain largely ice-free, despite the presence of ice streams extending westwards beyond the archipelago on either side.

Because of its ice-marginal location, St Kilda has preserved a superb array of periglacial landforms, including, for example, the *solifluction lobes* that are visible on the flanks of the central ridge of Hirta. These were formed when frost-shattering produced large quantities of weathered debris which became unstable and moved slowly downhill to create distinctive slope deposits. Other features formed more recently, such as the *protalus ramparts* associated with the Loch Lomond Stadial (about 13,000 to 11,500 years ago). At this time, permanent

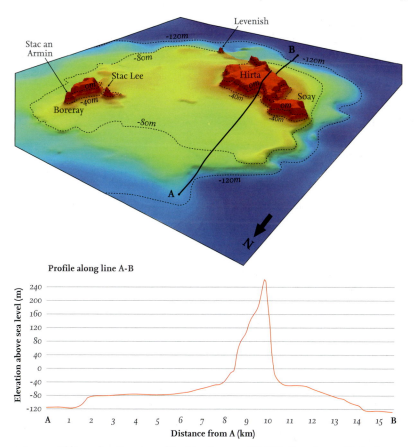

FIG 175. Oblique elevation view of the island group of St Kilda from the north, Contours of sea depth at minus 80 and minus 120 m are shown with colour shading from yellow (shallow) to blue (deep). The islands are marked in red but the highest peaks have been truncated by the computer to avoid obscuring the sea-depth pattern. An elevation profile along the line A-B is shown. The highest point on the large island of Hirta is 430 m above sea-level, well to the east of the profile.

snow or ice patches developed in the glen behind Village Bay, covering the slopes below the cliffs of Conachair and Mullach Sgar (the central ridge). Rocks falling from the cliffs slid down the snow fields and accumulated at their bases to form low ridges, which are clearly visible today. At the other side of the island, pollen preserved in deposits contains a very valuable record of vegetation (and therefore climate) changes in this region since these snow fields melted.

FIG 176. Village Bay, Hirta, in the foreground, with the settlement that was evacuated in 1939 at the request of the inhabitants. The Dun gabbro ridge is in the background. (© Patricia & Angus Macdonald/Aerographica)

A number of other landscape features in this Area also formed at or around the Devensian Glacial Maximum or during the Loch Lomond Advance, but to understand them we must first consider some other intriguing glacial landforms, now located offshore on the Hebridean Platform. Although these features do not themselves form part of the present-day scenery, their development is intricately linked with, for example, the formation of the cliffs of St Kilda and the coastlines of the Outer Hebridean islands.

At the height of the last glaciation the amount of ice, worldwide, locked up on land resulted in a decrease in global sea levels by about 120 m compared to today (Chapter 5, Fig. 40). However, as described in Chapter 5, in most Scottish locations the weight of the ice on land also served to depress the crust, so the actual history of sea-level change in most places is complicated by a glacial subsidence/rebound component. Unusually for Scotland, the western part of Area 9 (the St Kilda archipelago and the surrounding shelf) was sufficiently distant from the main Scottish icecap for the subsidence/rebound component to be quite small, so the relative sea-level history here broadly resembles the global (eustatic) curve shown in Figure 40. With this in mind, a number of interesting features can be identified in the St Kilda bathymetry, which is represented in Figure 175.

The sea floor around St Kilda consists of two submarine plateau surfaces, at different levels, each backed by steep cliffs. The deep plateau is at a depth of roughly 120 m below present sea level and it steps upwards to a shallower plateau with a cliff about 40 m high. The shallower plateau is about 80 m below present sea level and shoals gradually to around minus 40 m, before rising precipitously to form the cliffs of St Kilda (Fig. 175). These rock walls are the highest sea cliffs in Great Britain: those below Conachair on Hirta rise almost vertically from the sea to a height of nearly 430 m, and they also extend below the waves to a clearly defined base where they join the minus 40 m plateau. This is true of virtually all of the dramatic coastal features around these islands – the sea stacks, the arches and the geos (deep, narrow clefts in the cliff face). Stac an Armin, just north of Boreray, is the tallest sea stack in the UK at 196 m above sea level, but its bottom-to-top elevation difference is considerably greater, measuring 231 m from the base of its pedestal below the waves.

The back wall of the lower platform (roughly defined by the minus 80 m contour on Fig. 175) corresponds very closely to the outline of the still-buried part of the St Kilda igneous complex, the hard rocks of which seem to have weathered prominently to create a 40 m-high cliff line, now beneath the waves. This lower platform would also have been subjected to storm wave erosion during the Devensian Glacial Maximum, and probably during earlier glacial maxima as well, whenever global sea level was about 120 m below that of the present day. Similarly, the shallower platform roughly matches the sea level in this area between about 13,000 and 11,500 years ago, which corresponds to the Loch Lomond Stadial.

The currently accepted interpretation of these plateau surfaces is that they were cut into the Hebridean Platform around St Kilda by wave erosion during the cold phases of the Ice Age, particularly during the Devensian Late Glacial Maximum and the Loch Lomond Advance. During the latter, when the sea occupied the upper plateau surface, intense wave erosion began to exploit weaknesses in the St Kilda bedrock, producing some very spectacular coastal features that today rise from the plateau at minus 40 m. On the island of Dun (Fig. 176), just south of Hirta, a series of southwest/northeast-trending fault lines and dykes has been preferentially eroded to create a number of large geos that give the island its distinctive square-cut southwestern coastline. In places these geos extend into narrow caves which pass right through the island, essentially dividing it into a series of arches. One such example is Gob an Duin, which forms a natural rock arch over 50 m long and 24 m high.

As erosion continues, geos are broadened until the arches above them eventually become unstable and collapse, at which point the seaward side of the arch generally becomes a stack. Excellent examples of this process at different stages can be seen in the narrow sound separating Hirta from Soay, which contains several large stacks, including the narrow fin of Stac Shoaigh (61 m) and the steep tower of Stac Biorach (73 m). It is likely that these two were originally joined together to form an arch and, before that arch, the composite stack was probably joined to the main island of Hirta by another arch. At the present time, a small arch exists in Stac Shoaigh – and it is likely that this too will eventually collapse, dividing the stack again. Even further in the future, it is possible that the geos around An Campar, the northwesternmost tip of Hirta, will one day create new arches and ultimately form even more stacks. In this way, the sea is slowly breaking down and dividing the islands of St Kilda: during the Loch Lomond Stadial it is probable that Levenish, a small, isolated island 2.5 km east of Dun, was joined to the main island chain as an actively eroding arch or geo.

The observation that so many of St Kilda's coastal features rise from a now submerged wave-cut plateau of Loch Lomond Stadial age is very interesting, but also a little puzzling. The Loch Lomond Stadial lasted only 1500–2000 years, and yet the plateau surface associated with it at St Kilda is up to 6 km wide (Fig. 175). In contrast, sea level here has been relatively constant for the past 5000–6000 years, but there is virtually no platform whatsoever associated with the present sea level, despite St Kilda experiencing perhaps the highest wave-energy environment anywhere in the UK. It is possible that the Loch Lomond plateau surface has been occupied by the sea several times during the Ice Age, which might help to explain its large size. It has also been suggested that platform formation would have been more efficient during cold phases due to increased rates of frost-shattering in the cliffs and perhaps due to intense abrasion by floating icebergs. While more research is undoubtedly needed, it seems clear that the climatic conditions during previous glacial phases were conducive to plateau formation, more than those of today.

After the ice

After the Loch Lomond Stadial the climate began to warm, the glaciers shrank, and sea levels rose. As the ice retreated it deposited a layer of boulder clay, much, but not all, of which was eroded by meltwater streams and washed onto the Hebridean Platform. Today, boulder clay can be found around Village Bay on Hirta and in a few isolated patches on the Uists and Benbecula.

Pollen evidence suggests that, following deglaciation, the Outer Isles were colonised quite rapidly by a variety of tree species: first by birch and hazel and later by oak, elm and pine. A similar record for St Kilda shows an alternation between different types of heathland and grassland but no trees, perhaps because

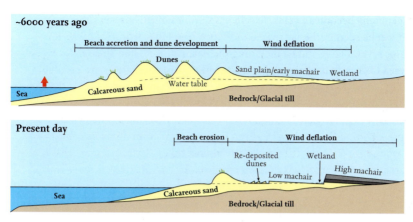

FIG 177. Profiles illustrating the formation and modification of machair with rising sea level. (After Hansom 2003 b, Fig. 9.3)

the climate there was too harsh or the soils too poor. By about 4400 years ago the pollen record shows that tree species in the Outer Hebrides had gone into decline, partly due to the increasingly wet climate and partly because of human activities. By 2600 years ago, most of the woodland in Area 9 had been replaced by the peaty blanket bogs that are present today.

The rising sea levels progressively flooded the Hebridean Platform from west to east, drowning the hummocky knock-and-lochan terrain of the Outer Isles to create numerous rocky islands, low cliffs and reefs, separated by broad bays. As flooding continued, the high wave-energy environment eroded and reworked interglacial marine sediments from the recently submerged parts of the Hebridean Platform, pushing them landwards into the bays to form sandy beaches. Much of this sandy sediment was calcareous, made up of millions of tiny shelly fragments. The prevailing wind, blowing predominantly from southwest to northeast, blew it further inland, where it became incorporated into the soils.

Evidence from North Uist suggests that there were two major influxes of calcareous sediment along the western coastlines of North Uist, Benbecula, South Uist and Barra: one about 8000 years ago and another about 5500 years ago. These influxes eventually led to a change in the near-coast soil chemistry to produce a very unusual grassland environment, now known as *machair* (Fig. 177). Machair is one of the rarest habitats in Europe, found only in the northwest of Britain and Ireland and supporting a very diverse range of flowers, birds and insects. Almost half of all Scottish machair is found in the Outer Hebrides, and by far the best and most extensive examples are located within this Area, along the western

FIG 178. Looking southeast from above Vallay, North Uist, towards the hills of North and South Lee, Note the machair sand accumulations of the Atlantic coast in the foreground. (© Patricia & Angus Macdonald/Aerographica)

FIG 179. Looking northeast from above Vallay, North Uist, showing machair sand coastal accumulations, and distant views of the hills of South and North Harris. (© Patricia & Angus Macdonald/Aerographica)

FIG 180. Looking southeastwards into Village Bay, Hirta, St Kilda. Note the smooth and gentle slope profiles of the landscape of Village Bay, in contrast to the storm-wave-cut cliff profiles in the foreground. (© Adrian Warren/lastrefuge.co.uk)

shorelines of North Uist, South Uist and Barra (Figs 178, 179). The calcareous dune deposits at Eoligarry on Barra are also remarkable for their size, extending inland to mantle bedrock over 100 m above sea level.

In contrast to the broad sandy bays and machair grasslands of the western shorelines, the eastern coastlines of the Outer Hebrides in this Area have a very different character. The drowning of the knock-and-lochan topography has still produced frequent small reefs and skerries, but the much lower wave-energy environment of the Minch coastline is not favourable for the formation of sandy beaches. Instead, this shoreline is typified by much smaller shingle coves with mud-flats and occasional patches of salt-marsh. This slightly more dissected coastline also has some very fine examples of drowned valley systems, such as Loch nam Madadh (Loch Maddy) and Loch Euphoirt, both of which support a variety of unusual flora and fauna.

On St Kilda, the rising sea level had relatively little impact on the towering coastal cliffs, but on Hirta the valleys of Glen Bay and Village Bay became flooded, the latter forming one of very few sheltered anchorages in the whole archipelago. Inland, in dramatic contrast to the island's vertiginous coastline, a very distinctive grassland habitat has developed, intricately linked to a fascinating and remarkable human history (Fig. 180). It is this combination of geological, geomorphological, ecological and sociological interest that led to the St Kilda archipelago being designated as Scotland's first World Heritage Site, in 1986.

CHAPTER 15

Area 10: Skye

THE ISLE OF SKYE is the most northerly and the largest of the Inner Hebrides. To the south are the Small Isles of Muck, Eigg, Rum and Canna. To the east the mainland includes the northern fringe of Ardnamurchan, Moidart, Arisaig, Morar, Knoydart, the Kyle of Lochalsh area, Applecross, Loch Torridon and up to the Gairloch area (Figs 181, 182).

The scenery of Area 10 is very varied, ranging from the stepped plateau landscape of northern Skye, Canna, Eigg and Muck, to the famously rocky peaked mountain groups of Rum and the Skye Cuillin, to the lower-lying hummocky ground of southern Skye and the highly indented coastline and mountain landscape of the mainland.

STORIES FROM THE BEDROCK

Figure 183 shows a simplified geological map of Area 10, and the main events in the evolution of the scenery are shown in Figure 184. This Area straddles the boundary between the Hebridean and the Northern Highland terranes described in Chapter 4, and the main rock-forming episodes are also discussed generally in that Chapter.

The oldest bedrock in Area 10 belongs to the Lewisian Complex, which outcrops today along the southeastern edge of the Sleat peninsula. Most of the remainder of the peninsula, along with large parts of Raasay, Scalpay, northern and eastern Rum and the mainland north of the Moine Thrust, are composed of Torridonian Sandstone.

Strongly folded and recrystallised Moine rocks, the eroded roots of the ancient Caledonian mountain belt, are found on the northwest coast of the Sleat peninsula and southeast of the Moine Thrust on the mainland. They are generally resistant to erosion, but less so where the rock is heavily jointed, folded or fractured. In places, particularly on the Morar peninsula, the Caledonian earth movements have

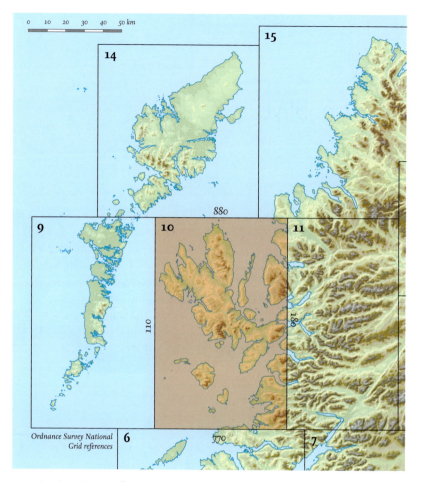

FIG 181. Location map for Area 10.

exhumed ancient Lewisian material, brought up from great depths in the crust.

Cambrian and Ordovician rocks are relatively rare in this Area, but do outcrop on the northern edge of the Sleat peninsula of Skye, in the Ord Window. Here, compressive movements associated with the Caledonian mountain building have exposed not only the Moine Thrust itself, but also a complex stack of folds and faults bringing the Cambro-Ordovician rocks up to the surface (Fig. 185). These rocks consist of shallow-marine limestones and mudstones which weather to produce low, boggy ground, together with tougher quartzites which have resisted erosion to form rounded hills.

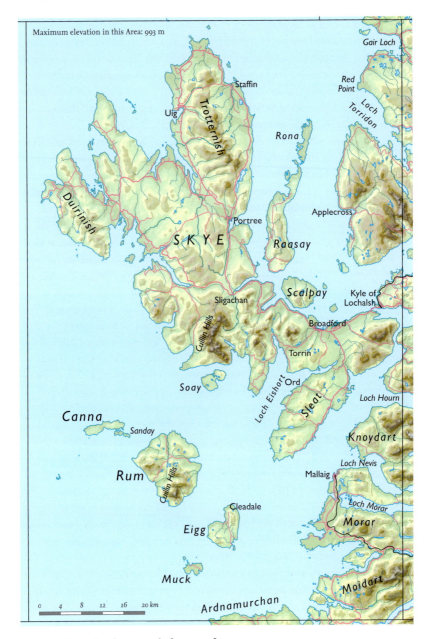

FIG 182. Natural and man-made features of Area 10.

Several kilometres to the northwest of Ord, on Skye, Cambrian and Ordovician limestones have been altered by hot liquids circulating from Tertiary igneous centres to produce the famous Skye marble. The limestone was originally rich in magnesium and also contained nodules of silica – impurities which combined to give the marble its distinctive green and yellow streaks. Skye marble was extracted from quarries at Strath Suardal for over 200 years, until their closure in 1912, and it is still quarried today just outside Torrin.

Bedrock of Devonian, Carboniferous or Permian age is not preserved anywhere in Area 10, suggesting that the region underwent net erosion during this long period. However, by the Mesozoic the crust appears to have been stretched, allowing two roughly parallel basins to subside, in which Jurassic and Cretaceous sediments began to accumulate. Most of the Cretaceous deposits were eroded away during a second uplift event 65 million years ago – when the Hebrides rose above sea level – to produce a largely flat land surface of Jurassic and older rocks. The coasts of Skye and Eigg contain particularly complete sections of the Jurassic rocks and provide excellent outcrops for studying the shallow marine, coastal, lagoonal and river environments that developed at this time.

During the early part of the Tertiary, between 61 and 58 million years ago, thick piles of horizontal or gently tilting basaltic lava flows were erupted in this Area, heralding an important episode of volcanic activity linked to the plate-tectonic opening of the Atlantic Ocean and the movement of Greenland and North America away from northwestern Europe (see Chapter 4). Today, the variably resistant lavas have produced a landscape of plateaus and regularly stepped cliffs often referred to as *trap topography*, using an old name for the fine-grained, compact lavas. The first flows formed are preserved on the islands of Muck and Eigg, while later, more extensive flows are now represented by the vast plateau of northern Skye and the Island of Canna (Fig. 186). The volcanoes responsible for this outpouring of lava were very large shield-shaped mountains which eventually connected Ireland to Scotland by an extensive lava plateau. Individual lava flows are commonly 10–15 m thick, and the overall pile was originally around 1200 m thick on Skye and up to 1800 m thick in the Hebridean Basin. Some of the recent fissure eruptions on Iceland give us an idea of what this region may have looked like at this time.

Basalt sills are another prominent feature of Area 10, particularly on the northeastern part of the Trotternish peninsula. They were extensively intruded mainly into the Jurassic strata below the lava plateau, forming gently inclined sheets up to 90 m thick. In many places, several sills have been stacked together to form a complex with a total thickness of about 250 m. Vertical columnar jointing is usually very well developed and is beautifully exposed at the famous

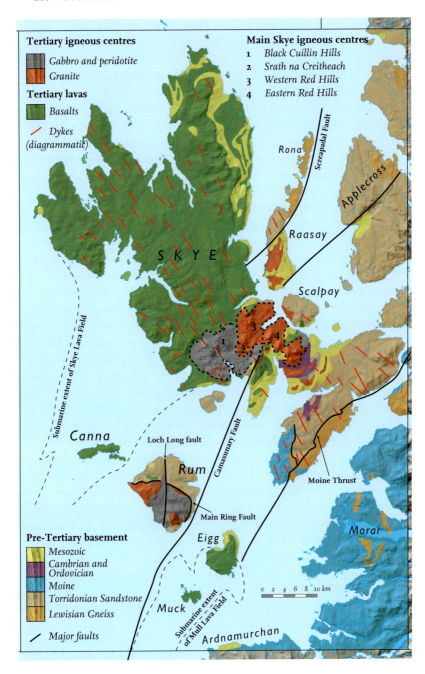

FIG 183 (OPPOSITE). Simplified geology and hill-shaded topography for Area 10. Numbers in the Central Igneous Complex of Skye refer to the volcanic centres.

Kilt Rock, south of Staffin on the Trotternish peninsula (Fig. 187). The bottom half of this 80 m-high cliff comprises horizontal layers of Jurassic rock, overlain in the upper half by a basalt sill, the vertical columns of which are reminiscent of the folds of a kilt. These hexagonal columns form during cooling, as the lava crystallises and loses volume. The surface of the flow cools first and the most efficient way for it to shrink is to do so into hexagonal shapes, leaving a crack between each hexagon. Eventually the lava will cool right through and leave deep hexagonal columns.

At roughly the same time as the plateau lavas were being erupted, localised igneous centres began to form where the Rum mountains and the Red Hills and the Cuillin of Skye now are. On Rum, magma rose through cracks in the crust and collected in a chamber a few kilometres below the surface, pushing the overlying rocks upwards to form a dome over a kilometre high and a few kilometres across. In time, the pressure on the domed rocks caused them to crack, producing a series of fractures which allowed the rocks of the dome to collapse downwards, forming a large, roughly circular crater known as a caldera (Fig. 188). The magma of the caldera was thick and sticky and so did not flow out easily. Instead, it was ejected in explosive eruptions, throwing out hot ash and fragments of volcanic rock that spread out across the caldera floor in searing-hot gas clouds called pyroclastic flows. Deposits from these flows are preserved today on the ridge between the summits of Ainshval and Sgurr nan Gillean.

As magmatic activity in this caldera waned, the silica-rich magma left in the chamber cooled slowly to form coarse-grained felsic granites, which today form the rounded western hills of the island. At roughly the same time, a second generation of magma, of different composition, rose into a slightly offset chamber, where it crystallised to form the gabbros that make up the larger, steeper peaks of the Rum Cuillin to the southeast.

On Skye, between about 61 and 55 million years ago, large volcanoes built up on top of the lava plateau, fed by deep magma chambers. The igneous rocks in this area make up the Skye Central Complex, which consists of four different volcanic centres (Fig. 183):

(1) The Black Cuillin (oldest)
(2) Srath na Creitheach
(3) The Western Red Hills
(4) The Eastern Red Hills (youngest)

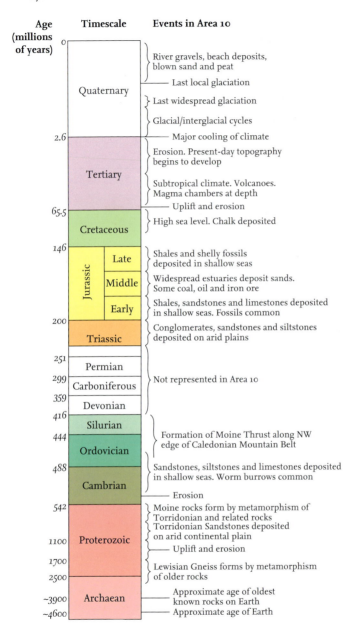

FIG 184. Timeline of bedrock and surface-layer events in Area 10.

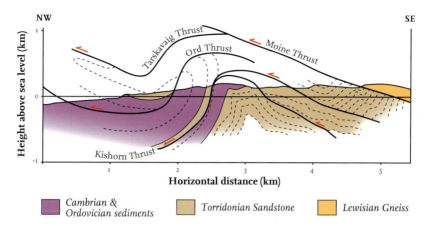

FIG 185. Cross-section through the bedrock of the Ord window (located on Fig. 182), showing that Caledonian (mid-Palaeozoic) fold and fault movements have also involved the movement of bedrock of the Lewisian Complex.

The large (approximately 15 × 10 km) Black Cuillin centre formed first, comprising mainly basic or ultra-basic magmas that eventually cooled to form the famous dark-coloured Skye gabbro. After magmatic activity had finished in the Black Cuillin, but before the emplacement of any other centres, a large number of fine-grained mafic (basaltic) dykes intruded across the region as a whole, cross-cutting the otherwise coarse-grained gabbro and the surrounding pre-Tertiary rocks. Volcanic activity then shifted eastwards and volcanoes built up around a number of smaller acidic centres which later cooled to form pinkish granites. First, the Srath na Creitheach centre was intruded into the Black Cuillin centre, followed by the emplacement of the two Red Hills centres, which together extend from Glamaig to Beinn na Caillich.

Figure 189 shows a cross-section through the area now occupied by the Skye Central Complex. It shows the structure and some of the processes operating at the time when the Black Cuillin centre was forming, and also shows how the top 2–3 km of the structure has been removed by subsequent erosion to expose the Black Cuillin and the Red Hills. The present form of this landscape on Skye is well illustrated by the aerial view of Figure 1, which was used to illustrate distinct landscape types at the beginning of this book. In the middle distance of that photograph, Jurassic sandstones and shales are overlain by flood basalts forming a line of steep cliffs not far above the road. The relatively smooth and low hills beyond this are part of the Red Hills centres, and behind them the rough-weathering Black Cuillin dominates the skyline.

FIG 186. The two-part island of Canna occupies the foreground and middle distance, linked to Sanday by a wooden bridge. Beyond is the island of Rum. Lava-flow layers (trap topography) dominate the landscape of the nearest part of Canna, although they produce an effect very like raised beaches. (© Patricia & Angus Macdonald/Aerographica)

Distinctive layering, on scales of centimetres to tens of metres, is characteristic of the gabbros of the Black Cuillin of Skye and the Cuillin of Rum. The layers of hard, pale-coloured rock stand out as distinct features of outcrops, separated by layers of brown crumbly rock on which grassy slopes have formed. This layering formed as magma cooled and crystallised within the magma chamber. On Rum and Skye, the first crystals to form were of the brownish-green mineral olivine, which sank to the base of the chamber and accumulated as a rock called peridotite, which now forms the soft, crumbly layers. As the magma continued to cool, another paler mineral – calcium feldspar – began to crystallise and sink alongside the olivine. This mix of minerals accumulated in large quantities to form a paler, harder rock called gabbro. This process (called *fractional crystallisation*) was repeated every time a new batch of hot magma was introduced into the magma chamber, producing alternating mafic peridotite and gabbro layers.

The final stage of volcanic activity in this Area formed the ridge of An Sgurr, which dominates the skyline of Eigg and represents the youngest volcanic rock preserved anywhere in Scotland (Fig. 190). The Sgurr is an irregular, lumpy ridge, reaching an elevation of 393 m, and underlain by thick layers of conglomerate which mark the position of a valley carved into the lava plateau. It is thought that, during one of the Rum volcano's last eruptions, a sticky lava of unusual

FIG 187. The Kilt Rock, northeastern Trotternish, Skye. The upper part of the coastal cliff, some 100 m high, has been eroded from a dolerite sill that had been intruded into the flat-lying Jurassic sediments. There is another sill at sea level. (© Adrian Warren/lastrefuge.co.uk)

composition flowed slowly along this valley, filling it to the brim. This lava cooled to form a pitchstone or volcanic glass, developing organ-pipe columns many tens of metres high in amazing fan-like patterns. Harder than basalt, the pitchstone has withstood erosion better than the surrounding rocks and now stands proud as a spectacular ridge. The base of the pitchstone and its contact with the underlying conglomerate are well exposed on the south side of the Sgurr Nose, where the base of the pitchstone is undercut to form a series of large overhangs, beneath which lies the baked and altered conglomerate.

MAKING THE LANDSCAPE

Tertiary valley evolution

Mapping the offshore sea depths of Area 10 has revealed a system of deep, elongate basins that have been carved in the bedrock. Such are the size of these basins that they appear to have been carved by long-continued river erosion during the Tertiary, when the offshore areas were not covered by the sea. Figure 191 shows the largest of these basins, and suggests how they may have been connected by rivers to some of the onshore river valleys.

During the Tertiary sea level was significantly lower than today and, instead of the sea, rivers flowed between the mainland and the Inner and Outer Hebrides. At this time, Torridonian and Moine bedrock was reduced to relatively low-lying hills, dissected by rivers which exploited weaknesses in the geological structure (e.g. faults, dykes and joints) to carve valleys. The portions of these valley systems currently visible on the mainland drain almost directly to the west, but the lower parts (now flooded by the sea) generally trend northwards in the north of this Area and southwestwards in the south (Fig. 191). Such diversions in the Tertiary drainage network are due mainly to large Caledonian-age faults (now offshore) with a southwest/northeast or south-southwest/north-northeast trend, and to the thick plateau lavas of the Skye lava field, which, along with the bedrock of the igneous centres, would have formed a barrier to westward flow.

The relatively warm, wet climate at this time resulted in intense weathering of the bedrock. Terracing began to develop in soils on the Torridonian and Jurassic sediments, with stronger layers forming crags and weaker layers forming heathery slopes in between. This has created a dip-and-scarp topography, well exposed throughout the Applecross peninsula and giving rise to northern Rum's well-known gently stepped landscape. Streams also developed on the young lava plateau, generally parallel to faults and fissures in the igneous bedrock. Intense river erosion eventually removed much of the original lava pile (although 300 m-high basalt cliffs are still found on Skye), finally carving the valleys now occupied by the major sea lochs of northwest and west Skye.

The trap topography of the lava plateau developed during the latter part of the Tertiary, principally due to the varying erosional resistance of different lava flows (Fig. 192). The top and bottom of a lava flow are generally softer than the central part, as these margins tend to cool and shatter during the motion of the flow, and also contain pockets of gas that are later infilled by easily eroded minerals. In addition, there was often a considerable time gap between the eruption of successive lava flows, meaning that they were subject to weathering and erosion which developed soft soil horizons, such as the red laterites found in the Storr screes. The net effect was that once igneous activity had ceased, the tops and bottoms of flows weathered much more easily than the hard central parts, producing a stepped topography of basalt cliffs and distinctive flat-topped hills. Two particularly fine examples of such hills are MacLeod's Tables, which dominate the uninhabited southern half of the Duirinish peninsula (Fig. 193). Legend has it they were used by a MacLeod chief to host a banquet for King James V on a royal visit, as part of a wager that nothing in MacLeod's Highland estate could compare to the grandeur of the King's court.

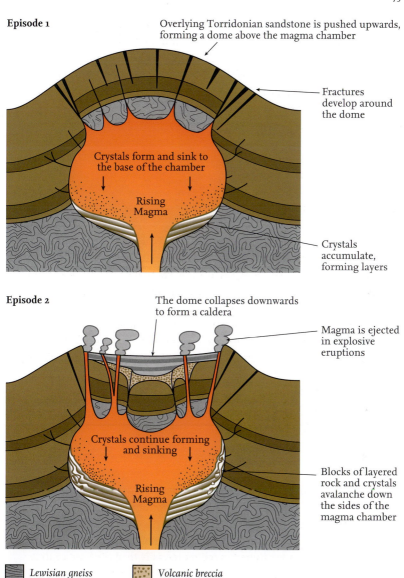

FIG 188. Two episodes in the history of the Rum caldera, illustrating the variety of surface and deep processes.

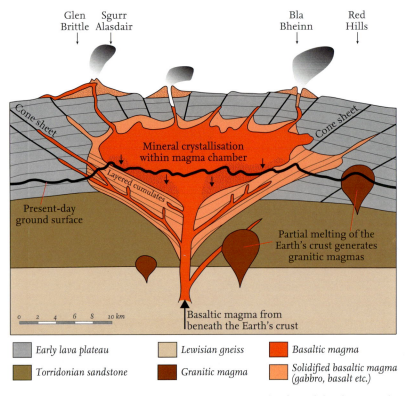

FIG 189. Diagram illustrating the structure and processes that formed the Skye Central Complex.

On Skye and Rum, late Tertiary erosion removed the tops of the Cuillin and Red Hills volcanoes to reveal the underlying sub-volcanic intrusions (Fig. 189). These coarse-grained igneous rocks were more resistant to erosion than the surrounding rocks, and so form the large, impressive hills that we see today.

River valleys often developed to exploit the soft, altered contacts between the harder igneous bodies and the surrounding rock, following lines of structural weakness. For example, Kilmory Glen on Rum largely follows the Loch Long Fault, which transects Rum in a north/south direction, whilst on Skye Glen Sligachan traces the contact between the Black Cuillin gabbro and the granite of the western Red Hills.

Within the Skye Black Cuillin, the gabbro weathered differently to the numerous basalt dykes which cross-cut it. The spectacular jagged outline of the Cuillin owes much to this differential weathering, where the dykes most

FIG 190. The striking An Sgurr ridge on Eigg, in the immediate foreground, is the remains of a lava flow that filled a former valley, and has now been isolated by subsequent erosion. The mountains of Rum, eroded from the basic igneous rocks of the Rum caldera, provide a spectacular background. (© Patricia & Angus Macdonald/Aerographica)

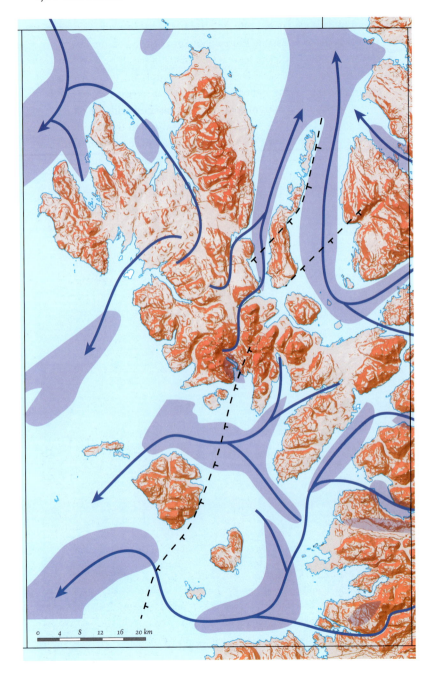

commonly tend to have weathered into notches in the gabbro ridge. One famous exception to this is the Inaccessible Pinnacle of Sgurr Dearg, formed by the weathering of two parallel dykes to leave a thin blade of basalt bedrock between.

In contrast, the Red Hills volcanic centres were emplaced after the dykes that are so abundant across this and other Hebridean areas (e.g. Areas 6 and 7). Their granites also contain a high proportion of potassium feldspar, which weathers more completely under warm, wet conditions than the calcium feldspars in the Cuillin gabbro. As a result, the granites have weathered more uniformly than the gabbros, creating characteristically smooth, rounded hills with few steep, rocky faces and extensive screes. In addition, the Red Hills volcanic centres were smaller than that of the Black Cuillin, explaining the smaller size of the Red Hills. This contrast in erosional development is illustrated on Skye, south along Glen Sligachan, with the Black Cuillin to the west and the Red Hills to the east.

FIG 191 (OPPOSITE). Slope map of Area 10, showing slopes greater than 7 degrees in red. The main offshore deep areas are also marked in darker blue, along with the drainage patterns that are likely to have formed them. Dashed lines indicate three important offshore faults.

FIG 192. Looking southeastwards over Loch Dunvegan, northwestern Skye. Trap (plateau lava) coastal landscape in the foreground, and Macleod's Tables in the background to the right. (© Patricia & Angus Macdonald/Aerographica)

FIG 193. Macleod's Tables in northwestern Skye. (© Patricia & Angus Macdonald/Aerographica)

Glacial evolution

During early periods of widespread glaciation, before some half-million years ago, most of the soils, sediments and weathered rocks formed during Tertiary and early Pleistocene times were swept away by ice, and Skye probably first became an island. During the repeated glaciations that followed, ice covered the majority of Area 10 as it flowed westwards from the higher ground further inland.

Rock fragments embedded in the bases of the ice sheets scoured and abraded the valley sides, smoothing any sharp obstacles in their path. Roches moutonnées covered in striae are found to the south of Kinloch Glen on Rum, indicating that ice once flowed from east to west in this area. During warmer phases, retreating glaciers deposited till which was then bulldozed into moraines by the re-advancing ice margins. Fine examples are seen in Glen Dibidil on southwestern Rum, and also in Glen Sligachan and on the descent from Loch Ainort towards Sconser in Skye, where the lower ground is made almost entirely of moraine ridges on top of lava.

On the mainland, ice flow took advantage of fault-lines, joints, shatter-belts and other lines of geological weakness to create knock-and-lochan topography, which is developed particularly well on the Applecross peninsula west of the Bealach na Ba pass.

The location of the knocks (rocky knolls) and lochans (small lakes) reflects the underlying bedrock and geological structure: hollows occur where shattered or less resistant rocks outcrop; more resistant rocks underlie the knolls. The hollows

FIG 194. Loch Nevis, between Knoydart and Morar on the mainland, looking eastwards. The inner rock basin of Loch Nevis is separated by a bedrock bar from the outer basin and the Sound of Sleat. (© Adrian Warren/lastrefuge.co.uk)

are often now occupied by small lakes linked by winding streams, or filled by peat bogs where these lakes became choked with vegetation. The rocky knolls are almost all bare, rounded, steep-sided hummocks. Their 'whaleback' shape is typical of glacial erosion, and their size can vary from a few metres to kilometres in length. Indeed, a large ridge of glaciated ground forms the backbone of South Morar, creating a rough terrain of rock benches, lochans and exposed, rocky summits.

On the Sleat peninsula on Skye the change in lithology from Lewisian Gneiss to Torridonian Sandstone across the Moine Thrust has been picked out by glacial erosion at Loch na Dal. Both rock types have been heavily weathered to give low, hummocky, well-rounded hills, but the gneiss has been more resistant and has formed bolder crags compared to the gentler slopes of the Torridonian. The Torridonian rocks also produce poorer, more acidic soils than those of the Lewisian, resulting in a subtle vegetation change across the fault from grassy Lewisian slopes to more heathery Torridonian.

Glacial scouring also resulted in the deepening and straightening of Tertiary drainage valleys to form glacial troughs, such as those now occupied by Loch Morar and Loch Nevis on the mainland (Fig. 194). This glacial carving led to the over-steepening of valley sides, making them unstable and resulting in rock falls and small landslides, which have produced a thin but extensive covering of scree on many valley walls, particularly below craggy sections.

During the Last (Devensian) Glacial Maximum, Skye was covered by an ice dome which enveloped all but the highest pinnacles. Reconstructions of the ice surface suggest that at the height of the glacial the ice reached a level of about 800 m in the Black Cuillin, leaving the top 50–100 m of the mountains protruding above the ice. The ice then descended gently across northern Skye, declining to an altitude of around 450 m across Duirinish, Waternish and the northern tip of Trotternish (Fig. 195). This is supported by the survival of thick accumulations of weathered, frost-shattered rock on hill tops along the Trotternish escarpment, which suggests that these summits, like those of the Black Cuillin, stood above the ice sheet as nunataks, and so escaped glacial scouring. On the other hand, in the Red Hills the ice dome covered most of the hill tops (all but the top 15 m of Glamaig is thought to have been covered), resulting in extensive ice erosion which has left smooth, rounded slopes with shallow arêtes and gentle corries.

Towards the end of the Late Glacial Maximum, meltwater from retreating glaciers dumped large amounts of sediment in fan-shaped deposits, seen for example near Loch nan Uamh, southwest of the Morar peninsula. Erratics left behind by the melting ice are also common throughout the landscape.

The lowlands of this Area have been largely ice-free since the Late Glacial Maximum of the Devensian, but the mountains of Skye and Rum have undergone a more recent episode of glacial modification during the Loch Lomond Stadial (some 13,000 to 11,500 years ago), when ice domes existed independent of the main Scottish ice sheet (Fig. 196). Today, the mountains of the Black Cuillin of Skye contain an outstanding array of glacial features, from deep, steeply walled corries, narrow arêtes and pointed horns, to 'textbook' glacial troughs such as Loch Coruisk (Fig. 197).

Landsliding

Where the plateau lavas are underlain by weaker sediments on the scarp landscapes around Eigg, and in particular Skye, some of the largest landslips in Britain can be seen. The underlying weak sediments have collapsed under the great weight of the overlying lava pile, causing massive blocks of lava to break off from the main cliff and slip downhill. The largest and freshest of these features formed within the last 15,000 years (since the Devensian glaciation), but landslide deposits occurring further away from the main escarpment moved much earlier, and have since been glacially smoothed and capped by till.

The Trotternish Ridge forms the backbone of the Trotternish peninsula and contains the widest and most famous array of these landslide features. Along the length of the ridge, enormous blocks of lava have slipped and rotated on curved

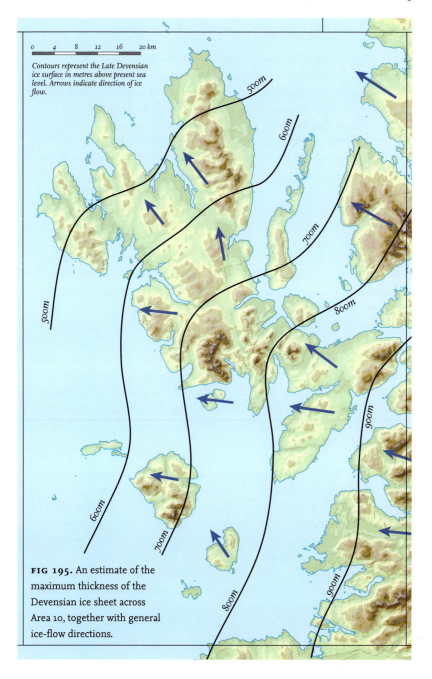

FIG 195. An estimate of the maximum thickness of the Devensian ice sheet across Area 10, together with general ice-flow directions.

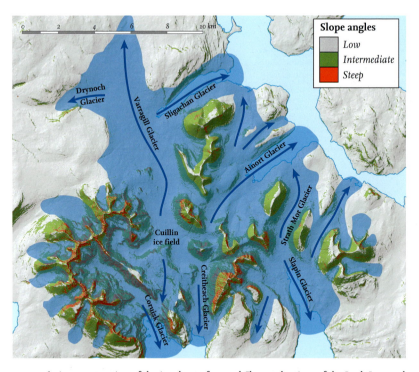

FIG 196. A reconstruction of the ice sheet of central Skye at the time of the Loch Lomond Stadial.

fracture surfaces which flatten out towards the east, so that the slipped blocks have been tilted towards the west (Fig. 198).

At the southern end of the Trotternish ridge, the Old Man of Storr is an isolated pinnacle of lava standing in front of the main escarpment of the Storr (Fig. 199). It is 50 m high and 15 m wide, perhaps the most impressive of the many pinnacles in this area, all isolated by weathering and erosion. The main part of the lava escarpment reaches its highest point here and represents at least 24 different lava flows. This cliff face is also cut by vertical gullies, which represent the weathering-out of younger basalt dykes.

At the northern end of the Trotternish ridge is the Quiraing, a huge area of landsliding where massive blocks have repeatedly detached themselves from the cliff face. The most famous of these blocks have been given names, and The Table is a green-clad plateau nestled in the midst of the Quiraing rocks. In the days of clan warfare this plateau was used to hide cattle, and in more peaceful times the Gaelic sport of shinty was played on the mostly level surface.

FIG 197. Looking north-northwest over the Black Cuillin of Skye. Glacially deepened Loch Coruisk is to the right, with the coast in the foreground. Note the typical roughness of the Cuillin bedrock surfaces. (© Patricia & Angus Macdonald/Aerographica)

Post-glacial evolution

After the ice departed, the stream drainage pattern became re-established and severe down-cutting into pre-existing valleys occurred. On the mainland, the development of many streams has been controlled by geological structures in the Moine rocks that were exaggerated by the ice, giving a dogleg appearance to some of the main water courses. For example, Borrodale Burn on South Morar has incised deeply into its valley along a southwest/northeast-trending fault, capturing waters from the main east-to-west flow.

In the areas covered by plateau lavas, the post-glacial drainage system is not well developed, with few mature rivers. This is in part due to the fact that the more mature, lower parts of the drainage system have been recently flooded by the sea during the Flandrian Transgression, leaving only the immature headwaters above sea level. As a result of this flooding, streams are generally incising in northern Skye, resulting in impressive gorges and waterfalls. Near the Kilt Rock, eastern Trotternish, Skye (Fig. 187), the Lealt River has created a dramatic cliff-edge waterfall where it descends from the edge of a large sill.

Dissolution features that developed at this time are also found in Area 10. They are particularly well developed where glacial scouring has removed the cover of soil and debris from the bedrock, exposing bare limestone to the

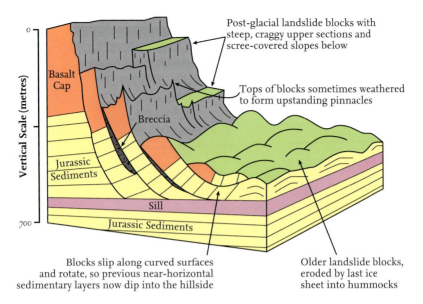

FIG 198. Diagram showing how landslipping of the exposed edge of the Trotternish slope has taken place due to rotational faulting on flat-lying, weak Jurassic sediments.

elements. This has resulted in the formation of karstic surfaces on Skye, where the Cambrian and Ordovician limestone has been dissolved along joints and cracks. Stream channels have also taken advantage of the soluble limestone, and on Skye an obvious change in the drainage pattern is seen where the Red Hills granites have intruded into Palaeozoic limestones to form marble, and streams flowing from the granite sink suddenly upon reaching the soluble marble, carving deep stream beds. A distinct vegetation change is also seen at this contact, with heather on the granite and short grass with a rich limestone flora on the well-drained marble.

Cave systems, thought to have formed during glacial/interglacial cycles, are also common in this area. Insoluble dyke rock locally forces streams to the surface, making networks of linked caves. High Pasture Cave, about 1.5 km southeast of Torrin, has over 320 m of navigable passages and is one of the longest cave complexes on Skye.

In the high mountains, the process of frost-shattering has continued since glacial times on the over-steepened valley sides and pinnacles, so that slopes everywhere are draped with scree. Perhaps the most famous example of this is the Great Stone Chute in the Black Cuillin of Skye, which falls for over 450 m from near Sgurr Alasdair's summit to the tiny tarn of Coire Lagan. Over time the

FIG 199. The Old Man of Storr and lava escarpments at the southern end of the Trotternish peninsula, Skye. (© Patricia & Angus Macdonald/ Aerographica)

rock fragments have been broken down further into finer, soil-like material, and freeze–thaw processes have sorted the particles into curious regular patterns, fine examples of which can also be seen near the summit of Orval on Rum. These features are still actively forming, whenever conditions are cold enough for ice to grow in the ground.

The formation of the coastline

The coastline of this Area is characterised by alternating high, vertical cliffs and low bays with headlands and sea stacks. The Duirinish peninsula on Skye, with its 130 km of coastline, has some of the highest sea cliffs in the Area, rising to 313 m at Biod an Athair ('Sky Cliff') and reflecting the hardness of the mafic basalt which forms most of them.

The positions of bays often correspond to changes in the bedrock geology. Applecross Bay, the location of the main settlement on the Applecross peninsula, has been carved from a soft outcrop of Jurassic limestone which has weathered recessively compared to the surrounding Torridonian sandstone (Fig. 184). In other places, such as at the Bay of Laig on Eigg and Bearreraig Bay on Skye, erosion of the Jurassic rocks by waves has created calcareous sandstone cliffs containing unusual carbonate concretions. The concretions themselves are as much as 2 m across, protruding from the cliff face and littering the rock platform below like giant cannonballs. They are thought to have formed by migration of calcium carbonate in solution that was then precipitated on a central core (concretionary growth) within the porous sediments after their burial.

In recent times sea level has fluctuated considerably, and remnants of beaches from periods of higher sea level are common around the coastal fringe. Two distinct sets of raised beaches are seen, all tilting gently west due to the glacial rebound in the east (see Chapter 5). Examples of note include a raised beach 30 m above present sea level near Broadford on Skye, from which sand and gravel are now quarried, and a wave-cut rock platform on Rum 30–40 m above present sea level that encircles almost the entire island. A lower set of raised beaches, 5–6 m above present sea level, has also been identified on Rum, at Harris, Kilmory Bay, Guirdil Bay and around Loch Scresort. In the Bay of Laig, on Eigg, a kilometre-wide stretch of raised beach, backed by high basalt cliffs, forms some of the best crofting land on the island (Fig. 200).

Some of these raised beaches are associated with long-abandoned caves, geos and sea stacks, such as those on southern Eigg, where a series of caves has been eroded out of the highly vesicular lava flows along the base of the cliffs.

FIG 200. Looking southwestwards over the island of Eigg, with the large Bay of Laig, backed by raised-beach deposits, opening to the right. On the ridge in shadow behind this bay is the Sgurr of Eigg (Fig. 190), with Ardnamurchan and the island of Muck in the distance behind. (© Patricia & Angus Macdonald/Aerographica)

CHAPTER 16

Area 11: Affric

Area 11 straddles the southern part of the spine of the Northern Highlands, extending from the Ben Nevis area (Lochaber), south of the Great Glen, to the Torridon and Loch Maree area of Wester Ross in the north (Fig. 201). The Area embraces some of the finest landscapes in Scotland, including the landward ends of many of the sea lochs of the highly indented western coastline, east of the Isle of Skye (Fig. 202).

A distinctive feature of the landscape of Area 11 is the way the central spine of the Northern Highlands is dissected by large valleys, many of them trending and opening to west and east. Some of them, such as Glen Affric and Glen Cannich, are famous in themselves, for their ancient woodland, river and loch scenery. The bedrock history of this part of northwest Scotland offers an explanation of why these distinctive valleys exist.

STORIES FROM THE BEDROCK

Chapter 4 summarised the bedrock history of Scotland as a whole, using a scheme separating nine successive episodes of bedrock formation. These episodes resulted in the main bedrock building blocks from which the history has been reconstructed. The principal bedrock types in Area 11 are shown in Figure 203, and a summary of events in the geological history of this Area is given in Figure 204.

The Greenland margin
In the northwest of this Area, west of the Moine Thrust Zone, three episodes are represented in what was labelled the Greenland margin of Scotland in Chapter 4. Two of the three episodes are amongst the oldest found in Britain.

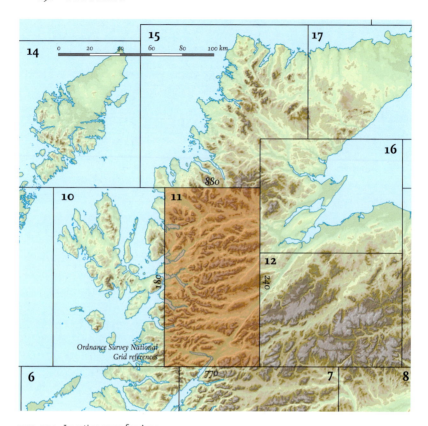

FIG 201. Location map for Area 11.

This crustal bedrock formed when northwest Scotland and southeast Greenland were part of one unified plate, before it was divided and separated by subsequent movements. Rocks of the Lewisian Complex were highly mobilised and altered during the Archaean, Mesoproterozoic and Neoproterozoic. They are the oldest metamorphic rocks preserved in Britain and have typically been eroded into the present-day knock-and-lochan landscapes that are so characteristic of the northwest Highlands.

East of the Moine Thrust Zone, bedrock surrounded by Moine Group bedrock has been interpreted as fragments of the Lewisian Complex that have been caught up and altered by later Caledonian movements.

Layered successions of Torridonian sandstones, many hundreds of metres thick, are exposed in Area 11, particularly in the large areas north and south of Glen Torridon, where some of the most dramatic mountain ranges of this

AREA 11: AFFRIC · 291

Maximum elevation in this Area: 1344 m

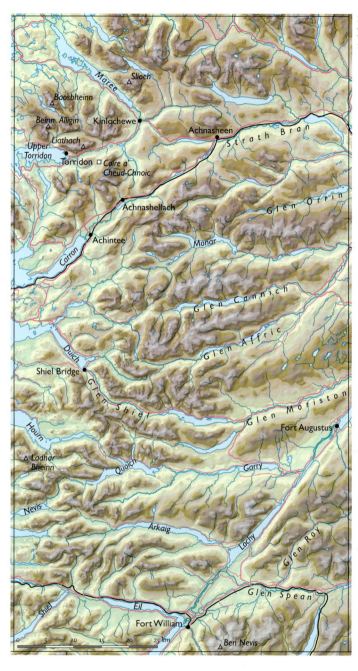

FIG 202. Natural and man-made features of Area 11.

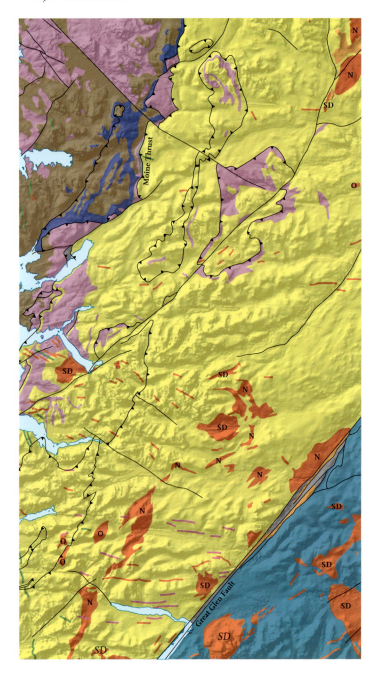

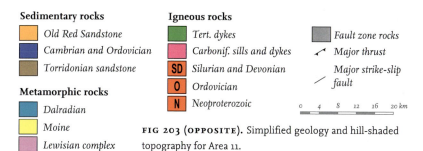

FIG 203 (OPPOSITE). Simplified geology and hill-shaded topography for Area 11.

material occur. Erosion of the slopes has picked out the very obvious layering, formed during the Mesoproterozoic and Neoproterozoic as the depositing rivers migrated to and fro across the alluvial surfaces that existed over much of the Hebridean Basin around 1 billion years ago.

Within the Moine Thrust Zone, distinctive Cambrian to Ordovician quartzites, shales and dolomitic limestones have often provided weak crustal materials that influenced the movements that occurred in the zone. These sediments were deposited under the shallow sea and coastal conditions that existed across northwest Scotland between 540 and 480 million years ago. The quartzites that were deposited on a landscape of much older Torridonian sediments produce almost snow-like white screes on the summit ridges of some of the mountains of this Area.

In the area around Loch Maree and Glen Torridon, and particularly on the mountain Slioch (Fig. 205), the unconformity between the Lewisian basement and the overlying Torridonian shows very clearly the contrast in the weathering and erosion behaviour of the two materials. It also provides vivid insight into the nature of the landscape some billion years ago when the Torridonian sediments were starting to accumulate on the Lewisian surface. This is because the present topography contains enough in the way of mountains and valleys to allow the contact to be traced in three dimensions, revealing ancient valleys up to 800 m deep that were eroded in the Lewisian, and then filled by sediment as the Torridonian accumulated between 900 and 800 million years ago (Fig. 206).

The core of the Caledonian mountains

Folded and altered sediments of the Moine and Dalradian supergroups occur to the northwest and southeast respectively of the Great Glen Fault Zone. They represent parts of the most deformed and metamorphosed central parts of the Caledonian mountain belt, and occur as the bedrock over most of Area 11. The most obvious fold trend is north-northeast to south-southwest, where it is picked out by mapping different rock types that have resulted from the alteration of sediments with different proportions of mud, sand and lime. These folds clearly represent major movement of the crustal rocks by compression in a west-northwest/east-southeast direction, but it is remarkable how little this fold trend is apparent in the slope patterns visible over a 1–10 km scale.

Coarsely crystalline igneous intrusions, often of granitic composition, but also locally more basic (gabbroic), occur scattered throughout the Area. These range in age of intrusion from Neoproterozoic, through Ordovician, Silurian and Devonian, and represent melting and intrusion of igneous material within the main core of the Caledonian metamorphic crust.

Britain's highest mountain, Ben Nevis (1344 m; Figs 207, 208), is the result of erosion of one of these intrusive igneous complexes, and the level of erosion has been just right to reveal that cauldron subsidence has taken place. A fragment of outer continental crust consisting of Silurian or Devonian lava, other volcanic material and sediment has subsided some hundreds of metres into the upper part of the intruding granite body during the activity of this igneous centre (Fig. 209).

Only minor amounts of Late Silurian to Early Devonian sedimentary bedrock are represented in this Area, except in the Great Glen Fault Zone, where the Lower Old Red Sandstone is locally present. It tends to have been preferentially eroded to form low ground during the making of the present landscape.

Post-Caledonian bedrock

Late Palaeozoic (Late Devonian, Carboniferous and Permian) and Mesozoic sediments are not represented in the bedrock of Area 11, except within the Great Glen Fault Zone, where it has been preserved, although preferentially eroded by Tertiary and Quaternary erosion.

In early Tertiary times, emplacement of dykes took place in many parts of Area 11, and this is the main evidence of activity associated with the important volcanic activity to the west in the area of the Isle of Skye (Area 10), as discussed in the next paragraphs.

MAKING THE LANDSCAPE

Tertiary landscape evolution

The remarkable series of east/west-trending, open-ended valleys are large erosional features of the landscape of the highland spine of Area 11, and suggest a long history of erosion, probably extending through much of the Tertiary. A north/south cross-section through Glens Cannich, Affric and Moriston (Loch

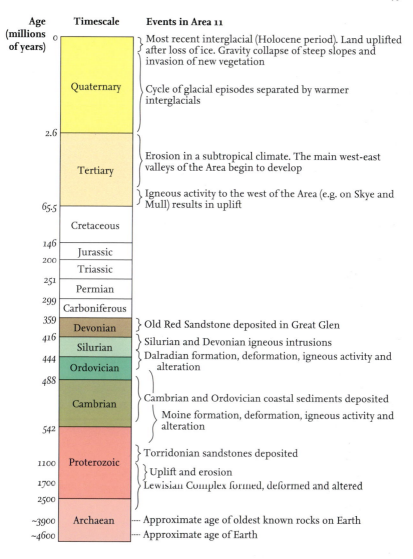

FIG 204. Timeline of bedrock and surface-layer events in Area 11.

Cluanie) illustrates the typical cross-sections of some of these valleys (Fig. 210).

To the west of Area 11, extensive Early Tertiary lava fields, dating from between 60 and 55 million years ago, are distinctive features of the Isle of Skye and other Hebridean islands, and are extensive in the sea-covered surroundings of these

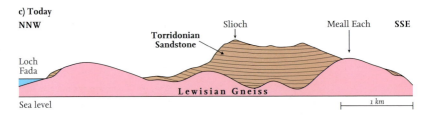
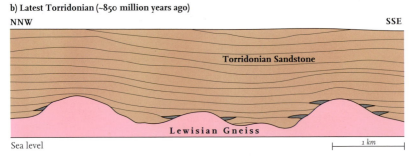
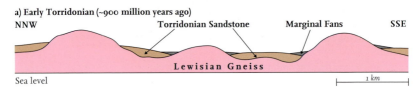

FIG 205. Cross-section through Slioch at the head of Loch Maree, suggesting the sequence of landscapes involved. Note the shaded triangles attached to slopes in the unconformity represent fans of conglomerate deposited by local Torridonian streams.

islands (Chapter 4 and Fig. 183). This extrusive volcanic activity was also associated with the intrusion of igneous sills, and both appear to represent a phase of vigorous igneous activity linked to Area-wide uplift of the surface of the crust. This uplift is likely to have generated a regional easterly slope across Area 11, which may in turn have been responsible for the remarkable series of Tertiary valleys that we now see trending to the east (Fig. 211).

Glacial landscape evolution

Our latest understanding of the history of climate fluctuations (see Chapter 5) has shown that about 2.6 million years ago, at the beginning of the Pleistocene period, general cooling became pronounced around much of the Earth. At the same time fluctuations in temperature became pronounced, and those showing

FIG 206. Liathach on the north side of Glen Torridon, looking west-northwest. The snow picks out the massive nature of the Torridonian Applecross Group mountains, and the near-horizontal layering that reflects the lateral movement of the rivers that deposited these Torridonian sandstones. (© Lorne Gill, Scottish Natural Heritage)

FIG 207. Looking northwest, with the Mamore ridge in the foreground and middle distance. Ben Nevis and Carn Mor Dearg are the higher peaks in the distance. (© Patricia & Angus Macdonald/Aerographica)

FIG 208. Looking south-southeast, the three ridge in the middle distance are Aonach More, Carn Mor Dearg and Ben Nevis. (© Patricia & Angus Macdonald/Aerographica/ Scottish Natural Heritage)

an average frequency of about a quarter of a million years are particularly clear. Detailed information on how these climate changes influenced conditions on land in Britain is limited to the last few hundred thousand years, because early evidence has tended to be removed by later cold periods involving glaciation. This is particularly so for Scotland, where most detailed evidence is restricted to the last few tens of thousands of years, the later phases of the Devensian glaciation.

Much of Area 11 was occupied by the ice field that developed during the Loch Lomond Stadial (between 13,000 and 11,500 years ago), and detailed patterns of retreat of this ice front have been suggested (Fig. 212). Outside the maximum extent of this ice field, directions of flow during the Late Devensian maximum are very generalised.

The details of the local retreat of this Loch Lomond Stadial ice sheet have been worked out by investigation of the deposits left behind locally, and the way these relate to features of the bedrock topography. A famous example of a large area of hummocky moraines is at the Coire a'Cheud-Chnoic ('Corrie of a Hundred Hills') in Glen Torridon (Fig. 213). Other examples of deposits left behind during the late stages of glacial retreat include patches of coarse rock debris that occur in some glacial corries, where they appear to be the results of the collapse of the back walls of the corries onto the snow and ice that were still present on the corrie floors.

Not only is the geographic extent of the Loch Lomond Stadial ice field known, but the maximum thickness of the ice has locally been recorded by *trim lines* on certain mountain tops. The trim line is over 900 m above sea level on Ladhar

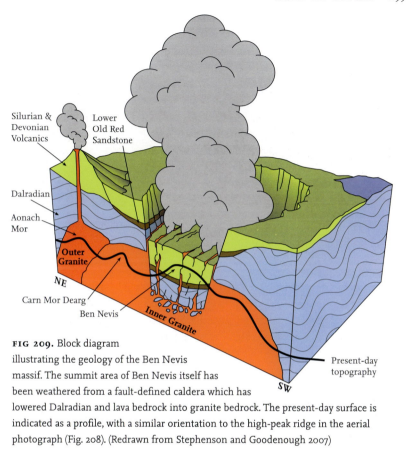

FIG 209. Block diagram illustrating the geology of the Ben Nevis massif. The summit area of Ben Nevis itself has been weathered from a fault-defined caldera which has lowered Dalradian and lava bedrock into granite bedrock. The present-day surface is indicated as a profile, with a similar orientation to the high-peak ridge in the aerial photograph (Fig. 208). (Redrawn from Stephenson and Goodenough 2007)

Beinn, to the south of Loch Hourn near the western edge of Area 11, but it has been measured at only 500 m near the Scottish north coast, showing the decline of the general elevation of the ice field in that direction.

Glen Roy, some 20 km northeast of Ben Nevis, is classic ground because of the 'Parallel Roads' that are so beautifully developed there, as a series of three parallel terraces cut into the bedrock of the slopes of the glen (Fig. 214). Similar terraces occur in nearby glens, although usually not so clearly a set of three. Charles Darwin visited the area shortly after his return from the *Beagle* expedition, during which he had seen striking evidence of upward movement of the land along the South American coast. Although he initially felt that the Glen Roy terraces were marine coastal features, he later accepted that they had been formed by the erosion of shorelines along the margins of lakes temporarily dammed up by

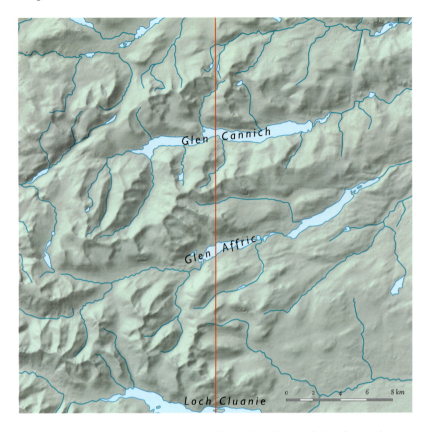

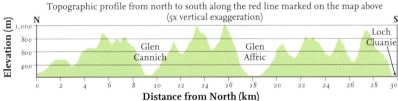

FIG 210. Hill-shade map of 30 × 30 km sample area, illustrating the topography of the Tertiary valley systems of Glens Cannich, Affric and Moriston (Loch Cluanie). A vertical topographic profile down the centre of the map, north to south along easting 215, is shown, with 5× vertical exaggeration.

local glaciers (Fig. 215). The Glen Roy terraces occur at elevations of 260, 325 and 350 m above sea level, and are thought to have been eroded as the local lake levels increased when glaciers advanced, changing the drainage configuration of the

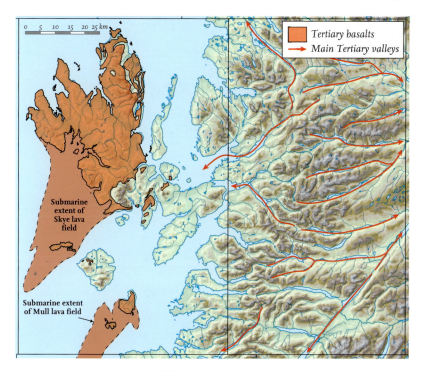

FIG 211. Areas 10 (Skye) and 11 (Affric), showing the extent of the Early Tertiary lava. The general trends of the large valleys of Area 11 may have been initiated by rivers flowing down the down-to-the east surface tilt generated after the extrusion of the lavas.

lakes and the outlets to the lakes. When the ice retreated there was a sudden and probably violent release of water, leaving the old lake shorelines high and dry.

The formation of the coastline

At its maximum extent (Chapter 5), the Late Devensian ice sheet is estimated to have extended up to 200 km west of the present coastlines represented in the sea lochs and coasts to the west of Area 11. It is not surprising, therefore, that erosional modification of the landscape at the base of this ice sheet has wiped out evidence for earlier coast features in this Area.

In the areas to the west (Area 11) and southwest (Area 7), relative sea level since the Devensian Late Glacial Maximum appears to have been about 50 m higher than at present. Since that time the crust has been rising or rebounding, due to the melting and unloading of the ice. Because the main ice load was centred on the present-day northwest Highlands (see above), the amount of uplift has been

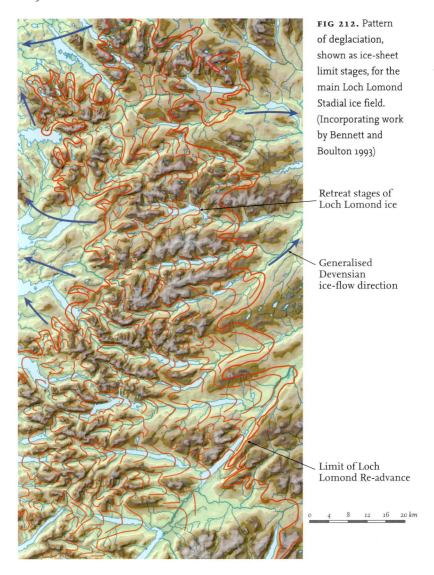

FIG 212. Pattern of deglaciation, shown as ice-sheet limit stages, for the main Loch Lomond Stadial ice field. (Incorporating work by Bennett and Boulton 1993)

Retreat stages of Loch Lomond ice

Generalised Devensian ice-flow direction

Limit of Loch Lomond Re-advance

greatest in the areas of thickest ice and has decreased rapidly westwards to almost nil in the area of the Minch.

A well-defined platform inland from a raised cliff line provides typically clear evidence in Applecross, southwest of Torridon, for recent rapid uplift of the land relative to sea level.

FIG 213. Ground moraine deposits left by the last stages of retreating ice, Coire a'Cheud-Chnoic, Torridon. (© Lorne Gill, Scottish Natural Heritage)

FIG 214. Three 'Parallel Roads' in mid Glen Roy at 260 m, 325 m and 350 m above sea level. (© Patricia & Angus Macdonald/Aerographica/Scottish Natural Heritage)

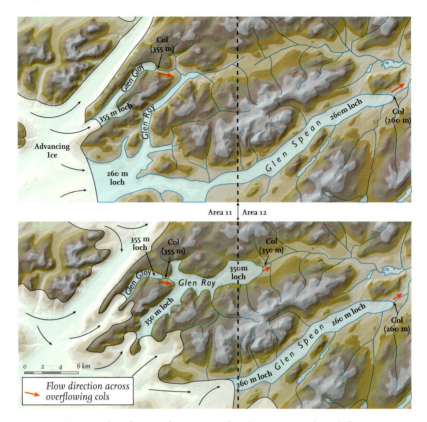

FIG 215. Two episodes of terrace formation in the Glen Roy area, where different configurations of glacier ice produced different lake levels with corresponding terraces and overflow cols. In Glen Roy itself, lake levels stood at 260 m elevation, and then stood at 325 m (not shown) and 350 m before retreat of the ice caused rapid draining of the lakes. (Redrawn from Peacock, Gordon and May 2004)

Post-glacial landscape evolution

The main evidence for the landscape evolution that has taken place since the Loch Lomond Stadial ice sheet disappeared comes from study of plant pollen preserved in the accumulations of recent lakes or bogs. An example of this sort of approach has shown how pine, birch and oak have become established after initial fluctuations over the last 10,000 years in the area of Loch Maree.

CHAPTER 17

Area 12: Cairngorm

THERE ARE NO PRESENT-DAY COASTLINES in Area 12, and the largest natural landscape features are the ranges of mountains and the valleys that separate them (Fig. 216). Large valleys that provide a useful first division of the Area are, from west to east, the Great Glen valley (Glen Mor), the Spey valley and the headwaters of the Dee (Fig. 217). Many other smaller valley systems form the upper parts of the Findhorn, Deveron, Don, North Esk, South Esk and Tay catchments, draining the edges of this Area (see Fig. 7, Chapter 2).

Near the centre of the Area are the Cairngorm Mountains, the 'Jewel in the Crown' of the eastern Grampians, and the largest area in Britain with an elevation greater than 4000 feet (1219 m) above sea level. These mountains are not only special in terms of their elevation, but also have unique features of local landscape and biodiversity, all linking back ultimately to their bedrock geology and landscape evolution. So it is natural that a special Cairngorms National Park was designated in 2003, and that many matters of planning and policy are now considered by the Cairngorms National Park Authority (CNPA) as well as other bodies.

Much less famous, but providing an interesting comparison, are the Monadhliath Mountains that lie between the Great Glen and Spey valley systems. It is intriguing to contrast the landscapes of these two mountain areas.

STORIES FROM THE BEDROCK

Metamorphic rocks

The oldest types of bedrock in Area 12 are metamorphic, and they form about 80 per cent of the Area (Fig. 218). Recent generalisation by the British Geological Survey of the geological mapping divide this bedrock into an older Moine

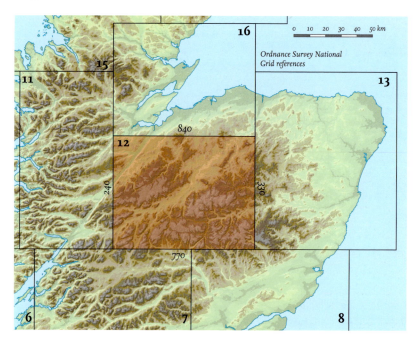

FIG 216. Location map for Area 12.

Supergroup to the northwest and north (in both the Northern Highland and Grampian Highland terranes), and a younger Dalradian Supergroup to the southeast (Fig. 219).

Most of this metamorphic bedrock was originally formed as mud or sand deposited in surface environments (Fig. 220). Material typical of the Moine Supergroup was deposited largely as layers of sand, with variable amounts of mud, and these were later altered into metamorphic *psammites* or *semi-pelites*. In contrast, the Dalradian Supergroup was deposited as a succession of more distinctive rock types, not only of sand and mud, but also of lime-rich sediments, glacial sediments, volcanic lavas and volcanic ashes. This greater variety of mineralogy and chemistry has resulted, after prolonged erosion and weathering, in local landscapes of more varied topography and vegetation, making it easier to follow distinctive layers across the landscape.

These metamorphic rocks were initially formed during the long period between about 1 billion and 500 million years ago, from the early Neoproterozoic to the Cambrian. However, it is clear that the original formation and subsequent alteration were far from steady or continuous. Ongoing studies of the complex histories of initial formation, folding and metamorphism have shown that

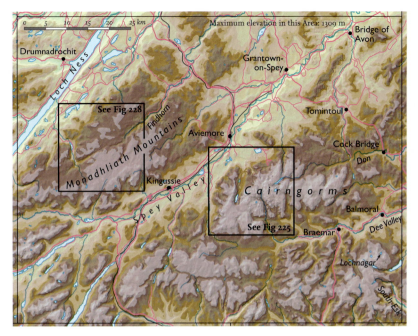

FIG 217. Natural and man-made features of Area 12.

episodes of movement and new mineral growth occurred at about 870, 800, 740, 600, 470 and 430 million years ago. Not only does this illustrate the complexity of the crustal evolution, in both space and time, but it also tends to show how fragmentary the evidence is. At least, evidence from elsewhere in Britain and Scandinavia for the Grampian (470 million years ago) and the Scandian (430 million years ago) episodes can be usefully integrated with general understanding of the evolution of the Caledonian convergent mountain belt across Britain and Scandinavia (see Chapter 4).

Caledonian intrusions

About 15 per cent of the bedrock at the present surface of Area 12 consists of coarse-grained igneous rock that was intruded from below, and then cooled and solidified before becoming exposed by surface erosion. Some of the intrusions are broadly of mafic (gabbroic) composition and were emplaced during Grampian Caledonian times (about 470 million years ago). These are mainly features of central and eastern Aberdeenshire, where they tend to have been eroded to produce landscapes at a similar elevation to the surrounding metamorphic bedrock.

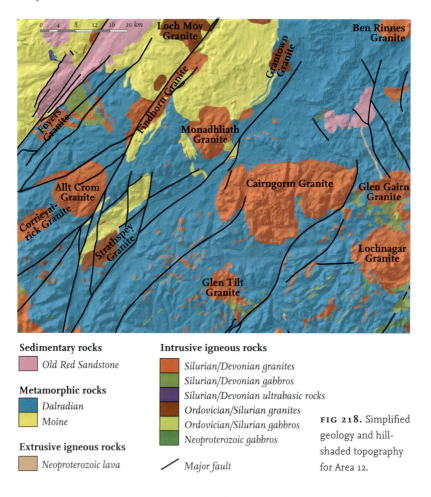

Sedimentary rocks
■ Old Red Sandstone

Metamorphic rocks
■ Dalradian
■ Moine

Extrusive igneous rocks
■ Neoproterozoic lava

Intrusive igneous rocks
■ Silurian/Devonian granites
■ Silurian/Devonian gabbros
■ Silurian/Devonian ultrabasic rocks
■ Ordovician/Silurian granites
■ Ordovician/Silurian gabbros
■ Neoproterozoic gabbros
／ Major fault

FIG 218. Simplified geology and hill-shaded topography for Area 12.

In contrast, many of the felsic (granite) intrusions are younger, and were often formerly known as the 'Younger Granites'. They have often resisted erosion because of their material properties, producing higher present-day ground. The two clearest examples of this are the Cairngorms Mountains, which have largely been eroded from one large granite intrusion, and the nearby massif of Lochnagar. These granites were intruded during Scandian Caledonian times (about 430 million years ago) and are grouped as 'Late Silurian and Devonian' (SD) on the latest British Geological Survey general map, UK North.

Some of these areas of intrusive bedrock have been cut by fractures or faults that have acted as channels for the upward passage of hot waters from within

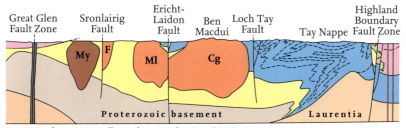

My: *Moy pluton* **F:** *Findhorn pluton* **Ml:** *Monadhliath pluton* **Cg:** *Cairngorms pluton*

FIG 219. Simplified cross-section showing the bedrock geology across Area 12, from northwest (left) to southeast (right). See Figure 218 for key to colours.

the deeper parts of the intrusion. These hot waters were rich in various chemical components that locally caused alteration of the surrounding rocks and the growth of ore bodies, sometimes rich in ore minerals, though these have rarely been economic in this Area.

Old Red Sandstone

Mudstones, sandstones, conglomerates and lavas of late Silurian and Devonian age (say 430 to 400 million years old) occur in often rather isolated areas across Area 12, mainly around the Great Glen and near Tomintoul. Apart from the conglomerates these deposits tend not to have resisted erosion, so outcrops are rare. The deposits have not been metamorphosed. They rest on the metamorphic rocks and Caledonian intrusions just described, showing that they were formed as a result of subsequent surface modification of a landscape made of these older rocks. They provide fragments of evidence of the landscape that existed after the main Caledonian movements were over.

Tertiary episodes

In Chapter 5, we used our introductory review of landscape history of the whole of Scotland to develop the idea that the large valley systems visible now have been eroded over tens of millions of years, stretching back through most of the Tertiary. Conditions of upwards movement of the Earth's crust, and of climate, have varied during this long period, and therefore so has erosion. Nevertheless it seems clear that landscape erosion of features, particularly the size of the major valleys, must be much older than the obvious erosion caused by Ice Age processes. The same may well be true of the small valley systems, but it has not yet proved possible to put numerical dates on the duration of these erosion histories.

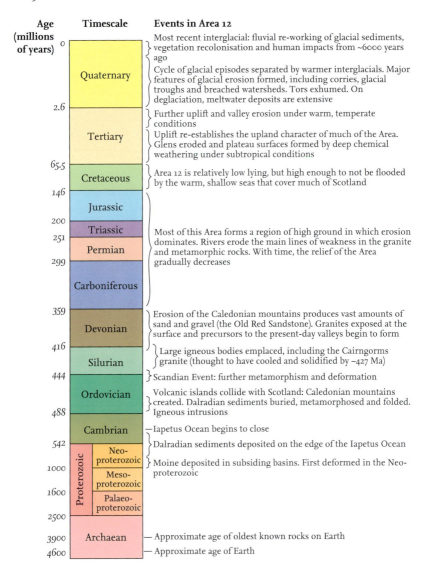

FIG 220. Timeline of bedrock and surface-layer events in Area 12.

Tors on the high granite plateau

Tors are distinctive isolated groups of jointed outcrops of granite, projecting from relatively flat or gently undulating landscape. Well-known examples of tors are those of Dartmoor in the southwest of England. The finest Scottish examples are from the northern and eastern Cairngorms. The summit plateau of Ben Avon (10 km north of Braemar) contains several distinct groups of tors, and the largest tors are probably those named the Barns of Bynack (15 km southeast of Aviemore), which reach up to 30 m above the local plateau surface. Figure 233 (Chapter 18) shows tors on the eastern granite of Bennachie, just over 30 km northwest of Aberdeen.

All these examples of tors are made of granite bedrock, and are cut by systems of joints or cracks typical of large volumes of granite bedrock that became fractured, either when the intrusive material cooled or when the confining pressure of overlying rock was removed by erosion, allowing the granite to expand. It is believed that widespread erosion has occurred across the granite landscape of these areas, perhaps under tropical conditions during Tertiary times, and possibly continuing during the very varied climatic conditions of the Ice Age. The tors appear to be occasional relicts of granite that have been left behind by this widespread erosion.

The Great Glen

There is ample evidence that this valley has developed by erosion along the Great Glen Fault Zone (Fig. 221). This zone stands out dramatically because of its straightness and its influence on the shape of the Scottish coastline, and it has been claimed to be the most obvious feature of British bedrock geology to be visible from space!

In late Silurian and Devonian times (around 430 to 400 million years ago), Old Red Sandstone accumulated along a valley that was oriented in the direction of the fault zone. Consideration of the regional geology shows that during this time the Northern Highland and Grampian Highland terranes were being forced together by widespread movement, which also involved fracture movement along, and parallel to, the line of the Great Glen. Left-lateral strike-slip movement was dominant, starting in Scandian, mid-Silurian times, about 430 million years ago. Movements along parallel faults, and in a similar left-lateral strike-slip sense, seem to have been a feature of much of the core of the Caledonian mountains at this time.

Fault scarps and deformed Mesozoic strata along the line of the Great Glen Fault Zone, north of Inverness (in Area 16), provide evidence of younger movement, mainly right lateral, during late Mesozoic and possibly even Tertiary times.

Contrasts in the bedrock types resulting from these episodes of movement in the crust must have produced contrasts in resistance to erosion that may explain the low-lying elongation of much of the Great Glen. However, in many parts, its

FIG 221. Looking southwestwards along the Great Glen, with Loch Ness in the foreground and Drumnadrochit and Urquhart Castle in the bay to the right. (© Adrian Warren/lastrefuge.co.uk)

form does not correspond to differences in bedrock, and must therefore be due to the channelling of river action during the millions of years of the Tertiary.

In Area 12, the central fault of the Great Glen Fault Zone runs along the length of Loch Ness, covered by its exceptionally deep waters. This major valley relief appears to be due to erosion by repeated ice streams during the Ice Age, and will be considered further below.

The Spey and Dee valleys

From Loch Laggan in the southwest, via Kingussie to Grantown-on-Spey in the northeast, the broad, slightly winding course of the Spey Valley forms a major low-elevation feature extending across the Grampian Highlands. So also does the course of the upper Dee, as it flows easterly towards the North Sea. In both cases the courses of the valleys are not straight, and curves relate to junctions with tributaries. The courses also locally show dramatic branches around hills that now stand as isolated erosional features of the broader valley, as at Ballater on the Dee, just east of the edge of Area 13 (Aberdeen). These features provide evidence of changes that have occurred in the complex history of erosion during many episodes of river, glacial and climate change.

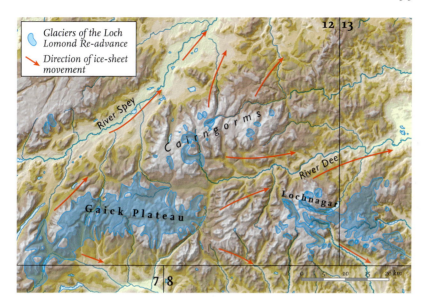

FIG 222. Overall ice-sheet movement for Area 12, and suggested limits of ice sheets during the Loch Lomond Stadial.

MAKING THE LANDSCAPE

During the Ice Age

Deep features of Scotland's surface provide strong evidence for glacial erosion by ice streams during the Ice Age. Apart from Loch Morar in Areas 10 and 11 (337 m deep), Loch Ness, partly in Area 12, is the deepest lake in Britain at 230 m. Its deepest point is thus about 215 m below sea level, and, traversing westwards, you would need to travel as far as the edge of the Atlantic continental shelf, a distance of about 300 km from the western edge of Area 12, before encountering a greater depth.

In Chapter 5, recent research was summarised that makes it clear that the there were large numbers of episodes of ice-sheet growth and retreat during the 2.6 million years of the Pleistocene. The last million years, or so, included several of these glaciations that are known, in a fragmentary way, from evidence in central and southern England, but are hardly known at all from evidence in Scotland. In Scotland, the last (Devensian) glaciation seems to have obliterated most earlier traces. However, the Devensian evidence from Scotland is fresh, and provides vivid evidence of the glacial processes that have been active (Fig. 222).

FIG 223. An aerial oblique view west-northwest across Glen Dee to the flat-topped plateau of Cairn Toul, with the beautifully regular corries eroded in its frontal face. Strathspey and the Monadhliath Mountains are beyond. (© Scottish Natural Heritage)

The valleys and mountains of Area 12 contain such an abundance of glacial features formed during the Devensian, that it seems best to select two smaller (20 × 20 km) sub-areas for examination (located on Fig. 217). The larger scale possible for these sub-area maps allows landscape details to be examined more fully, and we have selected parts of the Cairngorm and Monadhliath Mountains for this treatment.

Cairngorms

One of the remarkable kilometre-scale landscape effects in the Cairngorms is the contrast between the gently undulating landscapes of areas of high plateau and the distinct, sharp-edged corries with steep cliffs that have been eroded around the edges of those plateau areas (Figs 223, 224). The corries are often remarkably semicircular in the plan-view form of their cliffs. They most commonly face between north and east, and these directions would be expected because snow accumulates preferentially when sheltered more from daily heating by the sun. The corries range in width between some 300 m and over 1 km, and on the whole

FIG 224. Looking northwestwards across Glen Dee towards the plateau of Cairn Toul (1291 m) and Braeriach (1296 m) with the same corries as seen in Figure 223 facing towards the camera. (© Patricia & Angus Macdonald/Aerographica/Scottish Natural Heritage)

the larger corries are thought to be older. Much of the corrie erosion probably occurred in the latest Devensian and during the Loch Lomond Advance, between 13,000 and 11,500 years ago. The floors of the corries often show fresh end and side moraines, representing the last stages in the retreat of their small glaciers.

In contrast, the high, gently undulating plateau seems likely to be much older, if only because of the way its undulation surface is cut across sharply by the young corries. Another point is that the surface cover of most of the plateau areas of the Cairngorms lacks erratics from the areas of surrounding metamorphic bedrock. This suggests that these plateau areas were not overridden by thicknesses of ice capable of bringing such material from the south and west. Present-day patterns of ice distribution in partially glaciated areas in east Greenland and Spitsbergen often display high plateaus of limited extent with relatively thin ice that is often frozen solid to the underlying bedrock. These plateaus are often surrounded by deeply entrenched ice-stream glaciers that are typically fast-moving and wet or unfrozen on their bases. Occasional steep and narrow side glaciers may link the plateaus to the ice streams below. This may have been the situation in the high Cairngorm plateau.

The most obvious kilometre-scale features of the Cairngorm landscape (Fig. 225) are the elongate valleys, often with steep cliffed slopes and truncated spurs, that have given the valleys U-shaped cross-sectional profiles. These would

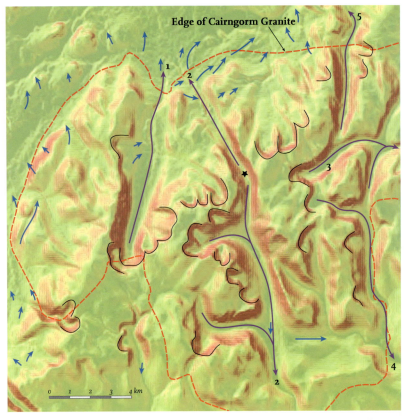

FIG 225. Slope map of 20 × 20 km Cairngorm sub-area, located on Figure 217. Note the major corries, ice-stream valleys, glacial breaches and post-glacial meltwater channels.

have been eroded by the major ice streams of the east Greenland and Spitsbergen model. Glen Einich, the Lairig Ghru and Glen Avon are some of the largest of these valleys in the Cairngorm sub-area, and they have clearly been eroded by active ice streams or glaciers. In the case of the higher parts of the Lairig Ghru, the U-shaped cross-sectional profile has been infilled by subsequent debris-flow deposits, with slopes of uniform angles that have recreated a V-shaped cross-valley profile (Fig. 226). Whereas Glen Einich is a northward-draining valley with a closed upstream end, the fame of the Lairig Ghru rests on the way it traverses

FIG 226. Looking southeastwards from near the summit of the Lairig Ghru pass. Note the apron of debris-flow tongues on the mountain side to the right. (© Lorne Gill, Scottish Natural Heritage)

across the high Cairngorm landscape, opening to north and south. This must reflect a history of erosion by two valley systems converging from both northerly and southerly directions. With changing climatic conditions, northward and southward ice streams must have alternated in importance, so that the bedrock summit moved its location, becoming lower. The present elevation is some 835 m, compared with the 1100 m, or more, of the plateau to west and east.

Monadhliath Mountains

The Monadhliath Mountains cover a rather similar area to the Cairngorms, but are further west (Fig. 217), and are much less visited because they lack many of the distinctive landscape features (Fig. 227). They are also even more lacking in tracks and roads for access. One exception, however, is the Corrieyairack Pass (764 m), famous for General Wade's military road, which was built in the eighteenth century to link Fort Augustus in the Great Glen, via Glen Tarff, to the Spey Valley near Garva Bridge and on to Laggan. This route cuts across the western edge of Area 12.

If kilometre-scale features of the Cairngorm sub-area are compared with those of a similar-scale sub-area in the western Monadhliath Mountains (Fig. 228), some interesting contrasts become clear. The Monadhliath Mountains consist of a range of bedrock types, though the mountains are made predominantly of Dalradian metamorphic bedrock and the granitic intrusions are smaller and

FIG 227. Over Kingussie, looking northeastwards down Strathspey, with the Monadhliath Mountains to the left. (© Patricia & Angus Macdonald/Aerographica/Scottish Natural Heritage)

more scattered. Probably because of this, the mountains are generally lower than those of the Cairngorms. The highest top, Carn Dearg, is only 945 m in elevation (compared with 1309 m for Ben Macdui, the highest point of the Cairngorms), and most of the tops range between 600 and 700 m. Slopes steeper than 20 degrees occur towards the Great Glen area, where they appear to have been formed by erosional contrast in the bedrock due to major intrusions.

In the central part of Figure 228, the steeper slopes around Glen Markie reflect active erosion by the local river systems where bedrock faults have resulted in straight erosional courses of the valleys. Further east the Findhorn dendritic-river valley system again provides steeper slope evidence of valley incision, which in the main Findhorn trunk river has been controlled to an extent by a fault system. To the southeast, branching corrie systems suggest glacial back-cutting from the main Spey valley, and there is an apparently fault-controlled linear valley flowing towards Laggan while the other end of the same fault system controls the linear direction of one of the main branches of the Findhorn system. Fault control of valley location and directions is clearly part of the formation of the Monadhliath landscape, and it seems likely that many of the faults were Scandian in age (see above). Breach-point summits occur between systems 2 and

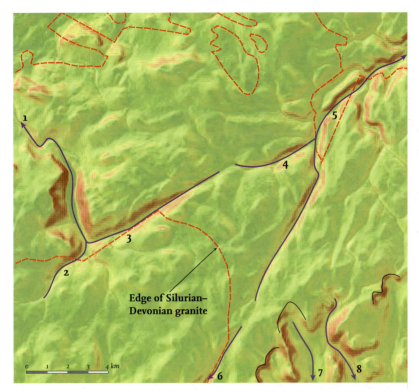

Slope

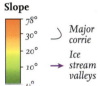

→ Ice stream valleys

↪ Major corrie

FIG 228. 20 × 20 km sub-area in the Monadhliath Mountains, located on Figure 217. Red dashed lines mark the outer limits of two groups of Silurian–Devonian felsic granite intrusive bodies in the southwestern and northern parts of the sub-area. Numbers indicate: (1) Fechlin, (2) Odhar, (3) northern Glen Markie, (4) Eskin, (5) Findhorn, (6) southern Glen Markie, (7) Gleann Lochain, (8) Gleann Ballach.

3, and 5 and 7, again suggesting alternations of ice-stream dominance in some of the valleys.

The main difference between the two sub-areas lies in the greater elevation of the Cairngorms, and the sharp distinction there between high plateaus and young corries. It may be that the Monadhliath Mountains received great precipitation, being further west, and suffered greater general erosion from rain, snow and ice than the Cairngorms, resulting in greater picking-out of fault lines and greater lowering of the topography by erosion.

Since the moving ice departed

A variety of smaller local features of the landscape, which have formed since the last departure of moving ice, are well developed in the high and empty ground of Area 12. Most of these reflect freeze–thaw movement of water in surface rock and soil materials, and they may still be active under present-day climatic conditions. Similar processes are widespread and active in Arctic areas today, where they are typical of periglacial conditions. Improving understanding of them is critical in the successful design of roads and pipelines, as well as housing.

The disappearance of the moving ice of glaciers and local sheets inevitably has caused changes in local drainage patterns, resulting in the dumping and erosion of the local quantities of unstable, loose material left by the ice. Area 12 contains abundant evidence of modification of the landscape in the form of abandoned river channels and valleys. River terraces represent fragments of old river flood plains and basins, now abandoned and stranded above the presently active river levels. In some places, large fragments of former river systems can be recognised, as, for example, on the Rothiemurchus Terrace, downstream from the northern mouth of the Lairig Ghru (Fig. 226).

Mass-movement is a term used to include a range of processes in which the boulders, pebbles, sand and mud of the soft surface layer move en masse. In debris flows or landslips masses of material move together, though flexibly, in contrast with movement of sediment in flowing water, where the sediment becomes sorted into discrete particles that move independently.

Flat areas of topography, when covered by a layer of soft material, sometimes develop remarkable patterns of polygons (honeycomb-like, from above). The individual polygon cells are a few tens of centimetres to a few metres across. In the present-day Arctic, these structures are common on flat ground, and are often called *frost polygons*. They also occur as relict features in parts of Britain. On high ground, the polygon patterns may still be actively developing today. When active, freezing and thawing of the pore water in the surface sediment causes rearrangement of the pebbles, sand and mud, resulting in pebble-rich 'walls' that form polygons around cores of finer-grained mud and sand. It is difficult to understand the underlying process, but it appears to result from the development, in the loose surface materials, of honeycomb-shaped cells of movement in which temperature-linked convection cells mimic the movement of boiling of water around steam bubbles in a kettle.

Frost polygons are found in areas of flat ground, and if this ground is followed across the landscape to an area of slopes, the polygons are seen to become more elongate, eventually becoming *downslope stripes*. This indicates that the movements that generate the polygons are being increasingly influenced by downslope gravitational processes.

In other situations downslope mass movement of surface material results in the formation of *terraces* or *lobes*, showing how material has moved under gravity. A general term for this sort of movement is *solifluction*. In some cases, *turf-banked terraces*, as much as a metre high, show the way that sediment-binding vegetation can colonise the fronts of the terraces while the upper, near-horizontal surfaces of the terraces are not colonised and reveal the mixture of mud and pebbles which makes up the internal body of the moving mass. '*Sheep-tracks*', often typical of steep faces in grassy lowland landscapes, are another example of the action of this type of process, although they may locally be further moved and developed by the passing of columns of walking sheep.

Steep slopes, for example on the back walls of corries or on the side walls of formerly glaciated U-shaped valleys, often develop gullies due to the frost detachment and fall of frost-loosened bedrock. This material will tend to choke constrictions in the gullies and form unstable plugs, which may become mobilised to form debris flows under conditions of thaw or heavy continued rain. Marvellous examples of the gullies and their debris-flow fans are common in Area 12, for example near the summit of the Lairig Ghru (Fig. 226), where this activity has turned a previously U-shaped valley, formed by ice moving along the valley, into a V-shaped valley.

Block fields are a particularly characteristic feature of the granite bedrock areas of the high Cairngorm plateaus. Chaotically jumbled areas of boulders, sometimes individually metres across, form something of a test of athleticism and nimble balance. These appear to be the remnants of areas where once tors existed, forming the highest points of the plateau. The tors have now been further degraded by erosion and weathering, until none of the bedrock is still precisely in its bedrock place. Granite bedrock always shows well-developed cracks or *joints*, due to forces generated at various stages since the granite solidified, so block fields are a natural product of further erosion and weathering of this jointed material. The details of the physics and chemistry of the processes are not well understood, and the variability of the local environments makes this a daunting challenge. Since Tertiary times these plateau areas have experienced a remarkable range of climate and groundwater conditions, from tropical to arctic, from dry to wet, and from ice-covered to being exposed to the atmosphere.

CHAPTER 18

Area 13: Aberdeen

In area 13, the coastline of scotland is dominated by the brutal elbow of land that projects out into the North Sea (Fig. 229). Inland, the Area is one of gently undulating hills that form the edges of the Grampian Highlands to the west and southwest. Wide river valleys drain the mountains and fringing hills, leading water and sediment down towards the coastline of the Moray Firth to the north and the North Sea to the east (Fig. 230).

Fishing and agriculture have supported the population in historic times, and given the Area a lively and distinctive culture, famous for its Northeastern Scots or Doric dialect. In the mid twentieth century, easily within present lifetimes, the sudden discovery of rich North Sea oil resources offshore transformed the economy, particularly of Aberdeen and its surroundings, turning it into the 'Oil Capital of Europe'. The present dwindling of the oil reserves seems unlikely to reverse the remarkable effect this has had on a regional economy that was previously famous for the tight-fistedness of its inhabitants!

STORIES FROM THE BEDROCK

Dalradian Supergroup

The oldest bedrock of the Area belongs to the Dalradian Supergroup of metamorphic rocks, and they form about 60 per cent of the land area (Fig. 231). Before these rocks were metamorphosed, they had accumulated as sediments, most abundantly as muds and sands, but also, less commonly, as lime-rich sediments, volcanic ashes and lavas (Fig. 232). Elsewhere in the Grampian Highlands, trilobite fossils have been found in the youngest part of the Supergroup. A general estimate of the age-span of the Dalradian Supergroup is

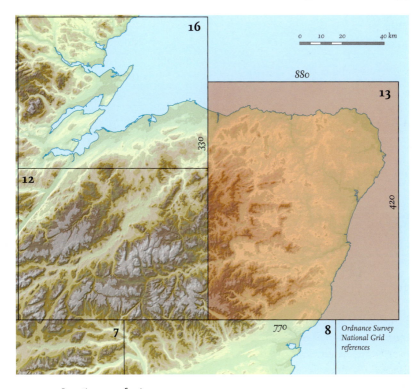

FIG 229. Location map for Area 13.

that it formed between the late Neoproterozoic and the Ordovician, over a period from perhaps 800 to 470 million years ago.

Because the different rock types of the Dalradian are relatively distinctive in their mineral contents, they can be recognised and have weathered differently. Mapping across Grampian Scotland has shown that the Dalradian consists of distinctive layers corresponding to formations representing episodes of Dalradian time. At least some of them can be followed across much of the width of the country (see Chapter 4), making it possible to estimate a total thickness of Dalradian material, and a figure of 16 km has been suggested. This great thickness is unlikely to have accumulated in one single basin, and it is more likely that it formed in a series of evolving basins during a long period of stretching of the crust, associated with normal faulting.

Folding, faulting and metamorphism of the Supergroup then followed, and it was while this was taking place that the Caledonian mountain building took place. The alteration or metamorphism of the rocks was not simple, and,

FIG 230. Natural and man-made features of Area 13.

particularly within northeastern Scotland, different histories of burial and heating have resulted in different histories of mineralogical change.

One remarkable feature of the Dalradian succession is the presence of pebble and boulder beds, now recognised as evidence of a widespread glacial episode in the mid-Neoproterozoic. The age is uncertain, but it was probably between about 700 and 600 million years ago. The best exposures are in Islay (Area 3) and the Garvellach Islands (Area 6) off the west coast, and other more highly altered occurrences are on Schiehallion (Area 8), Tomintoul (Area 12) and on the coast at

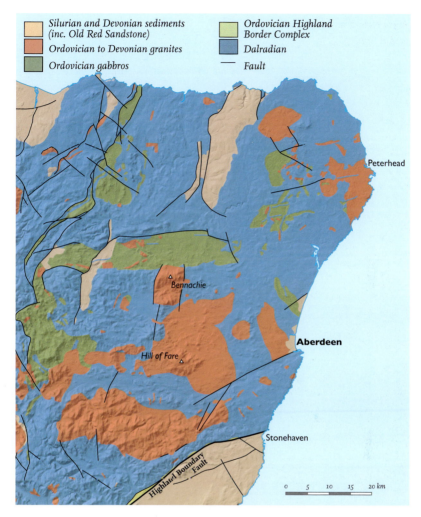

FIG 231. Simplified geology and hill-shaded topography for Area 13.

Macduff, east of Banff (Fig. 230). Neoproterozoic glacial deposits are found widely around the Earth, and have been used to suggest that this Neoproterozoic ice age was worldwide (the period of the so-called Snowball Earth).

Highland Border, Ordovician

One of the main terrane boundaries of Scotland, marked by the Highland Boundary Fault, separates the Grampian Highlands from the Midland Valley.

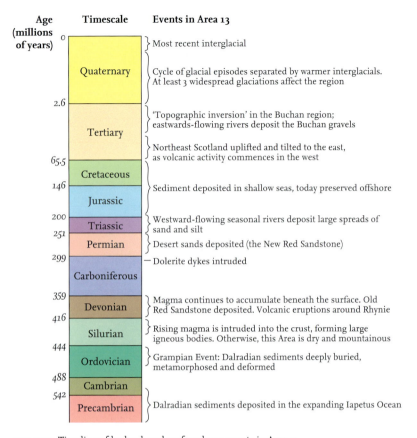

FIG 232. Timeline of bedrock and surface-layer events in Area 13.

Along this boundary, Dalradian rocks have fractured and moved against distinctive bedrock now assigned to the Highland Border Complex. Later the landscape of the time was eroded and Old Red Sandstone sediments were deposited. The generally straight boundary extends from the Firth of Clyde (Area 4) right across Scotland into the south of Area 13, trending northeastwards and crossing the coast near Stonehaven (Fig. 231).

The Highland Border Complex lives up to its name. It is poorly exposed, highly fractured and altered, and includes sediments thought to range from Cambrian to early Silurian in age, as well as igneous rocks, including basic pillow lavas perhaps representing fragments of ocean crust, and metamorphic sediments. Some of these Complex bedrocks are now serpentine-rich, and altered into carbonate-rich rocks, which can form small topographic features. However,

FIG 233. Bennachie, 30 km northwest of Aberdeen. The individual tops are formed by granite tors. (© Adrian Warren/lastrefuge.co.uk)

the Highland Border bedrocks have not usually produced high-elevation features themselves. It is the Dalradian metamorphics to the north and Old Red Sandstone conglomerates to the south that have usually formed the main hill topography of this border.

It is clear that this terrane boundary was a zone of movement and bedrock alteration from at least early Ordovician until late Devonian times (a period of well over 100 million years).

Caledonian intrusions

About 20 per cent of the bedrock of the land of Area 13 consists of large igneous rock *plutons* that came into position at different times during the Caledonian mountain building. Two different types of intrusions can be distinguished (see also Chapter 3).

The first type is *mafic* (gabbroic), thought to have formed in Ordovician times as a result of the incorporation of mafic intrusive bodies or even fragments of oceanic crust into the Caledonian mountain belt. These large intrusions tend not to form high ground, relative to the Dalradian metamorphic bedrock. They appear to have been preferentially weathered and eroded because of their rather unstable mineralogy of feldspar and dark silicate minerals, such as augite.

The second type of intrusion is *felsic* (granitic), formed of quartz, feldspar and minor amounts of dark silicates, and these tend often to form high ground relative to the Dalradian metamorphic bedrock. Many of the isolated broad hills of Area 13, such as Bennachie (Fig. 233) and the Hill of Fare, have been eroded from intrusions of granite, and most of them appear to have been intruded in late Silurian or even Devonian times.

The use of granite as a building stone has given a remarkably characteristic feel to the city of Aberdeen, and indeed to buildings across much of Area 13. Rubislaw Quarry, 142 m in depth and extending some 60 m below sea level, is only some 3 km west of the centre of Aberdeen, though well concealed by trees and fencing. It was the source of much of the grey granite used so extensively locally. The large granite intrusion that forms the bedrock around Peterhead is attractively red due to the colouration of its feldspars, and this contrasts with the more normal greyness of most of the late Caledonian granites. It was quarried largely from Stirling Hill, near Boddam, some 6 km south of Peterhead, and was again shipped widely according to architectural taste.

Old Red Sandstone

Conglomerates, sandstones and mudstones with some lavas have been mapped as Lower Old Red Sandstone, and form the bedrock in the northern triangle of land that extends southwards from the Highland Border where it intersects the coast at Stonehaven in the south of Area 13. Further south still, in Area 8 (Dundee), bedrock mapped as parts of the Upper Old Red Sandstone overlies the Lower Old Red. The coastal succession of Lower Old Red appears to span a time period from late Silurian to late early Devonian (some 425 to 400 million years ago), although there are clearly time-gaps within the succession. The early history of the Highland Border has been outlined above. Here we simply pick out some aspects of the Lower Old Red Sandstone episode.

Spectacular cliff outcrops occur along the coast in the southeast of Area 13, and define the northern limb of the Strathmore Syncline, the large downfold that runs several kilometres south of the Highland Border across much of Scotland. The coarse conglomerates below Dunnottar Castle, near Stonehaven, are parts of numerous sheets of conglomerate some 1000 m thick, though at Dunnottar the sheet has been folded so that the bedding is near vertical (Fig. 234). That implies strong local subsidence of the crust coupled with a supply of sediment from the erosion of a neighbouring area of uplifting high mountains, followed by uplift to the north to create the steep dips. Although mapping of the whole Lower Old Red Sandstone succession exposed along this coast has suggested a succession totalling some 9 km in thickness, more recent work based on the study of

FIG 234. Dunnottar Castle, 2 km south of Stonehaven, spectacularly built on a headland of Lower Old Red Sandstone conglomerate layers that have been tilted steeply to the south (left). (© Patricia & Angus Macdonald/ Aerographica/Scottish Natural Heritage)

organic traces in the sediments suggests that no more than 3–5 km of sediment accumulated in one place at a time. It therefore seems clear that the area of greatest accumulation of sediment moved while the succession was forming.

Other coastal outcrops, such as those at Crawton, 4 km south of Dunnottar, provide vivid views of the interaction of river-borne conglomerates and the mafic (andesitic) lava flows that were extruded periodically.

Recent work has surveyed the major unconformity that appears to represent most clearly the onset of sedimentation on the eroded flanks of the Caledonian mountains of northern and eastern Scotland. The unconformity is recognised as an ancient land surface of pre-Silurian and older bedrock that had been deformed and altered during the Caledonian mountain building, and was then covered by Old Red Sandstone (Late Silurian and Devonian) red sediments, formed primarily in rivers and lakes. This survey showed that the Caledonian land surface was more than 2000 m higher over the centre of the Grampian and Northern Highlands than over the Great Glen and Moray Firth. Information is largely lacking for the Atlantic margin and the North Sea around Scotland, but it is intriguing to see this independent evidence that the mountain landscape of the Highland areas was established by Devonian times, and has continued to exist for much of the following 400 million years.

A very remarkable inland patch of Lower Old Red Sandstone is preserved around the village of Rhynie, some 12 km south of Huntly (Fig. 230). Digging and drilling in the fields of the valley floors around the village has yielded remarkable information about the origin of the silica-rich Rhynie Cherts, known worldwide for their fossils of primitive plants and arthropods. It turns out that the fossils were preserved in the deposits of silica-rich hot springs that were themselves a product of local volcanic activity.

Offshore bedrock

Although Permian and Triassic bedrock is not exposed on land in Area 13, it is exposed near Elgin (Area 16), and has been mapped offshore on the sea bed all the way round the coast of Area 13. So closely does the unconformable base of the Permian and Triassic run parallel to the present coast in this Area, that it seems clear that the present-day coastline must inherit its form, at least to some extent, from the 250-million-year-old land surface of Permian and Triassic age. The mapping of the unconformities referred to above shows that the later land surface had only about half the relief of the earlier Caledonian surface, although, as discussed in the Old Red Sandstone section above, the Grampian and Northern Highland areas had by then become areas of relatively high topography.

Jurassic, Cretaceous and Tertiary bedrock forms much of the floor of the Moray Firth and North Sea in the offshore parts of Area 13. The Jurassic consists mainly of mudstones and sandstones, formed originally as muds and sands deposited in deltas where rivers brought sediments into the shelf seas of the time. In early Cretaceous times, mud and sand deposition was followed by deposition of the Late Cretaceous Chalk, the remarkable fine-grained, calcium carbonate sediment that blanketed most of the sea floors that existed across much of northwest Europe. In Tertiary times, muds and sands were again deposited widely across the floor of much of what is now the North Sea. These bedrock episodes are not represented directly on land in Area 13, but provide valuable clues about some of the events responsible for creating the landscape of the Area.

MAKING THE LANDSCAPE

The special landscape of Area 13 occurs in its northeastern part, historically known as Buchan (Fig. 235). It consists of rolling low ground that lacks high relief and contains no rugged bedrock outcrops. Some workers have regarded the area as defined by its relatively low elevation, usually of little more than 200 m above sea level, and recognised a low topographic Buchan surface. However, although this gentle landscape lacks drama, it contains valuable clues about the longer history of its evolution. Compared with most other parts of Scotland, where recent glaciation and crustal uplift have been vigorous, Buchan provides intriguing evidence of landscape events tens of millions of years ago.

One important type of evidence is provided by what have generally been called the Buchan Gravels. Examples of these occur at Windy Hills, 3 km northeast of Fyvie, and in the area of the Moss of Cruden, some 10 km southwest of Peterhead. The Gravels consist of different proportions of well-rounded cobbles of flint and quartzite in a fine-grained clay-mineral surround. The cobbles of flint appear to have been eroded from the Late Cretaceous Chalk which once occurred over this low-lying land. They may also have been eroded in the same way from the Chalk with flint growths that occurs in the offshore Cretaceous bedrock now found on the floor of the seas to the north and east. The cobbles of quartzite, which is a metamorphosed quartz-grain sandstone, are made of material similar to that now exposed in some of the local hills of Dalradian bedrock, and were probably therefore derived from the erosion of hills of this sort.

The Buchan Gravels now form the high ground in the local landscape, and appear to be a result of what is sometimes called *inversion of the topography*. They seem to have formed at a low elevation as a valley fill in a landscape that was then lowered generally by erosion. Because the Gravels formed a resistant material when subjected to general landscape erosion, they eventually formed relatively high ground while the surrounding landscape became the lower ground. Figure 236 illustrates the way this inversion process appears to have taken place, and suggests a timescale in which the initial flint gravels formed in early Palaeogene times (say Eocene), and the inversion that we see today occurred in the late Neogene, or late Tertiary.

The key to this is rates of erosion, and resistance to erosion by the materials at the surface. It is felt that subtropical climatic conditions in the early Tertiary in this part of Scotland may have played a critical role in this. Under these conditions the Dalradian and Cretaceous bedrock of the area was weathered chemically so that only the most resistant quartzite and flint materials survived and became concentrated in beaches and river beds, while other material from granites and the Dalradian Supergroup was reduced to clay minerals, leaving the Buchan Gravels as the final product. The bedrock that is visible in some other parts of the Buchan area provides evidence of deep chemical and mineralogical weathering that is not found in most Scottish bedrock.

At Den of Boddam, just southwest of Peterhead, numerous hollows in the ground surface mark a locality unique in Scotland, where Neolithic people, some 4000 years ago, extracted flint from gravels and worked it into flint tools.

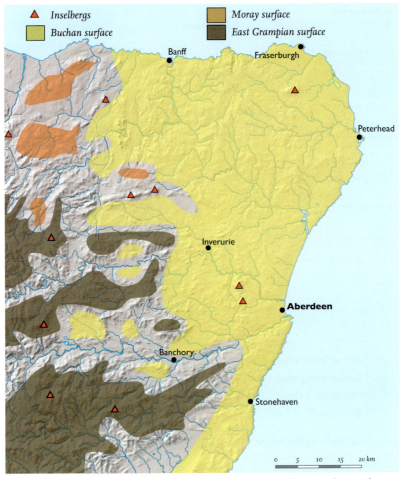
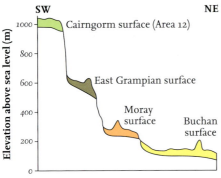

FIG 235. Topographic weathering surfaces recognised for Area 13. The surfaces have been plotted on a hill-shaded map of the topography, and some isolated peaks are picked out as inselbergs or erosional relicts. A profile shows the way the older weathering surfaces tend to be at greater elevation. (Lower diagram redrawn from Merritt and Leslie 2009)

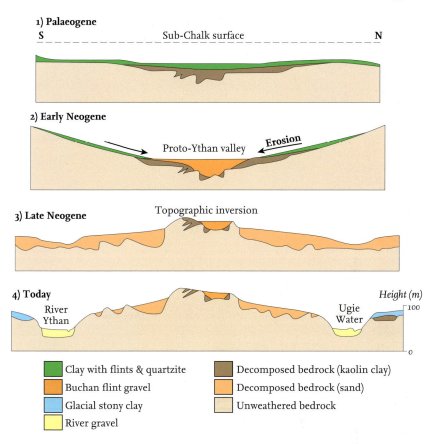

FIG 236. Sketch sections illustrating different phases in the evolution of the landscape of Buchan, showing how earlier valley deposits may now have become ridges at higher elevation (examples of 'inversion' of the topography). (Redrawn from Merritt and Leslie 2009)

This is remarkable evidence of the realisation by our ancestors of the value of this material, weathered from Cretaceous Chalk that is no longer visible locally but has been made available by its subsequent transport by rivers or even beach processes under very different environmental conditions.

During the Ice Age

Once again, the evidence of glaciation from Area 13 is rather different from that for other parts of Scotland. In most of Scotland, there is widespread fresh evidence of glacial activity during the last (Devensian) glacial episode, and this glaciation appears to have been so severe and general that it wiped out evidence from earlier episodes.

In contrast, in Buchan the soft surface layer contains deposits left by glaciers that are different enough in their material content and degree of weathering to suggest that they may represent pre-Devensian ice transport. In this respect Buchan appears to have been far enough east of the west-coast centres of Devensian ice accumulation so that only limited erosion and deposition by ice took place. Indeed, some workers have concluded that Buchan was ice-free when the rest of the land of Scotland was covered by ice. Whether this extreme situation occurred is not clear, but it is generally accepted that Buchan was marginal in terms of ice activity, rather like a local version of the situation in the Midlands and East of England, when the Devensian glaciation of northern England and western Scotland was at its peak.

The general pattern of Devensian ice movement across Area 13 is shown in Figure 237. The colours of the different glacial deposits here are a direct result of the materials that the different ice sheets have picked up during their movement. Thus blue-grey material has been picked up from the Jurassic bedrock of the floor of the Moray Firth, and this idea of its derivation is further supported by the presence of identifiable fossils and rafts of typical sediment, some of them hundreds of metres across. In contrast, the yellow and grey material of the central part of Area 13 has been derived from the granites and metamorphics of the Grampian high hills, and the red glacial materials owe their colour to the Old Red Sandstone, and possibly Permian and Triassic bedrock, that they have been carried over.

The pattern of movement arrows in Figure 237 suggest clearly that the general movement of ice across Area 13 was from the west, where the high mountains and deeply eroded valleys appear to have been the source areas for most of the ice. But the ice transporting both the blue-grey and red series shows diversions from this general direction in the areas of the present-day coasts. This suggests that ice sheets moving westwards across the North Sea from Norway caused deflection of the Scottish ice-flow directions. This idea is confirmed by bedrock fragments typical of present-day Norwegian outcrops that have been found near Peterhead, and erosional features due to ice movement across the floor of the North Sea.

Since the moving ice departed

The last (Loch Lomond Stadial) pulse of glacial advance and retreat came to an end about 11,500 years ago. Since then, climatic conditions have warmed generally, though fluctuating significantly, as reflected by evolving changes in

FIG 237. Generalised ice-flow direction for the Devensian glaciation of Area 13, superimposed on a hill-shaded map. Distinctively coloured glacial deposits are shown. (Redrawn from Merritt and Leslie 2009)

local vegetation cover. Changing sea level and coastlines are other key features in the evolution of the landscapes towards their present-day state.

In Chapter 5 we outlined the way that Scotland's coastlines have been influenced by changes in sea level relative to fixed points on the local landscape. With the melting of the main ice sheets of the world over the last 20,000 years, sea level as a whole has risen, but this has been offset in many parts of Scotland by the isostatic rebound of the land on losing its local load of ice. If Aberdeen is taken as a reference point on the present-day coast, it seems that there has been less change in sea level here than in Edinburgh (Fig. 238). This may reflect the smaller amounts of unloading due to ice melting in northeastern areas than was experienced at Rannoch Moor and further south around Edinburgh, perhaps a result of a southwest/northeast contrast in the shape of the ice sheet. The strong element of global sea-level rise experienced in southern England was masked, to an extent, by the rebound of the land of the area, but this was much less than further southwest in Scotland. Modelling the likely behaviour near Aberdeen suggests that sea level was some 20 m below its present level 10,000 years ago but changed to about 10 m above the present level about 6000 years ago, before dropping to where it is today.

Spey Bay

The northwestern part of the coastline of Area 13 consists of the remarkable gravel and sand beach that forms Spey Bay. This extends from near Lossiemouth (Area 16), eastwards for almost 17 km to Portgordon and Buckie in the east. About two-thirds of the way along this only slightly curved beach is a complex of actively shifting spits and channels where the River Spey enters the sea. The seaward part of the beach consists of a 'staircase' of descending beach ridges, each representing a younger phase of seaward growth of the beach as the sea level fell relative to the land.

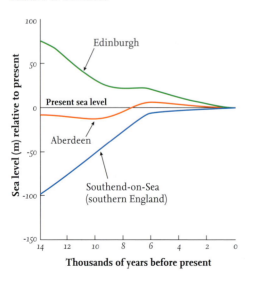

FIG 238. Graph showing the results of modelling sea-level changes over the last 14,000 years in the Aberdeen area, making assumptions about the way the land has risen in response to the melting of local ice. Curves for Edinburgh and Southend-on-Sea (Southern England) are shown for comparison.

Much more local study will be necessary to clarify the history of the development of this Spey Bay coastline. In addition to global sea-level changes, and vertical loading or unloading movements of the land, a further important variable is likely to have been the supply of sediment to the coastline. The Lower Spey has a well-known history of catastrophic flooding, and recent active movements of its many channels and islands can be judged from maps and the way the old railway bridge, near Fochabers, was designed for a different river pattern. All of this suggests large input of gravel and sand by the river. But longshore movement of sediment along the coastline, as well as onshore movement of sediment from the nearby floor of the Moray Firth, appear to have been dominant, suppressing any tendency for the river to build a large delta (Fig. 239).

Northern bedrock coastline

The coastline east of Spey Bay is predominantly one of cliffs with headlands, bays, fishing villages and small towns. For a few kilometres, midway between Banff and Fraserburgh, Old Red Sandstone bedrock outcrops along the coastline, because of down-faulting that probably took place at least partly at the same time as the Old Red sedimentation. Along this stretch of coastline, the Old Red cliffs of coarse sediments provide a distinctive backdrop to the cottages of Gardenstown, Pennan and Crovie (Fig. 240). Elsewhere, the cliffs are composed of the varied metamorphosed Dalradian bedrock, and the layering and cleavage provide structure that has been eroded by the sea to give form to the headlands, bays and offshore islands.

Northeastern coastline corner, Fraserburgh to Peterhead

Between these two burghs or townships, the coastline consists largely of wind-blown sand dunes and beaches, here and there developed into golf links, and extending over a distance of more than 25 km. At three points this coastline is deflected by low-lying reefs, islands of Dalradian metamorphic bedrock and accumulations of boulders, but these are minor topographic features in a coastal zone that is generally very low-lying, compared with the cliff lines of much of the rest of Area 13. The southernmost of these points is Rattray Head, near which is the Loch of Strathbeg. This loch is now freshwater but was formerly a tidal lagoon providing access from the sea to a small harbour at Old Rattray, which became isolated from the sea about 300 years ago. An unusually regular series of coast-parallel wind-blown dunes has built out on a foundation of gravel.

This is the area of coast that appears to have been overridden by Moray Firth ice, leaving its grey-green deposits, and which was then covered by the sea – which has since been retreating, over the last few thousand years. A question for

FIG 239. The mouth of the River Spey, 13 km east of Elgin. (© Patricia Angus Macdonald/Aerographica/Scottish Natural Heritage)

FIG 240. The village of Crovie, built in a bay eroded into Old Red Sandstone down-faulted against Dalradian metamorphic bedrock. (© Lorne Gill, Scottish Natural Heritage)

general landscape speculation is why does this protruding part of the Scottish coastline contain so little in the way of strongly eroded cliffs? Some of the answer may lie in the unusual history of weathering and low crustal rebound that has already been mentioned for the Buchan area. It may also be speculated that distinctive episodes of dumping of material in Tertiary and glacial times may have resulted in a particularly ready supply of gravel and sand.

Eastern bedrock coastline, Peterhead to Collieston

This 20 km-long stretch of coastline is largely one of cliffs, except at Bay of Cruden, where a sand-filled bay marks a valley, probably eroded from the landscape there by the ancestors of the Water of Cruden. North of this, around the Bullers of Buchan, some 9 km south of Peterhead, a stretch of coast has been chosen as a Geological Conservation Review site, because its cliffs provide a superb range of different forms (geos, arches, blow holes, stacks, caves, islands etc.) that are typical of storm erosion of a homogeneous hard igneous rock, the Peterhead granite (Fig. 241). One major feature of the erosion is the presence of planar joints or cracks in the otherwise homogeneous granite. In some cases these joints were formed by contraction during the original cooling of the granite, but they may also be due to the release of stresses in the granite during the period when it has approached the surface as landscape erosion has proceeded.

Sandy coastline, Collieston to Aberdeen

Almost 30 km of coast to the south of Collieston is lined by sandy beaches, providing excellent examples of deposition of large volumes of sand by the wind. Just south of Collieston is the Forvie National Nature Reserve, where the mouth of

FIG 241. The Bullers of Buchan, showing beautifully jointed pink Peterhead felsic granite, picked out by wave coastal erosion. (© Lorne Gill, Scottish Natural Heritage)

the River Ythan provides a wealth of varied habitats ranging from intertidal muds, sands and gravels to particularly extensive areas of wind-transported sand dunes, some of them stabilised by vegetation, particularly towards the north (Fig. 242).

Further south, along Balmedie Beach, is another fine development of wind-blown dunes landward of a continuous sandy beach, which is continuous as far south as the entry points of the Rivers Don and Dee. These rivers dominate the drainage of the eastern Grampians, and are likely to be flowing in valleys that were eroded in Tertiary times and have continued to evolve through the glaciations and subsequent post-glacial changes of sea level.

Coastal cliffs, Aberdeen to Catterline

This coastline continues for some 35 km further within Area 13, almost all consisting of cliffs, headlands and bays cut in bedrock. Even the major change in bedrock from Dalradian in the north to Highland Border series and Old Red Sandstone in the south makes little difference to the cliffed nature of the coast, or the general forms eroded along it by storm action.

Inland hills and valleys

The higher hills, largely carved from Dalradian metamorphic bedrock and granites, are unlikely to have been eroded significantly since the Loch Lomond cold episode came to an end about 11,500 years ago. But the local features of

FIG 242. Forvie National Nature Reserve and the mouth of the River Ythan. (© Patricia & Angus Macdonald/ Aerographica/Scottish Natural Heritage)

periglacial conditions, especially those generated by freezing and thawing conditions, will have continued to cause local movement and lowering of the surface of any soil layer present. Some of these features have been listed and described briefly in the treatment of Area 12 (Cairngorm), immediately to the west.

The major valleys, such as those of the Dee, the Don and the Ythan, have certainly been areas of active landscape development since the last 'permanent' or summer ice disappeared. Meander patterns in the more gently sloping valley floors and multi-channel or braided channel patterns in more steeply sloping valley floors have all been subject to change during river floods in historical times, and the amount of change was likely to have been greater in more immediately post-glacial times. The presence of bedrock hills as features present within valleys provides local evidence of important changes of valley routing, perhaps due to diversion by landslips. In the Dee valley, the town of Ballater occupies a southward meander in the main river, while a much more direct road bypassing the town runs along 'Macduff's Pass', a narrower, largely stream-free gorge further north, which appears to mark a now abandoned valley.

One of the distinctive aspects of some of the main valleys, particularly the Dee, is the variety of soils and vegetation, reflecting differences in the bedrock and surface layers. This adds greatly to the attractiveness of the landscape by providing colourful patchworks through the cycles of the seasons.

CHAPTER 19

Area 14: Lewis and Harris

LEWIS AND HARRIS (Area 14) are two parts of one large island, some 100 km in length, that forms the head of the Outer Hebrides chain of islands, facing out into the Atlantic Ocean (Fig. 243). Most of its northern part is composed of relatively flat and boggy ground, called the 'Isle' of Lewis, which then passes southerly into more mountainous landscapes, mostly parts of North and South Harris. Lewis and Harris together have an area of some 2100 km^2. They have a population of some 20,000, mostly living in or near Stornoway (Fig. 244).

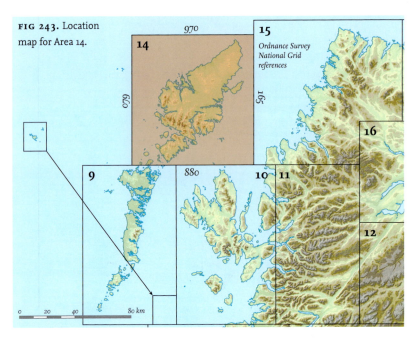

FIG 243. Location map for Area 14.

Lochs are numerous throughout Lewis and Harris (Fig. 245), and sea lochs penetrate deeply into the land, often with remarkably straight outlines. Between North and South Harris, the large island is cut almost in two at the isthmus of Tarbert (Fig. 246). A second major break in the chain occurs at the southern end of the large island, where the Sound of Harris cuts cleanly across the Hebridean chain with a particularly straight coastline where Northton and Leverburgh are situated (Fig. 247). Mapping of the bedrock, outlined below, shows that these landscape features are directly related to bedrock structures.

Distant islands add importantly to an understanding of the wider geological setting of the Outer Hebrides. The Shiant Isles, in the Minch, some 25 km east of Tarbert, Harris, will be discussed in this chapter. St Kilda, spectacularly well out in the Atlantic Ocean, some 100 km west of Tarbert, is discussed with Area 9 in Chapter 14.

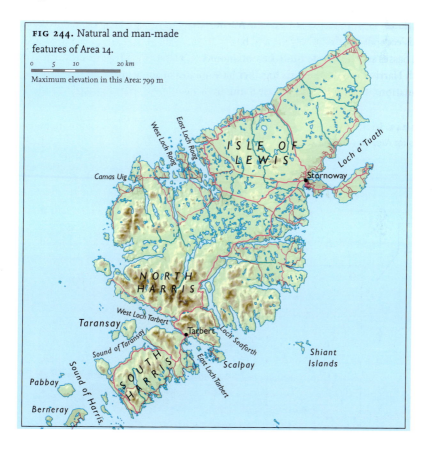

FIG 244. Natural and man-made features of Area 14.

Maximum elevation in this Area: 799 m

STORIES FROM THE BEDROCK

Pre-Caledonian bedrock episodes (the Lewisian Complex)
The bedrock of almost all of Area 14 consists of material of the Lewisian Complex (Fig. 248). This group of rocks consists primarily of coarsely crystalline gneisses, formed between 3.2 and 2.5 billion years ago. These highly altered metamorphic rocks are amongst the oldest rocks known in Europe, and appear to have formed when they were much closer to similar rocks in what is now southeast Greenland. Indeed, the Lewisian Complex of the northwestern Scottish crust is thought to have become separated from the rocks of the Greenland crust only around 60 million years ago, with the opening of the Atlantic Ocean.

The oldest rocks of the Lewisian Complex mostly started out as igneous rocks, formed by the cooling and crystallisation of hot, molten magma between 3.2 and 2.8 billion years ago. Then, 100 million or more years after their formation, they were buried deep in the Earth's crust, probably as two continents collided. They were then subject to numerous episodes of intense deformation and metamorphism, and new minerals formed under pressure and movement, leading to the banded appearance characteristic of gneiss. This period is referred to as the Scourian event, and it reached its peak around 2.7 billion years ago (Fig. 249). The hard, grey, streaky gneisses produced during this time are the most abundant rock type in Area 14.

After the Scourian, the gneisses lay buried deep within the interior of a relatively stable continent. Then, between 2.4 and 2.0 billion years ago, the continental crust began to stretch and rift apart and basic magma was intruded along crustal fractures, crystallising to form a set of dykes. The dykes are known as the Younger Basic Dyke Suite, and are thought to correlate with the Scourie dykes of the Scottish mainland (see Area 15). This period of extension resulted in continental rifting, and the Scourian gneisses became located at a continental margin, next to a newly created ocean. This ocean did not last for long, however: by about 1.9 billion years ago it began to close, and chains of volcanic islands formed above the subduction zone. Shortly after 1.9 billion years ago, the volcanic islands, together with fringing sedimentary deposits, collided with the continental margin. Volcanic, sedimentary and continental rocks became stacked up as thick slices and some were buried up to depths of 20 km, where they were intruded by hot bodies of mafic magma. Metamorphism followed: the mafic igneous rocks were converted to mafic gneisses, and the sedimentary and volcanic rocks into slate, soft graphite schist, hard garnet schist, quartzite, marble and amphibolite. Today, these stacked-up slices underlie the southern half of

FIG 245. Looking northeastwards across the Isle of Lewis from above the A858 road, some 20 km west of Stornoway and 5 km southeast of Callanish (Calanais). Note the boggy flatness and numerous lochs. (© Patricia & Angus Macdonald/Aerographica)

FIG 246. The isthmus of Tarbert, between North and South Harris, with the mountains of North Harris in the distance to the right. (© Adrian Warren/lastrefuge.co.uk)

FIG 247. The southern coastline of South Harris, with Leverburgh in the foreground. Chaipaval (Ceapabhal; 368 m) is in the distance with Northton (Taobh Tuath) and white machair coastal flats in its shadow. (© Adrian Warren/lastrefuge.co.uk)

South Harris: a 'core' of mafic igneous rocks, flanked on either side by northeast/southwest-trending belts of metamorphosed sedimentary and volcanic rocks. A large body of anorthosite underlies the mountain of Roineval (Roineabhal; Figs 248, 250). This is an unusual igneous rock made up primarily of feldspar, and it may have been part of the continental margin against which the younger rocks were moved.

The ocean continued to close, and, probably around 1.8 billion years ago, two continents collided and a mountain-building event occurred. This was the second and last main multi-phase episode of deformation and metamorphism of the Lewisian Complex, termed the Laxfordian. In contrast to the Scourian deformation, which was relatively uniform in its effects, Laxfordian deformation tended to be concentrated mainly in steep, narrow zones of intense shear along which adjacent gneiss blocks moved relative to one another. Today, the most conspicuous of these linear shear zones are northwest/southeast trending, crossing southern Harris and the Butt of Lewis. Another zone skirts the

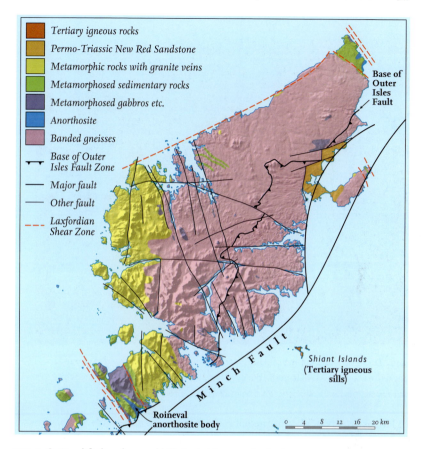

FIG 248. Simplified geology and hill-shaded topography for Area 14.

northwest coast of Lewis, and there is an obvious correlation between these lineaments and the form of the archipelago (Fig. 248).

Towards the end of the Laxfordian, some of the gneiss was buried deep enough that it began partially to melt. This produced small amounts of granitic magma, which cooled in irregular veins within the gneisses. At greater depths, temperatures were high enough for much larger volumes of magma to be produced. This then moved upwards and was intruded into the veined gneisses, forming abundant sheets of pink granite (up to several hundred metres thick) and pegmatite. Pegmatite is an interesting rock, composed of very large crystals within sheets and bodies several to tens of metres thick. Today, intense granite veining and abundant sheets of granite and pegmatite form a south-trending

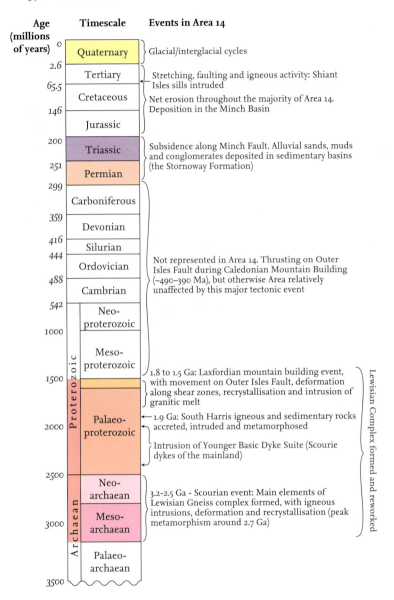

FIG 249. Timeline of bedrock and surface-layer events in Area 14.

FIG 250. Looking northwestwards across South Harris, with the village of Leverburgh in the middle distance. At the right is the mountain Roineval, with the anorthosite quarry works around Lingarabay. (© Patricia & Angus Macdonald/Aerographica)

complex, from the Uig Hills of southwest Lewis to South Harris. A narrow belt of pegmatites crosses the southern part of South Harris (from Finsbay to the island of Taransay), and there are numerous other bodies southwest of the main belt. These bodies are often responsible for smaller-scale landscape features, perhaps the most conspicuous being the well-exposed, 15 m-thick sheet that lies at a low angle on an eastern spur of Roineval. Feldspar crystals, which make up a large proportion of the body, average 60–90 cm in length here, and some are 1.5 m long. Another conspicuous, 25 m-thick body cuts across the slopes of Chaipaval, just northwest of Northton. Many of the pegmatite veins of Area 14 were exploited during the Second World War for their alkali feldspar.

About 1.5 billion years ago, the succession of episodes of intense alteration of crustal bedrocks (summarised in Fig. 249) dwindled and finally came to an end. This terminated a record of more than 1.5 billion years of activity in this crust, about one-third of the age-span of the Earth! Erosion then took over, and on the mainland the Lewisian Gneiss had reached the surface by around 1.1 billion years ago, when Torridonian Sandstone was deposited on top of it. The Outer Hebrides first came into being as a distinct crustal feature around the same time, flanked on the east by subsiding troughs into which Torridonian Sandstone was deposited. The Isles have remained at high levels since then: cover sediments would have been deposited from time to time, such as during the widespread marine flooding of the Cambrian and Ordovician, but there is no reason to think that they ever attained exceptional thickness. This may be partly due to the buoyancy of the Hebridean Platform, resulting from the unusually granitic composition of its basement. Today, Lewisian bedrock is wonderfully exposed in many parts of the Outer Isles, in particular in South Harris (Fig. 251) and the Uists (Area 9).

Many faults traverse the Lewisian of Area 14. Perhaps the largest and most significant of these, however, is the Outer Isles Fault. The base of the fault zone runs along the eastern side of the Area, dipping gently down southeastwards beneath the Minch. The fault zone itself is defined by deformed bedrock, sometimes involving a wide zone of crushing, shearing and even melting, sometimes much more limited in width. The fault is thought to have first been active as early as 1.7 billion years ago, possibly as the basement blocks of the Outer Hebrides and the Scottish mainland amalgamated. It was again active as a thrust during the Caledonian mountain building, and at various points throughout the late Palaeozoic and Mesozoic. As we shall see next, the fault zone formed a distinct zone of weakness that was exploited during Permo-Triassic extension, with important consequences for the formation of the southeastern coastline of Area 14.

Post-Caledonian bedrock episodes

By the end of the Caledonian mountain-building event, Area 14 lay within the massive Old Red Sandstone continent. The subsequent Devonian period was one of uplift and erosion, and by the end of the Devonian the level of erosion of the higher hills in the Outer Isles may have been no more than a kilometre or so above that of the present day. By Permian times, the region began to undergo extension and the Outer Isles resumed their old role as a high platform, whilst a fault-bounded basin (the Minch) developed on its eastern flank as a prelude to the opening of the North Atlantic. The Minch Basin is one of a series of roughly northeast/southwest-trending basins in northwest Scotland; it seems that as the region was subject to extensional stresses, major pre-existing faults became reactivated, with subsidence along these faults creating today's basins. The major bounding fault controlling subsidence in the Minch Basin is the Minch Fault, which hugs the east coast of the Outer Isles (Fig. 248; see also Area 9, Fig. 166). The Minch Fault and the Outer Isles Thrust Zone both follow the general trend of the length of the Outer Isles chain. When the region was

FIG 251. Lewisian Complex bedrock exposed in the knock-and-lochan landscape near Finsbay, 5 km east of Leverburgh, South Harris. (© Patricia & Angus Macdonald/ Aerographica)

subject to extensional stresses, the gentle dip of the Outer Isles Thrust Zone was too low for the fault to become the focus of extension. Instead, the Minch Fault developed, branching up steeply from the partially reactivated underlying Outer Hebrides Fault Zone (Fig. 252). The Minch Fault is therefore essentially a 'short-cut' fault, and has controlled subsidence and sedimentation within the basin since at least the Permian.

Thick sediments were deposited in the Permo-Triassic basins, and in Area 14 these sediments come onshore around Stornoway in north Lewis (Fig. 249). The 1.2 km-thick sequence, known as the Stornoway Formation, is made up of chocolate-red sandstones, conglomerates and mudstones, and contrasts strongly

(a) Topography and bathymetry

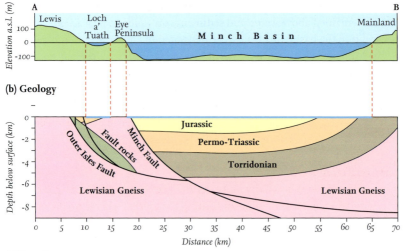

(b) Geology

(c) Location map

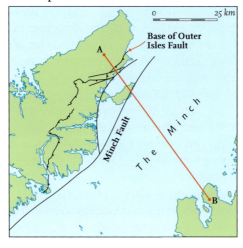

FIG 252. Cross-section of the Minch Basin.

with the highly altered, coarsely crystalline outcrops of the rest of Area 14. The sediments are coarse alluvial fan deposits (fan-shaped accumulations deposited by streams), including gneiss boulders up to 1 m, and exceptionally 3 m, in diameter. Elsewhere in Area 14, it seems that this time was one of net erosion, and Lewisian rocks were at least locally exposed and subject to erosion, any pre-existing cover rocks having already been cleared away.

Basin subsidence continued throughout the Jurassic, when the Minch was progressively flooded by shallow seas invading the region from the south. The Outer Isles remained above water, and sediment continued to be washed from them down into the basin, this time to be deposited in a marine environment. Today, the Minch contains up to 2.5 km of Jurassic sediments overlying some 3 km of Permo-Triassic sediments, with several kilometres of Torridonian beneath. The Minch Basin separates the Outer Isles from the mainland, and is therefore one of the primary controls on the coastline of Area 14. Indeed, much of the current coastline of Scotland is controlled by the presence of these offshore sedimentary basins, each dating from the Permo-Triassic.

Early Tertiary igneous episodes
The final phase of bedrock activity on Lewis and Harris occurred during the early Tertiary, when great stretching and rifting took place, separating the crust of Greenland and Scotland along the line of the newly created North Atlantic. During this extension, numerous fractures were created in the crust over a wide area, often aligned with pre-existing structures such as faults and shear zones. It is interesting to note in Figure 253 the similarity between the shape of the edge of the continental shelf and the edge of the Hebridean Platform, and the presence of a shear zone along at least parts of the latter. Onshore, a great number of faults dissect the Lewisian bedrock of Area 14 and, aside from the Outer Isles Fault, the majority of these formed some time after the Caledonian mountain building. A northwest/southeast or north-northwest/south-southeast trend is common, particularly for example in the remarkable set of close, straight fractures extending north-northwest from the Park (Pairc) district of Lewis to Loch Roag. This orientation is parallel to Tertiary dyke swarms elsewhere in the Hebrides, and it seems likely that some of these faults were developed during Tertiary igneous activity.

In places, dykes were emplaced along these joints and fractures and are visible today – for example on Scalpay. However, the most extensive outcrop of Tertiary igneous rocks in this Area is found in the Shiant Isles (Figs 244, 248), a small group of islands lying some 8 km southeast of the nearest coast of Lewis. In this part of the Minch Basin, magma rising through the sedimentary fill did not quite reach the surface, and instead was forced out sideways through the thick Jurassic sediments to form sills, sheets of igneous rock lying parallel to bedding layers. Some of these sills are very thick – most of Garbh Eilean, the main northern island, is composed of a single 130 m-thick sill. Geologically, the islands probably represent an extension of the suite of sills seen on the Trotternish peninsula of Skye (Area 10). As on Skye, one of the most distinctive features of the sills is

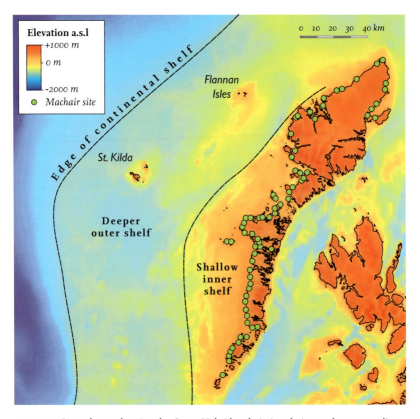

FIG 253. General map showing the Outer Hebrides chain in relation to the surrounding bathymetry. Machair coastal sites are also marked. (GEBCO bathymetry; machair sites are from Hansom 2003 b, Fig. 9.3)

the pronounced columnar jointing (discussed further in Areas 7 and 10), and hexagonal columns similar to, but much larger than, those on Staffa (Area 7) are well displayed in the numerous cliffs. On the whole, however, it is interesting to note the general lack of Tertiary igneous rocks in this Area, despite its proximity to the rift. Only two complexes penetrated the Outer Hebridean pre-Caledonian crust (at St Kilda and Rockall), whereas at least nine lie within or around the Caledonian crust of the Inner Hebrides. There seems to have been something special about the extremely old Outer Hebridean crust that inhibited the Tertiary igneous intrusions.

MAKING THE LANDSCAPE

Tertiary erosion

As described above, it seems likely that the Outer Hebrides have been at high levels compared to the surrounding land since Precambrian times. Only small thicknesses of cover sediments are therefore likely to have been deposited on top of the Lewisian Complex, which has probably lain at or close to the surface for much of its history. As a result, the main features of the landscape we see today in Area 14 may be the culmination of hundreds of millions of years of erosion, more so than in other parts of western Scotland. However, whilst the large-scale landscape features may have been initiated in pre-Tertiary times, perhaps one of the key phases of erosion took place at the start of the Tertiary. During early Tertiary igneous activity, not only were large volumes of igneous rock emplaced in western Scotland, but the region was uplifted. In the eastern part of this Area, the amount of uplift is estimated at around 3 km, decreasing southeastwards to less than 1 km on the western mainland. This uplift, combined with a warm, humid climate particularly favourable for deep weathering, resulted in some 1.5–3 km of bedrock being eroded from areas that are today near sea level. This period of erosion occurred some time between 65 and 50 million years ago, and it is uncertain whether it lasted 1 million years or 10 million years. Either way, the erosion rate is between 200 m and 2 km per million years, an order of magnitude higher than at most other times: between 750 m and 3 km were removed during the whole of the Mesozoic (some 185 million years), whilst during the rest of the Tertiary there was less than 1 km of erosion. Quaternary erosion, whilst very important scenically, reached a maximum rate of 150 m per million years only in the deepest troughs.

Surface uplift by itself only increases denudation in a secondary way, by enhancing relief locally where the catchments are well connected to sea level, and therefore capable of responding rapidly to a drop in local sea level due to crustal uplift on land. An important implication of this is that early Tertiary denudation was spatially variable, taking advantage of pre-existing drainage patterns, as well as lines and areas of weakness in the underlying bedrock. By the end of this erosional episode, it is very likely that the uplands, plains and large valley systems had become well-established features of the landscape, although they would be substantially modified by ice sheets during the last 2 million years.

During Tertiary times, relative sea level was much lower, and large rivers would have flowed both in the Minch and on the western part of the Hebridean Platform. Although the sea would not flood the Area until much later, the shape

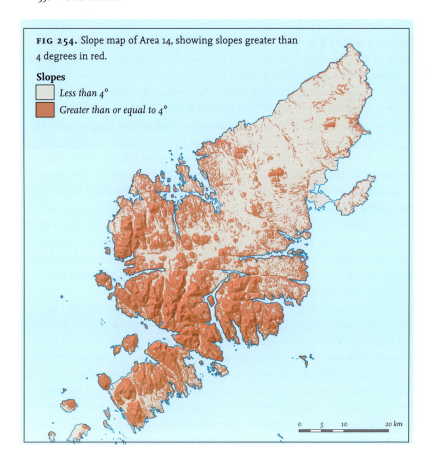

FIG 254. Slope map of Area 14, showing slopes greater than 4 degrees in red.

Slopes
- Less than 4°
- Greater than or equal to 4°

of what would become today's coastline probably started to become apparent at this time. The position of the present-day coastline correlates well with major Laxfordian shear zones and younger faults (Fig. 248). This suggests either that uplift has been concentrated along these zones, with the Outer Hebrides rising relative to surrounding areas, or that erosion was concentrated along these more fractured, weaker zones of rock. Either way, extremely ancient zones and fractures in the Earth's crust appear to have exerted an important control on some of the largest-scale feature of this Area.

As well as examining topographic maps, maps of slope angle provide a powerful way of examining shape patterns in the landscape. In looking at Figures 244 and 254, there is a striking difference in topography between the relatively low-lying, flat landscape of central and northern Lewis and the hilly country of southwest Lewis and much of Harris. In places, the location of this high ground may be due to the nature of the underlying bedrock: for example, the band of granitised gneisses running from the Uig Hills southwards to South Harris underlies generally hilly ground. However, the gneisses of east Harris and south Lewis are the same as those of north Lewis, yet the southern gneisses underlie the highest mountain in the Outer Hebrides, Clisham (An Cliseam, 799 m, located on Fig. 255), whereas the north of the island is a low, flat, marshy plateau rarely exceeding 120 m in elevation (Fig. 245). As bedrock contrasts cannot account for the differences in relief and elevation, it seems that tectonics must be the cause. A possible explanation is that the southwestern part of the Area was more uplifted than the northeastern half at the start of the Tertiary, lying as it did closer to the locus of igneous activity in northwest Scotland.

Another possibility is that there may have been differences in the structure of the underlying gneiss. The southwestern part of the Area appears to be dissected by a larger number of major faults than the northeastern part (Fig. 249), and so, during crustal movements, the blocks between these faults may have become uplifted or rotated, creating areas of high ground.

The numerous faults present in this Area have clearly influenced the direction of slopes and valley walls. Rocks within a fault zone are generally relatively soft, having been shattered or chemically altered during fault movement. During subsequent exposure, these faults then become etched out by water, and in Area 14 they are responsible for linear features ranging in size from small indentations within the broad, low plateau of the north, to precipitous gullies at the coast, to the largest valleys, often now infilled by long lochs. The correlation between faulting and topography is clear on Figure 248. For clarity, only the larger faults are marked on the map, and many more, smaller, faults are responsible for other linear features observable in the topography. The larger faults in Area 14 underlie not just one valley, but sets of valleys strung out along a line. For example, a fault underlies the set of valleys trending northwest from Loch Seaforth (which forms the northeast boundary of Harris) up to West Loch Roag. Another impressive fault-excavated valley bisects the Uig Hills of southwest Lewis along a remarkably straight north/south line. Although these valleys were gouged out to their present depths by the movement of glaciers, it seems very likely that they were initiated during the early Tertiary, if not earlier.

Faults have generally, therefore, been preferentially eroded to produce surface depressions. This is not the case, however, for the Outer Isles Fault Zone, which is associated in several places with prominent landscape features. The highest hill in northern Lewis is Beinn Mholach (292 m), some 10 km northwest of Stornoway. This is one of a pocket of closely spaced hills rising out of the otherwise largely flat, 100 m-high plateau. The little group of hills is closely encircled by the Outer Isles Fault Zone (Fig. 248), and it seems that the deformed rocks of the fault zone have resisted erosion more than the undeformed rocks to the west. The fault-zone rocks underlying these hills are slightly different from those of the rest of the fault zone in that they underwent brittle deformation during the Caledonian, and it seems that this has resulted in them weathering more prominently. In the Park region of southeast Lewis, it has also been suggested that rocks within the Outer Isles Fault Zone have been more resistant to erosion, and that the hilliness of this region may be due to the nature of the crush rocks in this part of the Zone.

Much of the Area is underlain by very similar hard bedrock, which on the whole has resisted erosion well. Although other rock types are rare, where present they tend to be weaker and more easily eroded than the gneisses, and so form topographic features. In South Harris, for example, the two bands of meta-sedimentary rocks have been more easily weathered than the metamorphosed igneous rocks, and today correspond to lower-lying regions. The same is true around Stornoway, where the much softer sandstones and conglomerates of the Stornoway Formation have been preferentially eroded to produce the lower-lying ground on which the capital of Lewis was subsequently built. This change in elevation occurs abruptly across the faulted contact between the Stornoway Formation and the surrounding Lewisian gneiss, and is visible in Figure 254. The Tertiary was also a time of erosion in parts of the Minch, which at that time would have been a major river valley. By a combination of uplift and erosion, the sills that now make up the Shiant Isles were exhumed, and again the hard igneous rocks withstood erosion more than the sedimentary rocks into which they had been intruded, and therefore began to form a positive topographic feature.

Glacial episodes

Since around 2 million years ago, Scotland has been subjected to repeated glacial and interglacial episodes that have extensively modified the pre-glacial land surface. As each successive glaciation has a tendency to rework the evidence of its predecessors, we know comparatively little about all but the most recent, Devensian, glacial episode. Area 14 is unusual in Scotland in that it does contain some evidence of earlier glaciations, perhaps reflecting the great distance (at least 80 km) of northern Lewis from the highest part of the last ice sheet (Fig. 255). Offshore glacial sediments provide the first evidence for glaciation in Area 14, demonstrating that an extensive ice sheet covered Scotland about 450,000 years ago, terminating westwards at the margin of the continental shelf. At this time, there may have been full ice cover over the Western Isles, possibly with ice flowing across

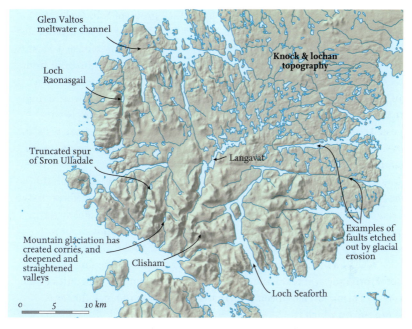

FIG 255. Hill-shade map of southern Lewis and Harris, picking out various glacial features.

the Area from the mainland. Glacially transported rocks originating from the mainland (*erratics*) have been found in both the northern and southern extremities of the Western Isles, supporting this theory, and it seems likely that the numerous sea-filled channels of the Western Isles, such as the Sound of Harris, were carved out by ice flowing westwards from the mainland.

Other features dating from before the last ice sheet are found along the northwest coast of Lewis, and some workers have proposed that part of northern Lewis remained ice-free during the last glaciation (Fig. 256), although this now seems unlikely from what is known about the offshore extent of ice. A pre-Devensian shore platform with backing cliff line appears to be the oldest feature, occurring discontinuously in northwest Lewis and on the Eye peninsula. It is best developed on the northwest coast of Lewis (between Galson, or Gabhsann, and Dell, or Dail), where it attains a width of 150 m. The platform lies between 7 and 10 m above present sea level, often stepping down to a lower intertidal platform at its seaward edge, and abandoned sea stacks occur on its surface. Glacial deposits rest on the shore platform, including pre-Late Devensian raised beach deposits and organic deposits of possible interglacial origin.

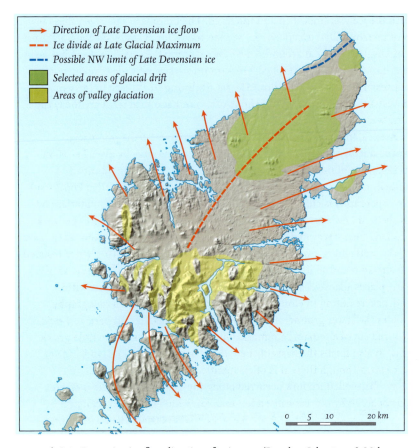

FIG 256. Late Devensian ice-flow directions for Area 14. (Based on Johnstone & Mykura 1989, and Gordon & Sutherland 1993)

The most recent glaciation, the Late Devensian, reached its maximum extent about 22,000 years ago. At this time the Western Isles supported an independent icecap with a central dome lying over the mountains of North Harris (Fig. 256). Ice flowed radially outwards from the dome, flowing westwards across the Hebridean Plateau into the Atlantic and eastwards into the Minch, where it combined with mainland glaciers to feed a large, fast-flowing ice stream (for a more regional reconstruction of Late Devensian ice-flow directions, see Area 9, Fig. 173). In North Harris and southeast Lewis, many of the hill tops would have protruded above the ice surface, as nunataks do today in Greenland. These exposed peaks were subjected to severe frost-shattering, while terrain lying beneath the ice was smoothed and moulded. The boundaries between these two types of terrain (called *trim lines*) can be seen today, for example on the northwest spur of Uisgnaval Mor at around 580 m. By mapping these trim lines, it has been shown that the last icecap reached a maximum surface altitude of about 700 m above present sea level over central Harris, declining in altitude to the west-northwest and east-southeast to heights of around 400 m at what are today the east and west coasts.

In Area 14, the most important modifications made to the pre-glacial landscape during the repeated Quaternary glaciations were by glacial erosion. Over the course of multiple glaciations, the bedrock was sculpted into a hummocky rolling surface across much of the region. This so-called knock-and-lochan topography is characteristic of lower-lying glaciated areas underlain by relatively hard Lewisian Gneiss. More extensively fractured patches of bedrock tend to have been excavated to form scoured depressions (the lochans, as they are often now water-filled), while more massive regions of gneiss have better resisted glacial abrasion and so underlie the rounded, ice-sculpted mounds (the knocks). In many places, glacial scouring occurred preferentially along faults within the bedrock, resulting in elongated hollows. Knock-and-lochan topography dominates the lower ground of this Area – in South Harris and parts of Lewis, the scoured surface remains a remarkable rocky wilderness where little grows (Fig. 251). It also forms the basis of the rather flat and featureless landscape of north Lewis, although there it is often mantled by younger deposits.

More channelled ice flow occurred along the Tertiary river valleys of Area 14, accompanied by more localised ice abrasion which both deepened and broadened these valleys. The Minch ice stream was perhaps the most erosive, cutting a 200 m-deep trough. Sediments recovered from within the Minch show that during the early Quaternary there was a terrestrial flood-plain environment with swamps and fens. As a deep trough was then carved out of the Minch Basin during successive glaciations, the region became flooded by the sea, and it seems likely that a channel has existed separating the Outer Isles from the mainland since around 18,000 years ago.

In the hilly ground of south Lewis and North Harris, glacial erosion was also concentrated along existing valleys, and the rocky topography here shows many features typical of glaciated upland terrain. Valley sides are often steep and rocky, and well-developed glacial corries, U-shaped valleys and rock troughs abound, particularly in the hills northwest of Clisham (Fig. 257). The pre-existing river valleys were not only deepened and broadened by ice scouring, but also straightened. Rivers can flow freely around corners, and so the upper course of a river valley tends to be made up of a series of interlocking spurs, ridges

FIG 257. Glaciated valley, now occupied by Loch Raonasgail, southwestern Lewis, looking south. (© Adrian Warren/lastrefuge.co.uk)

projecting from the valley sides into the valley bottom. Glacier ice cannot flow so freely around corners, and at the same time has more lateral erosive power than a river. As a result, glaciers carved through protruding edges of spurs, to form truncated spurs. Perhaps the best example in this Area, and the most famous, is Sron Ulladale (Fig. 255), carved by ice flowing down Glen Ulladale towards Loch Resort. It is reputed to have the highest overhanging cliff in Britain, steepened to its present shape by rock falls following the retreat of the ice.

As during the Tertiary, glacial erosion took advantage of zones of weakness within the bedrock. Faults are therefore generally very visible in today's landscape, having been etched out by glacial erosion both in the knock-and-lochan landscape of the lower areas and in the deeper U-shaped valleys and troughs. In addition, the different rocks of the South Harris Complex have

FIG 258. Looking northeast over Northton Bay (Traigh an Taoibh Tuath) towards the island of Taransay, with the mountains of North Harris in the background. (© Patricia & Angus Macdonald/Aerographica)

resisted erosion to different extents. For example, anorthosite in the southeast has weathered relatively prominently, and underlies the peak of Roineval, whose distinctive pale-coloured bedrock stands out in comparison with the darker-coloured gneisses of the rest of South Harris. To the northwest, the mafic gneisses underlie the more rounded hills around Bleaval, whilst the metamorphosed sedimentary rocks generally underlie lower-lying valleys that traverse the island. On a smaller scale, the Chaipaval pegmatite sheet stands out as a distinct ridge of rock running across the slope above Northton Bay (Traigh an Taoibh Tuath; Fig. 258).

The climate began to warm around 18,000 years ago, and by 14,000 years ago much of the ice from this Area had melted, although some glaciers may have persisted in favourable locations in North Harris. As this ice melted, it dumped its sediment load, although glacial deposits in this Area are generally fairly thin and localised compared to many other parts of Scotland. The largest glacial deposits are found in northern Lewis (Fig. 256), where much of the glacially scoured plateau north of Stornoway is overlain by a blanket of till.

Further south, the U-shaped valleys and hillsides closer to the ice centre are lined with boulder-strewn mounds and ridges, debris deposited by the retreating ice, or perhaps more likely during the Loch Lomond Stadial. At this time (between 13,000 and 11,500 years ago), small valley and corrie glaciers redeveloped in the mountains of North Harris, and material would have been deposited at their margins to form moraine. Moraine ridges are particularly well developed around the southern end of Loch Langavat (Langabhat; Fig. 255) and around Loch Voshimid (Bhoisimid), where they are comparable in shape and size to those forming at the margins of some Icelandic glaciers today.

As the Devensian ice sheet melted, large amounts of meltwater were released. This meltwater often had great erosive power, as streams carried heavy loads of pebbles and cobbles picked up by the ice, and often flowed under pressure under the ice. The combination of high pressure and entrained rock particles resulted in the meltwater acting like rock saws, producing deep, narrow gorges. Although there are few meltwater features in this Area, Glen Valtos (Gleann Bhaltois), near Uig on Lewis, is an excellent example of a meltwater channel, certainly the best in the Outer Isles (located on Fig. 255). It is a single narrow gorge some 2.5 km long, and at its maximum it is over 45 m deep . The tiny stream in its bottom is a good example of the misfit streams typical of meltwater channels – it is clearly incapable of having eroded such a remarkable feature. The channel was carved out of the bedrock under a glacier, and carried meltwaters eastwards towards Loch Roag. This flow direction implies that, at the time of melting, there was a thicker mass of ice off the west coast of Lewis than onshore, which is rather unexpected: one would expect the thicker ice inland near the mountain sources. In addition, crag-and-tail landforms and ice-moulded bedrock indicate that the last ice movement in the Uig area was to the northwest, and so this west-to-east flow is almost at right angles to that direction of ice flow.

The meltwater channel at Glen Valtos is part of a sequence of glaciofluvial features created by meltwater flowing from west to east. Glaciofluvial deposits are found at the channel mouth, by Miavaig, and around the bay of Camas Uig to the west. The latter deposits include a large arcuate ridge trending approximately southwest to northeast and terminating by Uig Lodge, thought to have been part of the sub-glacial drainage heading towards Glen Valtos. Sand and gravel deposits at the southern end of the bay (at Carnish, or Carnais) are thought to have been deposited in a large delta, with ice in the west creating a large lake. The surface of this terrace is kettled, i.e. it has depressions indicating the former positions of large blocks of ice, and the sand and gravel have been quarried. Another large mound of stratified sand and gravel is found north of the bay. Overall, the topographic situation of the glaciofluvial deposits in the Uig area suggest that, at the time of their formation, drainage northwestwards to the sea via Camas Uig must have been blocked by ice, and it is most probable that it was at this time that Glen Valtos was eroded.

After the ice

Global (eustatic) sea level has been rising over the last 18,000 years, as the melting of icecaps has caused an increase in the volume of water in the world's oceans. As explained in Chapter 5, throughout much of Scotland this increase in sea level has been more than cancelled out by the crustal surface rising, or rebounding, due to the melting of the ice sheets that weighed it down during glaciations. Thus, the raised coastal features that are common throughout much of Scotland are absent from the Outer Hebrides, and in fact there is evidence that the coastline has been progressively submerged by rising sea level. Buried intertidal peat deposits, for example, are relatively common (such as on Pabbay). It seems that Area 14 lay outside the uplift dome, and it is considered (along with Area 9) to be a classic example of a 'drowned' glaciated archipelago landscape.

Sea level was around 120 m lower during the Devensian glaciation, exposing the shallow, gently sloping parts of the Hebridean Platform (Fig. 253), as is found west of South Harris in particular (and in most of Area 9). This is in contrast to much of the Minch coastline, where a steep scarp, roughly coincident with the Minch Fault, drops off rapidly to over 100 m depth. As sea level then rose, the undulating knock-and-lochan topography of the Hebridean Platform was gradually submerged, with the knocks remaining above water to create the numerous rocky reefs and skerries seen today. Further south, it is thought that the Sound of Harris became submerged some 6000 years ago, separating the islands of the Outer Hebrides. Deep glaciated troughs were also flooded, creating the long, deep sea lochs that today penetrate far inland, such as Lochs Seaforth and Roag. As a result of this submergence, the coastline of Area 14 is highly indented. As Tertiary valley erosion was often controlled by underlying bedrock, which in turn guided glacial erosion, so the flooding of these valleys has created peninsulas, islands and sea lochs that coincide with the underlying bedrock structure, particularly major faults (Fig. 248).

Smaller-scale landscape features created by rising sea levels are shingle storm ridges, which often mark the crest of sandy beaches in this Area – as sea level has risen, beach material has been driven landwards over the undulating glaciated landscape. A number of lochs have become impounded by these storm ridges, such as the shallow Loch Mor Barvas (Loch Mor Bharabhais) in northwest Lewis.

Onshore, the land has seen a number of important changes since the end of the Devensian. As the final remnants of ice melted away, Area 9 would have supported open grassland vegetation, similar to some parts of northern Canada today. However, as temperatures warmed and soils matured, woodland became widely developed. This woodland then began to be replaced by blanket peat, possibly due to the climate becoming cooler and wetter, although the occurrence of charcoal in peat-bog records from South Uist (Area 9) suggests that deforestation by humans may also have contributed. Today, only tiny remnants of woodland remain, mostly on sheltered islands within lochs. Blanket peat is meanwhile widespread, particularly in the lower-lying regions. Peat is particularly well developed on Lewis, whose central northern plateau is covered by one of the largest undisturbed expanses of blanket bog in Britain, supporting a unique range of plant species and birds. It is likely that many of the rocky knolls and low hills now protruding above the peat were once covered too, as peat has been gathered for fuel for centuries. Each peat-cutting episode involves around 1 m depth, and most of the island has been worked over several times. Peat is still gathered today, and the peat banks from which peat is cut form obvious landscape features.

Although peat is widespread across Area 14, glaciated bedrock is often at or near to the surface, in places spectacularly so, giving rise to an almost lunar landscape. Lewisian gneiss is on the whole very impermeable, and this fact, together with the high rainfall experienced here, has led to the development of an extensive network of lochans. Pools and streams are common too on the blanket peat of north Lewis, but on a smaller scale to the bodies of freshwater further south in Lewis and Harris, where they really become one of the dominant landscape features. Indeed, the sheer number of these bodies of water is remarkable – the Outer Hebrides make up 1.3 per cent of the landmass of Great Britain, but contain some 15 per cent of the total area of standing water, despite the vast majority of the lochans having a surface area of less than 25 km^2.

An important feature of the coastal landscape of the Outer Isles is the presence of machair. This name is given to the gently sloping coastal plain composed of wind-blown calcareous shell sand. Machair is one of Europe's rarest landscapes and is unique to northwest Scotland and the west of Ireland, where its colourful summer flora and short-cropped grass cover present a memorable sight. The unusually shell-rich sand originated during the Devensian, when low sea temperatures killed off many of the carbonate-shelled marine animals. Subsequent onshore currents and wind then reworked this material, depositing it on the edge of the ice-scoured Lewisian platform as beach material, backed by dunes, with the machair plain beyond (see Fig. 177, Area 9). The composition of the sand is an integral part of the machair system, and the relative hardness of the Lewisian gneiss is therefore another important factor in machair formation: the lack of easily eroded rock means that little sediment is carried by rivers to the coast, and so the sands have a high percentage of offshore-derived shelly material. The high carbonate content helps create fertile free-draining soils, lacking in bulky organic matter. These are the most fertile soils on the islands, and have greatly influenced the location of the major settlements.

FIG 259. The bay of Luskentyre (10 km west of Tarbert): machair carbonate sediment forming bay and wind-blown dune field. (© Adrian Warren/lastrefuge.co.uk)

Although the most extensive machair of northwest Scotland is found in Areas 9 and 6 (the Uists, Barra and Tiree), important areas do occur in Area 14. The finest machair plains, most closely approaching the superb examples in the Uists, are found in South Harris, associated with the huge sandy beaches and dunes of Northton (Taobh Tuath) and Luskentyre (Losgaintir). Indeed, the area around Luskentyre is considered one of the finest examples anywhere of a geomorphological system that incorporates beach, sand dunes, machair and salt-marsh, and is an important location for the study of coastal evolution (Fig. 259). The sand dunes found on the north side of Luskentyre Bay are some of the highest in the Western Isles, being on average 14 m high. The southern part of Pabbay (Pabaigh) is also interesting, being home to the largest expanse of hill machair vegetation in the Western Isles. Hill machair is created when shell sand is blown up a hill, and the machair vegetation in Pabbay extends to the remarkable height of almost 200 m.

FIG 260. Ancient lazybeds by the coast near Camus Uig, west Lewis. (© Adrian Warren/lastrefuge.co.uk)

The distinction seen and discussed in Area 9 between eastern and western shorelines is also seen in South Harris. In general, the coastline facing the Minch has a low and subdued relief of hummocky gneiss bedrock, forming countless small reefs and skerries interspersed with occasional impersistent shingle beaches. Meanwhile, sandy beaches and machair tend to be well developed on the west-facing coast. Part of the explanation for this is that Atlantic storm action from the west provides a constant supply of sediment to the western coastline that is not available on the more sheltered southeastern coastline. However, the east–west distinction is not nearly as obvious further north, where the majority of the coastline is made up of rocky cliffs broken by small coves in which much smaller quantities of sand have accumulated. The northwest coast does have a higher number of these sandy bays than the southeast coast (Fig. 253), including the large and spectacular beach in Camas Uig, but they are by no means limited to this coastline. Indeed, the area north of Stornoway is unusual in that it is the only place in the Outer Hebrides in which machair occurs on the Minch coast.

It seems that offshore bathymetry has also played an important role in machair formation, and on Figure 253 it is clear that the Hebridean Platform is much wider west of the Uists and South Harris. It seems likely that more sediment will have accumulated offshore where the platform is shallower and more gently sloping, and that more of this sediment can therefore be pushed onshore to form machair.

In between the bays of North Harris and Lewis, spectacular cliff architecture is a common feature, particularly, for example, at the Butt of Lewis and Mangersta (Mangurstadh, west of Camas Uig). Around the latter area, a large area of bare sand extends well inland from the beach, illustrating the final stages of machair erosion. Sea stacks are also commonly seen, such as at the southeastern end of Garry Beach, near Tolsta, northeast Lewis. The abundance of sea cliffs and uninhabited islands in this Area has resulted in it, along with Area 9, having many of the UK's most important seabird colonies.

Some of the most recent landscape features are man-made, as humans have inhabited the Outer Isles for thousands of years. Remnants from ancient cultures are scattered around the islands in the form of brochs, Bronze Age burial mounds, stone circles and the famous standing stones of Callanish on Lewis, thought to have been a key ceremonial centre for island tribes since at least 2000 BC. The Callanish stones were excavated from 1.5 m of peat in 1851, demonstrating the minimum rate of peat growth over the 4000 or so years since the stones were erected.

Life has always been difficult on the Western Isles. As described above, the soils are generally nutrient-poor, acid and poorly drained, with widespread peat development. The main exception is machair, although this habitat is not nearly as extensive as in the southern Outer Hebridean islands. Even where soil is suitable for agriculture, it tends to be thin, as soil development is limited by climatic conditions. The human struggle with this inhospitable terrain is shown by the hard-won *feannagan* or lazybeds, parallel ridges of built-up soil separated by narrow drainage channels (Fig. 260). This method of arable cultivation is now largely extinct, as few people actively croft today, but was once widespread, as it is about the only way it is possible to grow crops on Lewis and Harris (and in much of northwest Scotland). The raised ridges were painstakingly constructed from the ditches alongside, where necessary after removing the covering peat, with seaweed and old thatch employed as fertilisers. For drainage purposes, the long ridges tended to be constructed following the contours of the land. Where well-drained soil was needed, such as where corn was grown for animal feed, the drainage ditches were waist-deep. Today, old lazybeds, though overgrown with grass and heather, form a distinctive feature of the lower-lying land in Area 14, and can even be seen on many of the small, uninhabited islands.

CHAPTER 20

Area 15: Cape Wrath

NOT ONLY IS AREA 15 one of the most remote in mainland Britain (Fig. 261), it has a remarkably empty coastline of cliffs and wide sandy bays. Inland, it has landscapes that combine rugged and bare bedrock with isolated mountains, giving the Area a special magical quality (Fig. 262).

FIG 261. Location map for Area 15.

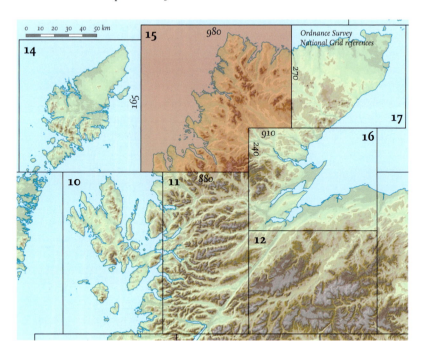

STORIES FROM THE BEDROCK

Chapter 4 summarised the bedrock history of Scotland as a whole, dividing it for convenience into nine successive episodes of bedrock formation. Here we comment on the episodes represented in Area 15 (Figs 263, 264).

Episodes of the Greenland margin

These three episodes are only represented in the Northern Highland terrane of Scotland (Chapter 4), and have similarities with episodes represented in southeast Greenland. Because of this, it seems likely that the crusts of these parts of Scotland and Greenland were united over the long periods of time involved, and only became separated when the extensive continent involved was split and started to drift apart as the Atlantic Ocean formed over the last 60 million years.

FIG 262. Natural and man-made features of Area 15.

Maximum elevation in this Area: 1119 m

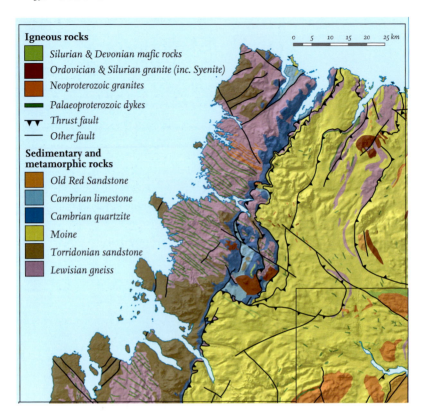

FIG 263. Simplified geology and hill-shaded topography for Area 15.

Episode 1: Formation of the Lewisian Complex
These metamorphic rocks record the oldest crustal events preserved at the surface in Britain. They were repeatedly mobilised and altered during the Archaean and the Palaeoproterozoic. Much of this complex history was first researched using the outcrops of Area 15. It was first realised here that metamorphic rocks that originated as igneous rocks in Archaean times (> 2.5 billion years old) could be separated from those of Palaeoproterozoic age (< 2.5 billion years old) by an event of dyke intrusion about 2.4 billion years ago that produced what are now called the Scourie dykes. Disentangling the sequences of crustal movement (folding, shearing and fracturing) is extremely difficult and involves the interpretation of field and geochemical (particularly age) evidence, and there are still disagreements about the details of the history. Researchers have used the names Scourian, Inverian and Laxfordian for events all recognised in different Area 15 localities (Fig. 264).

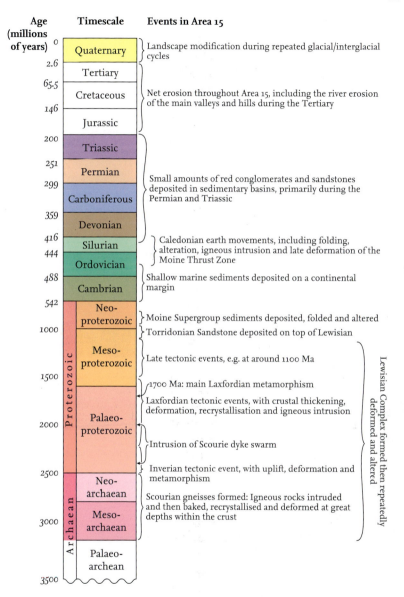

FIG 264. Timeline of bedrock and surface-layer events in Area 15.

FIG 265. Lewisian knock-and lochan landscape near Laxford Bridge, showing the widespread lack of superficial deposits on the Lewisian metamorphic bedrock. A widespread lineation from bottom-left to top-right is probably due largely to faulting, whereas the bottom-right to top-left lineation runs parallel to dyke intrusions. (© Adrian Warren/lastrefuge.co.uk)

The Lewisian generally has been eroded into present-day landscapes with the characteristic scale and roughness of topographic features that produce the knock-and-lochan landscape (Fig. 265).

Episode 2: Formation of the Torridon Sandstones
The landscape formed by the isolated, 'relict' mountains of horizontally layered Torridon Sandstones on a basement of knock-and-lochan Lewisian landscape is one of the most striking landscape features of Area 15 (Figs 266, 267). The name *monadnock* has been applied to isolated mountains of this sort, after Mount Monadnock in New Hampshire, USA, and it is a useful label to apply to some of the isolated mountains of the Inverpolly area (Stac Pollaidh, Cul Beag, Cul Mor, Suilven and Canisp), near Loch Assynt, further north.

FIG 266. Five 'relict' Torridonian mountains on the knock-and-lochan Lewisian landscape. From left to right: Canisp, Suilven, Cul Mor, Cul Beag and Stac Pollaidh. (© British Geological Survey/NERC. All rights reserved)

FIG 267. This photograph shows the clear unconformity between the Torridonian Sandstone of Suilven and the knock-and-lochan landscape of the Lewisian Complex. (© Patricia & Angus Macdonald/Aerographica/Scottish Natural Heritage)

However, it is notable that in the southern and northern parts of Area 15, Torridonian Sandstones are more continuously present at the surface than in the area of classic monadnock or relict scenery. For example, in the south, between the mountain range of An Teallach and Achiltibuie, north of Loch Broom, Torridonian outcrops are almost continuous. And much further north, north of Kinlochbervie (Fig. 262), large though relatively flat areas are also formed of Torridonian Sandstones. Possible reasons for this will be discussed below.

Episode 3. Cambrian and Ordovician sedimentation
Marine sediments of Cambrian and Ordovician age occur more or less continuously from near An Teallach in the south of Area 15 to Durness on the north coast. Not only are the outcrops largely continuous, but the succession is relatively uniform along the outcrop belt. The succession starts with Early Cambrian quartz-rich sandstones, followed by an interval of mudstones, then eventually by thick limestones with Early Cambrian, and then, after a break in the succession, Early Ordovician thick carbonates. The break in this carbonate succession is not sharp, nor does it involve any folding of the layers, making it clear that the sedimentation occurred during a time of crustal stability, or lack of crustal movement. Sea level and the surface of the crust remained within a few tens of metres of the present-day surface throughout this Cambrian to Ordovician episode.

During late Silurian or early Devonian times, when Caledonian compressive movements developed widely across Scotland, the presence of these relatively weak Cambrian and Ordovician sediments resulted in fracture failure and local folding that formed the Moine Thrust Zone.

Episodes of Caledonian mountain building
Episode 4: Making the core of the Caledonian mountains
East of the Moine Thrust Zone, most of the rest of Area 15 is underlain by outcrops of the Moine Supergroup, consisting very largely of metamorphosed sediments, although some folds may contain cores of material that originally formed part of the Lewisian Complex. Depending on the mineral composition of the original Moine sediments, the metamorphic rocks are more or less micaceous and/or carbonate-rich, and this has allowed some mapping of the folds and faults that have been formed at various times during the movement history of the Moines. Geochemical age work suggests that important episodes of movement and alteration took place some 800, 740, 470 and 410 million years ago, the most recent of which were parts of the Caledonian mountain building. The youngest of the events, at 410 million years ago (early Devonian), included the movement of the Moine Thrust Zone.

Igneous intrusions occurred at various times during this complex history of movement and alteration. Some of these were early enough to have been altered during phases of Caledonian or earlier metamorphism. One of these early intrusions resulted in the Carn Chuinneag granite (located on Fig. 262, although most of the intrusion is in Area 16), which created a zone of alteration of the surrounding Moine meta-sediments, in which the original sedimentary structures, such as cross-bedding and desiccation cracks, were preserved in such a way that they were not destroyed by later metamorphism, although this was severe.

Other intrusions took place later than the main phases of metamorphism, many being similar to the Caledonian late granite intrusions that are a feature of much of Scotland. Others are remarkable for the presence of minerals rich in potassium and sodium (alkalis). The large intrusions tend in most cases to be represented in the topography by high ground, a clear example being the alkaline intrusions that form the Ben Loyal massif, near Tongue (Fig. 262). The alkaline Borralan intrusion outcropping east of Ledmore contrasts with this because much of it has lower topography than most of the surrounding Assynt area. There has been speculation that the unique development of multiple thrust sheets in the Moine Thrust Zone of the Assynt area may be the result of the emplacement of these igneous intrusions here.

The Moine Thrust Zone was first mapped in detail by the famous British Geological Survey geologists Benjamin Peach and John Horne, with others, and the results were published in 1907. A stone monument to this work now looks out over Loch Assynt at Inchnadamph. Peach and Horne mapped in beautiful detail the way that low-angle reverse faults or thrusts had carried large sheets of older, deeper rocks over younger, more superficial rocks in response to compressive forces acting in the Earth's crust. This appears to have happened as one of the final phases of Caledonian movements in this part of Area 15 (Figs 268, 269). This was one of the first places in the world where it was demonstrated

FIG 268. Cross-section illustrating the repeated horizontal movement of sheets of older bedrock over younger bedrock.

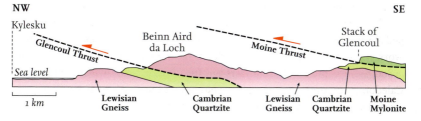

FIG 269. Glencoul Thrust on the north side of Loch Glencoul (the northwestern thrust in Fig. 268). (© Lorne Gill, Scottish Natural Heritage)

that compressional movements during mountain building can result in shortening of the crust of the Earth by many kilometres.

Episodes 5 and 6
Episode 5 is recognised as a distinct movement episode in the Southern Uplands of Scotland, but cannot be recognised as a distinct episode in the general Caledonian movement of northern Scotland, including Area 15. Episode 6, the deposition of the Lower Old Red Sandstone, is recognised widely across Scotland, resulting from a late phase of Caledonian mountain-building movements in which distinctive deposition occurred when much of the crustal surface was above sea level. However, only minor outcrops have been found within the boundaries of Area 15, though they are present over much greater areas to the south and east.

Post-Caledonian bedrock episodes
Episodes 7 and 8
Late Palaeozoic (Late Devonian, Carboniferous and Permian) and Mesozoic sedimentation is represented in Area 15 only by a number of relatively small areas in which red conglomerates and sandstones accumulated apparently in

response to fault movements that resulted from stretching of the crust in the coastal and offshore regions along the present-day north and west coast. Most of these sediments are now thought to have accumulated in Permian and/or Triassic times, but in some cases they may be Old Red Sandstone (Late Silurian or Devonian) or even Torridonian in age.

Episode 9: Tertiary volcanism
There is no evidence preserved within Area 15 that the important Tertiary volcanic activity to the southwest influenced the landscape here.

MAKING THE LANDSCAPE

Surface-modification episodes
Episode 10: Tertiary landscape evolution
The scale of the valleys, hills and mountains that form the best-known features of the landscape of Area 15, and the pattern of later glacial erosion, strongly suggest that river-valley erosion during the Tertiary made an important contribution to the topography, before the Ice Age caused the growth of ice sheets and glaciers.

Episodes 11 and 12: glacial and post-glacial landscape evolution
It is generally accepted that there were numerous distinct periods of cold climate during the Ice Age (Chapter 5), and that many of these saw ice sheets and glaciers covering and eroding the landscape of northern Scotland. In practice, evidence of the action of early glacial episodes is largely missing on land, and it is only the last (Devensian) glaciation that can be reconstructed in any detail. Even for this last main glacial episode, much of the evidence has come from investigating the retreat stages of the ice.

An exception to this is the occurrence of deposits found in caves. These are likely to be preserved even when surface deposits have been removed by erosion. Because of the importance of dissolution of limestones by freshwater streams, the caves of the Area occur mainly in areas of outcrop of Cambrian and Ordovician limestones (Episode 3, above). Those in the Durness Limestone at Creag nan Uamh, near Inchnadamph (at the east end of Loch Assynt, inland from Lochinver), have yielded a particularly rich fauna including brown bear, polar bear, arctic fox, northern lynx, lemming, reindeer and wolf, and also, remarkably, birds, fish and amphibians. These animals seem to have lived in the area in periods during the last glaciation, and have provided radiocarbon ages of between 44,000 and 9000 years.

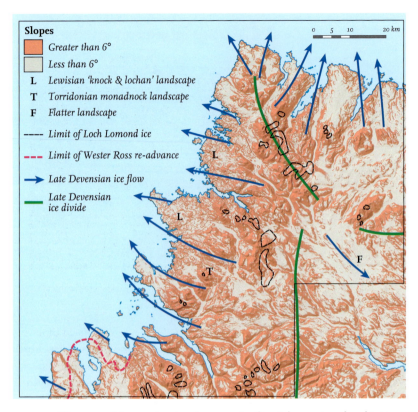

FIG 270. Slope map of Area 15, showing slopes greater than 6 degrees in red, and Late Devensian ice-flow directions and local development of ice during the Loch Lomond Stadial.

A generalised summary of the ice-flow pattern over Area 15 at the height of the Late Devensian glaciation shows the ice flowing outwards to the west, north and east from a central area that is similar to the present-day watershed (Fig. 270). Much of the detail of the last phases of this glaciation comes from investigation of the recent and relatively short-lived ice advance that occurred during the Loch Lomond Stadial, between about 13,000 and 11,500 years ago (Chapter 5). During this advance the only ice that built up in Area 15 consisted of small icecaps and isolated valley or corrie glaciers, although of course ice cover and erosion were much more widespread in the main Devensian glaciation and earlier in the Pleistocene.

The mountain range of An Teallach (Fig. 271), with its highest peak at 1062 m, consists of shapely peaks and corries of Torridonian Sandstones with small areas of Cambrian Quartzites down its eastern margin. It provides particularly good

FIG 271. Part of the An Teallach Range. (© Patricia & Angus Macdonald/Aerographica/Scottish Natural Heritage)

examples of glacial and periglacial features dating from Late Devensian times. Directional erosional features such as ice-generated chattermarks (regular chips) and striations, made on bedrock surfaces as ice-locked pebbles were sheared over the surface, show how the Late Devensian ice approaching from the south and east divided to flow around the An Teallach range. During Late Devensian times, the highest peaks of the range appear to have projected above the surface of the main ice sheets, and have been ice-shattered distinctly more than the lower slopes that were being covered by the ice sheets themselves. Wind transport of sand is another distinctive feature of the high ground on An Teallach, indicating the dry and unvegetated surfaces that must often have developed under really cold conditions.

This is a good point at which to consider why there is such a distinctive area of Torridonian monadnocks or isolated mountains in Area 15 (e.g. Fig. 266). In this area, from Stac Pollaidh in the south to Canisp in the north, the relatively uniform flow direction of the Devensian ice generated erosion to apparently just the level at which the unconformity between the Torridonian and Lewisian became exposed again for the first time since it was covered by Torridonian sediments some billion years ago. Further south, and near the north coast, the cover of Torridonian remained largely intact, and no monadnocks were formed. There may have been an important difference in the level of the Torridonian on Lewisian unconformity in this part of Area 15, and/or there may even have been a difference in younger vertical crustal movement. This latter may also be represented by the very different Moine Thrust Zone crustal thickness in the Assynt area east of the monadnocks, and the areas further south and north.

Slope mapping is a useful tool in seeking out different landscape types on a regional scale (Fig. 270). The knock-and-lochan pattern, so typical of the Lewisian Complex, shows up because of its large numbers of slopes of limited extent (less than 0.5 km), in contrast with the more extensive slopes that make up hills, mountain and valley sides of the more continuous Torridonian, Moine Thrust and Moine Supergroup landscapes. In the latter, there are distinct relatively flat areas, such as those on both flanks of Strath Tirry, northeast of Loch Shin. These flatter areas lack large slopes (at least steeper than 6 degrees), but contain minor ridge features that appear to be bedrock features either picked out by widespread glacial erosion or penetrating though a cover of glacial deposits. Whichever is the case, these flatter areas lack large, well-defined erosional valleys.

The Gairloch moraine, in the southwest corner of Area 15, consists of a sinuous low ridge of boulders and/or a boundary to the cover of boulder clay or drift. It extends for more than 10 km, in a generally north/south direction, across the empty interior of the peninsula. The topography traversed by the moraine undulates in elevation up to well over 200 m above sea level, and appears to represent the western limit of an ice-sheet front that has been described as a product of the Wester Ross Advance, which was probably slightly older than the Loch Lomond Advance.

Two lochs in the Inverpolly area where the sediments have been cored (Cam Loch, 2 km west of Ledmore, and Loch Scionascaig, 3 km north of Stac Pollaidh) have provided detailed vegetation records of lake and wetland environments from about 13,000 years ago to the present. These suggest considerable climate variations with pine- and oak-wood development, but evidence of climate deterioration over the last 4000 years. In contrast, similar work carried out on Loch an Druim, near Loch Eriboll on the north coast of Area 15, shows a distinctly more northerly history of vegetation, with no pine or oak.

Evidence of sea-level change along the coasts of Area 15 has been recognised in the Gairloch peninsula (in the south) and on the north coast around Tongue Bay, where there are erosional rock platforms distinctly above present-day sea level. However, the age of these is not clear, so it is not possible to interpret the balance between sea-level change and any crustal movement.

CHAPTER 21

Area 16: Inverness

THE MORAY FIRTH FORMS the central feature of Area 16 (Fig. 272). This triangular arm of the North Sea narrows southwestwards towards the city of Inverness. To the northwest and southeast of the Moray Firth, respectively, the mountains of the Northern Highlands and the Grampians provide symmetrical borderlands. At the point of closure at the southwestern end of the Moray Firth, the Great Glen Fault emerges from its traverse of the Scottish

FIG 272. Location map for Area 16.

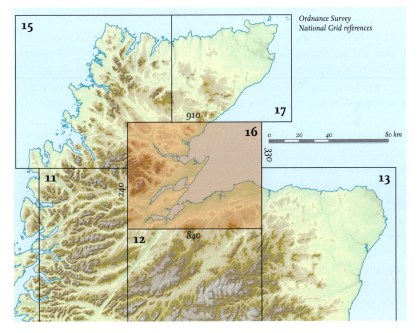

FIG 273. Natural and man-made features of Area 16.

Highlands, where it forms one of the great terrane boundaries of Scottish bedrock history (see Fig. 20, Chapter 4). The continuation of the Great Glen Fault can be followed northeasterly from the closure, shaping the strikingly linear coastlines of the Black Isle and the Fearn peninsula (Fig. 273).

The town of Inverness formally became a city in 2001. It is the administrative centre of the Highland council area, and is generally promoted as the capital of the Highlands of Scotland. With a growing population, now about 70,000, it is the central hub for northern road, rail and air communications. It is not unreasonable to claim that Inverness owes these key roles to its setting in Scotland's landscape, and that this, in turn, is the result of the history and position of the Great Glen Fault.

STORIES FROM THE BEDROCK

Moine and Dalradian Supergroups and their igneous intrusions

The metamorphic rocks that form the basement of most of Area 16 originally formed as sediments on the surface of the Earth (Fig. 274). These original

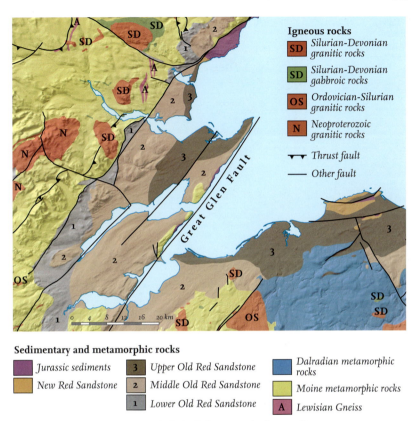

FIG 274. Simplified geology and hill-shaded topography for Area 16.

sediments were later altered (metamorphosed), or recrystallised, by one or more episodes of high crustal temperature, pressure and/or movement. No fossil evidence is available to help to date the original sediments, but geochemical (radiometric) dating has been helping to clarify the relationship of these rocks and their episodes to other metamorphic rocks in Scotland. It is concluded that all the metamorphosed sediments, at least within Area 16, were predominantly deposited during Neoproterozoic and Ordovician times (Fig. 275). They formed in one or more basins on the surface, accumulating sediment thicknesses of many kilometres, although subsequent crustal movements have changed the original arrangement so that it is now impossible to estimate the extent or shape of the basins or their thicknesses.

Before metamorphism the sediments were mainly bedded mixtures of sandstones and mudstones, with a small proportion of lime-rich rocks.

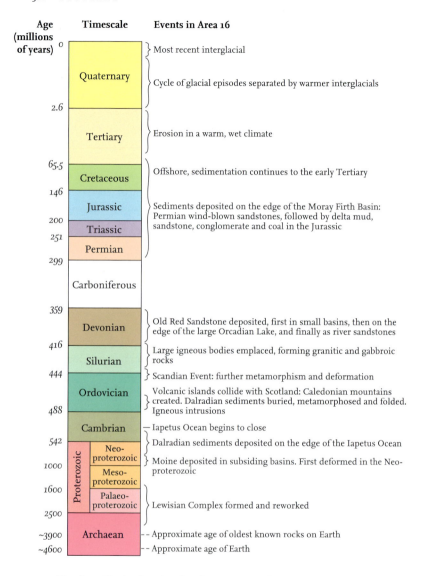

FIG 275. Timeline of bedrock and surface-layer events in Area 16.

In their metamorphic state, these have sometimes been given descriptive names incorporating classical Greek words, such as *meta-psammite* (altered sandstone), *meta-pelite* (altered mudstone) and *meta-semipelite* (altered mixed sandstone and mudstone). In addition, the term *quartzite* is often also used for altered, particularly pure, quartz sandstone. Sedimentary structures, such as ripples, are sometimes preserved in areas where the rocks have not been too strongly altered. The presence in some areas of folded layers with a high proportion of pelitic, altered mudstone has provided bedrock more readily attacked by Tertiary and Quaternary erosion, so that features of the present-day landscape have clearly been influenced by the original material properties of the bedrock.

All the metamorphic rocks of Area 16 appear to have acted as part of the core of the Caledonian mountain belt. British Geological Survey workers have simplified the labelling of these metamorphic rocks by using the term Moine Supergroup for rocks northwest of the Great Glen Fault. These rocks are regarded as Neoproterozoic in age. They have arbitrarily taken the line of the Great Glen Fault to separate them from the Neoproterozoic and lowest Palaeozoic metamorphic rocks of the Dalradian Supergroup to the southeast, though they also recognise an area of rocks southeast of Inverness which is Moine-like, and is taken to be equivalent to the earlier Moine Supergroup further northwest (Fig. 274).

Large areas of intrusive igneous rocks make up almost 30 per cent of the bedrock mapped at the present surface of Area 16. Most of these are of granitic coarse-grained material that was intruded after the metamorphic recrystallisation of the surrounding rocks. Arrival of granitic liquids from below must have been important in creating expansion of the crust, probably associated with the uplift of its surface in late Silurian to early Devonian times (from about 430 million years ago: the Scandian event – see Chapter 4). Earlier intrusions have also been mapped, dating from before some phases of the metamorphism of the area. The best known of these is around Carn Chuinneag (N on Fig. 274), in the west-central margin of Area 16, where intrusions extending over about 30 km, parallel to the general fold direction of the surrounding Moine metamorphics, occurred before the main metamorphism and were altered by it. As in the case of the great majority of these intrusions, the resistance of the intruded material to Tertiary and Quaternary landscape erosion has caused them to form high ground in the present-day topography.

Caledonian mountain evolution, and initiation of the Great Glen Fault and other transcurrent faults

Broad studies of the North Atlantic Caledonian mountain belt have led to greater understanding of mountain-belt processes generally, and a more complete understanding of the evolution of the belt in Scotland. In Northern Scotland (Chapter 4), episodes of rock alteration (metamorphism), igneous intrusion and rock surface uplift are often now thought to have been linked to continuing plate-margin convergence, with subduction and collisions, which punctuated the evolution of the Caledonian mountain belt.

Widespread left-lateral strike-slip fault movement in response to shear is now recognised as a late feature of the Caledonian mountain belt, probably starting in mid-Silurian times (430 million years ago: Scandian). In terms of local movement within Area 16, the Great Glen Fault was probably initiated during this episode, with parallel left-lateral movement on similar faults across the Highlands. However, in spite of various suggestions in the past, it is now generally agreed that it is not possible to pinpoint total movement on the Great Glen Fault during this important initial episode by matching bedrock features on the two sides. It seems to be the case that only certain later, and probably lesser, movements can be detected and measured, as will be described below.

Old Red Sandstone

The Old Red Sandstone was deposited on metamorphosed Caledonian rocks and associated intrusives throughout much of Highland Scotland. It consists of conglomerates (with rounded clasts) or breccias (with more angular clasts), sandstones and mudstones that appear to have been deposited on alluvial fans, on river flood plains and in lakes. It is generally red, indicating deposition in well-drained, oxidising, alluvial settings, although some of the mudstones are grey or even black, indicating deposition under chemically reducing conditions due to the presence of organic material in swamps or lakes. Latest work, based on fossil content, suggests that the Scottish Old Red ranges in overall age from mid-early Devonian (say 415 million years in age) to as young as earliest Carboniferous (350 million years in age).

For many years, researchers have distinguished Lower, Middle and Upper Old Red Sandstone divisions (1, 2 and 3 on Fig. 274).

Lower Old Red Sandstone

Some of the deposits may be as old as 414 million years, but most appear to be late early Devonian, about 402 million years old. Variable sediments include lake deposits, particularly in the Strathpeffer area (some 20 km northwest of Inverness), and suggest that crustal movements were forming a number of relatively small basins, some of which were folded and faulted, probably bringing to an end Lower Old Red sedimentation (e.g. faulting on Struie Hill, 18 km north of Alness), before the Middle Old Red basin was initiated.

Middle Old Red Sandstone

These deposits appear to range from about 397 to about 390 million years old, within the mid-Devonian, and are often called the Orcadian Old Red Sandstone. In Area 16 these sediments represent deposits along the southern edge of the large Orcadian river and lake basin that was centred in Caithness (Area 17) and Orkney (Area 18), and which extended further north as far as Shetland (Area 19). The remarkable fossil-bearing fish beds that formed in stable lake settings are described in those Area treatments.

Upper Old Red Sandstone
River-deposited sandstones predominate, starting in about the late mid-Devonian (388 million years ago) and continuing possibly until early Carboniferous times (350 million years ago).

Further development of the Great Glen Fault and other transcurrent faults
Detailed examination of the Old Red Sandstone has shown that the Lower Old Red Sandstone may have been deposited under the influence of the last stages of late Caledonian shearing and faulting, and that the variety, arrangement and deformation of the numerous small basins may be a reflection of this. In contrast, the deposits of the large Middle Old Red Sandstone Orcadian basin show little evidence of faulting during their accumulation. They also demonstrate that a distinct phase of fault movement on the Great Glen Fault system has taken place more recently than the late Caledonian phase described above. This later phase is discussed below.

Permian and Mesozoic
There is a gap in the time sequence of deposits after the Upper Old Red Sandstone (mainly Devonian) (Fig. 275), and it is not until the New Red Sandstone (Permian and/or Triassic) and Jurassic that sedimentary evidence has been preserved in Area 16. The new sedimentation left deposits at various coastal localities on the two margins that appear to represent events early in the life of a new basin, the Moray Firth Basin.

On the western margin, the largest of the bedrock areas extends between Golspie, Brora and Helmsdale on the downthrow side of the Helmsdale Fault. Further south, on the downthrow side of the Great Glen Fault, there are small fragments at Balintore and Eathie (Fig. 274). In the bedrock discussion for Area 17 (Caithness), a reconstruction has been provided of the way movements on the Helmsdale Fault caused the formation of remarkable debris-flow deposits of late Jurassic age. The same down-faulted coastal block extends for a further 20 km southwestwards into Area 16. The Late Jurassic deposits are estimated to be at least 500 m thick, and traversing southwestwards further down the coast, Jurassic deposits are exposed representing older and older deposits of middle and early

Jurassic age. Conglomerates, sandstones, mudstones and even coals are present in the Jurassic succession, formed in deltas, with local seawater and freshwater conditions. The coals were formerly the basis of mining at Brora, the only place in the UK where Jurassic coals were economic, at least for a period.

Along the southern margin of the Moray Firth Basin, fragments of Permian to Jurassic bedrock sediments occur on land north of Elgin, for some 12 km west of Lossiemouth. Much of the sediment consists of sandstones deposited by large wind-blown dunes, but river deposits also accumulated, and the Jurassic is represented in boreholes by mudstones with marine fossils. Fossil reptiles have been found in this succession, and some of them are displayed in the Elgin Museum.

These small land areas of Permian to Mesozoic bedrock on the two edges of the Moray Firth are the margins of a much more complete basin succession that forms the floor of the basin (Fig. 276). Sediments in the offshore parts of the basin have been investigated in detail by oil companies. The sediments extend from Permian through Triassic, Jurassic, Cretaceous and early Tertiary in age. The obvious sign of success in this work is the cluster of oil platforms over the Beatrice oil field, which is situated some 60 km northeast of Golspie and is visible just over 20 km offshore from the coast road further north (Fig. 277). The oil itself was probably derived from Middle Old Red Sandstone and Late Jurassic mudstones, and then migrated to the porous Middle Jurassic sandstones in a fold and fault structure of the Moray Firth Basin floor.

The faulting and folding of the sediments of the Moray Firth Basin provide evidence of the movement of the basin floor as the sediment was accumulating, and it is clear that some of this movement was linked to further transcurrent movement on the Great Glen Fault. Figure 278 uses a reconstruction of the Middle Old Red Sandstone outcrops to suggest that subsequent movement on this transcurrent fault was probably some 20 km in a right-lateral strike-slip sense.

MAKING THE LANDSCAPE

Tertiary

The discussion of Area 11 (Affric, Loch Maree to Ben Nevis) contains some consideration of the origins of the remarkable series of large east/west-trending, open-ended valleys that cut across the spine of the Northern Highlands. The conclusion was that Glens Cannich, Affric and Moriston are such major features that they have probably been forming by river erosion through much of the Tertiary, as well as the Quaternary. It was speculated that the erosion of these

AREA 16: INVERNESS · 391

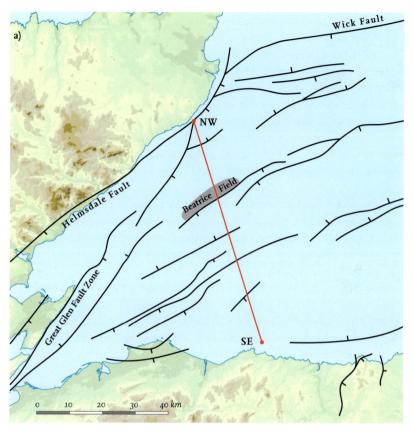

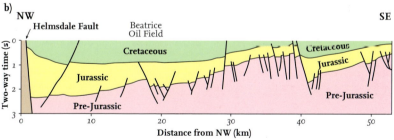

FIG 276. General map of the inner Moray Firth Basin, showing faulting pattern, and simplified geological cross-section, locating also the Beatrice oil field. The cross-section is based on seismic reflection studies by the oil industry. Two-way time is a measure of the speed of propagation of seismic waves and is used to estimate the thickness patterns of bedrock intervals of different ages. (From Hudson & Trewin 2002, Fig. 11.2)

FIG 277. Beatrice oil platform. (© Adrian Warren/lastrefuge.co.uk)

FIG 278. Diagram showing the 20 km of right-lateral movement along the Great Glen Fault that appears to have taken place between Devonian times and now.

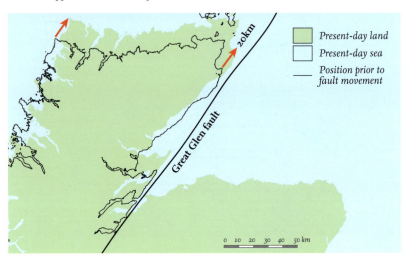

major valleys may even have been initiated by upward movement of the surface of the crust in the western Hebridean area, in response to the Early Tertiary igneous intrusions and extrusions that were taking place there.

The Ice Age

In Scotland most of the evidence for local erosion and deposition by ice has been left by the last main glaciation, the Devensian (Chapter 5). This started about 115,000 years ago and was largely over by about 10,000 years ago.

Figure 279 shows the generalised pattern of ice flow that is thought to have existed during the Devensian across Area 16. In the west of the Area, ice flowed broadly eastwards and northeastwards, parallel to the axes of the Dornoch and Cromarty Firths. Along the southern margin, major ice streams emerged flowing northeastwards along the Great Glen, paralleling those further southeast along the Findhorn and Spey valleys. These flows combined to produce flow northeastwards and then eastwards, paralleling the southern coast and margin of the inner Moray Firth. The flow pattern on this margin of the inner Moray Firth contrasts with that of the Dornoch and Cromarty Firth margin just described. This ice-flow stream, called the Kildrummie Ice Stream in this book, may reflect

FIG 279. Generalised ice-flow patterns for Area 16.

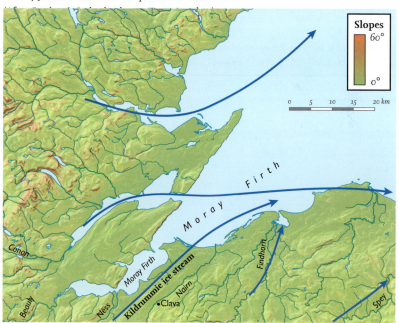

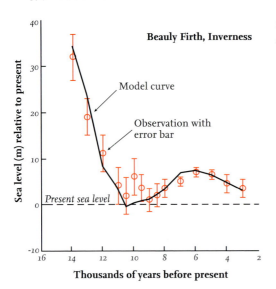

FIG 280. Sea-level curve for Area 16.

an ice-margin valley feature that was so large it was formed, not just by Devensian ice erosion, but in earlier Ice Age episodes as well.

The name Kildrummie Ice Stream comes from the Kildrummie Kames locality that extends for some 10 km southwest of Nairn. The most distinctive features are ridges of sand and gravel, called *eskers*, that appear to have been deposited in channels under the Devensian ice. Part of the evidence for this is that they appear in some situations to have been deposited by water flows that were travelling up-slope, presumably under the high water flow pressures that could have been produced below the ice, as if in a pipe. Other typical features, called *kames*, appear to have formed at the surface along the edges of ice sheets, where ice cliffs at the edges of large blocks and sheets of ice moulded the piles of sand or gravel deposits produced by the water emerging from the ice.

Certain localities have been found in the mixed glacial and river deposits of the Kildrummie Ice Stream that hint at relationships with the sea. One locality of this sort is at Clava (Fig. 279), some 9 km east of Inverness, where a clay pit at an elevation of about 150 m above sea level has revealed a 5 m-thick layer of muddy material rich in shells, identified as typical of arctic, or near-arctic, sea conditions. Some workers have felt that the deposits are older than the last Late Devensian glacial episode, and the elevation above sea level has been the cause of speculation. However, it has also been suggested that the whole layer at Clava may have been transported as a large glacial erratic. This would seriously change its significance!

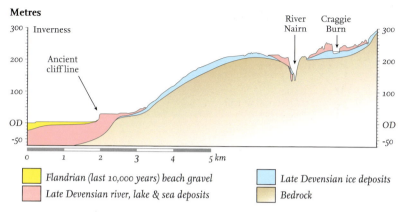

FIG 281. This schematic cross-section trending generally eastwards from Inverness represents the geometrical patterns of the young surface-blanket sediments.

After the ice

The landscape features described just above have been included in discussion of the Ice Age because, although formed by flowing water rather than flowing ice, they still were formed during the Ice Age, either below ice or at the margins of ice sheets.

The Area also contains many river terraces that represent fragments of sand and gravel flood plains that have been incised by more recent river activity, so that they are now elevated above present river level. These are highly characteristic of areas that have recently emerged from glacial conditions, and have been influenced not only by changing river flow patterns but also possibly by sea-level change.

Figure 280 shows predicted and observed values of relative sea level for the Beauly Firth. These data suggest that sea level was some 30 m above the present-day level about 14,000 years ago, and fell to near the present level 10,000 years ago, after which time worldwide sea-level rise matched the rise of the crust due to glacial unloading, and sea level varied by only a few metres (Chapter 5).

The cross-section in Figure 281 shows how recent sea level has modified the landscape created and left by late glacial events some 20,000 years ago. One of the remarkable features of the present-day coastline of the Moray Firth, across the whole of Area 16 and beyond, is the variety of the young coastal landscape forms developed beautifully along it. This coast is one of high sediment supply, due to strong sediment delivery by the rivers from their recently glaciated catchments, and also from the relatively shallow seas of the Moray Firth.

FIG 282. The Bar at Culbin, 5 km northeast of Nairn. (© Patricia & Angus Macdonald/ Aerographica/ Scottish Natural Heritage)

FIG 283. The Ardersier peninsula, 20 km northeast of Inverness, looking eastwards. Nairn is in the bay in the far distance, the eighteenth-century Fort George is in the foreground, and the offshore platform construction yard is in the middle distance amongst the wide expanse of intertidal coastal sediment. (© Adrian Warren/lastrefuge.co.uk)

Under these conditions, the active coastal landforms are particularly clearly developed, and prized by conservationists (Figs 282, 283). The name Culbin is famously associated with an extensive sand-blown dune system, now largely stabilised, but responsible in the past for periodic catastrophic covering of local settlements. But the same coastal stretch also shows fine active examples of gravel coastal plains and spits, and extensive intertidal sand-flats and salt-marshes, all tending to show longshore movement of sediment in response to tides, and to storms from the northern North Sea.

Areas influenced by strongly changing conditions will also have seen highly variable conditions of erosion and deposition, leading to great surface instability. So it is no surprise to find much evidence of debris flows and landslips. Indeed, debris-flow tongues and the scours left by their downhill movement are still active in present-day times, particularly on high ground, for example high on Ben Wyvis, some 30 km northwest of Inverness, where freezing and thawing of the ground material are still very active. At lower levels, many of the larger rivers have incised valleys that are full of varied terrace deposits, a clear indication of histories of active erosion and deposition since the main incision. Rivers such as the Nairn, Findhorn and Spey are spectacular examples of the formation of gorges in their middle reaches, and their histories of catastrophic flooding are a direct result of this pattern.

CHAPTER 22

Area 17: Caithness

THE OLD COUNTIES OF SUTHERLAND, in the west, and Caithness, in the northeast, are now part of the northern extent of the Highland Council area (Fig. 284). With a population of 25,000 in 2001 (from a peak of 45,000 in 1861), Area 17 is sparsely populated, and Thurso and Wick are the only towns with more than 7000 people. Although John o' Groats is known in the southern media as the top of the British mainland, it is simply a small settlement where the northerly running A99 trunk road ends abruptly, truncated by the northern coast. Dunnet Head, some 20 km to the west, extends several kilometres further north (Fig. 285).

First impressions of the landscapes of Area 17 can be gathered from the elevation map (Fig. 285). In the southeast, rounded hills several hundreds of metres high overlook the abrupt and straight coastline. This local landscape contrasts with the lower elevations, flatness and bleakness of the northeast corner of the Area between Latheron and Dounreay. Here the landscape is remarkable for the way the inland moors, devoid of many local features, contrast with sections of coastline with high and steep bedrock cliffs, sea stacks and caves. A traverse westwards along the north coast takes the traveller into another different landscape, with a coastline of headlands and highly indented bays. Here the inland landscape is drained by large numbers of northward-flowing river valleys. To the south of this landscape, midway between the two coastlines, the hills are more isolated, and separated by large elevated flat areas, often several kilometres across.

These variations of landscape are clearly closely linked to the bedrock history of the Area, as in the neighbouring Areas to the west (Area 16, Cape Wrath) and northeast (Area 18, Orkney). The same is true of the recent histories of surface modification.

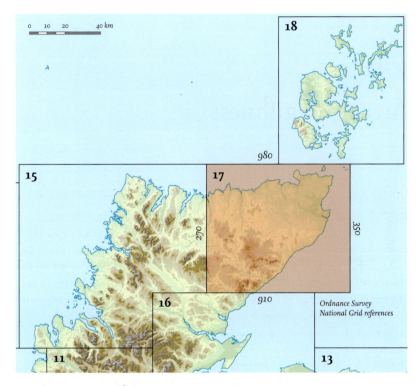

FIG 284. Location map for Area 17.

STORIES FROM THE BEDROCK

Moine Supergroup

The bedrock of the western part of Area 17 (Fig. 286) consists of metamorphic and intrusive igneous rocks that formed part of the core of the Caledonian mountain belt (Chapter 4). Like the rest of the oldest bedrock of the Northern Highland terrane, these rocks have been assigned to the Moine Supergroup (Fig. 287).

The alteration (metamorphism) of the Moine Supergroup occurred when original sediments were buried deeply, raising their temperature and pressure and causing the growth of new minerals such as mica, hornblendes, feldspar and quartz. The deep burial happened when Caledonian movements compressed and thickened the crust.

The rocks often show a clear layering or foliation, but it is unusual to find evidence that this layering formed as bedding in the original sediments. The

FIG 285. Natural and man-made features of Area 17.

layering is generally interpreted to result from recrystallisation of some of the minerals as the rocks were sheared during folding under conditions of strong crustal movement. In this Area the bedrock is often described as a *migmatite* or mixed rock, because it has been veined and intimately mixed up with molten rock that cooled to form quartz and feldspar-rich, granite-like, rocks that are often interpreted as the results of partial melting of older crust.

It seems that the deep-crustal conditions that caused the alterations may have occurred several times, during compressive phases in the Neoproterozoic as well as during the mid-Palaeozoic Caledonian mountain building. However, the history of the multiple phases has not yet been agreed, and it is difficult to relate events to those recognised in less altered rocks further south.

The bedrock variation in these metamorphic rocks is usually present on too local a scale to have created significant topographic features during the erosion of the present-day landscape. At Strathy, near Bettyhill on the north coastal road (A836), the metamorphic Strathy Complex provides an example of the way the Moine Supergroup material has resisted erosion relative to the neighbouring

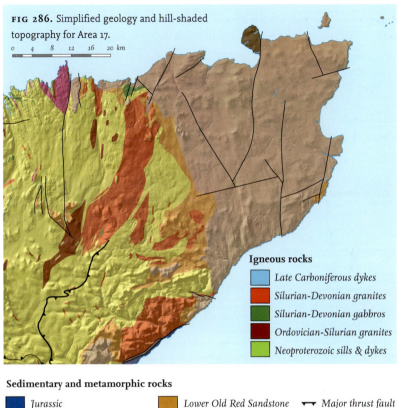

FIG 286. Simplified geology and hill-shaded topography for Area 17.

Igneous rocks
- Late Carboniferous dykes
- Silurian-Devonian granites
- Silurian-Devonian gabbros
- Ordovician-Silurian granites
- Neoproterozoic sills & dykes

Sedimentary and metamorphic rocks
- Jurassic
- Upper Old Red Sandstone
- Middle Old Red Sandstone
- Lower Old Red Sandstone
- Moine
- Mesoproterozoic gneiss

▼▼ Major thrust fault
— Other major fault

bedrock of Old Red Sandstone sediments. The Strathy peninsula appears to owe its existence to the contrast in erosional properties of the two bedrock types.

Numerous intrusive bodies have been recognised during the mapping of the Moine areas. Some of them, such as the Helmsdale Granite and the Strath Halladale Granite, were intruded later than any of the metamorphism. They are presumed to be Silurian (Scandian) in age, and are clearly Caledonian. Other intrusions have been metamorphosed, and were earlier, probably earlier Caledonian.

Old Red Sandstone

The Old Red Sandstone that forms the bedrock of much of the northeast corner of Area 17 (Fig. 286) is very different material from that of the Moine Supergroup

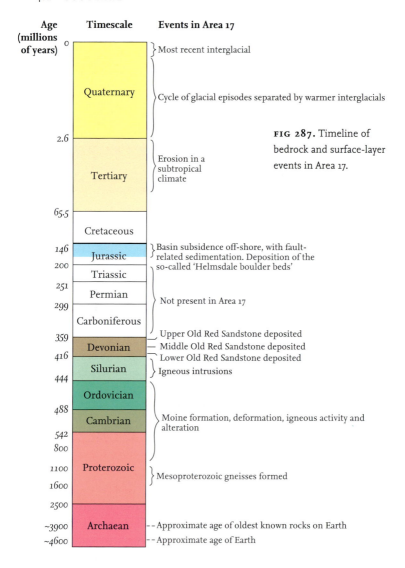

FIG 287. Timeline of bedrock and surface-layer events in Area 17.

and its intrusions. Remarkably flat-lying layers of mudstones and sandstones have been eroded to produce a generally flat inland landscape, and locally dramatic, near-vertical coastal cliffs.

The Old Red Sandstone sediments were deposited in three distinct episodes, the Lower, Middle and Upper Old Red Sandstone. These three episodes were

FIG 288. Middle Old Red Sandstone flagstones unconformably onlapping and covering a small hill top of migmatitic gneiss at Portskerra. (© N. H. Trewin)

deposited over a total time that ranged from about 420 million years ago to about 360 million years ago, starting in the Silurian period and ending at the end of the Devonian period.

The Lower Old Red Sandstone occurs widely over much of Scotland (see Fig. 27, Chapter 4), where it was often deposited along with volcanic lavas, and variably fine-grained to coarse-grained red sediments. The coarse-grained sediments, generally conglomerates, often suggest formation against slopes in the Devonian basement, and the slopes and valleys can sometimes be mapped. Topography of this sort suggests crustal movements and uplift, and the deposition of the Lower Old Red Sandstone has been grouped with the Caledonian mountain-building episodes (Episode 6) in Chapter 4.

The Lower Old Red Sandstone outcrops in small areas often around the edges of what must have been a more extensive Middle Old Red Sandstone basin extending from Caithness across Orkney (Area 18), and further east (see Fig. 28, Chapter 4). At Sarclet (Fig. 285; 8 km south of Wick), a small area of Lower Old Red Sandstone occurs, surrounded by outcrops of the Middle Old Red. It must have been raised by crustal movements, because it is now visible at the surface centrally within the surrounding Middle Old Red Sandstone.

The Middle Old Red Sandstone of Area 17, and Area 18 (Orkney) to the north, is the special feature of the bedrock of this northeastern part of Scotland. Whereas most of the Scottish Old Red Sandstone consists of red sandstones and mudstones that were deposited by rivers, the Middle Old Red Sandstone of Areas 17 and 18 is generally grey and more fine-grained. It accumulated in and around the waters of an extensive basin occupied by a lake or complex of many lakes (see Fig. 28, Chapter 4). Areas 17 and 18, between them, provide the best outcrops in Britain, of any geological age, that allow the deposits of ancient lakes to be studied, so that the landscape at the time can be reconstructed.

Conditions of deposition in and around these lakes varied with time. In places small hillocks of the metamorphic basement can be seen to have been covered by the general spread of Middle Old Red Sandstone sediments, as the basin developed. Most of the Middle Old Red Sandstone is very regularly bedded, much more so than would be expected in river deposits, where channels and river bars tend to disrupt the regularity. So regular is much of this bedding that it results in *flagstones* (Fig. 288), where the bedding can be split to produce slate-like sheets of the sediment, and indeed the flagstones have been widely used locally for paving and roofing, and to provide distinctive flagstone walls to fields. Sometimes water conditions in the lakes became stagnant near the lake floors, allowing the deposition of very finely bedded *laminites*. These special conditions, where very thin, probably seasonal laminae were formed, allowed the preservation of the bodies of unusually complete Devonian fish (Fig. 289) – in contrast to the very fragmentary remains that are all that tend to be found in the more active river deposits of much of the Old Red Sandstone of other parts of Britain and elsewhere. The most famous locality for these fish fossils is Achanarras Quarry, some 10 km south of Thurso, although its fame means that fossils are not now easy to find.

Lake deposits also tend to be rich in organic material, in this case probably largely the remains of algae, and the result is that grey or black pigments predominate in many successions, in contrast to the red, oxidised materials present in most Old Red Sandstone elsewhere. This content of plant organic material, when deeply buried in the Devonian bedrock that occurs below the present North Sea, has been altered to produce oil and/or gas, which under the right conditions has migrated and been trapped to form oil reservoirs – to the great benefit of the economy.

It has been suggested that some of the regular cycles of layers in many of the successions may be due to regular patterns of Devonian climate change caused by astronomical effects. This will be illustrated more fully in the discussion of Area 18 (Orkney).

The total thickness of the largely flagstone succession of this Middle Old Red Sandstone is estimated to be nearly 5 km, evidence of downward movement of the surface of the crust to this sort of extent during its deposition.

The Upper Old Red Sandstone only occurs around Dunnet Head, where it provides evidence of continuing subsidence of the Old Red Sandstone basin, with river and wind transport of sandy sediment into it.

Helmsdale Jurassic

Along the southern coast of Area 17 there is a distinctive strip of coastal land, rarely more than 1 km wide, where the bedrock consists of Jurassic sediments

FIG 289. Two largely complete specimens of the fossil fish *Osteolepis panderi* collected near Thurso. The white marks are man-made. (© N. H. Trewin)

(Fig. 286). This is of special interest because it helps to clarify the setting of the Jurassic bedrock under the northern North Sea that has been so important as a source of hydrocarbons for the British economy. Detailed examination of the Jurassic bedrock has also allowed the reconstruction of a fault-dominated submarine landscape that existed here in late Jurassic times.

The Helmsdale Jurassic bedrock is separated from bedrock of the Moine Supergroup and Old Red Sandstone by the Helmsdale fault zone. This zone runs northeast/southwest, parallel to the straight edge of the Moray Firth coast, where it forms the edge of the Northern Highlands. The fault zone runs only a little off parallel to the Great Glen Fault Zone, and appears to be related to the great family of faults that formed first in Scandian (mid-Silurian) times, in response to Caledonian compression (Chapter 4). This is a clear case where the present-day coast has been localised and oriented by coastal erosion of the bedrock contrasts formed by faulting, which, in this case, can be shown to have been active in late Jurassic times, about 150 million years ago.

The coastal strip in which these Jurassic sediments are visible around Helmsdale extends southwestward into Area 16 (Inverness) for a further 15 km. A total succession of Jurassic sediments, about 1 km thick, is visible along the coastal strip, and this is underlain by earlier New Red Sandstone, probably Triassic in age.

The most remarkable sediments in the Jurassic succession are known as the Boulder Beds. They consist of fragments of Jurassic and Old Red Sandstone bedrock surrounded by sandstones and mudstones that often contain Jurassic marine fossils. Some of the fossils indicate that deposition of these Boulder Beds occurred in late Jurassic, Kimmeridgian times, about 150 million years ago, in water depths of 100 m or more. Other fossils are of organisms that indicate shallower sea conditions, and appear to have lived on the top of the fault scarps that were being eroded at the time to produce the Boulder Beds. The Boulder

Beds accumulated as gravity-driven debris flows at the base of a fault scarp of one of the faults now mapped as part of the Helmsdale fault zone, as shown in Figure 290. The fragments in the Boulder Bed range in size from sand-sized, through pebbles and boulders up to the famous 'Fallen Stack' of Middle Old Red Sandstone flagstones (Fig. 291). This Fallen Stack was at one time thought to be the result of the toppling of a coastal stack similar to those seen being eroded by storms around the Caithness coast today (see below). However, it is now interpreted as a huge fragment that collapsed from the fault scarp when the scarp was a submarine feature. The collapse may have been triggered by fault or earthquake movement, or by erosion by the many catastrophic sediment flows that brought the Boulder Beds and other coarser sediments into place.

MAKING THE LANDSCAPE

Pre-Tertiary

In the case of Area 17, the western edge of a Middle Old Red Sandstone basin has been recognised as a feature in the landscape of some 390 million years ago, when ridges of Moine Supergroup materials provided a basin-edge slope against which the Old Red sediments were deposited. For example, on the mountain of Scaraben (Fig. 285), Moine quartzite materials were transported into the basin by local streams and debris flows. Other Old Red outcrops along the western edge of the Middle Old Red basin demonstrate a basin margin with numerous Moine Supergroup hills with slopes. The suggestion has been made that these hills acted together, however, to create a continuous barrier, because no large river input of sediment appears to have disturbed the fine-grained lake deposition typical of the Middle Old Red flagstones.

In late Jurassic times, say some 150 million years ago, an exposed and active fault scarp was present in the Helmsdale area, and this has been beautifully recorded in the sedimentary record. More recent landscape erosion in Tertiary and Quaternary times has redeveloped a modified version of the 150-million-year-old landscape.

In the absence of other clues from dateable sediments, evidence of early landscapes, determining the ages of other landscape features is very speculative. Seeking evidence for the sorts of erosional processes that have formed them can be an important approach.

Tertiary erosion

One of the conclusions reached in the review of Scottish landscapes carried out for this book is that much of the pattern of hills and valleys must have been

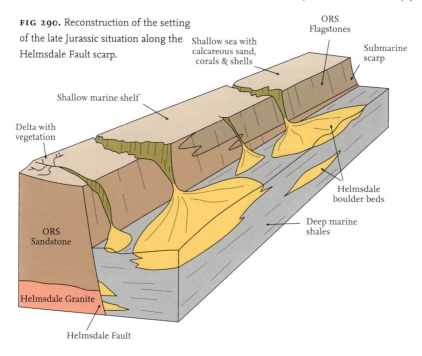

FIG 290. Reconstruction of the setting of the late Jurassic situation along the Helmsdale Fault scarp.

FIG 291. The 'Fallen Stack' is a large (34 × 27 × 9 m) fragment of Old Red Sandstone, now with its layering dipping steeply. It was deposited as part of the Helmsdale Boulder Bed (Kimmeridgian) at Portgower. (© P. F. Friend)

created by erosion over the last 50 million years. These 50 million years extend through much of the Tertiary and the whole of the Quaternary, essentially the period since the end of the vigorous early Tertiary igneous activity in the west (see Areas 6, Mull, and 10, Skye). It is important to bear this key point in mind when examining present-day landscapes.

Glacial activity

As with most of Scotland, evidence of the action of ice is overwhelmingly understood to be evidence from the (Devensian) glacial episode that was fully developed about 70,000 years ago, and may have started to develop some 115,000 years ago. In Area 17 (Caithness), two distinct ice-flow systems have been mapped using local indicators of ice-flow directions. The first of these involved flow northwards, eastwards and southeastwards from an ice sheet on the relatively high ground centred as shown on Figure 292, some 40 km south of the north coast of Area 17. The second system was restricted to the eastern part of Area 17, the tip of the historic county of Caithness. This eastern system left deposits of boulder clay that often contain sea shells, supporting the conclusion that this ice flow originated in the Grampian Highlands, considerably to the south, and traversed the floor of what is now the Moray Firth before flowing northwards, onwards across Caithness.

These two flow systems seem now to be well accepted by most researchers, but there is still debate about the extent and timing of the glaciations in Area 17. There is good evidence that the local (western system) was active, before the arrival of the shell-bearing system from its more distant ice source. It has been suggested that the shell-bearing system may have been diverted to flow across northeastern Caithness by the arrival of Norwegian ice from the east, but Figure 35 (Chapter 5) demonstrates the uncertainty about these broader patterns.

After the ice

Cliffs, between 30 and 70 m high and remarkably steep, are major features of the coastal landscapes of Caithness (Fig. 293). Sea stacks often provide vivid evidence of the continuing retreat of the coastline by isolation and attack on headlands. As shown in the Duncansby photograph (Fig. 294), it is obvious that the steep faces on these cliffs are often a response to the flagstone layering of the Old Red Sandstone bedrock, particularly because most of the layers have an inherent fracture tendency both parallel to and perpendicular to the layers. The well-defined layering assists erosion by attacking storm waves. The fact that much of the layering is near-horizontal, reflecting the lack of folding since the Devonian, has resulted in a steep orientation of the perpendicular bedding fractures, producing steep cliffs.

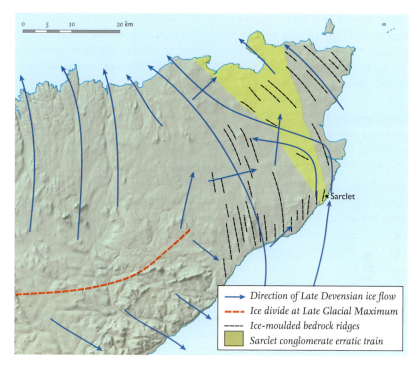

FIG 292. Late Devensian ice movement directions and limits in Area 17.

It has been estimated that relative sea level in Area 17 was about 80 m lower than present some 15,000 years ago, when the Devensian ice was dwindling, although the Loch Lomond Advance had still to happen. By 10,500 years ago most ice had gone, and the relative sea level was about 50 m below present. By 6000 years ago sea level had risen to very nearly its present level. Since then the present coastline and cliffs have been evolving and retreating under the action of storm waves.

Inland, many slope features in the landscape will have been influenced by the rapid changes of climate just described. This is particularly evident in the way weak materials such as boulder clay and soils tend to have collapsed and flowed downslope under variable conditions of rainfall, flooding and freezing.

Slope mapping of Area 17

Although one of the less dramatic of Scottish Areas in terms of its landscapes, hill-shade (Figs 286, 292) and slope mapping (Fig. 295) do much to distinguish areas with distinctive local landscapes.

FIG 293. Dunnet Head, with the lighthouse in the distance on the northernmost point of mainland Scotland. The massive red sandstones are of Upper Old Red Sandstone. (© Patricia & Angus Macdonald/Aerographica/Scottish Natural Heritage)

FIG 294. Sea stacks southeast of Duncansby Head, 2 km southeast of John o' Groats. (© Patricia & Angus Macdonald/Aerographica/Scottish Natural Heritage)

The northwestern coastal region of Area 17 is remarkable for the series of sub-parallel valleys from Strath Naver in the west to Strath Halladale in the east. These generally trend parallel to lithological contrasts in the metamorphic bedrock of the local Moine Supergroup, and their erosion demonstrates some control by these contrasts. Glacial flow directions also ran parallel to these features and must have helped to develop them. Finally the name *strath* and the slope map (Fig. 295) show how they tend to have a flat flood-plain floor distinct from their valley-margin slopes. This provides evidence that the complex carpet of sediment left on the surface during the last glaciation has been redistributed by more recent floods, depositing at least some of their load in the valleys in response to the rising sea levels since.

A similar strath morphology has been formed around Latheron on the east coast, where the A9 trunk road to Thurso heads inland shortly to enter the catchment of the Thurso River. In contrast to the northwestern straths, the bedrock here is flat-lying Old Red Sandstone, so there is no question of control by large material contrast in the bedrock, although fracture patterns may have had some influence. Flow directions in the eastern ice system, however, may have been important in developing some of the valleys.

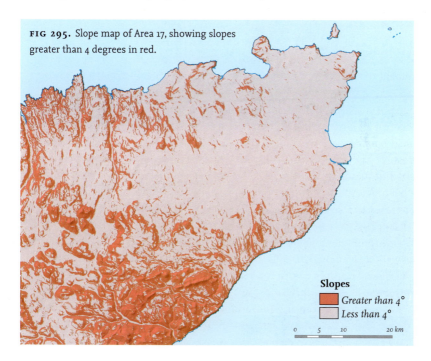

FIG 295. Slope map of Area 17, showing slopes greater than 4 degrees in red.

FIG 296. Aerial photograph of a classic piece of flow country. (© Patricia & Angus Macdonald/ Aerographica/Scottish Natural Heritage)

The southern landscapes in Area 17 consist of generally higher ground underlain by Moine Supergroup metamorphic rocks and related intrusions, so the higher general elevation and greater cover of sloping landscape reflects a persistent resistance to erosion, and perhaps a tendency to upward movement on the part of this crust. In late Caledonian, Devonian times, this area became the landscape that formed the margin of the Middle Old Red Sandstone basin, and in Jurassic times, movement was limited to fractures along the Helmsdale zone, perhaps because of the crustal structure of this mountainous area.

The lack of slopes in much of the northeast of Area 17 appears to reflect generally the flatness of the bedrock surface both before and after the deposition of the Old Red Sandstone, and the fact that there has been no general folding of the crust since. The main crustal movement detected in the Helmsdale area was the movement of the near-vertical fault zone, and this did not disturb the flatness of the general landscape. Quaternary deposition of ice-related deposits created some topography on this plain, but not enough to colour up the slope map to any degree.

The 'Flow Country' of Caithness and Sutherland is believed to be the largest expanse (some 4000 km^2) of blanket bog and peat in Europe (Fig. 296), and much interest has been generated recently by the realisation that this environment is special and should be conserved. Local programmes of drainage and forestation have been put into reverse, and the Royal Society for the Protection of Birds nature reserve at Forsinard (Fig. 285) is a symbol of this new awareness.

These large expanses of wet peat formation depend fundamentally on maintaining a high enough water table at least locally to create ponding, the very opposite of developing efficient drainage. The abundance of areas underlain by a flat surface in the bedrock is a key requirement in the formation of this environment, and reflects the erosional history of the Area not only in Tertiary and Quaternary times, but also in Devonian and Jurassic times as just outlined. The presence of local ice- and ice-sheet-related surface blanket materials will also have played a key role in allowing this special environment to form.

CHAPTER 23

Area 18: Orkney

THE NEAREST ORKNEY ISLAND is only some 14 km from Dunnet Head on the Scottish mainland coast in Area 17 (Caithness), so can easily be seen from there under most conditions (Fig. 297). There are some 70 significant islands in the Orkney group, and 21 of them are inhabited (Fig. 298). The total population of Orkney (Area 18) is just over 20,000, of whom some 7000 live in Kirkwall and 2000 in Stromness.

FIG 297. Location map for Area 18.

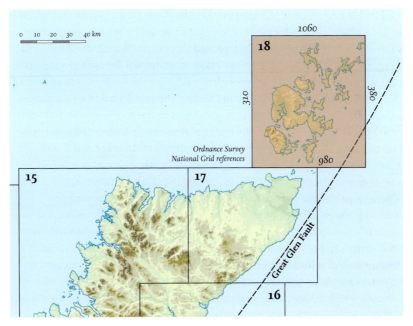

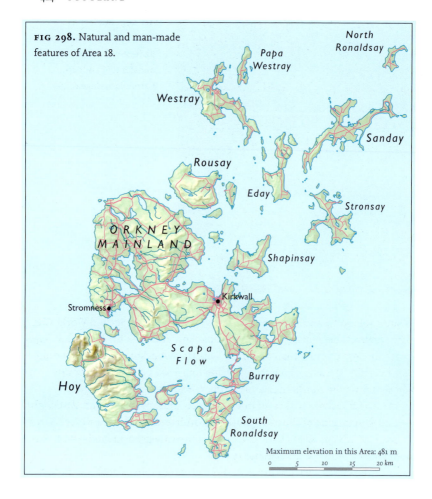

FIG 298. Natural and man-made features of Area 18.

The islands have a particularly long record of settlement, extending over perhaps the last 8000 years. The Mesolithic and Neolithic heritage of settlements and structures is exceptionally rich, perhaps partly because of the remote setting of the islands. For some 600 years, between 875 and 1472, Orkney was most closely linked, culturally, to Scandinavia. During this period, in 1137, work began on the building of St Magnus Cathedral in Kirkwall, using red and yellow building stone from the Orkney Old Red Sandstone (Fig. 299). Subsequently the islands came under the control of the Scottish crown, and then became British.

Scapa Flow was used as the North Atlantic sanctuary for the Royal Navy during the First World War, and at the end of that war large numbers of German naval

FIG 299. St Magnus Cathedral, Kirkwall, Orkney, made of red and yellow-red sandstone. (© Adrian Warren/lastrefuge.co.uk)

ships surrendered there and were then scuttled. Early in the Second World War, a German submarine managed to enter Scapa Flow and sank the battleship *Royal Oak*, with the loss of more than 800 men. This tragedy resulted in the building of the Churchill Barriers, which now provide four road bridges from South Ronaldsay across the southern islands to the Orkney Mainland (Fig. 300).

In map-view, Orkney makes an interesting contrast with Shetland. Although the overall dimensions of the two groups are similar, Orkney has a wider scatter of islands. The islands of Shetland are more compactly grouped and tend to have a more elongate, north/south, geometry.

Most of the Orkney islands are low, and the topography is gently rounded with few notable slopes. Fertile soils have encouraged widespread use of the land for livestock (Fig. 301). An exception to this is the higher topography of the large southwestern island of Hoy (Fig. 302).

STORIES FROM THE BEDROCK

Moine Supergroup

Crystalline metamorphic rocks occur in a number of small areas, 1–3 km across, along the western edge of Mainland, some 20 km west of the Kirkwall area (Fig. 303). There is no reason to regard these as anything but extensions of the Moine

FIG 300. Churchill Barriers, Orkney, linking the island of Burray (in the right foreground), via Lamb Horn and Glimps Horn (in the middle distance) to Mainland (in the far distance). (© Adrian Warren/lastrefuge.co.uk)

FIG 301. Aerial oblique view looking southwest over North Ronaldsay, with Sanday in the distance. Note the low-lying, intensely farmed landscapes with only local low cliffs. (© Adrian Warren/lastrefuge.co.uk)

FIG 302. Aerial oblique view showing the Old Man of Hoy and neighbouring cliffs on Hoy. The Scottish mainland is in the distance to the right. (© Adrian Warren/ lastrefuge.co.uk)

Supergroup that underlies most of the Northern Highland terrane, particularly dominating most of Areas 11 (Affric), 15 (Cape Wrath) and 17 (Caithness).

On Orkney these small outcrop areas are surrounded by much larger areas of Old Red Sandstone bedrock which was deposited around and on the Moine (Figs 303, 304). It seems clear that they represent the tops of distinct hills that must have formed features on a low ridge towards the edge of the Old Red Sandstone basin, rather like the local situation revealed in the coastal outcrops near Portskerra in Caithness (Area 17, Fig. 288).

Old Red Sandstone

The Old Red Sandstone forms almost all of the rest of the bedrock visible in Orkney. On the whole, the layering of these sediments is generally flat-lying, showing that subsequent tilting movement has only been rather local. When combined with Old Red Sandstone evidence more widely across northeast Scotland (Areas 16–19), a picture of a basin emerges that was at least 400 km across (see Figs 27 and 28, Chapter 4) and accumulated sediment up to some 5 km thick. The way that different levels in the Old Red Sandstone now occur as bedrock in different places shows that local earth movement and surface erosion have been active since the basin was filled (Fig. 305). Although some of the basin fill has been removed by later erosion, the later earth movements have certainly played a role in determining where material, and how much material, has been removed. This Old Red Sandstone accumulated during the late Silurian and Devonian periods between about 420 and 360 million years ago.

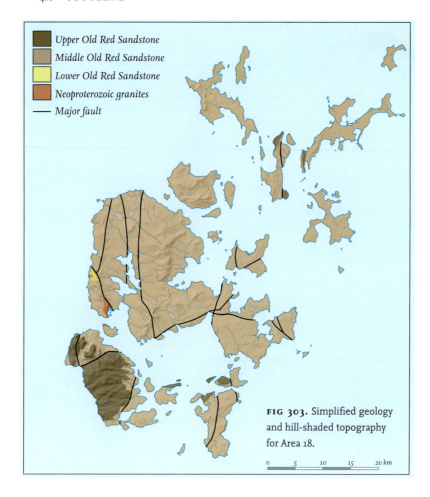

FIG 303. Simplified geology and hill-shaded topography for Area 18.

The sediments equivalent to the Lower Old Red Sandstone of the rest of Scotland are of very limited extent within Orkney. They are limited to the same western end of the Orkney Mainland in which the Moine Supergroup bedrock also occurs. They consist of sandstones, siltstones and coarse breccias that appear to represent deposition by rivers, lakes and wind-blown dunes in and around alluvial fans derived from the crystalline hills that existed in the western marginal part of the great northeast Scotland basin.

The Middle Old Red Sandstone of Area 18, and of Area 17 (Caithness) to the south, provides striking examples of a distinctive basin-filling episode. Whereas most of the Scottish Old Red Sandstone consists of red sandstones and

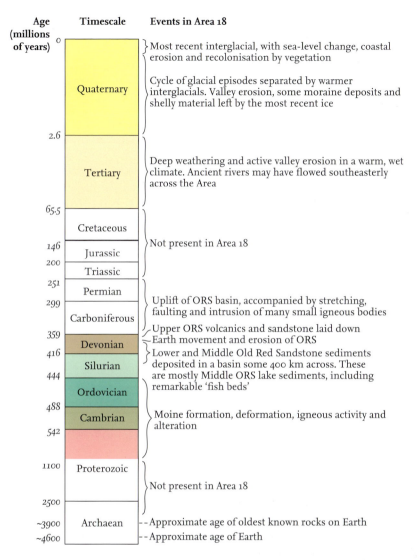

FIG 304. Timeline of bedrock and surface-layer events in Area 18.

mudstones that were generally deposited by rivers, the greyness, fine grain-size and clear layering of the Middle Old Red Sandstone is very different. These features have been discussed in the previous chapter (Area 17), with the general conclusion that the sediments were the result of deposition in and around the

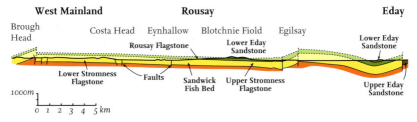

FIG 305. Cross-section from Mainland to Eday, showing true-scale geometry of layering, faults and folds.

margins of one or more lake basins. Two aspects of this are discussed further here, because they illustrate particularly fascinating discoveries made in these remarkable lake deposits.

'Fish beds' make up a very small percentage of the total successions of Middle Old Red Sandstone sediments, but they provide remarkable clues on the local environments and the state of animal evolution at the time. The material that makes up these fish beds is often called *laminite* or *rhythmite*, because its dark, calcium–magnesium carbonate material is often laminated or layered with laminae that are less than 1 mm thick. This very fine and regular lamination reflects the stagnant-water conditions in the deeper waters of lakes a few metres or tens of metres deep, where organic plant and animal detritus created oxygen-starved conditions in which bottom-living organisms were unable to live, and did not therefore burrow through and destroy the fine layering as they would have done in better-oxygenated water. This allowed the beautiful preservation of whole and part carcases of the fish that swam in the upper waters of the lake, and sank to the bottom on death (Fig. 289, Area 17). Their preservation became famous from the publications of Hugh Miller, which were extremely popular in the nineteenth century, including *The Old Red Sandstone* (1841) and *Footsteps of the Creator* (1849). The best-known fish-bed locality is Achanarras Quarry in Caithness (Area 17), where one of the main fish beds in the northeast of Scotland occurs. A continuation of this bed is also visible in the western Mainland of Orkney, where it is called the Sandwick Fish Bed. Further extensions that may have been linked to this same distinctive fish bed have been found in Shetland (Area 19) and the Moray Firth area (Area 16), so that this single episode of deep-lake deposition appears to have occurred over an area at least 400 km across. Most fish beds are thought to represent only a few thousand years of deposition, and many thinner ones represent shorter periods.

Thicker cycles of sedimentation, varying in thickness from a few metres to a few tens of metres, are typical of the Middle Old Red Sandstone successions.

The fish-bed rock type, although particularly distinctive and interesting, is merely one component of the thicker cycles, representing an episode of relatively deep and stagnant lake conditions. The overwhelmingly dominant sediments present contain varying amounts of silt and sand, with mud cracks, ripple marks and other indicators of deposition on mud- and sand-flats that must have surrounded the lakes and formed during varying wet and dry conditions. Careful work measuring long successions of sediment, for example around the coasts of Mainland, Rousay and South Eday, has resulted in the counting of some 40 of these cycles, starting from the Sandwick Fish Bed. The relative thicknesses of these cycles appear to demonstrate regular patterns of variation, suggesting that climatic changes of wetness and dryness occurred on scales that represented time periods of 25,000, 100,000 and 400,000 years. These periods are now well known to be responses to cycles of astronomical Earth rotational behaviour, as pointed out by the Serbian engineer and meteorologist Milutin Milankovitch (1879–1958), but it is remarkable to find evidence for them in Devonian lake-basin sediments.

The Upper Old Red Sandstone of Orkney consists of the Hoy Volcanic Rocks and the Hoy Sandstone, found mainly on the large southwestern island of Hoy. The Hoy Sandstone is a rather uniform sandstone, lacking the fish beds and flagstone cycles just described from the Middle Old Red Sandstone, and it appears to have formed largely by deposition from braided rivers. A distinct unconformity between the Middle and Upper Old Red was formed by a period of earth movement and erosion in late Devonian times. In much more recent times, the Upper Old Red Sandstone has been eroded to form dramatic coastal scenery, including the Old Man of Hoy (Fig. 302), and also provides the highest ground in Orkney (Ward Hill at 481 m). At the end of this discussion of Area 18, reasons for the present-day topography of Orkney will be considered.

Complex patterns of faulting cut through the usually flat-lying Old Red Sandstone strata, and these appear to have been linked to some local folds in the strata that have influenced present-day landscapes. There is evidence that some of the faulting occurred during the deposition of the Middle Old Red Sandstone. But much of it occurred after the youngest preserved Old Red had formed, in response to stresses and movements in the crust. The great thicknesses of the Old Red that accumulated, the presence of igneous intrusions and lavas in both the Middle and Upper Old Red Sandstone, and the state of alteration of organic materials in the sediments all suggest that the northeast Scotland Old Red basin subsided by several kilometres after sediment started to form about 400 million years ago, and then rose again about 300 million years ago, as the stretching and intrusion described in the next paragraph took place.

Carboniferous or Permian igneous intrusions

Over 200 small intrusions, mostly dykes, have been mapped in Orkney, mostly of olivine and augite-rich materials, broadly classified as *lamprophyres*. They are thought to be late Carboniferous or Permian in age, and their orientation suggests crustal stretching in a north-northwest direction. Only locally do these small intrusions influence the landscapes.

MAKING THE LANDSCAPE

Pre-Tertiary

Bedrock evidence from Orkney has demonstrated that the margin of the large northeast Scotland Devonian basin ran northerly roughly 20 km west of the westernmost part of the Orkney island group (see Figs 27 and 28, Chapter 4). Hills of Moine Supergroup crystalline bedrock, a few tens of metres high, were surrounded by actively accumulating Devonian sediments in this marginal area.

Tertiary

In common with the rest of Scotland, it seems likely that wide valleys were eroded in the Orkney area before the Pleistocene glacial activity that started more than 2 million years ago. These valleys were initiated in Tertiary times some 60 million years ago, after the end of the Tertiary igneous activity in western Scotland. For much of the Tertiary, warm climatic conditions favoured deep weathering and active valley erosion.

Glacial activity

Work on the history of glaciation in Orkney has shown dominant ice-flow directions to the northwest, although there is uncertainty about whether this pattern represents conditions in the late Devensian (during the Late Glacial Maximum), or whether this occurred in the earlier Devensian. There can be no doubt that this phase of glaciation eroded the sides of the Tertiary valleys to some extent. Moraines left by ice have only been identified clearly in the high ground of the island of Hoy. In the eastern Orkney islands, shelly material in the glacial deposits shows that the ice had moved across surfaces that had earlier been sea floor (Fig. 306).

After the ice

Since the general disappearance of ice, local mass movement down slopes has occurred very widely across Scotland. The commonest movement has taken the

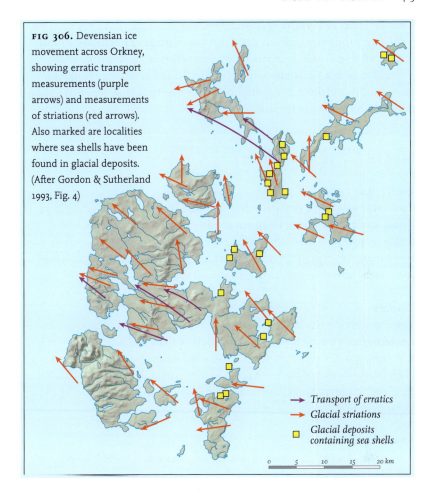

FIG 306. Devensian ice movement across Orkney, showing erratic transport measurements (purple arrows) and measurements of striations (red arrows). Also marked are localities where sea shells have been found in glacial deposits. (After Gordon & Sutherland 1993, Fig. 4)

form of relatively gradual creeping, producing terraces, often looking like sheep tracks, and sometimes exaggerated by sheep, or more catastrophic landslips or mud-slides. In all cases these movements are likely to have been most active under periglacial conditions, when the porous soil layers were being moved frequently downslope by freezing and thawing, or by loading and lubricating with water under conditions of heavy rain. In Orkney, the steep slopes are most common in the southwest, and it is on the island of Hoy that good examples of periglacial terracing have been described.

The southwest coast of Orkney is famous for its high and near-vertical cliffs carved in the Old Red Sandstone, and there is no doubt that these steep cliff

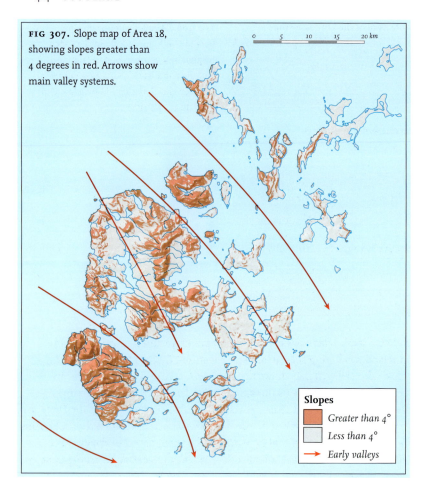

FIG 307. Slope map of Area 18, showing slopes greater than 4 degrees in red. Arrows show main valley systems.

Slopes
- Greater than 4°
- Less than 4°
- → Early valleys

features are being actively created and modified under storm-wave attack at the present day. The near-vertical faces are a direct result of the flat-lying Old Red Sandstone strata and the way that fractures tend to occur perpendicular to the flat strata, resulting in vertical joints and faults. However, similarly well-bedded strata occur over most of Orkney, so the predominance of high cliffs in the southwest seems likely to be a response to the strength of storm waves that approach the islands from the Atlantic Ocean to the west. The Old Man of Hoy (Fig. 302) is the best-known of a number of spectacular sea stacks and arches on this coastline, rising some 137 m above sea level. Only some 200 years ago the Old Man was part of an arch, which then collapsed to leave the present needle-like tower.

a) Deposition of the Hoy sandstone

FIG 308. Sketch diagram showing how the high ground of Hoy has been formed by a combination of faulting and the contrast in bedrock properties between the Upper and Middle Old Red Sandstone of Orkney.

b) Normal faulting

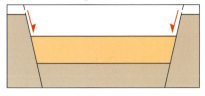

c) Selective erosion of the Hoy hills

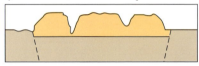

Relative sea-level changes are likely to have played an important role in creating and modifying coastal landscape features. In Chapter 5 (Figs 43, 44), evidence was reviewed that shows that the Earth's crust in a distinct area in western Scotland, called by us the Rannoch Rebound Dome, has risen up (or rebounded) during the last 18,000 years as a result of the melting of the Devensian ice that had depressed it during the maximum glaciation. Outside the area of this Rannoch dome, the crust did not rebound but was subjected to the worldwide rise in sea level caused by the release of meltwater to the oceans. Orkney appears to have been well outside the area of the Rannoch dome. There is some local evidence of slightly high sea levels before the Devensian glaciation, and evidence of the uplift of the land since this glaciation is not widely recognised.

LANDSCAPE OVERVIEW OF ORKNEY

The slope map (Fig. 307) only picks out slopes greater than 4 degrees, but shows very clearly certain patterns in the distribution and extent of these slopes, providing a direct overview of this important feature of the landscape.

The island of Hoy, in the southwest, has already been mentioned as containing not only the highest hill top but also the highest cliffs, not to mention the Old Man of Hoy. The island provides much the most extensive area in Orkney of the Hoy Sandstone, the youngest preserved unit of the Upper Old Red Sandstone. The Hoy Sandstone consists of massive sandstones, relatively more uniform than the underlying sandstones and flagstones of the Middle Old Red Sandstone. So it is natural to assume that the relative strength of this material, compared with much of the rest of the Orkney bedrock, has played an important role in the face of landscape erosion. However, it is also clear that faulting has played a special role, as shown in Figure 308, and the linear faulted margin of the southeastern edge of the Hoy mountains confirms this.

A linear submarine step edge, probably reflecting erosion of a fault, has been identified as the edge of the platform on which the islands of Orkney stand, from South Ronaldsay to Sanday. It has been claimed that this scarp is parallel to the probable line linking the Great Glen Fault of the Scottish mainland to the Walls Boundary Fault line in Shetland (see Fig. 22, Chapter 4). It may therefore be the result of wave erosion during repeated low-stands of the sea.

Mainland, Rousay and Westray show land slopes of moderate extent, compared with those of Hoy, and although these are locally clearly related to intervals of resistant sandstones, detailed examination would be needed to verify this. It may also be that these northwestern islands have undergone upward earth movement, relative to the much flatter islands to the southeast. This would be consistent with the fact that the Moine 'basement' and the local areas of Lower Old Red Sandstone are also restricted to the northwestern islands, and provide evidence that the margin of the Devonian basin was in this direction.

On Figure 307 a number of large arrows mark the positions of relatively continuous topographic lows, combining knowledge of submarine depths with knowledge of low ground on land. These have been suggested to be valleys of ancient rivers (see Pre-Tertiary and Tertiary, above) that flowed southeasterly and east-southeasterly, and have survived, although often flooded by sea-level rise.

The distinctive scatter of the relatively low islands of Orkney seems to be explained in terms of their origin as a fragment near the western margin of the large northeast Scotland Old Red Sandstone basin. Since this origin hundreds of millions of years ago, surface modifications have eroded the upper parts of the basin fill, with the amount of erosion and elevation varying with the resistance of the bedrock present at the surface, and the faults and folds that formed during and after deposition. Glaciation and repeated changes of sea level have continued the erosion and added the final touches to the present-day pattern of this island archipelago.

CHAPTER 24

Area 19: Shetland

THE MAP-VIEW OF THE COASTLINE OF SHETLAND (Fig. 309) differs so much in its overall shape from that of Orkney (Area 18) that it immediately hints at radical differences in the landscape history of the two groups of islands. The many Orkney islands provide samples of a single large sedimentary basin of Middle Old Red Sandstone age. These samples have been only slightly moved or tilted since their sediment was deposited in Devonian times, some 400 million years ago. In contrast, the Shetland coastline has a very different, more compact, irregular and elongate form (Fig. 310). The islands have a much greater variety of bedrock, and contain evidence of a very long and varied history of movements involving folding, faulting and rock alteration. So varied and interesting is their geological history that the islands of Shetland have been awarded the status of European Geopark for the remarkable diversity of their easily accessible geology and landscape, all packed into a comparatively small area.

In spite of the remote locations of the Northern Isles of Orkney and Shetland, prehistoric human relics are remarkably numerous and rich in cultural significance. One of the most remarkable sites is Jarlshof, near Sumburgh, the southernmost headland on the Shetland Mainland, close to the main Shetland airport. At Jarlshof an occupation mound has been excavated, including extensive buildings attributed to Bronze Age, Iron Age, Viking and medieval people, covering at least 4000 years of settlement. In medieval times, Shetland's cultural links were strongest with Scandinavia, reflecting the seafaring prowess and energy of the people and the relative proximity of the Norwegian coast. After many centuries, Scottish and then British government took over, although the islands are still proud of their Scandinavian heritage.

The mid-twentieth-century discovery of rich hydrocarbon resources, mainly beneath the North Sea to the east, saw Shetland favoured as the location for a

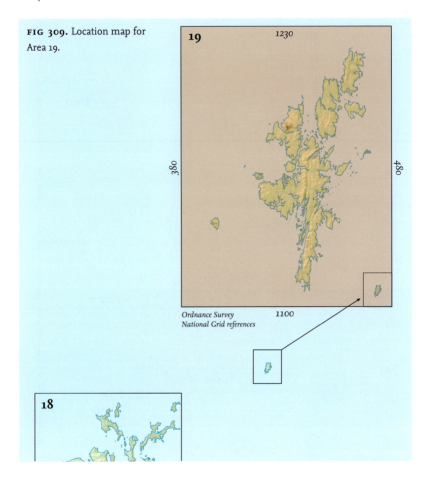

FIG 309. Location map for Area 19.

major oil terminal at Sullom Voe (Fig. 311), and led to a remarkable change in many aspects of Shetland life, resulting from the economic boom that followed.

STORIES FROM THE BEDROCK

Faulting
The bedrock mapping of Shetland has revealed a complex pattern of folded, faulted and altered sedimentary, igneous and metamorphic rocks (Figs 312, 313). The islands have a geology that is probably unrivalled in complexity in the whole of the British Isles. One key feature of this complexity is the presence of many faults, particularly

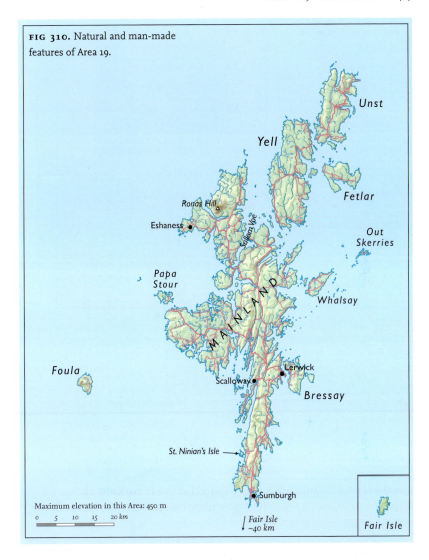

FIG 310. Natural and man-made features of Area 19.

north/south trending, that extend across the whole island group. The extent of these faults suggests that they were responses to crustal stresses acting over areas at least as large as the island group and its sea-covered surroundings.

The most discussed of these large Shetland faults is the Walls Boundary Fault. This is often suggested to be a continuation of the Great Glen Fault, one of the major terrane boundaries of mainland Scotland (Chapter 4, Fig. 20).

FIG 311. Looking south over Sullom Voe oil terminal. (© Adrian Warren/lastrefuge.co.uk)

The Great Glen Fault is remarkable for the way it cuts straight across the Highland landscape of Scotland, clearly visible as the most obvious geological feature on satellite imagery. It is often interpreted as an ancient Scottish equivalent of the San Andreas fault of California, with a similar lateral movement caused by two crustal plates sliding horizontally past each other. Fragments of crust altered by plate-margin compression and collision are now present on both sides of the North Atlantic Ocean. The main mountain building occurred from Ordovician to Devonian times, say from 475 to 400 million years ago, whereas the Atlantic Ocean started to appear by ocean-floor spreading only some 250 million years ago. The Great Glen Fault of northern Scotland is generally believed to have been particularly active, with left-lateral largely horizontal movement, in late Caledonian (?early Devonian) times.

It is difficult to find independent evidence for the timing and sense of movement of the large faults that traverse the islands of Shetland. Even if there was continuity with the Great Glen Fault of mainland Scotland, the route taken by the fault or its branching pattern cannot be followed across the area now covered by sea between Shetland and the Scottish mainland. However, it is generally concluded that Shetland represents an area with an unusually long and varied crustal history (see below), and that the deformation involved largely horizontal fault movements. Moreover, there is evidence that the major faults moved more than once, and that the fault movement was both left- and right-lateral at different times.

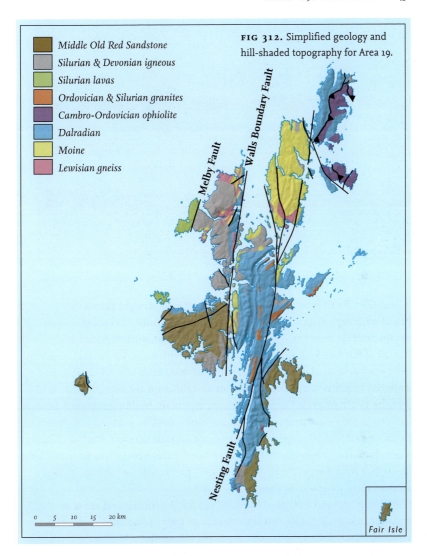

FIG 312. Simplified geology and hill-shaded topography for Area 19.

- Middle Old Red Sandstone
- Silurian & Devonian igneous
- Silurian lavas
- Ordovician & Silurian granites
- Cambro-Ordovician ophiolite
- Dalradian
- Moine
- Lewisian gneiss

Lewisian Complex

Coarsely crystalline metamorphic rocks (gneisses) occur in the Northmaven peninsula of the Mainland, and also in the Ve Skerries, northwest of Papa Stour. These have been grouped with other metamorphic rocks in the northern Mainland and along the northern edge of the Walls peninsula, and correlated with the Lewisian Complex (Archaean and Palaeoproterozoic) of the Hebridean

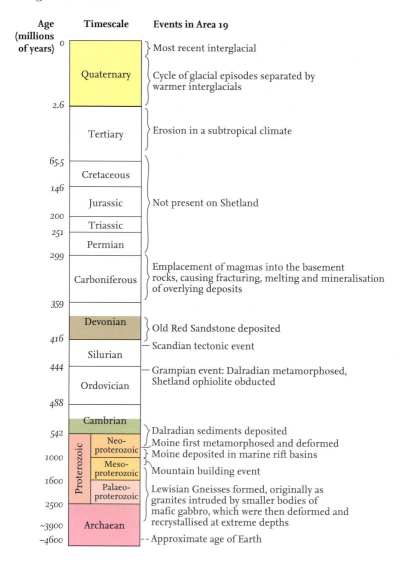

FIG 313. Timeline of bedrock and surface-layer events in Area 19.

terrane (see Fig. 20, Chapter 4). There is some radiometric evidence for this, and it seems likely that the oldest rocks and events that form the basement in the Hebridean terrane are also represented in Shetland, particularly in the above west Shetland localities, to the west of the main area where the crust has been involved in Caledonian mobilisation. The Wester Keolka Shear Zone has been interpreted as a northern continuation of the Moine Thrust, and the local Shetland equivalent, therefore, of the fault that acted as the boundary of the Caledonian belt.

Moine Supergroup

In Chapter 4, the Moine Supergroup of metamorphic rocks that forms the bedrock of much of the Northern Highland terrane was interpreted as part of the core of the Caledonian mountain belt. Several areas of bedrock in Shetland appear to have been deposited and deformed over the same complex Caledonian succession of events (Chapter 4, Episode 4). These include depositional events between about 1000 and 900 million years ago (Mesoproterozoic and Neoproterozoic), and then at least three different episodes of alteration and crustal movement starting with an episode in the Neoproterozoic (Knoydartian on the Scottish mainland) about 900 million years ago. This first episode was then followed by mid-Ordovician movements (Grampian, say 470 million years ago) and mid-Silurian movements (Scandian, say 430 million years ago). All three of these events are represented in Shetland in what is broadly referred to here as Moine bedrock, though only the last two would conventionally be regarded as Caledonian.

Dalradian Supergroup, and other eastern metamorphic rocks

The Dalradian Supergroup includes the metamorphic rocks that provide most of the basement of the Grampian Highland terrane of mainland Scotland (see Figs 20 and 22, Chapter 4). These were originally deposited as sandstones, mudrocks, limestones and volcanic rocks between Neoproterozoic and Ordovician times and have been moved and altered, particularly in the Grampian (mid-Ordovician, about 470 million years ago) and Scandian (mid-Silurian, about 430 million years ago) episodes of the Caledonian mountain building. Some areas of Shetland bedrock, particularly on Mainland, have been correlated with the Dalradian Supergroup of mainland Scotland. The range of metamorphic rock types present, e.g. quartzites, schists, marbles and meta-volcanics, is similar to that of the Grampian Highland terrane, and the rock types present have weathered at the surface in a similarly varied way.

The differences in erodibility of the varied Dalradian bedrock units have resulted in a remarkable landscape of linear hills and valleys that forms a central belt running north/south across Mainland. This is particularly clear on the slope map (Fig. 314). The fertile valley that extends northwards from Scalloway towards Tingwall is a clear example of the preferential erosion of one of the carbonate (marble) units in the succession (Fig. 315). Not only is this inland linear pattern of hills and valleys clear, but so is the coastline pattern of coastal ridges and

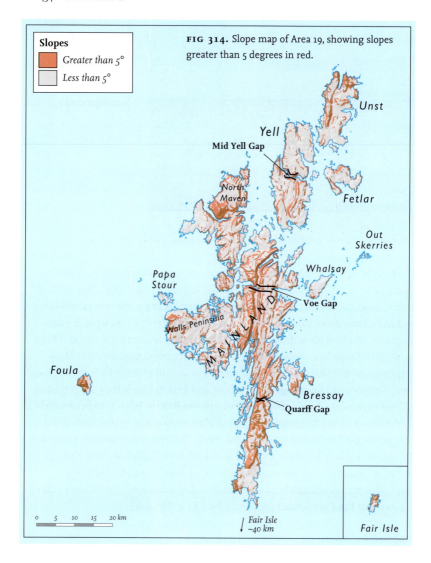

FIG 314. Slope map of Area 19, showing slopes greater than 5 degrees in red.

water-filled straits (or voes). It is unusual in British landscapes to be able to pick out fold curvatures in the bedrock over the distances that can be followed in this Mainland central belt, but the S-shaped map pattern of the landscape-bedrock features is really clear in this case.

The Shetland ophiolite of Unst–Fetlar is a particularly remarkable feature of Scottish bedrock geology. Ophiolites are associations of bedrock types found in

FIG 315. Scalloway township, with ridge-and-voe landscape behind. (© Adrian Warren/lastrefuge.co.uk)

many of the mountain belts of the world, and are now generally understood to be slabs of the Earth's crust formed as oceanic crust that have then been *obducted* or pushed onto continental crust during the compressive plate movements that created mountain belts. The ophiolites themselves consist of mafic and ultrabasic igneous rocks with sediments that were formed as oceanic crust, and they appear to have been hot enough at the time of their obduction to cause local alteration (metamorphism) of the continental crust onto which they were forced. All these features can be recognised in Unst and Fetlar, where they are regarded as the best examples of ophiolite preserved in the British Isles. Careful analysis of mineral histories in this ophiolite suggests that its material crystallised about 490 million years ago (late Cambrian) and was obducted about 470 million years ago (mid-Ordovician) as part of the Grampian (Caledonian) episode. This obduction happened when a volcanic arc collided with a continent, and then suffered further collision of continents in the Scandian (mid-Silurian, 430 million years ago) episode of the Caledonian mountain building (Fig. 316).

Old Red Sandstone

The pattern of broadly north/south-trending faults that traverses the bedrock of Shetland has been summarised in Figure 312, and the suggestion made that the islands represent a complex of crustal slices brought together into their present positions, long before the present landscape was formed by surface processes. It might be hoped that the Old Red Sandstone, which forms the youngest sediments of the Shetland bedrock, could help to provide information on the late episodes of this bedrock story.

FIG 316. The northern point of the island of Unst at Hermaness, and the island and lighthouse of Muckle Flugga. Unst and Fetlar consist of Caledonian metamorphic rocks, including the Shetland ophiolite described in the text. Note the layers sloping down to the right, and the seabird colonies, strongly influenced by the layering. (© Patricia & Angus Macdonald/Aerographica/Scottish Natural Heritage)

Distinct bedrock of Old Red Sandstone sediments and associated volcanics occurs in different parts of Shetland, and it is very largely of mid-Devonian age, with some earliest Upper Devonian possibly present (Fig. 317).

West of the Melby Fault, on Eshaness and Papa Stour, there are extensive outcrops of volcanics, both mafic and felsic in composition and consisting of lavas and ash deposits. These overlie the Melby Formation, which consists of unmetamorphosed sediments, hundreds of metres thick. Fish beds in the sediments contain fish fossils reminiscent of the famous fish beds of Achanarras and Sandwick in the early Middle Devonian of Caithness and Orkney (Areas 17 and 18). The island of Foula reveals some 1800 m of sandstones above sea level resting on metamorphic basement. But it is not clear how this thick succession of sediments relates to the Devonian sediments and volcanics west of the Melby Fault.

Between the Melby Fault and the Walls Boundary Fault, the bedrock of the Walls peninsula consists predominantly of strongly folded and altered (locally slightly metamorphosed) grey sandstones, mudstones and volcanics, which are strikingly different from the less deformed Old Red Sandstone of other parts of Shetland. This deformation and alteration may be the result of the later intrusion of a large granitic body in southern Walls. The Walls sedimentary succession

AREA 19: SHETLAND · 437

FIG 317. The Neap, a headland with numerous islands and sea stacks made of Eshaness volcanic bedrock. Hillswick and the Ness of Hillswick are in the middle distance, and the Mainland forms the skyline. (© Adrian Warren/lastrefuge.co.uk)

was once thought to be more than 20 km thick, having been formed in a distinct and continuously subsiding basin, but a re-examination of the succession has suggested that this idea was based on a misunderstanding of the way the basin was filled. The Walls sediments are of later Middle Devonian age, and were deposited in a lake basin. There are similarities with the 3 km-thick succession of Old Red Sandstone that makes up the island of Fair Isle.

East of the Walls Boundary Fault, and visible down the east coast of Mainland, is a third area of Old Red Sandstone, also now dated as late Middle Devonian. The sediments consist of sandstones and conglomerates, with occasional fish beds. The arrangement of these strata suggests that the high ground of the spine of the southern Mainland (Fig. 318) was a ridge of hills, forming, probably amongst other ridges, in the marginal parts of the Middle Old Red Sandstone Orcadian Lake (see Fig. 28, Chapter 4). There is therefore evidence of a basin-margin landscape in Devonian times in Shetland, rather similar to that seen west of Orkney and Caithness further to the south.

Granites

Intrusions of coarse-grained igneous rock, mostly several kilometres across and of granitic, felsic composition, are features of the Shetland Mainland, as they are through much of the Caledonian mainland of Scotland. The upward movement

FIG 318. Sumburgh Head and lighthouse at the southern tip of the Shetland Mainland. Steeply tilted Devonian strata are part of the East Mainland Old Red Sandstone succession that was deposited against a ridge of metamorphic bedrock now forming the topographic spine of this part of the Mainland. (© Adrian Warren/lastrefuge.co.uk)

of felsic coarse-grained igneous liquids was clearly a widespread process in later Caledonian mountain building. Some of the Shetland intrusions solidified after arriving in crust of Moine and Dalradian metamorphic rocks, and one major body (the Sandsting Complex) was intruded into the deformed Walls Devonian sediments.

In terms of landscape effects, the highest hill in Shetland (Ronas Hill, 450 m) has been eroded from one of the larger granite intrusions, providing evidence of the resistance of some of this material to young weathering and erosion (Fig. 319).

Mesozoic history

Although the most important, larger movements (say at least 100 km of relative displacement), involving folding, faulting, metamorphism and intrusion of bedrock in Shetland, appear to have come to an end in the late Caledonian times (mid-Devonian), later movements were also important, and signalled the emergence of the islands as a persistently elevated feature of the crust.

In these post Middle Devonian times, relative elevation of the Shetland area is indicated by subsidence in many of the offshore regions surrounding Shetland. Some 40 km west of the westernmost islands, the Claire Basin subsided and

FIG 319. Eshaness lighthouse, on cliffs of Devonian volcanic, is in the foreground. Ronas Hill, eroded from late Caledonian granite, forms the skyline to the northeast. (© Adrian Warren/lastrefuge. co.uk)

accumulated thick sandstones, of Late Devonian into Carboniferous age (say 370 to 350 million years ago), that have proved to be an oil-exploration target, due to the presence of hydrocarbons, although these are often of high viscosity. In Permian and Triassic times (say 270 to 230 million years ago), thick sediment accumulated in basins to the west and east of an identifiable Orkney–Shetland platform (see Fig. 30, Chapter 4), and further transcurrent movement occurred on the Walls Boundary and Nesting Faults. This time the movement was right-lateral, and the associated Great Glen Fault of the Scottish Mainland moved in the same sense, linked to growth of the Inner Moray Firth Basin (see Fig. 278, Area 16).

MAKING THE LANDSCAPE

Tertiary erosion

In much of mainland Scotland, large valleys that extend across 10 km-wide areas of land are recognised to be the result of erosion by rivers that began their carving at least by mid-Tertiary times. In contrast with mainland Scotland, nowhere in Shetland is more than 5 km from the sea, so there is simply not enough space to be able to recognise whether a low-lying area is part of a Tertiary valley system or not. The only possible signs of ancient valley erosion are a few 'gaps' that have been identified in the north/south topographic spine that runs northwards through Mainland and Yell (the Quarff, Voe and Mid Yell gaps; Fig. 314). These gaps traverse the generally north/south-trending hill ridges that have formed as erosion has picked out the material contrasts due to the layering and structure of the bedrock.

The Ice Age

The pattern of glaciation that has been revealed in the mapping of the islands has been based on measuring the orientation of ice-scoured features, and, to a lesser extent, the identification of ice-transported debris. The pattern is a relatively simple one in which an ice divide has been recognised, with ice flow to the west and east on the opposite sides of the topographic spine that runs from north Unst in the north to Sumburgh in the south (Fig. 320).

It seems most likely that the glaciation represented in this map was the last main glaciation of the Ice Age, the Devensian, which reached a maximum extent about 20,000 years ago. It is also possible that some of the ice-scouring features and movement of erratic material may have occurred during the Loch Lomond Advance between 13,000 and 11,500 years ago (see Chapter 5).

A few kilometres north of Sumburgh airfield, an erratic boulder was found, estimated to be some 1.5 tonnes in weight, and it has been named the Dalsetter Erratic. This is famous because it is made of a rock type unique to an area south of Oslo, Norway. This erratic is taken to provide evidence for a glaciation, earlier than the Devensian, in which ice from Scandinavia was able to transport debris at a time when there was no local southern Shetland source of ice. Erratics from the Old Red Sandstone of the southeast Mainland coast are also found to have been transported over the present spine of the southern Mainland, supporting the idea of early glacial conditions with overriding ice flow to the west.

After the ice

Many of the hill slopes of Shetland show evidence of mass movement, or slumping of the ground surface, that may well be continuing under present climatic conditions, but was certainly more active in the periglacial conditions that existed as the last ice was melting.

Much of the land surface of Shetland has a covering layer of peat deposits that has formed over the last few thousand years of the Holocene, since the departure of the last ice. This has had a mantling effect on the landscapes, and has made economic farming very difficult over much of the land.

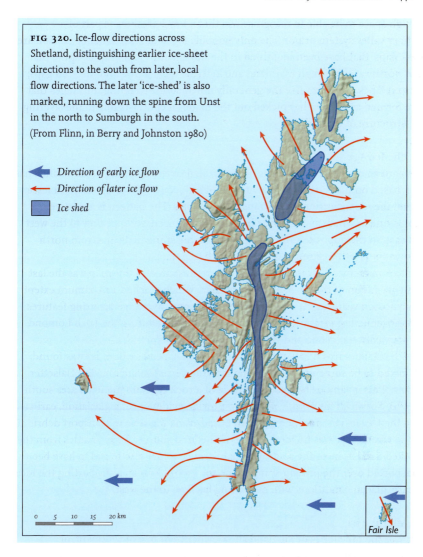

FIG 320. Ice-flow directions across Shetland, distinguishing earlier ice-sheet directions to the south from later, local flow directions. The later 'ice-shed' is also marked, running down the spine from Unst in the north to Sumburgh in the south. (From Flinn, in Berry and Johnston 1980)

⬅ Direction of early ice flow
← Direction of later ice flow
▨ Ice shed

In Chapter 5, the general pattern was established that the Ice Age consisted of long glacial episodes alternating with short interglacials. Global modelling has suggested that each of the main glaciations caused worldwide lowering of sea level of the order of 150 m. The other effect discussed in Chapter 5 was the way that the crust of some western parts of Scotland, where the ice was thickest, was lowered by the load of this ice. This ice-loading effect is usually taken to have been weak in the area of Shetland, at least during the last Devensian glaciation, and this is supported by the general absence of raised beaches and other evidence of uplift of the land since the Devensian ice melted.

Assuming that loading by ice was relatively minor in Shetland, then the dominant difference in relative sea level here would have been that it was lower by some 150 m during much of the Ice Age. Under conditions of worldwide post-glacial melting, the sea would have then risen, flooding the exposed shelf and changing a much larger single island of Shetland (including Foula) into the present cluster of islands.

In general, it is often coastal landscapes that show the clearest evidence of recent landscape-changing activity. In the islands of Shetland, because of their setting in the stormy North Atlantic Ocean, the contrast in this activity between the outer coasts and the inner coasts is particularly clear.

The outer coasts, particularly those facing into the prevailing storms from the west and southwest, often show distinct lines of cliffs, providing evidence of erosion of the bedrock by the fierce attack of storm waves. Some of the cliffs that are of relatively modest height (say 10–20 m) have become the sites for accumulation of boulders on their tops, providing remarkable evidence of the strength of the wave attack. In other cases, vegetation has frequently been stripped from high cliff tops. Many of the outer cliff lines lack beaches of sand, gravel or boulders, in spite of the evidence that they are being actively eroded by waves. In these cases, debris generated by storm action must be transported into areas further offshore by the same fierce storm action. The west coast of the island of Foula provides a most magnificent example of actively eroding sea cliffs. The Kame, a cliff some 376 m high, is second only in height in Britain to the highest sea cliffs on St Kilda (Area 9).

In contrast, inner coasts have been generated by the flooding of low-lying land as sea level has risen relative to the land. In most cases the inlets created by the flooding have more or less sheltered coastlines that tend to have relatively low cliffs, or even areas of sediment accumulation, in the form of beaches, bars and spits that connect to islands, called *tombolos* (Fig. 321). The relatively gentle wave action is further demonstrated by the presence in places of low cliffs that have been eroded in peat, but where the waves have not been able to attack the bedrock that exists further landward. On Whalsay, freshwater peats, dated by radiocarbon methods as between 6000 and 7000 years old, are below sea level, and it is estimated that the sea has risen by some 9 m over that period.

One form of natural event that has been rarely recognised in any record of past events is the tsunami, or catastrophic ocean wave. Yet there is now evidence for several tsunamis that have recently caused devastation in the northern North

FIG 321. St Ninian's Isle: a tombolo, where the growth of sediment spits has linked two bedrock cliffs. This remarkable feature (located on Fig. 310) is some 14 km north-northwest of Sumburgh Head on the generally exposed west coast of the Shetland Mainland, but the sheltering effect of the outer island has been enough to allow the sediment of the tombolo to accumulate. (© Adrian Warren/lastrefuge.co.uk)

Sea area. Most people became aware of events of this type after the Boxing Day 2004 tsunami, which caused more loss of life around the Indian Ocean than any event in living memory. Whereas the Indian Ocean event was a result of a very powerful earthquake off Sumatra, the North Sea tsunami was a result of a submarine landslip or slide at Storegga, northwest of Trondheim in Norway. An offshore area the size of present-day Iceland, and composed largely of unstable glacial sediments, is believed to have collapsed from the edge of the Norwegian continental shelf, in at least three episodes, the largest of these occurring some 7900 years ago. The size of the tsunami wave must have been particularly great in Shetland, only a few hundred kilometres from the site of the collapse. Estimates suggest that the tsunami waves may have been as much as 10 m in height as they approached some parts of Shetland, and may have reached heights of 25 m where the wave increased in size as it travelled up some of the coastal inlets.

CHAPTER 25

Overview

In the first part of this book, we illustrated the sorts of processes that have been creating the natural landscapes of the Earth's surface. We began by considering the ways that slopes, rivers and coasts have often been the active sites in the *surface modification* of landscapes (Chapter 2). We then went on to demonstrate the underlying importance of *solid Earth movements* in the Earth's crust, caused by processes generated within the Earth (Chapter 3).

In this overview chapter, we take a rather more global view than was possible in the Area chapters that have made up most of this book. We want now to look at Scotland, and its neighbours England and Wales, in their wider context, as they have moved relative to each other and other continents. Using studies of the way oceans have changed their shapes, and also measurements of past rock magnetism, we follow the changing latitudes through which these areas have moved in the past.

We also want to revisit how the interplay between surface modification and Earth movements determines landscapes. We want to stress how closely we find these two factors have often been linked, and how they often balance each other. For example, internal movements may cause mountains to be formed that are then modified by glaciation and/or landslides, both of which act to reduce the size of the mountains. Another example is the modification of the Earth's surface by the deposition of sediment by water, ice or wind, which may then result in subsidence of the Earth's crust in response to the new local load of material on its surface.

We wish to simplify and generalise the Area treatment used in much of this book. To achieve this, we present four key steps in the creation of Scotland's present landscapes, labelling them as four acts in an evolving drama. We shall begin with Act 1, dominated by solid Earth movements, in which Caledonian plate convergence occurred, culminating in the collision of Scottish terranes with the terrane of England and Wales. This was followed by Act 2, in which steady northward drift of the combined British continental areas saw them passing through equatorial latitudes and becoming united with large southern continental fragments, producing the single mega-continent of Pangaea. In Act 3 of the drama, Pangaea started to split as divergent movements caused North America and the British Isles to separate and the Atlantic Ocean to form. The final act (Act 4) has occurred much more recently, when global cooling led to Scotland being repeatedly overridden by icecaps and glaciers.

ACT 1: CALEDONIAN PLATE CONVERGENCE

Very active plate-tectonic convergence occurred between around 470 and 420 million years ago (Ordovician to Devonian), bringing together the terranes that make up Scotland (see Figs 19–22, Chapter 4) and England.

The convergence involved the moving together of areas of continental crust from the Laurentian continent (Greenland and North America), three small terranes now incorporated in present-day Scotland, and crust from the Avalonian continent now represented in England and Wales (Fig. 322). Horizontal movement of these components occurred over thousands of kilometres, taking place over the relatively short period (50 million years) here called the Caledonian Convergence. This convergence act is very short indeed compared with the age of the Earth (4.6 billion years), and also very short compared with the earliest pre-convergence events recorded in the history of the terranes and fragments themselves. It was, however, a key period in the history of Scottish landscape formation.

The boundaries of the five Scottish terranes (see Fig. 20, Chapter 4) correspond generally to distinctive features in the landscapes, reflecting differences in the boundary histories.

The Hebridean terrane is special for its very distinctive Archaean and Proterozoic basement with its complex history of metamorphic alteration between 3.2 and 1.1 billion years ago. With its cover of Torridonian Sandstone (1.2 to 0.95 billion years old) on the Scottish mainland, followed by Cambrian and Ordovician sediment (580 to 470 million years old), this terrane is regarded as a fragment of the Laurentian mega-continent.

In contrast, the Northern and Grampian Highland terranes are the metamorphic core of the Caledonian Convergence, folded and strongly altered during Ordovician and Silurian times (particularly 470 and 430 million years ago), long after the basement alteration in the Hebridean terrane. The broadly northeast/southwest trends of folding movements in these terranes seem to be characteristic of the Caledonian convergence and, along with the terrane boundaries, formed high mountain landscapes made of rocks resistant to erosion, which have controlled surface modification of the landscapes ever since. The same directional trend is broadly followed by the Great Glen Fault, involving horizontal fault movement that occurred apparently in response to shear stresses caused by the general convergence.

The Midland Valley is largely a response to younger solid Earth movements, although evidence of earlier Caledonian movements is present in the form of fragments of rock brought to the surface by younger volcanic events.

The Southern Uplands appear to have formed in response largely to surface modification in Ordovican to Silurian times (470 to 430 million years ago) when an accretionary prism of sediment built southeastwards from the main core of the Caledonian terranes during an episode of plate subduction.

The Iapetus Suture is the name given to the feature that marks the boundary of the last Caledonian terrane closures. To the southeast of this are other areas of solid Earth movement and modification, such as the Lake District and Wales, that were part of the Avalonian terrane.

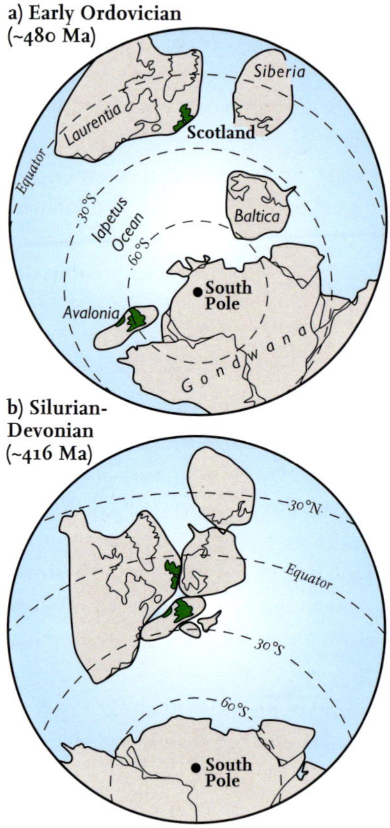

The Lower Old Red Sandstone that occurs in all the terranes just discussed (except the Hebridean) can be regarded as the last evidence of surface modification of the Caledonian Convergence. It consists entirely of sediment deposited above sea level, evidence of the relatively high elevation of the continental surface, and contains local evidence of solid Earth movements as well as evidence of subduction-related volcanism.

FIG 322. South Polar view of the Earth showing the pattern and locations of continents at two stages (roughly 480 and 416 million years ago) during the Caledonian Convergence (Act 1). (From Stone 008)

ACT 2: PANGAEAN DRIFT THROUGH THE TROPICS

The events described here took place in Devonian to Triassic times, 420 to 200 million years ago.

Pangaea is the name often given to the single large continent that appears to have started to develop after Caledonian Convergence had taken place. The Convergence assembled northern and southern Britain by closing what has sometimes been called the proto-Atlantic, or the Iapetus Ocean. As far as Scotland is concerned, the mid-Devonian, early Carboniferous, Permian and Triassic saw surface modification with the growth of subsiding basins. It is important to realise, however, that the extent of the movements was much smaller than those of the Caledonian Convergence. Indeed, the super-continent of Pangaea became a feature on a single plate, lacking any plate boundaries traversing it. In this respect it has similarities with present-day Australia, a large area of continental crust, stable in terms of large movement boundaries. Northern Pangaea, like present-day Australia, moved northward through tropical latitudes (Fig. 323), and this is reflected in the accumulation of sediment in the basins of the British Isles that show many features of sedimentation in low-latitude, tropical conditions. These sediments include coals, limestones, tropical soils and red mudstones and sandstones.

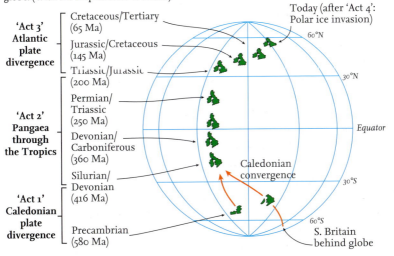

FIG 323. Changes in the latitude of Scotland, southern Britain and – later – the British Isles through time. The initial position of southern Britain was on the concealed face of this globe. (With the help of Alan G. Smith)

Some of the Midland Valley and Southern Uplands Area summaries in this book have shown beautiful examples of the importance of Carboniferous igneous activity on the present landscape of Scotland. Indeed, relict igneous intrusions and extrusions, picked out by subsequent erosion, dominate many local landscapes. These tell us much about the crustal movement processes active in the Carboniferous, but still do not detract from the conclusion that the movements at this time involved much less total movement than the Caledonian Convergence of Act 1.

ACT 3: ATLANTIC PLATE DIVERGENCE

Act 3 covers the period from about 200 million to 2.6 million years ago (Jurassic to Quaternary).

In terms of global continental movements, the next important event for Britain was the initiation of the Atlantic Ocean, which began spreading northeastward in Jurassic times, a plate divergence that has been continuing ever since (Fig. 324). Though of great importance in the North Atlantic region, these divergent movements are much less extensive than those of the contemporaneous Mediterranean–Himalayan belt, in which large continents and many varied micro-continents and terranes have been involved.

In terms of more local solid Earth movements, the pattern of basin boundaries that developed during this time was highly significant for the British Isles, in that we see a real shift towards the present-day shape of the British coastline and offshore bathymetry (Fig. 325). We have seen how components of Scotland's shape

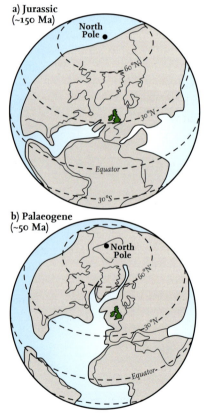

FIG 324. Equatorial to North Polar view of the Earth in Jurassic and Palaeogene (early Tertiary) times (Act 3). (From Stone 2008)

are clearly inherited from the form and structure of the Caledonian convergent plate terranes. Now the Mesozoic basin boundaries can be seen to add a new component. They define many of the features of the west, north and east coasts and offshore bathymetry, and have resulted in a landscape pattern which is very much what we see today.

Other important events followed the formation of this basin pattern, also related to the Atlantic plate divergence, although the centre of the divergence had shifted considerably to the west of the British Isles, with ocean-floor spreading focused on the Mid-Atlantic Ridge. It seems likely that Jurassic volcanism in the central North Sea represents a branch of the divergent movement pattern, causing basin subsidence that formed the North Sea and controlled the distribution of much of its hydrocarbon wealth. The linkage between Atlantic divergence and the early Tertiary volcanism down the west coast of the British Isles has also been frequently demonstrated, and this has strongly influenced the surface modification of the areas involved.

The tilting of the British Isles, downward towards the east, is another important part of this solid Earth movement divergent pattern. We have seen its role in controlling the Tertiary erosion pattern, generating the eastward-flowing major valleys that characterise Scotland's rivers.

ACT 4: POLAR ICE INVASION

Our final act covers the events of the last 2.6 million years (Quaternary to present day).

There is good evidence of cooling of the Earth's climate by around late Tertiary times, and after about 15 million years ago it is clear that the South Polar region was cool enough for ice sheets to develop. In northwest Europe, the Ice Age is normally estimated as starting about 2.6 million years ago. This cooling tendency was particularly likely to have been felt in northwest Europe, where the northernmost parts of Scotland reached a latitude of about 60 degrees north (Fig. 323).

CONCLUSION

In this overview chapter, we have simplified the development of Scotland by picking out four 'acts' of distinct importance. Now we shall conclude by comparing them in terms of their contributions to the present-day landscape. These acts have been distinguished as (1) Caledonian plate convergence,

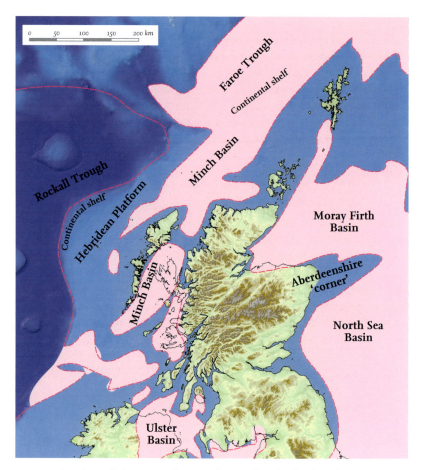

FIG 325. Permian and Mesozoic sedimentary basins of Scotland and northern England. The basins are shaded in pink. GEBCO data have been used for general submarine topography. (Basin pattern from Ziegler 1982)

(2) Pangaean drift through the tropics, (3) Atlantic plate divergence and (4) Polar ice invasion. In Act 1, the Caledonian plate convergence involved *solid Earth movements* of fragments of crust (terranes), with movement distances horizontally of hundreds and even thousands of kilometres, and vertical movements that generated mountains and basins many kilometres in height and depth. Vigorous *surface modifications* must have been taking place throughout this act. Act 2, Pangaean drift through the tropics, created coal and oil deposits that have been of great importance economically to Scotland, and to the British Isles as a

whole, but by the end of this act landscapes were relatively subdued and surface modification relatively gentle. The Atlantic plate divergence of Act 3 saw the development of most of the shape of the British Isles, related to solid Earth movements but only producing local surface modification in these islands.

In the Area chapters, abundant evidence has been presented of the recent surface modification of Scottish landscapes by ice (Act 4). This ranged from the scouring out of corries in the Cairngorms and the sharpening of peaks in the Cuillin in Skye, to the covering of large river basins in the Borders with drumlin fields. Recent dating work has shown that ice was still active in Scotland a mere 12,000 years ago, whereas it is almost 500,000 years since parts of southern England were modified by ice, and much of the rest of southern England escaped all ice modification. This remarkable contrast in surface modification does much to explain the contrasting landscapes of Scotland and England, and demonstrates the overwhelming importance of the polar ice invasion that repeatedly occurred in response to variations in the Atlantic margin climate with latitude and altitude over the last million years or so. Furthermore, it is the relatively recent timing of these climatic effects that is chiefly responsible for making Scottish landscapes so much more dramatic than the older landscapes further south and east in the British Isles, and the widespread appeal of Scottish landscapes is in large measure a reflection of this.

Further Reading

Because this book touches on such a large and diverse range of different topics, we have had to be selective in suggesting material for further reading. The reading suggested here ranges from material suitable for the general readership to specialised reviews of a more or less technical nature. Many local organisations are now producing excellent leaflets on specific local topics, and we have generally not attempted to list these, although many of them are very good.

SOURCES OF MAPS AND BOOKS

British Geological Survey Sales Desk: mail order and counter sales.
  BGS, Keyworth, Nottingham NG12 5GG. 0115 936 3241, sales@bgs.ac.uk, shop.bgs.ac.uk.
BGS Edinburgh: counter sales, mail order (Scotland only). BGS, Murchison House, West Mains Road, Edinburgh EH9 3LA. 0131 667 1000, scotsales@bgs.ac.uk.
BGS London: enquiries, counter sales, local mail order. BGS, Natural History Museum, Cromwell Road, London SW7 5BD. 0207 9038 8462, bgslondon@bgs.ac.uk.
Geo Supplies Ltd, 49 Station Road, Chapeltown, Sheffield S35 2XE. 0114 245 5746, www.geosupplies.co.uk.
The Map Shop, 15 High Street, Upton upon Severn, Worcestershire WR8 0HJ. 01684 593146, themapshop@btinternet.com.
Stanfords, 12–14 Long Acre, London WC2E 9LP. 020 7836 1321, www.stanfords.co.uk.

GEOLOGICAL AND BATHYMETRIC MAPS OF SCOTLAND AND SURROUNDING SEAS

British Geological Survey (1977) *Quaternary Geology: North Sheet*. 1 : 625,000 scale.
British Geological Survey (1991) *Geology of the United Kingdom, Ireland and Continental Shelf: North Sheet*. 1 : 1,000,000 scale.
British Geological Survey (1996) *Tectonic Map of Britain, Ireland and Adjacent Areas*. 1 : 1,500,000 scale.
British Geological Survey (2008?) *Bedrock Geology of the UK: North Map*. 1 : 625,000 scale, 5th edition, and booklet (2008, by P Stone).
GEBCO (General Bathymetric Chart of the Oceans) is available digitally and at various scales, using website search engines.
Ziegler, P. A. (1982) *Geological Atlas of Western and Central Europe*. (Book with pocket of map enclosures). Shell International, Amsterdam.

BGS REGIONAL GUIDES COVERING SCOTLAND

These books from the British Geological Survey provide specialised reviews of the geology of the main regions, as it was known at the date of publication.

Grampian Highlands (4th edition, D. Stephenson, 1995).
Midland Valley of Scotland (3rd edition, I. B. Cameron, 1995).
Northern Highlands of Scotland (5th edition, G. S. Johnstone, 2004).
(See also 4th edition, G. S. Johnstone and W. Mykura, 1989.)
Orkney and Shetland (W. Mykura, 1976).
Palaeogene Volcanic Districts of Scotland (C. H. Emeleus, 2005).
The South of Scotland (3rd edition, D. C. Greig, 1971).

SCOTTISH LANDSCAPE AND GEOLOGY: BOOKLETS BY SNH AND BGS

These beautifully illustrated and clearly written booklets, each subtitled 'a landscape fashioned by geology', cover much of Scotland. They are pitched at a readership with general curiosity and less technical background than the BGS Regional Guides listed above. These booklets are obtainable from BGS (see above) or from Scottish Natural Heritage (www.snh.org.uk/pubs).

Argyll and the Islands (D. Stephenson and J. Merritt, 2010).
Arran and the Clyde Islands (A. McAdam and S. Robertson, 1997).
Ben Nevis and Glencoe (D. Stephenson and K. Goodenough, 2007).
Cairngorms (J. Gordon, R. Wignall, N. Brazier and P. Bruneau, 2006).
East Lothian and the Borders (D. McAdam and P. Stone, 1997).
Edinburgh and West Lothian (D. McAdam, 2003).
Fife and Tayside (M. Browne, A. McKirdy and D. McAdam, 2001).
Glasgow and Ayrshire (C. MacFadyen and J. Gordon, 2006).
Glen Roy (D. Peacock, J. Gordon and F. May, 2004).
Loch Lomond to Stirling (M. Browne and J. Mendum, 1995).
Moray and Caithness (C. Auton, J. Merritt and K. Goodenough, 2011).
Mull and Iona (D. Stephenson, 2011).
Northeast Scotland (J. Merritt and G. Leslie, 2009).
North West Highlands (J. Mendum, J. Merritt and A. McKirdy, 2001).
Orkney and Shetland (A. McKirdy, 2010).
Rum and the Small Isles (K. Goodenough and T. Bradwell, 2004).
Scotland: the Creation of its Natural Landscape
    (A. McKirdy and R. Crofts, 1999).
Skye (D. Stephenson and J. Merritt, 2006).
Southwest Scotland (A. McMillan and P. Stone, 2008).
The Outer Hebrides (K. Goodenough and J. Merritt, 2007).

GENERAL BOOKS ON EARTH PROCESSES

Allen, P. A. (2009) *Earth Surface Processes.* Blackwell, Oxford.
French, H. M. (2007) *The Periglacial Environment,* 3rd edition, Wiley, Chichester.
Gradstein, F. M., Ogg, J. G., and Smith, A. G. eds (2004) *A Geologic Timescale 2004.* Cambridge University Press, Cambridge. (The latest international geologic timescale can be found on www.stratigraphy.org.)
Holmes, A., and Duff, D. (1994) *Holmes' Principles of Physical Geology,* 4th edition. Chapman and Hall, London.
Leeder, M. R. (1999) *Sedimentology and Sedimentary Basins: from Turbulence to Tectonics.* Blackwell, Oxford.
Skinner, B. J., Porter, S. C., and Park, J. (2004) *Dynamic Earth: an Introduction to Physical Geology,* 5th edition. Wiley, Chichester.
Van Andel, T. H. (1994) *New Views on an Old Planet: a History of Global Change,* 2nd edition. Cambridge University Press, Cambridge.
Yarham, R. (2010) *How to Read the Landscape.* Herbert Press, London.

GEOLOGICAL CONSERVATION REVIEWS

There are more than 40 volumes in the Geological Conservation Review Series, produced by the Joint Nature Conservation Committee and providing general review and local site survey information. We have particularly used the following:

Gordon, J. E., and Sutherland, D. G. (1993) *Quaternary of Scotland*. Geological Conservation Review Series, No. 6. Chapman and Hall, London.
Stephenson, D., Bevins R. E., Millward, D., et al. (1999) *Caledonian Igneous Rocks of Great Britain*. Geological Conservation Review Series, No. 17. Joint Nature Conservation Committee, Peterborough.
May, V. J., and Hansom, J. D. (2003). *Coastal Geomorphology of Great Britain*. Geological Conservation Review Series, No. 28. Joint Nature Conservation Committee, Peterborough.

BOOKS REVIEWING LANDSCAPES AND/OR GEOLOGY OF SCOTLAND OR BRITAIN AS A WHOLE

Gillen, C. (2003) *Geology and Landscapes of Scotland*. Terra, Harpenden.
Kempe, N., and Wrightham, M., eds (2006) *Hostile Habitats: Scotland's Mountain Environment. A Hillwalkers's Guide to the Landscape and Wildlife*. Scottish Mountaineering Trust, Nairn.
McKirdy, A., Gordon, J., and Crofts, R. (2007) *Land of Mountain and Flood: the Geology and Landforms of Scotland*. Birlinn, Edinburgh; in association with Scottish Natural Heritage. This beautifully illustrated and clearly written book is suitable for a non-technical readership.
Sissons, J. B. (1967) *The Evolution of Scotland's Scenery*. Oliver and Boyd, Edinburgh and London.
Stamp, L. D. (1947) *Britain's Structure and Scenery*. New Naturalist 4. Collins, London.
Stone, P. (2008) *Bedrock Geology UK North: an Explanation of the Bedrock Geology Map of Scotland, Northern England, Isle of Man and Northern Ireland – 1 : 625,000*, 5th edition. British Geological Survey, Nottingham. This is a very valuable up-to-date review.
Toghill, P. (2000) *The Geology of Britain: an Introduction*. Swan Hill Press, Shrewsbury. This is an excellent introduction for general readers.

Trewin, N. H. ed. (2002) *The Geology of Scotland*, 4th edition. Geological Society, London. This is the most complete available review of knowledge of Scottish geology, at a professional level.

Upton, B. (2004) *Volcanoes and the Making of Scotland*. Dunedin Academic Press, Edinburgh.

Woodcock, N. H., and Strachan. R. eds (2000) *Geological History of Britain and Ireland*. Blackwell, Oxford. This provides a lively account at an intermediate level.

PROFESSIONAL AND/OR LOCAL STUDIES CITED

Astin, T. R. (1990) The Devonian lacustrine sediments of Orkney, Scotland: implications for climatic cyclicity, basin structure and maturation history. *Journal of the Geological Society*, **147**, 141–51.

Bennett, M. R., and Boulton, G. S. (1993) Deglaciation of the Younger Dryas or Loch Lomond Stadial ice-field in the northern Highlands, Scotland. *Journal of Quaternary Science*, **8**, 133–45.

Berry, R .J., and Johnston, J. L. (1980) *The Natural History of Shetland*. New Naturalist 64. Collins, London.

British Geological Survey (1997) 1 : 50,000 Scotland Sheet 84W, Fortrose. British Geological Survey, Nottingham.

British Geological Survey (2004) *Exploring the Landscape of Assynt: a Walkers' Guide and Map Showing the Rocks and Landscape of Assynt and Inverpolly*. Map at 1 : 50,000 scale. British Geological Survey, Nottingham.

Dawson, A. G. (1991) Scottish landform examples. 3: The raised shorelines of northern Islay and western Jura. *Scottish Geographical Magazine*, **107**, 207–12.

Flinn, D. (1980) Geological history. Chapter 2 in Berry and Johnston 1980 (see above).

Hansom, J. D. (2003a) Hard-rock cliffs: GCR site reports. Pages 55–128 in Geological Conservation Review Series No. 28 (see above).

Hansom, J. D. (2003b) Machair. Pages 471–514 in Geological Conservation Review Series No. 28 (see above).

Hudson, J. D., and Trewin, N. H. (2002) Jurassic. Pages 323–50 in Trewin 2002 (see above).

Kokelaar, B. P., and Moore, I. D. (2006) *Glencoe Caldera Volcano, Scotland*. Classical Areas of British Geology. British Geological Survey, Nottingham.

Lambeck, K. (1993) Glacial rebound of the British Isles. *Geophysical Journal International*, **115**, 941–90.

Lloyd, J. M., Shennan, I., Kirby, J. R., and Rutherford, M. M. (1999) Holocene relative sea-level changes in the inner Solway Firth. *Quaternary International,* **60,** 83–105.

Peach, B. N., Horne, J., Gunn, W., Clough, C. T., and Hinxman. L. W. (1907) *The Geological Structure of the North-West Highlands of Scotland.* Memoirs of the Geological Survey of Great Britain. HMSO, Glasgow.

Salt, K. E., and Evans, D. J. A. (2004) Superimposed subglacially streamlined landforms of southwest Scotland. *Scottish Geographical Journal,* **120,** 133–47.

Smith, D. E., Wells, J. M., Mighall, T. M., et al. (2003) Holocene relative sea levels and coastal changes in the lower Cree valley and estuary, SW Scotland, U.K. *Earth and Environmental Science Transactions of the Royal Society of Edinburgh,* **93,** 301–31.

Stoker, M. S., Leslie, A. B., Scott, W. D., et al. (1994) A record of late Cenozoic stratigraphy, sedimentation and climate change for the Hebridean Slope, NE Atlantic Ocean. *Journal of the Geological Society,* **151,** 235–49.

Stone, P. (1999) Shoulder O'Craig (NX663 491). Pages 556–9 in Geological Conservation Review Series No. 17 (see above).

Index

Note: page numbers in *italics* refer to figures and tables.

Aberdeen (Area 13) 322–41
  bedrock 322–30
  Buchan Gravels 330–1, *332, 333, 334,* 339
  Caledonian intrusives 327–8
  coastline formation 335–7, *338,* 339–41
  Dalradian Supergroup 322–5
  glacial landscape 324–5, *333–6*
  Ice Age 333–4
  landscape 330–1, *332, 333–7, 338,* 339–41
  man-made/natural features 324
  Old Red Sandstone 328–30, *337,* 339
  post-glacial landscape 334–6
  sea-level change 336
  unconformity 329, *330*
Acadian episode 40
accretionary prism *42, 43*
Achanarras Quarry (Caithness area) 404, 420
Affric (Area 11) 289–304
  bedrock 289–90, *291–2,* 293–4, *295, 296*
  Caledonian mountain core 293–4
  coastline formation 301–2
  glacial landscapes 296, *297, 298*–301
  Greenland margin 289–90, 293
  landscapes 294–302, *303, 304*
  lava fields 295–6, 301
  location of area 289, *290*
  man-made/natural features 291
  post-Caledonian bedrock 294
  post-glacial landscape 304
  terrace formation 299–301, 304
  topographic profile *300*
  valleys 294–5, *300,* 301
  vegetation 304
  volcanic activity 295–6
agriculture 369, 415, *416*
Ailsa Craig 71, *72,* 78, 83, 90
alkaline intrusions 377
aluminium extraction 160
An Teallach (Cape Wrath area) 380–1
angular unconformity *162, 163, 164*
Annan, River (Southern Borders) 101, *102*
Annandale valley (Southern Borders) 98
anorthosite 346, *347, 349,* 363
anticlines 23
Applecross peninsula (Skye area) 274, 280, 287, 302
arches 259–60, 339
Ardersier peninsula (Inverness area) 396
Ardnamurchan peninsula (Mull area) 180, *182,* 188, *189, 191,* 198
Areas 3–5
Arran 111–32, *133, 134–7*
  bedrock 111–19, 120
  coastline formation 132
  Devensian glaciation 126
  glaciation 126, 129–30
  granite 118, *119,* 124
  igneous rock 124–5
  sills 119, *120,* 124
  valleys 129–30
  volcanic activity 118–19, 124
Arrochar Alps (Rannoch area) 219, 226

Arthur's Seat (Edinburgh) 165, 169, 174
asthenosphere 16, 18, 19
Atlantic Ocean initiation 448
Atlantic plate divergence 447, *448–9,* 451
aureoles 68, 183
Awe, Loch 218, 226
Ayr, River 85

Ballachulish granite 206, 208
Ballantrae Complex 67, 78
Baltica 39, 41
Banks, Joseph 202
Barra (Area 9) 241–63
  bedrock 241–4, *245–6, 248,* 250
  glacial landscape 252, *253,* 254–60
  landscapes 247, *249,* 250–2, *253,* 254–61, *262,* 263
  post-glacial landscape 260–1, *262,* 263
  sandy beaches 261, *262,* 263
  sea-level change 261
  slope map *247, 249*
  vegetation 260–1
bars *442, 443*
basalt
  columnar 193, *195,* 201–2
  sills 267, 269
basins
  boundary pattern *448, 449*
  Old Red Sandstone *421, 426*
  rock 56
  sedimentary 353, *450*
  Solway Firth *97, 98*
  subsidence 353, *421,* 437, 438–9
  see also Minch Basin; Tweed Basin
Bass Rock (Edinburgh area) 165, *175*
bays 89
  Aberdeen area 340
  Cape Wrath 370
  Coll 202
  Galloway 91
  Jura to Arran 136–7
  Shetland *442, 443*
  shingle 368
  Skye area 288
  Tiree 202
  see also raised beaches; sandy beaches
bedrock 1–2
  Cambrian sedimentation 37–8
  Carboniferous to Tertiary 144–7
  Devonian 45–7
  Grampian Highland terrane 214–15
  groups 31, 35
  history 29, 30, 31, 32–3, 34, 35, 36–41, *42, 43*–51
  horizontal movement of sheets 377
  mapping of patterns 23–4
  Mesozoic sedimentation 48–9
  metamorphism 228–9
  Midland Valley 142, 208, 214
  Ordovician sedimentation 37–8
  Permian 45–6

post-Caledonian episodes 35, 45–8, 45–50
pre-Caledonian Greenland-margin episodes 31, 34, 35, 36–8, 39
river catchments 11–12, 13
Southern Uplands terrane 41, 43, 142, 178
Tertiary 49–50, *51*
weathering 72, 274
see also named Areas; rock types and groups
Ben More (Mull) 198, *199*
Ben Nevis (Affric area) 294, *297, 298, 299*
Black Cuillin (Skye) 271, 276, 279, 282, 285
  Great Stone Chute 286
Black Isle (Inverness area) 384
blanket bog 85, 137, 226, 365–6, 412
block fields 321
blow holes 339
bogs, eccentric 200
boulder beds 324–5, 405–6, *407*
breccias, Old Red Sandstone 388
British Geological Survey 29, *30*
British Isles, tilting 449
Buchan Gravels (Aberdeen area) 330–1, *332, 333, 334,* 339
Bullers of Buchan (Aberdeen area) 339, *340*
Bute (Jura to Arran) 114, 122, *123,* 124

Cairngorm (Area 12) 305–21
  bedrock 305–12, 317–18
  Caledonian intrusives 307–9
  glacial landscape 312, *313–21*
  landscapes 313–21
  man-made/natural features 307
  mass movement 320–1
  metamorphic rock 305–7
  Old Red Sandstone 309, 311
  periglacial conditions 320–1
  post-glacial landscape 320–1
  slope map 316
  valleys 305, 309, 312, 315–17, *318*
Cairngorm Mountains 305, 314–17
Cairngorm National Park 305
Cairnsmore of Fleet (Galloway) 68, 76–7
Caithness (Area 17) 398–412
  bedrock 399–406
  Helmsdale Jurassic 404–6
  Moine Supergroup 399–401, 406, 411, 412
  Old Red Sandstone 401–4, 406, 412
  Boulder Beds 405–6, *407*
  coastline formation 406, *407,* 409, 411
  glacial landscape 408–9
  landscape 406, 408–9, *410,* 411–12
  slope mapping 409, 411, *411*
calderas 200, 269, 275, 277
  see also Glencoe caldera (Rannoch area)
Caledonian convergent boundary 22–3, 449
Caledonian intrusives 230, 307–9, 327–8
Caledonian Mountain Belt 35, 70, 307
Caledonian mountains
  igneous intrusions 41
  metamorphic rocks of Inverness area 387

INDEX • 459

mineral growth 207
mountain-building events 205–10, 376–8, 387–8
  core-building episode 38–41, 42, 43–5, 293–4
  movement patterns 206, 216, 228, 229
Caledonian plate convergence 444–6, 447, 450
Callanish standing stones (Lewis) 369
Calton Hill (Edinburgh) 169
Cambrian sedimentation 37–8
Canna (Skye area) 267
cannonball concretions 202, 287–8
Cape Wrath (Area 15) 370–82
  bedrock 371–2, 373, 374, 375, 376–9
  Caledonian mountain-building 376–8
  Greenland margin 371–2, 373, 374, 375, 376
  post-Caledonian episodes 378–9
  glacial landscapes 379–82
  landscape 379–82
  Lewisian Complex 372, 374, 375, 382
  man-made/natural features 371
  marine sediments 376
  sea-level change 382
  slope map 380, 382
  Torridonian Sandstone 374, 375, 376
  vegetation 382
Carradale Water (Kintyre) 122
Carrick Hills (Galloway) 69
Carsphairn Valley (Galloway) 80
Carstairs Kames (Glasgow) 154, 155, 156
Castle Rock (Edinburgh) 169, 172, 173, 174
cave systems 286, 288, 339, 379
chattermarks 381
Cheviot Hills 95, 96, 97, 98, 99
  bedrock 166, 169
  faults/folding 166
Cheviot Igneous Area 165
Churchill Barriers (Orkney) 415, 416
Claish Moss (Mull area) 200
cliffs
  Aberdeen area 339, 340
  Caithness area 408, 409
  Cape Wrath 370
  erosion 442
  Galloway coast 90
  Lewis and Harris 369
  Orkney 417, 423–4, 426
  outcrops 328–9
  Shetland 439, 442
  St Kilda 259
climate 87, 449
  change since Devensian Late Glacial Maximum 57–8
climate indicators 52–3, 54, 57–8
Clyde Beds (Glasgow) 156
Clyde, River (Glasgow) 158–9, 160
Clyde Valley (Glasgow) 153, 156, 157–8
coal deposits 70, 146, 160
  Pangaean drift 450–1
coastline formation 14, 15, 89
  Aberdeen area 335–7, 338, 339–41
  Affric area 301–2
  Britain 449
  Caithness area 406, 407, 409, 411
  Dundee area 240
  Galloway 87–91
  Inverness area 395, 396, 397
  Jura to Arran 131–2, 133, 134–6

Lewis and Harris 365, 367
Mull area 200–3
Orkney 425
Shetland 427, 442–3
Skye area 287–8
Southern Borders 109–10
St Kilda 259–60
  see also sea-level change
Coire Gorm lavas (Mull) 188
Coll (Mull area) 180, 182, 198, 202
columnar jointing 193, 195, 202, 353–4
Comrie granite 206, 208
cone-sheet complex 244
conglomerates, Old Red Sandstone 388
continental crust 19, 20
continental shelf 353, 354
Corrieairack Pass (Cairngorm area) 317
corries 298, 314–15, 318, 321, 359
Corryvreckan whirlpool 202
Cowal (Jura to Arran) 114, 128, 128, 130
Cowal Flat Beds (Jura to Arran) 116
crag-and-tail formation 107, 154, 172, 173, 174, 177
Craig Varr (Kinloch Rannoch) 219
Cree river valley (Galloway) 73, 85, 91
Criffel-Dalbeattie body 67–8, 70
Cromarty Firth (Inverness area) 393
Cruachan granite 210
crust 19–20
  melts 183, 184
  movement measurement 22–8
  rebound 27, 339
  thickening 24
  uplift in Affric area 296
  vertical movements 24–7
  see also tectonic plates
Cuillin (Skye) 1, 2, 271
  see also Black Cuillin (Skye)
Cuillin of Rum (Skye area) 269, 272, 276
Culbin (Inverness area) 396, 397

Dalbeattie body 65, 76–7
Dalradian Supergroup 38–40, 112–15
  Aberdeen area 322–5
  Caledonian mountains 205, 206
  Dundee area 227–9
  erosion resistance 215, 217
  folding 128–9, 323–4
  Inverness area 384–7
  Jura to Arran 120–2, 123, 124, 128–9, 136
  limestone downcutting 226
  Loch Lomond 150
  metamorphism 323–4
  Mull area 182, 193, 195
  Rannoch area 214–15, 219, 221
  Shetland 433–5
Dalsetter erratic (Shetland) 440
dams/damming 86–7, 108–9, 156
Darwin, Charles 299–300
debris-flow fans 317, 321, 389–90, 397
Dee river valley (Aberdeen area) 341
Dee river valley (Cairngorm area) 305, 312
Dee river valley (Galloway area) 73, 85
deforestation 85, 160, 366
deglaciation
  Affric area 302
  Barra 260–1
  Dundee area 239–40
  Edinburgh area 177
  Glasgow area 154, 155, 156, 158–9

Loch Lomond Stadial 302
Southern Borders 107
St Kilda 260–1
Uists 260–1
deltas, sediment 235
deposition
  coastal 14, 15
  Torridonian Sandstone 36
  vertical crustal movements 25–6
  see also glacial deposition
Devensian glacial episode 53–4, 55
  Aberdeen area 333–4
  Affric area 298
  Barra 255–6
  Cairngorm area 313–14
  Cape Wrath area 379, 380, 381
  Edinburgh area 170, 171, 172
  Galloway landscape 75
  Glasgow area 151–2
  Hebridean Platform 259, 365
  ice-flow direction 82–5
  ice sheet 55–6, 57, 61, 62, 252, 254
  Inverness area 393
  Jura to Arran landscape 125–6
  Lewis and Harris 360
  Mull area 197–8
  Orkney 422, 425
  Rannoch area 219
  Shetland 442
  Skye area 282, 283
  Uists 255–6
Devil's Beeftub (Southern Borders) 101, 102
digital elevation 7–8
Digital Elevation Model (DEM) 5
dip-and-scarp topography 274
dissolution features 285–6
Don river valley (Aberdeen area) 341
Doon, Loch (Galloway) 86–7
Dornoch Firth (Inverness area) 393
downslope movement 8, 9, 12, 14
downslope stripes 320–1
drainage network
  Aberdeen area 340
  Cairngorm area 305
  Firth of Forth 178–9
  Lewis and Harris 364
  Rannoch area 210, 213, 219
  Skye area 285, 286, 287
  Tweed Basin 179
drumlins
  Edinburgh area 171, 177
  Galloway 79
  Glasgow area 152–4
  Midland Valley 79
  Solway Firth area 99
  Southern Borders 107
  superimposed 153
  swarms 79
  Tweed Basin 171
Dundee (Area 8) 227–40
  bedrock 227–31, 232, 233–6
  coastline formation 240
  glacial landscape 237–8
  Ice Age 237–8
  landscape 236–40
  man-made/natural features 229
  sea-level change 238–40
  slope map 233, 238
Dundee city 227, 230
Dundee Law 235

Dungeon, Loch (Galloway) 84
Dunnet Head (Caithness area) 398, 400, 404, 410
Dunottar Castle (Stonehaven) 328, 329
Dunscansby Head (Caithness area) 410
dykes 119
    Affric area 294
    Cape Wrath area 372
    Etive Complex 210
    Glasgow area 147
    Glencoe 224
    Jura to Arran 119
    Lewis and Harris 353
    Mull area 192, 195, 202–3
    ring 189, 190, 191, 198
    Skye 271, 276, 279
    Southern Borders 97
    St Kilda 244, 259

Earth
    cooling of climate 449
    mass measurement 217–18
    movement within 6, 7, 16, 17, 18–28
    surface movement measurement 22–4
earthquakes 6, 7, 18, 21, 22
Eaval (North Uist) 251
Edinburgh (Area 5) 161–79
    bedrock 165–6, 167
    glacial landscape evolution 170, 171, 172, 173, 174–6, 177
    landscape 166–70, 171, 172, 173, 174–9
    location 161, 162
    man-made/natural features 163
    post-glacial landscape 176–9
    sea-level change 176, 336
Eigg (Skye area) 267, 272–3, 277, 287, 288
epidiorites 182
erosion
    Aberdeen area coast 339, 340
    Buchan Gravels 331
    cliffs 442
    coastal slopes 14, 15
    Dundee area 237
    Edinburgh area 168
    Glasgow area 145–6
    Hebridean Platform 251
    Hoy hills (Orkney) 425
    lava fields 192–3, 194
    Lewis and Harris 352, 355–8, 364
    meltwater 364
    Midlothian Valley 168
    Mull bedrock 192–3, 194, 195
    Rannoch area rivers 210, 213–15, 216, 217–19
    river 237, 274, 390, 393
    sediment 25–6, 185
    Skye area 274
    South Uist 250
    Tertiary landscapes 33, 51
    Tweed Basin 168
    unloading of crust 27
    vertical crustal movements 25–6
    wave 339, 340
    see also glacial erosion
eskers 81, 154, 176, 394
Etive Complex 210, 214–15
Etive granite 206, 210, 214
Etive, Loch (Rannoch area) 226
eustatic curve 60

Fallen Stack (Caithness area) 406, 407
faults
    Caledonian Mountains 206, 216
    Cheviot Hills 166
    Dalradian Supergroup 323–4
    Glasgow area 140, 149
    Glencoe 224, 225
    Lewis and Harris 356, 357–8
    Lewisian Complex 350, 353
    mammal bones in Clyde peats 152
    mapping 23–4
    margin 233–4
    Moray Firth Basin 390, 391
    Old Red Sandstone 421, 426
    Pentland Hills 166
    ring 224, 225
    Shetland 428–30, 431
    St Kilda 259
    Tertiary valley erosion 365
    see also named faults
fauna during last glaciation 379
Fearn peninsula (Inverness area) 384
feldspar crystals 349
felsic intrusions 22
    Aberdeen area 327
    Cairngorm area 308, 317–18, 319
    Mull area 191–2
    Skye area 269
    St Kilda 244
Fife Ness (Dundee area) 227, 228
Fingal's Cave (Staffa) 193, 194, 195, 201–2
Firth of Forth 175–6, 178–9
Firth of Lorne 197, 201
fish beds 420, 421, 436
fish fossils 96, 142, 234, 404, 405
    Moray Firth 420
    Orkney 420, 421
    Shetland 420, 436
flagstones 403, 404, 406, 407, 408
Flandrian Interglacial 57, 199, 202, 287
Fleet intrusion 68
flints 331, 333
floodplain 13, 14
Flow Country (Caithness area) 412
folds/folding 23–4
    Affric area 293–4
    Arrochar Alps 219
    Caledonian Mountains 205, 206, 216
    Cheviot Hills 166
    Dalradian Supergroup 323–4
    Jura to Arran 116, 117, 128–9
    Moray Firth Basin 390
    Mull area 181–2, 195
    Pentland Hills 166
Forth, River 178–9
    estuary 159, 175–6, 179
    sea-level change 60–1, 62, 158
Forth Valley 152, 158, 175–6
Forvie National Nature Reserve (Aberdeen area) 339–40, 341
fossils
    Aberdeen area bedrock 322, 330
    Caithness area 404, 405
    Glasgow area 142, 146
    reptile footprint 96
    Rhynie Cherts 330
    trilobite 322
    see also fish fossils
fractional crystallisation 272
freeze-thaw processes 12, 14, 226, 286–7, 397

frost polygons 320
frost shattering 84, 360–1
Fruid Reservoir (Southern Borders) 108

gabbros
    Aberdeen area 327
    Rum 269, 272
    Skye 271, 272, 276, 279
    St Kilda 244, 251
Gairloch moraine (Cape Wrath area) 382
Galloway (Area 1) 63–91
    beaches 91
    bedrock 64–72
    climate 87
    coal deposits 70
    coastal cliffs 90
    coastline formation 87–91
    damming 86–7
    Devensian ice-flow direction 82–5
    drumlins 79
    glacial landscape 75–85
    granite 70
    human occupation 63–4
    hydro-electric power 86
    igneous rock 90
    landscape 72–91
    lava fields 69–70
    low-lying area 78
    man-made/natural features 64
    post-glacial landscape 85–7
    raised beaches 90, 91
    rivers 85
    sea-level change 88
    sediment 69–70
    tidal marshes 85, 86
    vegetation establishment 85
    volcanic vents 69, 78
Geographic Information System (GIS) 5, 6–7
geological history episodes 29–30, 33
geos 259–60, 288, 339
glacial deposition
    Aberdeen area 334
    Arran 130
    cave systems 379
    Clyde estuary 159
    Edinburgh area 177
    Forth estuary 159
    Galloway 79–81
    Glasgow area 152–4, 157, 159
    Lewis and Harris 359, 363–4
    Orkney 422
    sediment 80–1, 107, 282
    Skye area 282
    Southern Borders 107
glacial episodes 52, 53–6
    temperature curve 53–4
    see also Devensian glacial episode; Late Glacial Maximum; Loch Lomond Stadial
glacial erosion
    Aberdeen area 334
    Arran 130
    Cape Wrath area 381
    Forth Valley 152, 175–6
    Galloway 75–8
    Jura to Arran landscape 126
    Lewis and Harris 359, 361–2, 362–3
    Rannoch area 219–22, 223, 224
    Skye 281

INDEX • 461

Southern Borders 100–1, 102, 103
Southern Uplands 72
  valleys 12, 103
glacial erratics 83, 282, 359, 394, 440
glacial landscapes
  Aberdeen area 324–5, 333–6
  Affric area 296, 297, 298–301
  Barra 252, 253, 254–60
  Cairngorm area 312, 313–21
  Caithness area 408–9
  Cape Wrath area 379–82
  Dundee area 237–8
  Edinburgh area 170, 171, 172, 173, 174–6, 177
  Galloway 75–84
  Glasgow area 151–4, 155, 156–8
  Hebridean Platform 258
  Inverness area 393–5
  Jura to Arran 125–31
  Lewis and Harris 358–65
  Mull area 196–9
  Orkney 422
  Rannoch area 219–22, 223, 224
  Shetland 440–2
  Skye area 280–2
  Southern Borders 99–107
  St Kilda 256–9
  Uists 252, 253, 254–60
glacial scouring 127–8, 281, 285–6, 361
glacial till deposition 80, 104, 106
glaciation 113
  Highlands 82–3, 151–2
  Snowball Earth 113, 325
  see also valleys, glacial
glaciofluvial deposits 81, 107
  Glasgow area 154, 155, 156
  Inverness area 394
  Lewis and Harris 364
Glasgow (Area 4) 138–60
  bedrock 139–47, 149
  coal deposits 146, 160
  deforestation 160
  faults 140, 149
  fossils 142, 146
  glacial landscape modification 151–4, 155, 156–8
  human impact 160
  landscape 147, 148, 149, 150, 151–4, 155, 156–9
  Midland Valley basin development 142–4
  post-glacial landscape modification 158
  rivers 158–9
  sea-level change 156, 157–8
  volcanic activity 146, 147
Glen App Fault (Galloway) 74
Glen Fyne granite 208
Glen Roy (Affric area), Parallel Roads 299–301, 303, 304
Glencartholm (Southern borders) 96
Glencoe (Rannoch area) 212, 221–2, 223, 224
Glencoe caldera (Rannoch area) 209, 210, 211, 212
  glacial erosion 222, 223, 224
Glencoul Thrust (Cape Wrath area) 378
gneiss see Lewisian Gneiss
gold 71
gorges, river 397
Grampian Event 142

Grampian Highland terrane 32, 39, 40, 41, 111, 322–3, 445–6
  Aberdeen area 325
  bedrock 214–15
  Dundee area 227
  movements 182
  Mull area 182
  Rannoch area 204, 205–6, 208, 219
  river valleys 213
  strike-slip movement 208
granite 23
  Aberdeen area 328, 339, 340
  Affric area 294
  Arran 118, 119, 124
  block fields 321
  Cairngorm area 308, 310–11, 321
  Caithness area 401
  Caledonian mountains 208–9
  cracks 321, 339
  Dundee area 230
  Galloway 70, 76–7
  joints 321, 339
  Lewis and Harris 347, 349
  Monadhliath Mountains 317–18, 319
  Mull area 182–3, 191–2, 195, 200
  plutons 67–8, 77, 208, 327
  quarrying 200
  Rannoch area 208–9, 219, 221
  Shetland 437–8, 439
  Skye area 269, 279
  St Kilda 244, 251
  tors 130, 310–11, 327
graptolites 66
gravel ridges 394
Great Eucrite (Ardnamurchan) 189, 191
Great Glen (Cairngorm area) 305, 309, 311–12
Great Glen (Inverness area) 393
Great Glen Fault 30, 32, 35, 41, 180, 182, 205, 218
  Affric area 293, 294
  Cairngorm area 311–12
  directional trend 446
  initiation 387–8
  Inverness area 383–4, 387–8, 389
  magma intrusions 208
  Moine Supergroup location 387
  Orkney area 413, 426
  right-lateral movement 392, 439
  Shetland 429–30
Greenland margin
  Affric area 289–90, 293
  Caledonian Mountain Belt 35
  Cape Wrath area 371–2, 373, 374, 375, 376
  pre-Caledonian episodes 31, 34, 35, 36–8, 39
Grey Dog tidal race (Lunga, Mull area) 202
Grey Mare's Tail waterfall (Southern Borders) 100, 102, 103
gullies 321

hachure shading 7
hanging valleys 103
Harris see Lewis and Harris (Area 14)
Hebridean Platform 247, 251, 258, 259, 261, 450
  Devensian episode 255–6, 365
  machair formation 369
  plateau surfaces 259, 260
  shear zone 353, 354
  St Kilda 250–1, 259–60

Hebridean terrane 32, 34, 37, 431–2, 445
Helmsdale Fault Zone 389, 391, 405, 406, 407, 412
Helmsdale Granite 401
Helmsdale Jurassic 404–6
Hermaness (Shetland) 436
Highland Border Complex 142, 227, 229–30, 325–7
Highland Boundary Fault 116–17, 208
  Aberdeen area 325–7
  Bute 123, 124
  Dundee area 227, 229–30
  Glasgow area 142
  Rannoch area 214
Highlands
  glaciation 82–3, 151–2
  uplift 72
hill-hole pair 157
hill machair 367
hill-shade 6–7
hills, Aberdeen area 340–1
Holocene 57
Horne, John 377
hot waters, Cairngorm area 308–9
Hoy island (Orkney) 425–6
Hoy Sandstone 421, 425, 426
Hoy Volcanic Rocks 421
human impact
  coastline formation 89
  damming 86–7, 108–9
  Glasgow area 160
  Jura to Arran 137
  Lewis and Harris 366, 369
  Mull area 200
  Southern Borders 108–9
  vegetation 85, 108
Hutton, Charles (mathematician) 218
Hutton, James (geologist) 161, 162, 164, 174–5
Hutton's Section 174–5
hydro-electric power 86

Iapetus Ocean 67, 93
  closure 140, 142, 208
Iapetus Suture 32, 43, 67, 94, 97, 446
ice, surface modification 451
Ice Age 52–6, 57, 252
  Aberdeen area 333–4
  Cairngorm area landscape 313–21
  Inverness area 393–5
  northwest Europe 449
  Shetland 440–2
ice flow
  Aberdeen area 334, 335
  Barra 253, 255
  Cairngorm area 313
  Caithness area 408, 409, 411
  Cape Wrath area 380, 381
  Dundee area 238
  Edinburgh area 172, 173, 174, 175
  Inverness area 393–4
  Jura to Arran 126
  Lewis and Harris 358–9, 360, 361
  Mull area 197–8
  Shetland 440, 441
  Skye area 280, 283
  Solway Firth 99
  Southern Uplands 83–4, 99
  Tweed Basin 171, 172
  Uists 253, 255

ice sheets 151–2
  development 449
  extent 55–6, *57*, 252, 254
  loading 27, 59
  melting 59, 61, 62, 83–4
  movement patterns *254*, 255
  unloading 59
ice streams 56
  Cairngorm area 317, 319
  Glasgow area 152
  Great Glen Fault 312
  Highlands 82–3
  Inverness area 393–4
  Jura to Arran 126
  Lewis and Harris 360
  Minch Basin 361
  Monadhliath Mountains 319
  Mull area 197–8
  Rannoch area 219
icecap 360, 361, 380
  extent of Devensian glacial episode 252, 254
igneous activity 50
  Carboniferous 448
  Edinburgh area 165
  Lewis and Harris 344, *354*, 355
  Mull area 183–4, 198
  Post-Caledonian episodes 47–8
  Skye area 267, 269, 271–3
  St Kilda 244, *246*, 250–2
  Tertiary 49–50
igneous intrusions
  Affric area 294, *296*
  Caithness area 401
  Caledonian mountain-building 41
  Cape Wrath area 377
  Dundee area 235–6
  Inverness area 384–7
  Orkney 422
  Shetland 437–8, 439
  see also lava entries; mafic intrusions
igneous rock 22
  Aberdeen area 327–8
  Arran 124–5
  Cairngorm area 307–8
  Caledonian mountains 208
  downslope movement 8
  Dundee area 233–4, *235*, 235–6
  Edinburgh area 168–9
  Galloway area 90
  Glasgow area 140
  Inverness area 387
  Kintyre 125
  Lewis and Harris 344, *354*, 355
  Shetland 437–8, 439
  Shiant Isles *347*, 353–4
  Southern Borders 95–6
Innerwick Fault *166*, 168
Inverness (Area 16) 383–97
  bedrock 384–90
  Caledonian mountain-building 387–8
  Dalradian Supergroup 384–7
  Mesozoic deposits 389–90
  Moine Supergroup 384–7
  Permian deposits 389–90
  coastline formation 395, *396*, 397
  glacial landscape 393–5
  Great Glen Fault 383–4, 387–8, 389
  igneous intrusions 384–7
  landscape 390, 393–5, *396*, 397
  man-made/natural features 384

oil reserves 390, 391, 392
Old Red Sandstone 388–9
  post-glacial landscape 395, *396*, 397
  sea-level change 395
Inverness city 384
inversion of topography 331
Islay 111–32, *133*, 134–7
  bedrock 111–19, 120
  coastline formation 132, *133*, 134–6
  Dalradian Supergroup 113
  knock-and-lochan topography 128
  limestone 113
  population 120
  rock platforms 132, *133*, 134–6
isthmus of Tarbert (Harris and Lewis area) 343, *345*

Jarlshof (Shetland) 427
Jura to Arran (Area 3) 111–22, 123, 124–32, *133*, 134–7
  bedrock 111–19, 120
  coastline formation 131–2, *133*, 134–6
  flooded valleys 136
  glacial landscape evolution 125–31
  human impact 137
  landscapes 120–2, 123, 124–32, *133*, 134–7
  population 120
  post-glacial landscape 136–7
  rock platforms 132, *133*, 134–6
  sea-level change 131–2, 134, 135–6
  vegetation 137

kame-and-kettle topography 81, 156
kames 154, *155*, 156, 394
karstic surfaces 286
Kentra Moss (Mull area) 200
kettle holes 81, 156, 221
Kildrummie Ice Stream 393–4
Kilt Rock (Trotternish peninsula) 269, *273*, 287
Kintyre (Jura to Arran) 114, 122, *125*, 129, 131
Knapdale (Jura to Arran) 128–9, *137*
Knapdale Steep Belt (Jura to Arran) 116, 120–1
knock-and-lochan landscape 34, *36*, 77, 263
  Cape Wrath area 374, *375*, 382
  Coll 182
  Glasgow area 152
  Jura to Arran 128
  Lewis and Harris 351, 359, 361, 365
  North Uist 255, *256*
  Skye area 280–1

Lairig Ghru (Cairngorm) 317, *321*
lake deposits 404, *420*, 421, 437
laminites 404, *420*
Lammermuir Fault 165, *166*, 168, 175
lamprophyres 422
landforms 1–2, 6
landscapes 1–2
  cycles 6
  history 2
  human influence 2–3
  plate boundary effects 23
  surface modification 444
  vertical crustal movement impact 25–6
  see also glacial landscapes; knock-and-lochan landscape; Tertiary landscapes

landslides 226, 282, *284*, 286, 423
Late Glacial Maximum 57–61, 62
Laurentia 39, 41
lava escarpments *284*, 287
lava fields 47, 49–50
  Affric area 295–6, 301
  Dundee area 233–4, *235*
  erosion 192–3, *194*
  Galloway 69–70
  Glasgow area 145–6
  Jura to Arran 114, 117
  Midland Valley 70–1
  Mull area 182–3, 184, 186, *187*, 188–93, *194*
  Skye area 267, 301
lava flows 267
lava, mafic 182, 184, 186, 233
  see also mafic intrusions
lava pinnacle (Skye) *284*, 287
lava plateaus 287
  Caledonian mountains 209
  Glasgow area 149
  Lorne 209, 210, 214, 219, 226
  Skye area 274
Laxfordian deformation 243, 346–7, 356, 372, *373*
lazybeds 368, 369
lead 23, 71
Leadhills (Galloway) 71, *72*
Leven-Blackwater valley (Rannoch area) 222
Lewis and Harris (Area 14) 342–69
  basin subsidence 353
  bedrock 343–4, *345*, 346–7, 348, 349–54, *358*
  early Tertiary igneous episodes 353–4
  post-Caledonian episodes 350–3
  pre-Caledonian episodes 344, 346–7, 348, 349–50
  coastline formation 365
  faults 356, 357–8
  glacial landscape 358–65
  human impact 366, 369
  ice flow 358–9, *360*
  landscape 355–69
  lazybeds 368
  Lewisian Complex 344, 346–7, *348*, 349–50, 353
  machair 346, *354*, 366–9
  man-made/natural features 343
  sea-level change 354–5, 365
  slope map *355*
  topography variation 356–7
  vegetation 365–9
Lewisian Complex 31, 34, *36*, 37
  Affric area 290, 293, *296*
  Barra 241–3, 245–6
  Cape Wrath 372, 374, *375*, 382
  faults 350, 353
  Lewis and Harris 344, 346–7, 348, 349–50, *351*, 353
  melting 183
  Mull area 180–1, 182
  Shetland 431–3
  Skye area 264
  Uists 241–3, 245–6
Lewisian Gneiss 256
  Affric area 290, 293, *296*
  Lewis and Harris 344, 347, 357
  Skye 281

INDEX · 463

Liddesdale (Southern Borders) 98, 103, 105
limestone 113, 182, 286
   caves 379
   downcutting 226
   overlaying Cambrian/Ordovician sedimentation 38
limestone pavement 226
Linnhe, Loch (Mull/Rannoch areas) 180, 182, 226
   Great Glen Fault 218
   ice flow 197, 219, 226
lithosphere 16, 18, 19
   see also crust; tectonic plates
loading, vertical crustal movements 26–7
Loch Doon intrusion 67, 77
Loch Doon pluton 77
Loch Lomond Stadial 58–9, 84, 298–9, 302
   Aberdeen area 334
   Affric area 298, 302
   Caithness area 409
   Cape Wrath area 380
   Gencoe 222
   Glasgow area impact 151, 156–8
   Jura to Arran landscape 125–6, 129–30, 135
   Mull area 198–9
   Rannoch area 220, 221, 222, 223, 224
   Shetland 440
   Skye area 282, 284
   Southern Borders impact 100, 104
   St Kilda 256, 259–60
Loch Tay fault 218
lochans 366
   see also knock-and-lochan landscape
Locharbriggs (Southern Borders) 96
lochs 226, 343, 345, 365, 366
   see also knock-and-lochan landscape
Lomond Hills (Dundee area) 236, 237
Lomond, Loch 152
   see also Loch Lomond Stadial
Lorne, Firth of 197, 201
Lorne lava plateau 209, 210, 214, 219, 226
Lower Old Red Sandstone 43–5, 446
   Aberdeen area 328–30
   Affric area 294
   Caithness area 403
   Dundee area 231, 233–4, 235
   Edinburgh area 165
   Galloway 69, 78
   Glasgow area 144
   Inverness area 388
   Jura to Arran 117
   Loch Lomond 150
   Mull area 182–3
   Orkney 418
Lowther Hills (Galloway) 71, 72, 73, 75–6
Luce Bay-Loch Ryan 73, 89
Luskentyre (Harris) 367
Lyon, Glen 218

MacCulloch's Tree (Mull) 187, 188
machair 202, 261, 262, 263
   hill 367
   Lewis and Harris 346, 354, 366–9
MacLeod's Tables (Skye) 274, 279, 280
mafic intrusions 22, 327, 344, 346
   see also lava, mafic
magma
   Caledonian mountains 208–9
   columnar jointing 193, 195, 202

granitic 347
Lewis and Harris 344, 347
Minch Basin 353
Rum 269, 272
Skye 272
St Kilda 244
magma chambers 188–90, 191
mammal bones, Clyde peats 152
mantle 19
maps 3–5
   digital 6–8
marble, Skye 267
margin faults 233–4
Maskelyne, Nevil (Astronomer Royal) 217–18
mass movement 320–1, 422–3, 440
Medwin Water (Glasgow) 159
Megget Reservoir (Southern Borders) 108–9
Melby Fault 431, 436
meltwaters 154, 155, 156, 359, 364
Mendelssohn, Felix 202
Mesozoic sedimentation 48–9
metamorphic rock 8, 31, 323–4
   Aberdeen area 327
   Cairngorm area 305–7
   Caithness area 400–1
   Cape Wrath area 377
   Inverness area 384–7
   Lewis and Harris 344, 346, 347, 348
   Shetland 433–5
Mid-Atlantic Ridge 449
Middle Old Red Sandstone 45, 46, 420
   Caithness area 403, 406, 412
   flagstones 403, 404, 406, 407, 408
   Inverness area 388–9
   Orkney 403, 418–21, 426
   Shetland 437, 438
Midland Valley 70–1, 79, 87, 149, 160
   basin development 69, 142–4
   bedrock 142, 208, 214
   Devensian ice-flow direction 82
   Dundee area 227
   Edinburgh area 165
   Galloway 63, 67
   Glasgow area 140, 142–4
   Old Red Sandstone 208, 214
   Rannoch area 214
   solid Earth movements 446
Midlothian Basin 168, 169
Midlothian Valley, erosion 168
migmatite 400
Milankovitch, Milutin 421
Miller, Hugh 420
Minch Basin 350, 352, 353, 361, 450
   sills 353–4, 358
   subsidence 353
Minch Fault 247, 347, 350, 351, 352
minerals/mineral veins 23, 71
   Cape Wrath area 377
   Dundee area 229
   Mull area 183–4
   ore bodies in Cairngorm area 309
   Southern Uplands 68
mining 87, 160
   see also coal deposits
mixed magma intrusions 244
Moffat Hills, ice accumulation 99
Moffat Water (Southern Borders) 98, 103
Moffatdale (Southern Borders) 103, 104

Moine Supergroup 38–40, 181–2, 183, 202
   Affric area 290
   Cairngorm area 306–7
   Caithness area 399–401, 406, 411, 412
   Cape Wrath area 382
   Grampian Mountains 205–6
   Great Glen Fault 387
   Inverness area 384–7
   Orkney 415, 417
   Shetland 433
   Skye area 264–5
Moine Thrust Zone 34, 36, 37, 38, 377–8
   Affric area 290, 293
   Cape Wrath area 376, 382
Monadhliath Mountains (Cairngorm area) 305, 317–19
monadnocks 374, 375, 381–2
moraines
   Affric area 298, 303
   Cape Wrath area 382
   Glasgow area 157
   Glen Torridon 298, 303
   Jura to Arran 130
   Lewis and Harris 359, 364
   Loch Dungeon 84
   Loch Lomond Stadial 58–9, 157
   Loch Ryan 84
   Orkney 422
   rogen (ribbed) 80
   Skye 280
   terminal 100, 101, 157
Morar, Loch (Skye area) 281
Moray Firth (Aberdeen area) 334, 337
Moray Firth (Inverness area) 383, 393, 395, 420
Moray Firth Basin (Inverness area) 389, 390, 391, 439, 450
More, Ben (Mull) 198, 199
Morvern (Mull area) 180, 182, 198
mountain building 24, 28
   Caledonian mountains 205–10, 376–8, 387–8
   core-building episode 38–41, 42, 43–5, 293–4
Muck (Skye area), lava flows 267
mud-flats 91, 109
mud-slides 423
mudstones 388
Mull (Area 6) 180–203
   bedrock 180–4, 185, 186, 187, 188–92
   erosion 192–3, 194, 195
   coastline formation 200–3
   crustal movement 180–1
   glacial landscape 196–9
   human impact 200
   landscape formation 192–3, 194, 195–203
   lava fields 182–3, 184, 186, 187, 188–92
   erosion 192–3, 194
   location 180, 181
   peat deposits 199–200
   sea-level change 199, 200–1, 202
   volcanic activity 182–3, 184, 186, 187, 188–92
Mull Central Complex igneous intrusions 198

Neolithic people 331, 333
Ness, Loch (Cairngorm area) 312, 313
Nevis, Ben (Affric area) 294, 297, 298, 299
Nevis, Loch (Skye area) 281

New Red Sandstone 48, 96, 117–18, 405
Nith river valley (Galloway) 73–4, 75, 81, 82, 85
North Ronaldsay (Orkney) 416
North Sea 449
  tsunami 442–3
North Sea Basin 450
North Uist 251
  knock-and-lochan landscape 255, 256
  machair 261, 262, 263
Northern Highland terrane 32, 39, 41, 371, 445–6
nunataks 198, 199, 222, 282, 360–1

oceanic crust 19–20
Ochil Hills (Rannoch area) 209
oil reserves 450–1
  Aberdeen area 322
  Inverness area 390, 391, 392
  North Sea 449
  Shetland 427–8, 430, 439
Old Man of Hoy (Orkney) 417, 421, 424, 425, 426
Old Man of Storr (Skye) 284, 287
Old Red Sandstone
  Aberdeen area 326, 328–30, 337, 339
  basins 421, 426
  Cairngorm area 309, 311
  Caithness area 401–4, 406, 412
  Caledonian mountains 208
  Dundee area 231, 233–4, 235
  Inverness area 388–9
  Jura to Arran 124
  Midland Valley terrane 208, 214
  Orkney 403, 414, 415, 417–21, 423–4
  Shetland 435–7, 438
  Southern Uplands 95
  see also Lower Old Red Sandstone; Middle Old Red Sandstone; Upper Old Red Sandstone
ophiolite 434–5, 436
Orcadian Lake Basin 45, 46
Ordnance Survey National Grid references 4
Ordovician sedimentation 37–8
ore bodies 309
  see also minerals/mineral veins
Orkney (Area 18) 383, 413–26
  agriculture 415
  bedrock 415, 417–22
  coastline formation 425
  fish beds 420, 421
  glacial landscape 422
  islands 413, 414, 415
  landscape 422–6
  man-made/natural features 414
  Old Red Sandstone 403, 417–21, 423–4, 426
  pre-Tertiary landscape 422
  sea-level change 425
  settlement 413, 414
  slope map 424, 425, 426
Orkney-Shetland platform 439
Orwell, George 202
Outer Hebrides 261, 262, 263, 349–50
  see also Barra (Area 9); Lewis and Harris (Area 14); St Kilda; Uists (Area 9)
Outer Hebrides Fault Zone 351, 352
Outer Isles Thrust Zone 243, 246, 247, 250, 251, 350–1

outwash plains 81
oxygen isotopes 52–3, 54, 57–8

Pabbay (Lewis and Harris) 367
Pangaea supercontinent 146–7, 447–8
Pangaean drift 447–8, 450–1
Paps of Jura 120, 121
Patna Hill (Galloway) 78
Peach, Benjamin 377
peat
  buried intertidal 365
  Caithness area 412
  Galloway 85
  Glasgow area 152
  Jura to Arran 137
  Lewis and Harris 365–6
  Mull area 199–200
  Rannoch Moor 226
  Shetland 440, 442
pebble beds 324–5
pegmatite 347, 349, 363
Pentland Fault 166, 168, 169, 170
Pentland Hills (Edinburgh) 165, 166, 168–9
periglacial conditions 12, 14, 256–9
Peterhead granite (Aberdeen area) 339, 340
pitchstone 273
place names, Southern Uplands 64
plate tectonics 16, 17, 18–22
  see also tectonic plates
plutons 77, 208, 327
  concentrically zoned 67–8
Polar ice invasion 449
pools 366
population centres 3
protalus ramparts 256
psammites 307
pseudotachylites 247, 250

quarrying
  Aberdeen area 328
  anorthosite 349
  Galloway 87
  Glasgow area 160
  granite 328
  Lewis and Harris 349
  Mull area 200
  Rannoch area 206
  Skye marble 267
  slate 200, 206

rainfall, river catchments 11
raised beaches
  Ailsa Craig 90
  Arran 132
  Dundee area 239
  Galloway 90, 91
  Glasgow area 158
  Skye area 288
Rannoch (Area 7) 204–26
  bedrock 205–10, 214–15, 217
  blanket bog 226
  drainage 210, 213, 219
  glacial erosion 219–22, 223, 224
  landscape formation 210, 213–15, 216, 217–22, 223, 224, 225, 226
  man-made/natural features 205
  post-glacial landscape 224, 226
  river drainage 210, 213, 219
  river erosion 210, 213–15, 216, 217–19
  sea-level change 224, 226

slope map 214
valleys 213, 218
vegetation 226
Rannoch granite 206, 208
Rannoch Moor 215, 221, 222, 223, 226
Rannoch Rebound Dome 61, 62, 132, 239, 425
Red Hills (Skye) 269, 271, 279, 282
reefs 365, 368
relict mountains 374, 375, 381–2
reptile footprint fossils 96
reservoirs, Southern Borders 108–9
Rhinns peninsula (Islay) 111–12
Rhins of Galloway 73, 79, 83, 84, 89
Rhynie Cherts (Aberdeen area) 330
rhythmite 420
ridge-and-voe landscape 435
ring dykes 189, 190, 191, 198
ring fault 224, 225
ring intrusion 209
river(s)
  Aberdeen area 340
  Edinburgh area 177–8
  erosion 237, 274, 390, 393
  flow rates 11
  Glasgow area bedrock formation 144, 145
  gorges 397
  Holocene 158–9
  Inverness area 397
  Jura to Arran 136
  Lewis and Harris 354–5, 361
  meanders 177–8
  Rannoch area 210, 213–15, 216, 217–19
  Skye area 287
  Southern Borders 108
river catchments 9, 10, 11–12, 13, 14
river channels 12, 13, 14
river terraces 395
roches moutonnées 280
rock basins 56
rock glacier 131
rock platforms 132, 133, 134–6, 158, 201
  wave-cut 288
rogen (ribbed) moraines 80
Roineval (Lewis and Harris) 346, 347, 349
Ronas Hill (Shetland) 438, 439
Ross of Mull 183, 195, 202
Rum (Skye area) 269, 272, 276, 277
  calderas 269, 275, 277
  freeze-thaw processes 287
  igneous activity 269
  wave-cut rock platform 288
Ryan, Loch (Galloway) 84, 89

Salisbury Crags (Edinburgh) 169, 174–5
salt-marsh 90, 91, 109, 367
sand, wind transport 381
sand dunes 202
  Aberdeen area 337, 340
  Galloway area 91
  Inverness area 396, 397
  Lewis and Harris 367
  Mull area 202
sand-flats 90, 91, 109
sand ridges 394
Sandsting Complex (Shetland) 438
sandy beaches
  Aberdeen area 339–40
  Barra 261, 262, 263
  Lewis and Harris 366, 367, 368, 369

INDEX • 465

Uists 261, 262, 263
Scapa Flow (Orkney) 414–15
scarps, fault-controlled 149
Schiehallion (Rannoch area) 206, 216, 217
Scottish Enlightenment 161
Scottish National River Flow Archive 9, 10
Scourian event (dyke swarm) 243, 344, 372
scree 84, 104
sea cliffs *see* cliffs
sea-level change 28, 59–61, 62
   Aberdeen area 336
   Affric area 301–2
   Barra 261
   Cape Wrath area 382
   Dundee area 238–40
   Edinburgh area 176, 336
   eustatic 60, 365
   Firth of Forth 176
   Forth Valley 158
   Galloway 88
   Glasgow area 156, 157–8
   Inverness area 395
   Jura to Arran 131–2, 134, 135–6
   Lewis and Harris 354–5, 365
   Mull area 199, 200–1, 202
   Orkney 425
   Rannoch area 224, 226
   Shetland 441–2
   Skye area 274
   Solway Firth 88, 89, 109, 110
   Uists 261
   see also coastline formation
sea lochs 343, 365
sea stacks
   Aberdeen area 339
   Caithness area 406, 407, 410
   Lewis and Harris 369
   Skye area 288
   St Kilda 259–60
seaearths 160
sediment
   Aberdeen area bedrock 322
   accretionary prism 42, 43
   accumulation on coastlines 442
   Affric area deposition 293
   Cairngorm area deposition 307
   Caithness area deposition 404–5
   Caledonian mountains 205
   Cambrian 37–8, 376
   Carboniferous 235
   coastal deposition 14, 15, 89
   deltas 235
   deposition 25–6, 36
   Dundee area 227–8, 235, 240
   Edinburgh area 165
   erosion 25–6, 185
   Galloway 64–6, 69–70, 91
   glacial deposition 80–1, 107, 282, 358, 363
   Glasgow area bedrock 144, 145
   Inverness area 385–7, 390
   Jura to Arran 117, 118
   layering 399–400
   Lewis and Harris deposition 351–2
   loading 27
   Lower Old Red Sandstone formation 44–5
   Mesozoic 48–9
   Mull area 183, 185
   Ordovician 37–8, 376
   post-Caledonian episodes 45–6

Shetland deposition 439
Southern Borders coast 109–10
thickness measurement of layers 28
Torridonian Sandstone 36
sedimentary rock 8, 64–6, 140
sedimentation
   cycles 421
   Middle Old Red Sandstone 420–1
   Orkney 420–1
   Solway Firth basin 97, 98
semi-pelites 307
An Sgurr (Eigg) 272–3, 277
sheep-tracks 321, 423
Shetland (Area 19) 383–443
   bedrock 428–39
   Dalradian Supergroup 433–5
   granite 437–8
   Lewisian Complex 431–3
   Mesozoic history 438–9
   Moine Supergroup 433
   Old Red Sandstone 435–7, 438
   coastline formation 427, 442–3
   faulting 428–30, 431
   fish fossils 420
   gaps 440
   glaciated landscape 440–2
   human occupation 427
   Ice Age 440–2
   islands 415
   landscape 439–43
   man-made/natural features 429
   oil reserves 427–8, 430, 439
   ophiolite 434–5, 436
   post-glacial landscape 440–3
   slope map 434
   tsunami waves 442–3
   Walls Boundary Fault line 426, 429, 430, 431, 436–7, 439
Shiant Isles (Lewis and Harris area) 343, 343, 347, 353–4, 358
Shiel, Loch (Mull area) 200
shingle beaches 368
shingle ridges 135–6, 365
shore platforms 88, 359
shoreline features, old 61, 62
Shoulder o' Craig (Galloway) 69
Shuttle Radar Topographic Mission (SRTM) 5
Siccar Point (Edinburgh) 161–2, 163, 176
sills
   Affric area 296
   Arran 119, 120, 124
   basalt 267, 269
   Dundee area 235–6
   Jura to Arran 119, 120, 131
   Midland Valley 70–1
   Minch Basin 353–4, 358
   Mull area 192, 202
   St Kilda 244
silver 71
Skene, Loch 100, 101, 103
skerries 365, 368
Skye (Area 10) 264–88
   bedrock 264–5, 267, 268, 269, 270, 271–3
   cave systems 286
   coastline formation 287–8
   freeze-thaw processes 286–7
   glacial landscape 280–2, 283
   karstic surfaces 286
   landscapes 273–4, 275, 276, 277–8,

279–82, 283, 284–8
   landsliding 282, 284
   lava fields 267, 301
   man-made/natural features 266
   post-glacial landscape 285–7
   sea-level change 274
   Sleat peninsula 264–5, 281
   slope map 278
   vegetation 286
Skye Central Complex 268, 269, 271–2, 276
Skye marble 267
Slapin, Loch 1
slate quarrying 200, 206
Sleat peninsula (Skye) 264–5, 281
slopes 8, 9
   failure 226
slumps 226
Snowball Earth 113, 325
solid Earth movements 59, 444, 446
   Atlantic plate divergence 448
   Caledonian plate convergence 450
   tilting of British Isles 449
solifluction lobes 256, 321
Solway Firth 90–1, 99, 109, 110
   basin 97, 98
   sea-level change 88, 89, 109, 110
Sound of Harris 359, 365
South Uist 250
Southern Borders (Area 2) 92–104, 105, 106–10
   bedrock 92–6, 103, 105
   coastline formation 109–10
   glacial landscape 99–107
   human impact 108–9
   landscape 97–104, 105, 106–10
   post-glacial landscape development 108–9
   reservoirs 108–9
   rivers 98, 108
   Tertiary erosion 97–8
   vegetation 108
Southern Uplands Fault 63, 64, 74–5, 165
Southern Uplands terrane 41, 42, 43
   bedrock 41, 43, 142, 178
   deformation 67
   Edinburgh area 165, 166, 168
   formation 94–5, 446
   Galloway 64, 67
   glacial erosion 72
   glaciation 72, 83–4, 99, 151–2
   granite bodies 67
   hill-front 175
   ice flow 83–4, 99
   mineral veins 68
   place names 64
   uplift 72, 97
   valleys 73
Spey Bay (Aberdeen area) 336–7, 338
Spey valley (Cairngorm area) 305, 312
spits 442, 443
Sron Ulladale truncated spur (Lewis and Harris) 359, 362
St Kilda 241, 245, 252, 257, 263
   coastline formation 259–60
   glaciation 256–9
   grassland 263
   human history 263
   igneous activity 244, 246, 250–1
   periglacial conditions 256–9
   post-glacial landscape 260–1, 262, 263
   sea cliffs 259

sea floor 257, 258–9
vegetation 257, 260–1
volcanic activity 250–1
St Magnus Cathedral (Kirkwall, Orkney) 414, 415
St Mary's Loch (Southern Borders) 103, 104
stacks *see* sea stacks
Staffa, Isle of 193, 194, 195, 201–2
step edge 426
Stinchar Valley Fault (Galloway) 74
stoping of Mull granites 183
storm ridges 90
Stornoway Formation 351–2, 358
Strath Halladale Granite 401
strath morphology 411
Strathy Complex (Caithness area) 400–1
streams 366
striations 381
strike-slip movement 208, 311, 388
Strontian granite 183–4
strontianite 184
subduction 20, 21, 446
  accretionary prism formation 42, 43
Sullom Voe (Shetland) 428, 430
Sumburgh Head (Shetland) 438
surface blanket 2, 12, 14
surface modification episodes 51–9, 444, 450–1
synclines 23

Talla Reservoir (Southern Borders) 108
Tay Estuary (Dundee area) 227, 228, 239
Tay, Loch 218
Tay, River 11
tectonic plates 16, 17, 18–22
  Caledonian plate 444–6
  convergent 19, 20, 22, 444–6
  deformation 22–3
  divergent 21
  movement 18–19, 38, 39, 50
  plate boundaries 18, 20–3
  subducted 20, 21
  transform boundaries 21
temperature curve, glacial episodes 53–4
Tentsmuir (Dundee area) 239, 240
terrace formation 13, 14, 299–301, 304, 321, 423
terranes 29, 32
Tertiary landscapes 49–50, 51
  Affric area 294–6
  Cairngorm area 309
  Caithness area 406, 408
  Cape Wrath area 379
  Dundee area 236–7
  Edinburgh area 167–8
  erosion 33, 51
  Glasgow area 147, 148, 149, 150
  Inverness area 390, 393
  Jura to Arran 120–2, 123, 124
  Lewis and Harris 355–8
  Mull area 195–6
  Orkney 422
  Rannoch area 213–14, 218–19
  Shetland 439–40
  Skye area 273–4, 275, 276, 277–8, 279
Tertiary volcanism episode 49–50, 51
Thames Estuary, sea level change 60, 61, 62
thermal expansion/contraction, vertical crustal movements 27

Three Sisters of Glencoe 224, 225
tidal marshes 85, 86
tides 110, 202
tillites 113
tin 23
Tiree (Mull area) 180, 182, 198, 202
tombolos 136, 442, 443
Torridonian Sandstone 34, 36–7
  Affric area 290, 293, 296, 297
  Cape Wrath area 374, 375, 376
  Lewisian Complex contact 36, 37
  Skye 281
tors, granite 130, 310–11, 327
trap topography 202
  Mull area 185, 192, 193
  Skye area 267, 274, 279
Tresnnish Isles (Mull) 186, 188
trilobite fossils 322
trim lines 361
Trotternish Ridge (Skye) 282, 284, 286
troughs, glaciated 365
truncated spurs 359, 362
tsunami waves 21, 442–3
Tweed Basin
  drainage network 179
  drumlins 171
  Edinburgh area 165, 168, 171, 172, 177
  ice flow 171, 172
  Southern Borders 106–7
Tyndrum Fault 206, 210, 218

Uists (Area 9) 241–63
  bathymetry 250
  bedrock 241–4, 245–6, 248, 250, 350
  glacial landscape 252, 253, 254–60
  landscapes 247, 249, 250–2, 253, 254–61, 262, 263
  post-glacial landscape 260–1, 262, 263
  sandy beaches 261, 262, 263
  sea-level change 261
  slope map 247, 249
  topography 247, 250
  vegetation 260–1
unconformity 236, 293, 329, 330
  angular 162, 163, 164
unloading, vertical crustal movements 26–7
Upper Old Red Sandstone
  Caithness area 404, 410
  Dundee area 234, 236
  Glasgow area 144
  Inverness area 389
  Jura to Arran 117
  Orkney 418, 421

valleys 11, 12
  Aberdeen area 340–1
  Affric area 294–5, 300, 301
  Arran 129–30
  Cairngorm area 305, 309, 312, 315–17, 318
  flooded 88–9, 136
  glacial 11, 12, 56, 103, 219, 315–17
  Glasgow area 154
  Lewis and Harris 361–2
  glacial till deposition 104, 106
  hanging 103
  Lewis and Harris 361–2
  Monadhliath Mountains 318
  Orkney 424, 426

processes 9, 10, 11–12, 13, 14
Rannoch area 213, 218, 219, 226
Shetland 440
Skye area 273–4
Southern Uplands 73
Valtos, Glen (Lewis) 359, 364
Varsican mountain building 39, 47–8
vegetation
  Affric area 304
  Barra 260–1
  Cape Wrath area 382
  Galloway 85
  human impact 85, 108
  Jura to Arran 137
  Lewis and Harris 365–6
  Rannoch area 226
  Skye area 286
  Southern Borders 108
  St Kilda 257, 260–1
  Uists 260–1
volcanic activity
  Affric area 295–6
  Arran 118–19, 124
  calderas 209, 269, 275, 277
  Caledonian mountains 208–9
  Dundee area 233–4, 235–6
  Edinburgh area 165, 169, 172, 173, 174, 175
  Glasgow area 145, 146
  Lewis and Harris 344
  Mull area 182–3, 184, 186, 187, 188–92
  North Sea 449
  Skye area 267, 271
  St Kilda 250–2
  subduction-related 446
volcanic glass 273
volcanic plugs 70–1, 72
volcanic vents 69, 78
volcanoes 6, 7, 21, 22
  Dundee area 233, 234, 235–6
  Glencoe 209
  Mull area 182–3, 184, 186, 187, 188–92
  Post-Caledonian episodes 47
  Skye area 267, 271
  St Kilda 250
  Tertiary 49–50

Walls Boundary Fault line (Shetland) 426, 429, 430, 431, 436–7, 439
waterfalls 287
wave-cut rock platform 288
weathering 72, 274
  Aberdeen area 339
  anorthosite 363
  Black Cuillin 276, 279
  Edinburgh area 168
  Glasgow area 145–6
  Jura to Arran 120–1
  Red Hills (Skye) 279
  Skye area 274
  Southern Borders 97–8
Wester Keolka Shear Zone (Shetland) 433
Wester Ross Advance 382
Whin Sill (Bamburgh) 165
whirlpools 202
Wigtown Bay (Galloway) 89

Younger Basic Suite 243
Younger Dryas cold phase 58
Ythan, River (Aberdeen area) 339–40, 341

The New Naturalist Library

1. *Butterflies* — E. B. Ford
2. *British Game* — B. Vesey-Fitzgerald
3. *London's Natural History* — R. S. R. Fitter
4. *Britain's Structure and Scenery* — L. Dudley Stamp
5. *Wild Flowers* — J. Gilmour & M. Walters
6. *The Highlands & Islands* — F. Fraser Darling & J. M. Boyd
7. *Mushrooms & Toadstools* — J. Ramsbottom
8. *Insect Natural History* — A. D. Imms
9. *A Country Parish* — A. W. Boyd
10. *British Plant Life* — W. B. Turrill
11. *Mountains & Moorlands* — W. H. Pearsall
12. *The Sea Shore* — C. M. Yonge
13. *Snowdonia* — F. J. North, B. Campbell & R. Scott
14. *The Art of Botanical Illustration* — W. Blunt
15. *Life in Lakes & Rivers* — T. T. Macan & E. B. Worthington
16. *Wild Flowers of Chalk & Limestone* — J. E. Lousley
17. *Birds & Men* — E. M. Nicholson
18. *A Natural History of Man in Britain* — H. J. Fleure & M. Davies
19. *Wild Orchids of Britain* — V. S. Summerhayes
20. *The British Amphibians & Reptiles* — M. Smith
21. *British Mammals* — L. Harrison Matthews
22. *Climate and the British Scene* — G. Manley
23. *An Angler's Entomology* — J. R. Harris
24. *Flowers of the Coast* — I. Hepburn
25. *The Sea Coast* — J. A. Steers
26. *The Weald* — S. W. Wooldridge & F. Goldring
27. *Dartmoor* — L. A. Harvey & D. St. Leger Gordon
28. *Sea Birds* — J. Fisher & R. M. Lockley
29. *The World of the Honeybee* — C. G. Butler
30. *Moths* — E. B. Ford
31. *Man and the Land* — L. Dudley Stamp
32. *Trees, Woods and Man* — H. L. Edlin
33. *Mountain Flowers* — J. Raven & M. Walters
34. *The Open Sea: I. The World of Plankton* — A. Hardy
35. *The World of the Soil* — E. J. Russell
36. *Insect Migration* — C. B. Williams
37. *The Open Sea: II. Fish & Fisheries* — A. Hardy
38. *The World of Spiders* — W. S. Bristowe
39. *The Folklore of Birds* — E. A. Armstrong
40. *Bumblebees* — J. B. Free & C. G. Butler
41. *Dragonflies* — P. S. Corbet, C. Longfield & N. W. Moore
42. *Fossils* — H. H. Swinnerton
43. *Weeds & Aliens* — E. Salisbury
44. *The Peak District* — K. C. Edwards
45. *The Common Lands of England & Wales* — L. Dudley Stamp & W. G. Hoskins
46. *The Broads* — E. A. Ellis
47. *The Snowdonia National Park* — W. M. Condry
48. *Grass and Grasslands* — I. Moore
49. *Nature Conservation in Britain* — L. Dudley Stamp
50. *Pesticides and Pollution* — K. Mellanby
51. *Man & Birds* — R. K. Murton
52. *Woodland Birds* — E. Simms
53. *The Lake District* — W. H. Pearsall & W. Pennington
54. *The Pollination of Flowers* — M. Proctor & P. Yeo
55. *Finches* — I. Newton
56. *Pedigree: Words from Nature* — S. Potter & L. Sargent
57. *British Seals* — H. R. Hewer
58. *Hedges* — E. Pollard, M. D. Hooper & N. W. Moore
59. *Ants* — M. V. Brian
60. *British Birds of Prey* — L. Brown
61. *Inheritance and Natural History* — R. J. Berry
62. *British Tits* — C. Perrins

63. *British Thrushes* — E. Simms
64. *The Natural History of Shetland* — R. J. Berry & J. L. Johnston
65. *Waders* — W. G. Hale
66. *The Natural History of Wales* — W. M. Condry
67. *Farming and Wildlife* — K. Mellanby
68. *Mammals in the British Isles* — L. Harrison Matthews
69. *Reptiles and Amphibians in Britain* — D. Frazer
70. *The Natural History of Orkney* — R. J. Berry
71. *British Warblers* — E. Simms
72. *Heathlands* — N. R. Webb
73. *The New Forest* — C. R. Tubbs
74. *Ferns* — C. N. Page
75. *Freshwater Fish* — P. S. Maitland & R. N. Campbell
76. *The Hebrides* — J. M. Boyd & I. L. Boyd
77. *The Soil* — B. Davis, N. Walker, D. Ball & A. Fitter
78. *British Larks, Pipits & Wagtails* — E. Simms
79. *Caves & Cave Life* — P. Chapman
80. *Wild & Garden Plants* — M. Walters
81. *Ladybirds* — M. E. N. Majerus
82. *The New Naturalists* — P. Marren
83. *The Natural History of Pollination* — M. Proctor, P. Yeo & A. Lack
84. *Ireland: A Natural History* — D. Cabot
85. *Plant Disease* — D. Ingram & N. Robertson
86. *Lichens* — Oliver Gilbert
87. *Amphibians and Reptiles* — T. Beebee & R. Griffiths
88. *Loch Lomondside* — J. Mitchell
89. *The Broads* — B. Moss
90. *Moths* — M. Majerus
91. *Nature Conservation* — P. Marren
92. *Lakeland* — D. Ratcliffe
93. *British Bats* — John Altringham
94. *Seashore* — Peter Hayward
95. *Northumberland* — Angus Lunn
96. *Fungi* — Brian Spooner & Peter Roberts
97. *Mosses & Liverworts* — Nick Hodgetts & Ron Porley
98. *Bumblebees* — Ted Benton
99. *Gower* — Jonathan Mullard
100. *Woodlands* — Oliver Rackham
101. *Galloway and the Borders* — Derek Ratcliffe
102. *Garden Natural History* — Stefan Buczacki
103. *The Isles of Scilly* — Rosemary Parslow
104. *A History of Ornithology* — Peter Bircham
105. *Wye Valley* — George Peterken
106. *Dragonflies* — Philip Corbet & Stephen Brooks
107. *Grouse* — Adam Watson & Robert Moss
108. *Southern England* — Peter Friend
109. *Islands* — R. J. Berry
110. *Wildfowl* — David Cabot
111. *Dartmoor* — Ian Mercer
112. *Books and Naturalists* — David E. Allen
113. *Bird Migration* — Ian Newton
114. *Badger* — Timothy J. Roper
115. *Climate and Weather* – John Kington
116. *Plant Pests* – David V. Alford
117. *Plant Galls* – Margaret Redfern
118. *Marches* – Andrew Allott